Powers of Distinction

Powers of Distinction
On Religion and Modernity

Nancy Levene

The University of Chicago Press :: Chicago and London

The University of Chicago Press, Chicago 60637
The University of Chicago Press, Ltd., London
© 2017 by The University of Chicago
Published 2017
Printed in the United States of America

26 25 24 23 22 21 20 19 18 17   1 2 3 4 5

ISBN-13: 978-0-226-50736-1 (cloth)
ISBN-13: 978-0-226-50753-8 (paper)
ISBN-13: 978-0-226-50767-5 (e-book)
DOI: 10.7208/chicago/9780226507675.001.0001

Published with the assistance of the Frederick W. Hilles Publication Fund
of Yale University.

Library of Congress Cataloging-in-Publication Data

Names: Levene, Nancy, author.
Title: Powers of distinction: on religion and modernity / Nancy Levene.
Description: Chicago; London: The University of Chicago Press, 2017. |
  Includes bibliographical references and index.
Identifiers: LCCN 2017011913 | ISBN 9780226507361 (cloth: alk. paper) |
  ISBN 9780226507538 (pbk: alk. paper) | ISBN 9780226507675 (e-book)
Subjects: LCSH: Religion—Philosophy. | Modernism (Christian theology)
Classification: LCC BL51 .L477 2017 | DDC 200.1—dc23
  LC record available at https://lccn.loc.gov/2017011913

♾ This paper meets the requirements of ANSI/NISO Z39.48-1992
(Permanence of Paper)

For Kathryn, home land
For Kinneret, promised land

Why, then, inquire
Who has divided the world, what entrepreneur?
No man. The self, the chrysalis of all men
Became divided in the leisure of blue day
And more, in branchings after day. One part
Held fast tenaciously in common earth

And one from central earth to central sky
And in moonlit extensions of them in the mind
Searched out such majesty as it could find.

WALLACE STEVENS, "An Ordinary Evening in New Haven"

Contents

1

The Principle of Modernity

One is always wrong, but with two, truth begins.

Friedrich Nietzsche, *The Gay Science*

Can one divide human reality, as indeed human reality seems to be genuinely divided, into clearly different cultures, histories, traditions, societies, even races, and survive the consequences humanly?

Edward Said, *Orientalism*

You must wager. There is no choice, you are already committed.

Blaise Pascal, *Pensées*

Religion and Modernity × Two

To take distinction as the organizing concept of this book is to take on the distinction that has served since antiquity to ground speculation about the nature of reality and the human task within it: the one and the many. It is an old construct, ostensibly long since replaced by more sophisticated ways of conceiving the real. Yet it persists in sinews of thinking and organizing—the embrace of plurality over fusion, the multiple over the singular, difference over sameness. It is rarer in our epoch to incline the other way, but there are always also claims for unity, similarity, singularity. What matters is that the embrace of multiplicity and unity skims over the conceptual and political challenges of the number two. Three things can be construed as equally distinct, and thus like four, or five, or six. They might also be partners in a common position, and thus like one. It is easy enough to imagine the world as multiple—so many things, so many connections, possibilities, angles. So much work to do to understand it all, and yet all part of one world. Infinite, singular.

The harder job is to divide.

It can readily be done, of course. Those who grow up with the PBS television show *Sesame Street* know the song, "One of these things is not like the others." One knows how to divide and isolate and categorize. Scholarship may be no more than the mandate to do so. But *Sesame Street* is just as conscious as scholarship that what works for pencils and suitcases and telephones is decidedly not what works for persons and societies. One does not divide and classify persons or societies without cost and thus without great delicacy. Canons may be rich sites of distinction. The social, geographic, or intellectual divisions they express are less obviously fruitful unless one leaves the moving parts as benignly distinct, different without cost (multiple), but also without fundamental—that is, human, and thus contested—relation.

One can, then, cluster anything in any way using attributes such as time, place, language, gender, religion: this one has these attributes and that one has those and everything and everyone has some attributes and it need not get political. But to look at difference at an elementary level—in concept, in history, this is less automatically upbuilding terrain. For this reason two, the basic unit of division, is the number worth obsessing over—difference of x and y, distinction between this and that, how many things there are at root, how to count beyond one and many. How, in short, to find the missing place of two. It may be that to find the place of two, of distinction, is to be pressed to rescue it from what Edward Said calls Orientalism, or what might more generally be identified as the logic of us and them. It is first, though, to know what one is looking at. Three might be the number of history, one the space of philosophy. It might be the reverse. What matters is that periodically the wheels of our multiples be checked for stability. On this score there is work to do to understand one, two, and three—in scholarship and in worlds. To continue to pitch always further into the unspecifiable multiple is to go perhaps not even as far as one.[1]

This is a book on religion and modernity, two concepts with enormous reach. Each has seemed usable without too much precision, although each is also constantly being redefined. New projects in the humanities and social sciences regularly hinge on an author's fresh account of one or the other or both. The theological origins of modernity. The modern provenance of religion.[2]

THESIS

I argue that, while religion and modernity indeed belong together, their relation calls for conceptual scrutiny to expose the nature of their power. Such scrutiny is focused not on identifying novel concepts but on distinguishing two versions each of religion and of modernity, as well as the difference between them. These distinctions work to clarify where the power of the terms is obscured. But because there are several operative distinctions, and a refusal to take refuge in either the peace of indifferent multiplicity or the luster of a new theory, the work to unravel the plot is tough at times. The aim, however, is simple and momentous: to reorient the understanding and task of modern life.

To begin, I identify two concepts of religion. One concerns a dual relation between the natural world and a supernatural realm, in which either the supernatural provides a standard of value for a naturalism that is its reflective counterpart or the opposite—the natural provides the standard for the supernatural. In each case the terms are opposed, though they may also be identified. They are reversible. The second concept of religion advances a principle of reality inclusive of ideals, in which the standard of value is creative of what is and must continually be realized. In this case the terms—here *real* and *ideal*—are affirmed together in the mutually sustaining and mutually critical embrace of two. Each concept of religion may also be a secularism.

The second concept of religion (and the secular) is also a concept of modernity as the embrace of history and interpretation over against naturalism and supernaturalism. This modernity is an epoch distinguished in time, as modernities are. But its time encompasses biblical concepts of reality, which support and are supported by the more usually marked modernity of innovations in science, technology, politics, law, and economics.

Both religion and modernity, then, have two versions, but they are connected only through the second concept of religion. There is thus a difference between religion and modernity, as follows. In concepts of religion, it is from the standpoint of only one of the two concepts that one may observe the distinction between them. It is the second concept of religion, the principle of a reality inclusive of ideals, that "sees" that there are two concepts and invites a difference of value between itself and the contradictory logic of naturalism and supernaturalism, which one can call nonmodern. In concepts of modernity, by contrast, neither the time of modernity in biblical concepts nor the modernity of scientific and political innovation sets the standard for the other. One may observe the distinction between them from either position, and this distinction is also a fundamental continuity. Modernity is two in possessing two beginnings. But these beginnings will tend to draw apart, losing their connection. Religion in the second version is a key term enabling one to identify the nature of their relation. Once again, in connecting biblical and scientific/revolutionary modernity, religion might also be a secularism.

The point with modernity is to see that the "what" of modern innovation is in partnership with the principle of the religion of interpretation—that the truth or God exists in the world to be taken up as the human, historical task. This religion, no less a secularism, is constituted in the call to Abraham to leave his homeland for a promised land; to constitute community based not on privileges of rank, whether natural or spiritual, but on the promise to make communities of righteousness—to make home land, as I write the difference. It therefore makes no sense to identify modernity with a critique of religion unless one also recognizes that such a critique is a position of religion itself insofar as it is understood as a commitment to the realization of ideals, to truth in history. Modernity is religion × two in recognizing the difference between a religion of supernatural naturalism and a religion of reality. Religion is modernity × two in recognizing the relation of the biblical work of critique to the innovations that carry out its charge and, in turn, help us enact the work of criticism, secular and religious.

This is to contribute to debates about religion and secularism by reconstructing the question. The question here is not whether religion survives in modernity in the form of secularism—whether secularism is some transposed religion. The question is not whether or why religion survives at all, or returns, or what to do about this or that religion. The question is posed in the light of there being two principal forms of religion. In modernity the question is, Which one is at issue? But this is equally to ask about modernity itself, which has two principal times. The wager is that the distinction of the elementary ideas will identify—and enact—the power to be had in the concepts and in their worlds.

The argument requires readers to attend to two ways of thinking about "two," two dualisms. In the first dualism, which structures the first concept of religion, two terms (one and many, reason and history, soul and body) are either identified or opposed. In the second dualism, which structures the second concept of religion, the two terms are understood in mutually supportive relation, however paradoxically so. The missing distinction of modernity is the distinction between these dualisms. It is the rescue of the position of two whereby its terms are mutually engaged, mutually true. Truth and interpretation. Reason (or God) and history. Equally self and other, whose work as interpreters is to enact and augment truth in common.

This work, and this way of speaking, is familiar, but it is easy to confuse. Religion and secularism are standard forms of the confusion insofar as they assimilate the two dualisms. Either religion and the secular each express only the first dualism, despite their apparent contrast with one another, or each works from the second dualism but through its confusion with the terms of the first. In religious terms, this confusion is to place God outside of or identical to history (mastery or teleology); in secular terms it is to place truth or the good outside of or identical to history (rationalism or historicism). Critics of dualism likewise see only one "two," the perennial distinction of the one and the many, by the logic of which truth, God, essence, oneness is opposed to manyness and its cognates. It is therefore ironic that the critique of dualism, in quest of the one or (more usually) the many, merely recapitulates one of two dualisms, the dualism whose two terms, opposed or identified, can yield only one term, with the other an empty postulate to be deferred or denied.

Dualisms are products of the human mind in its confrontation with the reality of which it is part. There is no escape from the challenge of two, of doubleness, but there are two different ways to inhabit and conceive it.

Insofar as the one is not opposed to the many, that is, insofar as one takes up the charge of religion in and as modernity, we are each called to join in making values collective. This position refuses dualism as either opposition or identity, whether religious or secular. What the dualism of paradoxical relation mandates can be stated bluntly. Truth appears. Equally, God exists. What one values is not elsewhere than where one begins to think and exist, which does not mitigate but indeed engenders the challenge of making good on this beginning. Readers mindful only of the difference between truth and God, or anxious to make one the standard of the other, will miss the underlying structural question of where they appear in a system. The second dualism—religious and secular—gives us a system inclusive of critiques of it, a reality that is alive to what might enlarge and empower it. This second dualism, the second concept of religion in its relation to modernity, calls for interpretation as subjects/minds/readers are not simply opposed to their ends and to each other but are called to forge them in cooperation. One must wager for the truth and reckon with the wagers of others.

Yet this second dualism of truth and interpretation, ideal and real, God and existence also risks violence, since, once the truth or God is not elsewhere or nowhere, as in supernaturalism or naturalism, anyone can claim its mantle over against others, as against oneself. This is not to say violence is unique to the dualism of mutual relation. There is nothing more violent than the position that truth is outside what you can know, or that there is no truth but what is given. It is only by excluding the logic of identity (one) and opposition (many) that the second dualism is creative of an actual two, one that is open to others, to all. Without this work, this critique, the co-involvement of two is inconceivable. Dualism will be merely two in opposition, and thus merely one (and many).

What is notable is that the refusal of one and many, supernaturalism and naturalism, does not in itself end confusion or violence. These contradictory positions simply become the fantasies by which is abrogated the hard work of making what is true for you true for all. Once each term is constituted in and through the other, it is newly possible to polarize their distinctness from each other, replicating the structure of the first dualism by opposing the terms, refusing their intimacy and its obligations. In short, once the distinction of two is in existence and not between what exists (many) and what is the standard of existence (one), it is tempting either to reerect standards outside existence or to refuse standards altogether, both of which flee from the difficulty of enacting them together. There will be imagined nothing more supernatural than the God of history, nothing more natural than the death of this God, as thinkers and citizens struggle with what is required—with the human task.

In biblical terms, this task is to make good on the charge to Adam and Eve to take up the difference of good and evil: the difference of knowing both good and evil, which knowledge makes human beings like God, and the difference between good and evil, in the face of which human beings are enjoined to commit to the first, despite toil and pain. It can seem a solution of a kind to deny knowledge altogether in submission to a God who issues the contradictory command not to know. But as this very God acknowledges in the creation of the world, knowledge is good, and there is no going back.

It is not, then, that religion haunts modernity and secularism. It is that religion in modernity is confounded in the beginning by its own temptations, its own golden calf. Human beings, confused by their own powers in distinguishing good and evil, disavow these powers in acts of violence. God, confused by the bargain struck, drowns his grief at the terrible proximity of good and evil in acts of violence.

It might seem possible to say that, once history expresses the truth of interpretation, there can then be nothing but one interpretation advanced arbitrarily against another, a reinvestment of might makes right now pitting self against other, your truth against mine, epoch against epoch. But this work is a profanation of a principle it behooves us to continue to restate: that insofar as the truth is constituted in common, in history, it expresses the truth *of* history and thus the golden rule that history is the scene of both self and other, the interpretations of the good that can be made common. The paradox is that the temptation of the one and the many—the logic of opposition and identity—can appear only in a system that is already in critique of it. It can thus confuse only in a system that has the power to rectify the confusion.

The argument is supportive of a broadly Hegelian account of history, with a caveat. Hegel gives us history as the concept of the other, the mutually constituted, if also mutually struggling, terms of human relationship as human beings realize their being—their truths, their ideals, their otherness—in time and with one another. What Hegel made so shocking is the stipulation that this concept of history is itself historical. It requires us to found history as a site of innovation, not as a naturalism or supernaturalism that has always been in the world or that is simply coincident with thinking. This claim risks the gravest of dangers—that in marking history's parameters one will leave some positions outside history—whole civilizations, religions, cultures. Would this move not betray the very commitment to otherness that history ostensibly wagers?

First, yes. The move to make the concept of history specific does potentially betray the very commitment to otherness it expresses. Hegel's shock has only increased in force as readers come to terms with the guilt embedded in the claim. Yet it is not enough to leave it there—to say history is tragic, or to set aside this concept of history altogether as offensive, racist, wrongheaded. Hegel must not be defended against the arrows of post-Enlightenment disgust at what seems nothing so much as the systemic egoism of the West, the white man, the European, the Concept. What is called for is a reckoning with the position. Now that we see just what it costs, we must call anew for rectification.

There is no way to escape the dangers of history insofar as it is understood as the work of truth, of God, of mind. There is nothing outside this concept of history but a naturalism, which decomposes spirit into might makes right, or a supernaturalism, which indefinitely postpones the work to make good on the principle that the good might be shared in common. Indeed, the profanation of the work of history in violence is nothing less than the illicit recourse to naturalism and supernaturalism as history's alter egos. It is only by refusing this recourse that what history bears can once again come into view: not distinction as what divides me from you, but distinction as what liberates us for one another. This is the modern. It is only in distinguishing—history from natural-supernaturalism, religion from the dualism of opposition and identity, modernity from the immobility of station, rank, class, kin—that one is free to form histories in common. Therefore, and second, no, the move to make history specific does not simply resign us to tragedy. It forms the condition, lifeless without our alertness to its dangers, to make an inclusive world.

This is to say, then, that although religions, but no less secularisms, distinguish between us and them, insiders and outsiders, religions, and no less secularisms, may also distinguish, and be distinguished by, the principle of inclusion. They may also include not just us but also them. Inclusion is a distinction, a distinction both from positions that distinguish invidiously and from those that do not distinguish at all. It is paradoxically distinction by which inclusion comes to be possible. Such a distinction, while different from distinctions that divide invidiously, is nevertheless a risky intellectual and political work. In contemporary thinking about religion, scholars and thinkers tend to collapse these distinctions into one, consistent with religious and secular assimilation of the dualisms. Either include or distinguish. Either include everyone or distinguish everyone.

My claim, rather, is that inclusion is a distinction. It is a principle in whose realization not all positions are equally germane. Given the urgent pressure on pluralism in late modern democracies, the idea that pluralism is principled remains a vexing observation. There is a great deal of confusion about what the move entails, so powerful is the desire to include and so complex is the work of doing so without imperialism, egoism, or ignorance. It will seem that the choice is between violence and inclusion. But inclusion will bring its own violence. The conceptual history that endeavors to understand, and thus to address, this consequence is the work of this book.

The distinction of inclusion, the principle of modernity, is associated with values the West prizes—with democracy, pluralism, and critique. But it is not the property of the West per se. This is not a vague globalism. It is a point about the West's own distinction as well as its confusion. For one must ask, If modernity is given in biblical antiquity, why does it take so long to realize?

On the one hand, thinking takes time. Even more, thinking whose work is in time takes a great deal of it. More precisely still, time is a concept the struggle for which time alone cannot resolve. As I show in reading Saint Anselm, Spinoza, and Kant, we miss the modern in concept, and the discourses of the religious and the secular compound the time it takes to reckon with it. On the other hand, it is central to understanding the distinction of religion and modernity to observe that we miss the modern in concept because the West is divided between nonmodern and modern positions. It is divided, that is, between the two concepts of

[handwritten margin note: WEST IS CONFUSED BY ITS OWN PRINCIPLE OF INCLUSION/ MODERNITY, WHICH IT EXPRESSES]

religion (as of the secular), the one a dualism of opposition and identity and the other a dualism of inclusion and critique. The West is confused by and in this division, which it expresses without seeing it. The division is not a function of temporal period. Abraham is modern. Plato is not. God is confused. The Forms are not.[3]

Twentieth-century social and political thought has focused on the deleterious aspects of Western thought and culture, whether embodied in instrumental reason, global capitalism, or imperialism. Such thinking continues apace in the current century, and it is as important as ever. However, it is just as important to observe what is involved in a West confused about its own principle, but therefore creative of self-critique—a position that provides the standard for itself and its errors. Not all conceptual positions do so. Some must borrow such standards, where they access them at all. Scholarship on religion and in the humanities more generally believes it can avoid the distinction of "not all," the investments of inclusion and division.[4] Certainly the distinction will arouse the threat of violence. As in Hegel's concept of history, what could be more imperialist than to consign some positions to conceptual dependence on others? Nevertheless, this is the claim. The aim is not to conquer nonmodern positions, Western or otherwise. It is to understand modernity as that position that will be confused about its principle, to clarify why this is, and to resist it. It is to anatomize the missing distinction of modernity in order to have more of what modernity is at its most powerful.

[handwritten margin note: AIM]

[handwritten note: anatomize missing dist. of modernity]

Models of Truth

Let me conceive in elementary form what this is to say.

In the model in which truth appears, the refused positions are what opposes truth and appearance and what identifies them. The terms religion and secularism can express either the model or the positions it refuses.

[handwritten margin note: accepted truth v. other.]

[handwritten margin note: modernity principle]

In the model in which a (single) collective is constituted by and held accountable to a principle of inclusivity, the refused positions are what identifies inclusivity with the collective and seeks either to expand by domination or to exclude by membership and what identifies inclusivity with the erasure of the (single) collective. The terms religion and secularism can express either the model or the positions it refuses.

[handwritten margin note: collective v. excludes collective.]

The refused positions in the two models are mutually supportive. Insofar as appearance is not where the truth is (appearance is not true) or insofar as truth is merely whatever appears, a collective can only be rooted in and can extend only as far as the representation and conquest of natural or accidental generation: kin/tribe/ethnos/race/empire.

The refused positions structure many frameworks of social and intellectual life. Their refusal is modernity. In the light of modernity, what is refused is or becomes nonmodern. It also becomes the temptation of modernity as it flees from its own principle.

Modernity is the name for the principle expressed in the two models: truth is included in what appears, and its appearance signals the value of inclusion over against the appearance that inclusion as the value of all is impossible. Truth's appearance signals the value, and not only the givenness, of appearance. What appears is the truth that truth is inclusivity, that there can be inclusivity and not just collectivity. Modernity is the name for the critique of the refused positions, which become its temptation. It is not only a principle but an epoch, and not only an epoch but also the source of epochs—the epoch in which epochal thinking is inaugurated, acts of mind to delimit and, in delimiting, to constitute reality as a value, as the site of value.

In modernity, truth appears. The work this event calls for is history. History is thus also a refusal, a claim. History is capacious. It includes facts and interpretations. It addresses a past that is completed and a past that might be or mean new things. What history claims is that the truth of what appears—the truth of appearance—is relative to value, to the aims of human beings, both the ones telling history and the ones who are its subjects. What history thereby refuses is that the truth of appearances is elsewhere. It refuses the truth that would be elsewhere. It therefore refuses the division of duties that would put philosophy in charge of truth and history in charge of what appears. It refuses the resignation of truth and embrace of pure appearance (change, contingency). History is the claim that, insofar as truth appears, there is one duty: to account for, to understand, and to build up this principle.

The word truth might have signified that what is the case lies beyond (its) appearances, which case would be insusceptible of conception insofar as concepts partake of images—the appearance of things. The word appearance would then have signified the position against which the truth is juxtaposed—things as they are conceivable but not necessarily as they truly are. In lying beyond concepts, what is the case could be accessed, if at all, only through progressive moves to denude oneself of the confusion of what seems. Alternatively, appearances could be affirmed as what is the case, accessible in denuding oneself of the confusion that there is something truly there. In the premise that is modernity, the truth, in appearing, throws its pursuer into confusion. But this is now neither because she is confused on the way to the truth beyond appearances nor because she is stuck in appearances that shall not be true. It is because she is faced, in appearance, with the imperative to recognize, to understand, (its) truth. What is required?

This is a double question: What is required to discover the truth? What does the truth require? What truth, in appearing, means to begin with is that appearance can be true. But therefore the question is not Where is the truth such that I might find it? (it is in appearance) but, for any given truth claim, True for whom, why, and when? True for what end? It does not follow that therefore truth is merely divisive, merely yours and not (necessarily) mine. If truth insofar as it lies beyond appearance would be universal in being untainted by the limits of appearance, truth insofar as it appears is universal in being subject to the limit that it include all appearances. This is to say that the truth, in appearing, can be made universal, can bespeak a universal *whom*, a universal *why*, a universal *when*. Truth, in appearing, is nothing other than the value, the good, the inclusivity of appearance.

Doubtless history testifies largely to the forfeiture of this good, to the profanation of what can be made valuable, to the resignation to the given. Nevertheless, the good of truth's appearance as inclusivity is history's subject and its struggle. If history aims to pursue all cases, the concept of case is limited by this principle of inclusion: that history include as much as there is and that history's story, the case of history itself, is of the struggle to include and (for the most part) its forfeiture. In this forfeiture, history is (the story of) violence. History would be an accounting of the violence of exclusion or history would itself be violent, or both. But it is not only so. History's case is an instance limned by what is made possible in truth appearing: the inclusion in the totality of what appears of the value of appearance as a totality and therefore the question of the specific—valuable for whom, why, and when. It is only insofar as truth appears that the specifics of what appears are significant in the question of what is the case. It is only in the realm of specifics, their "visions and revisions," that history can ameliorate (its) violence.[5]

History is not moral philosophy by another name—that which subordinates specific cases to general rules or that which generates rules from specific cases. But neither is history mere, and thus indifferent, specificity. History is not subordinate to principle. History is principled. Truth is not elsewhere. But neither is truth merely whatever appears. Truth appears. So then questions of accuracy are paramount. Who fired the gun? But such questions are in pursuit of a story. Did he fire the gun on hearing an intruder or to shoot his wife? Did she fire the gun in self-defense or to get his attention? Courts work to determine what is the case in order to render judgment. The difference of history is that there is no end but the one the historian delivers, knowing it can be overturned at any time, now unto the end, as the catechism has it. The pressure on the courts is to achieve justice. The pressure on history is to achieve understanding. But no less the reverse. Courts seek understanding. History is the achievement of justice, the fidelity to a case that bequeaths to it maximal specificity. History itself is therefore specific in being the frame of the truth insofar as it appears. In history, as in the law, the facts are part of a story in which all parties have investments. The historian wants to know what is really the case, even as what is the case evades what seems. This desire is no less that of the subjects, even as what is the case involves their evasion or repression. What is the case in either case requires not only specificity but decision. Consistent with the appearance of truth, history is a distinction.

If appearances were devoid of truth, if the world as human beings experience it conformed merely to chance or to fate, pure change or pure stasis, if it expressed, in scientific parlance, nature alone or, in theological-philosophical parlance, God or reason alone, then it would be as it was for Oedipus: something to bring to the foot of the oracle. The laws of nature, the laws of God. In contrast, history presumes, and is the presumption of, subjects who are subject to the oracle that is their own mind, their take on the case together with the take of others. In history there is no "what is" separate from this taking. But the formulation always needs reformulation. It is not that "what is" is therefore only how things are taken. It is that, in the case of the subject, she cannot get to what is without taking it some way or other, and this taking is her story, the one history is empowered to tell as it pursues what is really the case. But the historian, then, stands in the story. For she, too, takes it some way or other.

What is the case requires a decision.

History is the work of modernity insofar as modernity is the appearance of the truth. The truth that appears, the truth of appearance, is that appearances can be made true, valuable, to human beings. Human beings are not, that is, stuck only with appearances. Appearances are also what human beings make for their ends, and insofar as human beings have ends, they are realizable in appearance and only in appearance. A concomitant of the maxim that truth appears is that human beings can realize their truths, but then that truth is not only personal but also public, also inclusive of others. That truth is not elsewhere but is here, is mine, means that, in being here, it is also yours. Truth, in appearing, can be ours. I might like this, in sharing common projects with you. Or I might not like this, in denying you your truth. Either way, what is true is not for one of us to determine outside of including or excluding others. No one has privileged accessed to what is, since truth appears. No one has recourse to ignorance, since truth appears. If there is no universal truth that is not subject to you and to me, we are together subject to the principle that truth is for all.

This makes history's story one of value as historians pursue the vicissitudes of human decision, human investment, inclusive or exclusive. (This need not be conceived as purely personal decision. One can speak of history deciding, of events happening with unidentifiable actors.) It also makes history a work of decision. The historian, no less than her subjects, is subject to—that is, in fundamental relationship with—the principle of inclusion. How much will she take into account in taking what she sees as what is? How long will she linger on what she sees in relation to how others have seen—the same thing, the thing taken otherwise, the question of what thing? How will she evaluate what you say when you say, through the evidence, "I fired the gun in self-defense"? All the usual analogies are in operation with this question. The historian is detective, jury, snoop, reporter. All these are kindred tasks in the pursuit of the real. But again, then: How will she decide?

"Love believes all things—and yet is never deceived."[6] Kierkegaard's maxim is surely diabolical. And yet it is the maxim of history.

What is history's principle? In modernity truth appears and history is fidelity to it. History is fidelity not to the truth in itself nor to appearances in themselves, which positions modernity refuses as illusory or confused. History is fidelity to the truth insofar as it appears and thus requires history to tell its story. The story, once again, is not of the truth alone nor of appearances alone, but of their inextricable relationship. History is fidelity to the truth *that* truth appears, equally the truth that *what* appears can be made universally true, universally valuable. This double principle implicates the historian in the history she pursues, for it means that there are no facts in history outside the values these facts, that is, subjects, enact, which values the historian commits to realizing (understanding) and to criticizing in taking them as she will. Thus the historian may take the case as she will, but she is absolutely constrained in two respects. If it is the case she is after, she is absolutely constrained by it. In taking the case one way or another, however, she is absolutely constrained to critique it. Did the Reformation happen? Is what happened a reformation? There are elements to consider, facts and words by which one is unqualifiedly constrained.

But in history the historian is also free. What, of what she learns, shall she believe?

In the first place, history is to believe all things. This belief, this all, refers not just to the value of hearing out the case to the end of the evidence, taking into account maximal facts and angles on them. It refers to the principle of inclusion not only as method but also as substance. She says she fired the gun in self-defense. Other evidence shows she may have fired it to get him to stay. But determining what is the case is the work not only of discerning what is the case *in* the case, but of committing to the case as a case in which truth is at stake, the truth, namely, that truth can be staked, can be committed and enacted. If truth is elsewhere, the confusion about what is the case can never be resolved, since no positions are true. If truth is merely whatever appears, then the case need not be resolved, since all positions are true. The first is: We cannot know why she fired the gun. Even she does not know! The second: What can be known is the truth that all answers are possible. This impasse might sound like a quagmire native to the practice of history, but history's quagmire is otherwise. It is the ineradicable, perhaps diabolical challenge of navigating the truth of appearance. This is a challenge shared by subject and historian alike, since although the subject may not know why she fired the gun, it can be known as the specific answer that first she, and then the historian, commits to.

That these may not be the same answer, and that together they may far from exhaust the case, is the second part of the historical maxim: that by the standard of love, the standard of inclusion, the historian shall also, shall indeed therefore, never be deceived. In committing absolutely to the case, to the truth of the case's appearance, the historian finds that her work is also the critique of it.

Modernity is the wager that critique is possible only in light of the commitment to the principle that truth appears. The condition of finding the subject's errors is believing him, believing in him as navigating exactly the same challenge as the historian. What is the case? History brings to this question tools of detection that a subject may not bring. A subject's tools may simply be different ones. But there are no tools that exempt either party from the challenge, also the value, they share—that the world is one in which the truth can be known, albeit with great difficulty. Modernity is the maxim that historical constraint may also be or become the good of inclusion. Modernity is the imperative: You shall risk both generosity (love believes all things) and criticism (decision) because, with appearance neither merely itself (hence critique) nor empty of itself (thus believe!), you can.

Two things follow.

First, once there is modernity, there is confusion. Modernity's principle emerges in positions that will struggle not to reduplicate the refused positions. Modernity emerges in the marketplace, one might say, and is immediately assimilated to, taken for, its refusals. This is not only because modernity models an exception that is hard to hear over the din. It is also because it is a product of what modernity models that it will be confused with the positions it criticizes. What modernity models—that truth appears, that the collective may also be inclusive, the specific universal—is that the truth that appears is that appearance is the only site for truth, which is therefore not pristinely available, not in itself, but must be realized, enacted. It is liable, then, to be confused. If truth is not in itself, where and what is it? What is to be done? If truth is not in itself, therefore it must not be at all.

Second, therefore, modernity requires ongoing clarification as the very substance of its critique.

Two Distinctions

Notwithstanding these exertions, that truth appears, however much it is latent or confusing, can seem a banality. Surely every conceptual position holds this, every myth, every religion, every philosophy, from *Game of Thrones* to the *Tibetan Book of the Dead*, from the *Wall Street Journal* to the *Fundamentals*, from the *Laws of Manu* to the Constitution of the United States to the histories of it to the name Kardashian. Isn't this—that truth appears—just what thinking is, just what formal or systemic thinking is designed to express, and what all instances of thought presuppose? If not, what kind of difference is being noted?

The principle of modernity names two distinctions. It names, first, the distinction between modernity and nonmodernity, which is reflected in the two concepts of religion. Modernity invents itself and nonmodernity as the distinction between the principled exception of inclusion and the routine exclusion that is a function of all other positions. Modernity is the exception in making collectivity possible on grounds other than kin/tribe/ethnos/race. Modernity is the concept of history as neither nature nor supernature, the concept of religion as inclusive of ideals. In so being, modernity excludes nonmodernity, not for the purpose of domination or privilege but to refound it as included in and by modernity's principle.

The principle of modernity names, second, the distinction between modernity and itself. Modernity invents itself—twice—as the principled exception of inclusion, once in biblical concepts and once in engines of scientific, economic, and political innovation. But modernity is liable to confusing itself with nonmodernity, which muddles not only when but what it is. Insofar as modernity distinguishes nonmodernity in order to dominate or exclude with reference to privilege or membership, or insofar as it interprets inclusion as a warrant for domination, it betrays its principle. Indeed, confused by its principle, modernity assails the principle (of) itself in the name of what it refuses.

This distinction of modernity with itself requires a project of clarification, making modernity known to itself and thus in accord with itself. It concerns exposing modernity's violence, which stems from its failure to keep faith with its own refusals.

The distinction between modernity and nonmodernity is putting modernity to the test. Can you distinguish in order to include? Can you distinguish the position of modernity, without which the principle of inclusion is unthinkable, as a condition of including its refused positions on new grounds? Can you distinguish the specific position of inclusion—inclusion of the specific as a regime of value—without making the exclusion of other positions merely the replication of exclusion as a principle? Modernity, once again, is the principle that a (single) collective is constituted by and held accountable to a principle of inclusivity. The refused positions are these: what identifies inclusivity with the collective, which seeks either to expand by domination or to exclude by membership, and what identifies inclusivity with the erasure of the (single) collective. Yet how is modernity not just another collective in default of the accountability of principle? Or another universal in blindness to the irrevocability of collectives?

It is because modernity is both a refusal of positions and also liable to confusing itself with what it refuses that the clarification of modernity is an intervention in the study of domination and violence. Modernity is in need not of refusal, but of rehabilitation. In principled terms, modernity is as much a political as a metaphysical claim, concerned as much with the conditions of inclusion and exclusion as with where or what is truth. It is concerned, that is, to establish that the metaphysical and the political involve each other. Modernity stands for the concept of political inclusivity on the grounds of a critique of metaphysics qua the opposition or identification of truth and appearance. It is equally the concept of truth embodied in human aims on the grounds of a critique of politics qua triumphal collectives.

Insofar as modernity is confused, its political principle of inclusion becomes a triumphalism—political, not to say metaphysical, arrogance and terror. It is not correct to identify the principle itself as corrupt. This would be the preeminent guise of modernity's self-destructive confusions. Yet that it is so mismanaged, corrupted, and bastardized in its own home does nothing to win champions for the principle. It does not matter that modernity "knows" this is the wages of its emergence. It is the responsibility of modernity's paragons to attend to its deconstruction.

In the story of the Grand Inquisitor, composed by Ivan and relayed to his brother Alyosha in Dostoevsky's *The Brothers Karamazov*, the Inquisitor, in the midst of the ritual burning of heretics, apprehends and arrests a figure who has wandered into town and is "recognized" by the people as the one who is "promised to appear at the end of time."[7] The set piece of the story is the confrontation between the Inquisitor and his prisoner as the Inquisitor slips into his cell and challenges him face to face. " 'Is it you? You?' " The prisoner is silent, and the Inquisitor quickly changes tack, exhorting the prisoner to "be silent" and launching an accusatory speech pleading abandonment, breach of contract, and the Inquisitor's right to interpret the fine print as he will.[8] To which end, he observes, "I . . . joined the host of those who have *corrected your deed*."[9]

The Inquisitor is speaking of his diabolical overturning of the principle of the good. The principle brought by the prisoner, he recalls, is that human beings do not live by bread alone but are charged first and last with freedom—with freely knowing and enacting the difference between good and evil. This principle is too difficult, laments the Inquisitor, at least for most of humankind. "Man had henceforth to decide for himself, with a free heart, what is good and what is evil, having only your image before him as a guide." This he cannot do, and he will eventually overturn that image and its truth as impossible. Therefore the Inquisitor has taken on, in the name of love, the salvation of those beings who would otherwise be lost, giving them "miracle, mystery, and authority" in place of the agony of their own hearts and minds.[10] In so doing he sacrifices his own devotion to the principle but also, perversely, goes further than it does, nay, surely, corrects it, he says, in loving them as they *cannot* love themselves.

What the Grand Inquisitor reveals at the end of the story, however, is that this correction is forged in bitterness, not in love. The Inquisitor admits that he too encountered the truth of the freedom of good and evil. "I, too, was in the wilderness, and I, too, ate locusts and roots." But he "awoke and did not want to serve madness."[11] He would instead serve the other side. Consider, though, he insinuates by the revelation of his own case: Would not the other side to an impossible demand be not evil but good? It depends. Milton's Satan has it that with "all hope excluded thus," the only commitment left is to the dark side: "Farewell remorse: all Good to me is lost; Evil be thou my good."[12] Evil can be your good, undoubtedly. But it thereby marks the difference between them.

The Grand Inquisitor poses the question, Is the refusal of the principle the protest that the principle is outside possibility, divine not human, in recognition of which one either leaves the quest constitutively incomplete or embraces a fatal division of oneself? Or is the refusal the protest that it is merely impossible, something the possible has never heard of? The embrace of the principle would then be madness, perhaps, but could also refound possibility to include not only impossibility but also, by that fact, possibility itself. This the Grand Inquisitor seems to know. In confessing that he went to the edge of the possible and would not go further, he is silent on the heart of this drama—that he thereby lost not only impossibility but all possibility too; that his love of humankind, his assignment of it to its possible, is nothing so much as despair.

It is a familiar story. Although the prisoner is not named, Alyosha, the novice monk, knows well what and who Ivan is talking about. Ivan means the thinly disguised tale as a joke and a provocation. A reading. So, too, *Philosophical Fragments*, in which Søren Kierkegaard's pseudonym Johannes Climacus gives an account of the "Teacher" who brings the condition for the truth in bringing himself into the world, the condition that truth, in being in and of the world, requires the learner to do likewise. Or to be in offense. Johannes Climacus, poet of the story, admits he steals it from another poet.[13]

And so here too. Isn't the story of modernity the uncanny of this familiar, and aren't its stakes the ones we have tried to suppress in correcting them? For the question what kind of difference is being noted can be observed through the questions When is modernity? Where is modernity? Or as Kierkegaard asks of the stolen poem, "But who then is the poet?"[14] Insofar as modernity is the principle of the good of inclusion, of love, surely nothing is more diabolical than to give an answer to these questions—to locate some time, some place, hence someone outside love. Surely what is called for here is the silence of Ivan's prisoner, the pseudonymity of Kierkegaard. Perhaps, too, the flight of Jonah, the lament of Job. The fear, or the refusal, of God.

And yet. The Grand Inquisitor represents the prisoner's silence. Kierkegaard's pseudonym speaks, badly, he allows, but at length. Jonah eventually drags his feet to the task. Job gets a hearing for his lament and hears God's in turn. The principle, God, if you like, calls forth. Its learners, in fearing offense, offend the clarity of its purpose—critique, from the good to the good. There is no choice but to speak of it. In refusing to speak, one cedes matters only to worse speech—to the corrections that pass for principle, the confusions that would resign the position. Either faith or offense, says Climacus. Either commit or betray your commitment, says Pascal.

On the one hand, it is correct to say that modernity invents the positions it refuses and confuses. It does not arise out of them, is not an improvement on or emendation of them, and it does not understand them except through its own lens. Modernity arises as refusal, and the refused positions arise simultaneously with it. It is not necessary to ascertain whether these refused positions exist as modernity imagines them. They serve modernity as postulates and indeed as modernity's own position insofar as it is confused. They might simply be left as abstractions. On the other hand, they have names, whether of continent (Africa, Asia), region (East), culture (Indic), or civilization (ancient Greece, indigenous). With one exception, these names coincide with formations modernity has, in the confusion of its critique, worked to dominate. The exception, ancient Greece, is confused by moderns in another way, not as target but as origin, even as the principle of modernity is unknown in the Greek position moderns ironically recall as their own.

This is to acknowledge that all formations are fictions, that is, invented for some purpose. Yet the view that all formations are fictions is consistent with the distinction of modernity, which refounds collectives as mobile, subject to deconstruction through both delimitation and openness. If all formations are fictions, this is distinctly true of modernity, which, in inventing itself, makes invention the paradoxical sign of its ongoing project. This has not spared modern formations from confusion. These confusions can go by yet another set of names: Judaism, Christianity, Islam, secularism, the West. In identifying modernity as its subject, my book elaborates two distinctions: the distinction of the principle from what it renders nonmodern, a distinction of two "twos," and the distinction between the principle of modernity and its confusions and betrayals—that one "two" will ape the structure of the other to escape its own burdens. Each of these moves creates havoc. It is possible to see modernity as itself the villain in the story, a formation whose internal confusions pale in comparison with the modern adventures of conquest and conversion relative to its others. But that story has been told repeatedly. The question here is the distinction that makes this critique possible.

The notion that all formations are fictions, without reference to whether such fictions are a concept of all formations, is central to the premise that cultures are hybrids, identity is hybrid, that diversity, mixing, impurity, borrowing, translation, and invention are the norm in human populations and in human personality. The self would be no less an amalgam of persons and positions than culture is. This premise, attractive and true, is nevertheless no more self-evident than what it replaces. It is a good description that (and because it) supports pluralist thinking, openness, mobility, mutability, all of which are surely preferable to imagining that culture is homogeneous and static, the dream of fascists. That culture is homogeneous, that simplicity or singularity is the premise, can be an unattractive truth. Must it thus be incorrect, even if this is the self-image of cultures themselves? Granted, the expression political correctness is to be abjured as reactionary. But it is valuable to observe the confusion of the value of inclusion with inclusion as a forcible act of description. Persons and cultures can be endlessly creative in depicting themselves now this way and now that way; so then also, by the logic of culture as fiction, in being now this way and now that way, now mobile and now static. But there are also constraints.

As Said observes, we divide in the context of finding the world divided. Culture may be invented. But it is invented from something, from yet another culture, yet another language.[15] Or it invents itself. The notion that culture is invented is designed to combat the idea of a cultural identity, and thus cultural supremacy, founded in the nature of things.

But cultures, persons, languages—human formations—obey the logic of the materials they themselves generate, which tend to the conservation of collectives.[16] Not all articulate principles of diversity, invention, and inclusion. Indeed, most do not. The question is, if it is true that human beings tend to prize their own collective over that of others, if it is true that they do so largely in deference to a dualism of opposition, is it thereby erroneous to conceive a position not endemic to all cultures, or to culture as such, that works to deconstruct this most common of human moves?

I call this position, this principle, modernity. The position is one of critique, critique from a particular standpoint. The standpoint is (the) one that recognizes that critical standpoints may be empowered and not only refuted by their specificity; not only subject to, in being refutable by, yet another critique but the principle of critique as a standpoint in recognition of others. It is lamentable that such a position may then acquiesce in the ostensible right to prize itself over others, to become itself the benighted source of triumphal collectivism. But if it is always correct to condemn distinctions that make one thing preeminent over others, that invidiously divide one person from another, us from them, high from low, and so on, is it always wrong to distinguish at all, even where distinction is the condition of understanding, not to say responding, to what is the case? To the extent that response is integral to the work of understanding, one gambit, expressive of a leeriness to distinguish, assumes the identification of all positions—in being identically distinct. One and many. The position of modernity, the position this book fights for, is another gambit: inclusiveness as the condition of supporting distinctness, consistent with the principle, the distinction, that identifies inclusion as a value.

This is a reason to use, if not to belabor, the names modernity has named in its refusal. There is a bloody history involved in the identification of the nonmodern. But to summarily correct it does not rectify this history.[17] It does not rectify it to evade the work of distinction. What is called for, rather, is to formulate the conditions of inclusion. In the light of the prestige of modernity and in the face of modern patterns of domination, it is risky, perhaps extravagantly so, to distinguish positions (whole continents, entire civilizations, fictive nonentities) as lying outside modernity. Such a move will tend to produce the bitter laugh of the Grand Inquisitor. But although this is not to claim the position of the prisoner, who is, indeed, precisely silent, making this move is a part of the work of clarification. This too the Inquisitor knows, in pressing forward in his speeches, in allowing himself to be seen in his devilry—in thus upending Satan's upending of the good by showing, with Milton, that the good, in being the standard of both itself and evil, cannot permanently be upended. As Pascal puts it in the wager, commit, for you are already committed.[18] Decide which of good or evil it shall be.

The positions of nonmodernity are not themselves confused, where or to the extent that they exist at all. Modernity, in its conflation with its own (invented or real) other, is. The distinction of and with ancient Greek metaphysics is valuable in marking the scene of confusion insofar as Greek concepts/practices of reason are taken to epitomize philosophical thinking. That the Greeks had or invented a notion of philosophy is not in doubt. That there are no "ancient Greeks" outside the cultural mixing of the ancient Mediterranean region is not in question. That this moniker refers to a historically and geographically invented golden age whose disagreements and nonhomogeneity are no less striking than its integrity—that thinking is hybrid, that no cultures are pure (no cultures are cultures) and, above all, that biblical religions have repeatedly propagandized themselves as grateful to the Greeks but finally triumphing over them, much as Christianity finally triumphs over Judaism and secularism over Christianity—neither these observations nor the disapproval they represent are in dispute here.

What is at issue is modernity's move to read into the Greeks its own image, to find in the ancient Greek concept of reason the meaning of reason wherever it travels. That thinkers, philosophers, theologians, and scholars throughout history have symbolized Greek reason as the thing that unifies the ancient and the modern, the religious and the secular, or alternatively as the thing that carves out the secular and the modern in opposition to the religious and the ancient—all such images are indisputable. They are true to the thinkers, philosophers, theologians, and scholars who find them true. They are false to the distinction of modernity.

The Greeks are identified by modernity in the difference between the good and the true insofar as these can be known in themselves and the good and the true as what one enacts or fails to enact in existence: what appears, what is achieved and betrayed. The difference is between the "pure knowledge," for which "we must escape from the body and observe matters in themselves with the soul by itself," and the knowledge that is practiced in the world, the practical reason of a good will, a commitment to the other.[19] The Greeks symbolize the confusion between what modernity refuses—that the truth is purely in itself—and what is nevertheless alluring—this truth precisely insofar as it cannot be known.

This distinction is not native to the Greeks themselves. They would say the truth can be known. This is what philosophy is, the love and pursuit of wisdom as the good, the true, the beautiful. Modernity, by contrast, identifies this pursuit as contradictory in the conception of the good in itself in opposition to the person who seeks it. Socrates knows this in knowing that he is ignorant of the truth and the good. But he does not know, he cannot know, what truth, what good he is ignorant of. He does not know the truth of his ignorance, which in modern terms would place him in flight from and not on the way to what he seeks. For this flight, one requires a concept of beginning, like Adam and Eve, with the knowledge of good and evil.

The notion that the West is divided is a position allied with the very nomination of the West. It is advanced in nineteenth-century comparative philology to lift up the Greeks over the Semites in the struggle for the creation of an Aryan, Christian Europe.[20] It is advanced wherever the Renaissance is understood to give birth to an ancient modernity, a recovered secular, a humanism finally fully realized.[21] This is the invention of the West as divided before the East ever enters into it, Athens and Jerusalem, a division that might involve the rescue of one side or the other, or the elegant merger of the two, from Philo to Bahya ibn Paquda, from Aquinas to the Cambridge Platonists to the contemporary philosophy of religion.

For modernity too the issue is distinction, but of another kind. It is not the reversal of the protagonists, the Greeks now the enemy in favor of a revalued Semitism. Abraham the modern, though he is. The distinction is of a modernity that would refuse the divisions underwritten by Greek metaphysics—between truth and appearance, between universals and collectives. These are divisions in which the very distinction between Hebraic Jerusalem and Greek Athens replicates the Athenian division, expressed in Plato's *Euthyphro*, between what the gods love and what is loved by the gods; between revelation and reason in which each is opposed to the other.[22] The question Socrates asks Euthyphro is whether something is pious because the gods love it, or whether it is pious in being beloved by the gods—thus pious in itself. This might be the relation between revelation—what is pious is what is God's will—and reason—what is pious (or true) is what submits all to its standard, gods and humans alike. Many religious and secular thinkers have cast the difference of religion and reason in this way. But it is on the Athenian ground of opposition and identity, in which human minds are not involved.

The biblical relationship of God and human beings, by contrast, is one of covenant, in which God might issue commands but they are not for that reason good, being subject to human interpretation and critique. Nor is God disempowered relative to what is good in itself. The good is constituted in common. "Choose life," says God in Deuteronomy, by loving God and keeping the commandments.[23] But these commandments must be those by which one can freely live, a principle that tests God himself when he notes, in punishing disobedience, that he gave the Israelites "laws that were not good and rules by which they could not live."[24]

Modernity is the power of distinction by which it can be determined what is good and what is evil, with the truth's image as a guide. Modernity is therefore distinct from the opposition between what is true because God imagines it so and what is true in itself. Modernity is the truth that truth is historical, revealed and enacted in collectives of interpretation and critique. This is not to conceive modernity as pure of divisiveness. Quite the contrary. It is to banish the contradictory logic of purity from its own house by tearing down the house of the West, making purity the temptation of a projected, mythic past. Modernity is distinct in founding the ineluctable relation of two—truth and appearance, thus interpretation; collective and universal, thus critique; self and other, thus history, love, and betrayal. If modernity nevertheless becomes yet another victim to the violence of purifying impulses, this is possible precisely because of what modernity refuses and confuses: the pure in itself, the good in itself, the division between the corrupt what is and the perfect what was and will be, the gnostic dualism of good versus evil, the two truths in perfect opposition, that is, identity.[25] Modernity is not pure. It does not invent the idea of purity. It invents the difference between this idea and the principle that what is corrupt may be so only in fundamental relation to what is not only so. Modernity invents its own temptation and then, as with the golden calf, gives in to it. This calls for critique.

Plan of the Book

Criticism does not await a certain method to complete it. The critic uses whatever methods work to communicate, which methods are finally limited to and by concepts. Nevertheless I want to identify, if not a question of method, then one of form. In the main this book takes the form of standard essayistic writing. I also use nonstandard forms, whether aphorisms or, in places, a kind of interrogative *more geometrico*, to use Spinoza's term. This is in order to elaborate a series of conceptual moves as plainly as possible, with questions, distinctions, contestations, and clarifications.

What makes this writing nonstandard is, negatively, that there is no effort to write continuous prose; positively, that there is an effort to identify the shape of positions in relation to and distinction from one another and to give discrete points of access to an argument as it is being built. In some respects criticism faces off with scholarship. Criticism is in pursuit of what might be (a) well-known, but is (b) requiring modification and restatement, while being (c) resistant to modification by the scholarly requirement to encompass the well known with its tributaries known and less known, the commentaries thereupon, the nature of one's departure therefrom, and only then the modification, strictly tentative. Scholarship is built on the foundation of fidelity to other voices. Nothing can advance without it. And yet there can be a concurrent need to power out of the cacophony, in quest either of what is known, but not well, or of what is imagined as unknowable in confusion of the limits of knowledge. The critic stands as dealer in what is worth knowing, again and anew.

The field of this criticism is the humanities. I also write in the context of religious studies, which has the merit of being mobile in its intellectual character and thus open to experiment. Yet the division between religion and its study, so dear to the field as the price of entering the humanities, is no more an elementary one than the concept of religion itself. Although the difference between a thing and the study of that thing might seem of obvious significance, this difference is not profound when the thing in question is religion, or like constructs such as art, ethics, or politics. Religion is not an object. It is a concept. It is not a concept as opposed to a practice, but a concept whose practice involves judgments and commitments. Although these commitments may take forms alien to the judgments and commitments required of scholarly study, they do not necessarily do so. Attempts to establish scholarship as some other kind of thing, distinguished by, for example, "objectivity," "history," or "secularism," collapse in incoherence, for the question is how to account for the judgments and commitments of thinking anything.

The elements of a study of religion are concepts of religion in the various human worlds, including one's own. But what is religion? Religion, concerned, like art, ethics, and politics, with the nature and value of reality, enacts boundaries in and distinctions of the real. These concerns are not exclusive to religion. Thinking divides, differentiates, chooses, and catalogs. But religion makes a specialty of these foci, instituting images and schemes to manage and systematize a reality that threatens from the side of familiarity or banality no less than from the side of immensity. These images and schemes, together with their institutions, texts, and practices, form the content of religion. This does not make religion a generic concept, hovering above particular vocabularies and histories.

History elucidates concepts of religion as they are expressed in the construction of and confrontation with borders, geopolitical and theological, imaginative, and also practical and social. But whereas history will tend to signify the many, I use it to ask about two. There are many religions, but there are only two elementary ways of structuring borders. Equally, although there is only one word, religion, there are two elementary concepts.

"Powers of distinction" refers to the power and disempowerment of distinctions constituted in social and imaginative formations. It also refers to the power of criticism. Together with Said, I wager that we need to pose the questions both of what we find and what we make. What is the value of inherited distinctions regarding the formations of religion and modernity? What are the distinctions this inheritance produces, or that we produce? Religion and modernity are each cause for contest and strife. I pursue their relationship in recognition of the stakes Said makes all too plain: that distinction is a question of survival and also a threat to it. Together with Wallace Stevens, muse throughout, this will be to find in distinction not only the burden to make better worlds, but also the power, as one does, to affirm the one that is.

Chapter 2, "A History of Religion," identifies the quest to formulate religion as a generic category, inclusive without distinction. Such a religion is constituted for the purpose of escaping the domination and distortion of narrowly Christian models of thinking. But it has unsalvageable consequences. I work instead for a history of religion that roots both religion and secularism in the distinction of modernity. The terms religion and modernity are formations and fantasies whose borders, and thus contents, are unsettled. The geographical-conceptual complex of modernity, dubbed Western, possesses a twofold symbolic identity: as an internally diverse repository of universalizable cultural riches and as an exemplar of cultural domination, monolithic in its relations with its symbolic partners—the ancient, the East, the primitive.

The West, one might say, is simply a name for one half of the globe, modernity but a description of historical period, religion an identifier of community. But these ascriptions, also divisions, are never so simple. Our cultural schizophrenia about religion's parameters and the proper attitude toward it provides an opportunity for revision on all these fronts. Distinction as a conceptual and historical operation anchors equally the questions religion poses to reality and those we thinkers and readers pose to religion and related formations. When is religion? Where is religion? What is religion? What difference do these decisions make? The distinction of the two dualisms, the one of opposition/identity and the one of relationship and inclusion, but also confusion, supports the effort to reconsider the humanistic tendency to multiply distinctions in the face of political danger.

Chapter 3, "Artificial Populations," investigates the work of the eighteenth-century humanist Giambattista Vico to conceive of history in the distinction of the Hebrews. I begin with two theorists who fought such distinctions, in line with their fields of study in the humanities and the social sciences. Durkheim corrects for distinction insofar as it undergirds Christian-Western dominance of the terms of social scientific study by conceiving forms of religion shared by all societies, indeed the form of religion that is society as such. Said advances an alternative solution, whereby distinction is robbed of its power through magnification of its operations with the help of a secular history. Ironically, it is Vico whom Said credits for this concept of history. If Durkheim's elementary form of the religious life is designed to rectify what Vico distinguished as the God of the Hebrews, the critique of Orientalism embraces Vico's distinction, but in reverse. It shall now be the nations distinguished from the Hebrews, distinguished, that is, from distinctiveness, who take up the charge of eliminating invidious distinction in commitment to a history purged of God altogether.

To open Vico's *New Science* is to be reminded just how much we live in Durkheim's and Said's world and not in Vico's. Yet Vico's distinction between the Hebrews and the gentile nations—alarming to present sympathies in its apparent cultivation of a Judeo-Christian triumphalism—proves paradoxically a more capable resource than either a generic religion or a critique of Orientalism in addressing both the violence of distinction and the work of inclusion. The chapter takes its title from Stevens's poem "Artificial Populations," in which "the Orient and the Occident embrace," "two poles" of "a state of mind."[26] Vico has been taken up in the study of religion as alternately a naturalist and a supernaturalist, a precursor of secular history and a Catholic defender of sacred history. It is crucial to encounter these interpretations in coming to understand Vico's alternative to both positions, his commitment to history as the site of wisdom and critique, the work and the good of knowing others.

Chapter 4, "The Collective," revises what Said calls the West, what the study of religion calls Christianity, and what Vico calls the Hebrews. With Durkheim, I connect religion and society in elementary forms. With Said, I stand alert to the danger of distinction. But with Vico, I call upon the Hebrews to bear the elementary distinction of modernity. Let it now be the figure of Abraham with whom distinction reckons—the one who is called to leave his land for another that is promised. In this chapter I employ questions with often multiple, sometimes alternative, answers. This form works with the second dualism, in which two things that might seem opposed can both be true—that is, more strongly, that each might be true only insofar as the other is true. This is to confront the temptation to oppose or identify in the light of the imperative to hold contrasting truths together—not as a logical feat but as an existential work in support of distinction and of mutuality. This is not meant to abrogate decision or to defer it. It is to decide not "all of the above" but these and those must work together, and readers, thinkers, and collectives must see how for themselves.

At the same time, there are distinctions to be made, and not all alternatives are equally in play. The issues this book confronts—religion, history, truth, critique—are of epic importance. In working with them, I make claims about how they can be conceived and suggest strongest versions. This acknowledges that these terms do not always bring out the best—in worlds, in readers, thinkers, citizens. One can say yes, this is how to capture what is ideally at issue in democracy or religion. But such wagers do not displace a darker sense that religions will be problematic, readers will be confused, citizens and collectives will choose violence. At times I leave in this darker eventuality on the grounds that faith in the good of self and other, in interpretation, in history, in democracy, and in love must be made and remade. One loses faith. The loss of it needs a voice too.

Religion is not a stable word, but it is empty to say that it can therefore be employed any old way. Instead I give readers constraints. My decisions embed in the framework, which shows that thinking takes place in the light of commitments that may multiply under pressure and may at times be confused. There is choice in the framework. In some cases I want readers to decide. Will religion always threaten a complex polity? Partly it depends on what you mean by religion. Here are options. But also, it depends on what you do. That must be open.

Having confronted the structure of modernity and religion in their web of distinctions and connections, I turn in the next two chapters to readings of thinkers with whom this critique is powered. I pursue the paradoxes of modernity through a consideration of some of its stories, its temptations, and a few of its key figures—students and critics of religion, historians and paragons of modernity. In chapter 5, "Images of Truth from Anselm to Badiou," it is Anselm, figure of medieval Christianity, who gives us the principle that truth appears in the maxim that

God exists, the commitment, astonishing for him no less than for us, that testifies to the centrality of the mind in and as history. In putting Badiou's commitment to the time of the concept in this view, one gains not only a longer history of ideas but a richer conceptual story up to the present. In chapter 6, "The Radical Enlightenment of Spinoza and Kant," it is these Enlightenment critics who give us the principle that both religion and secularism are subject to the elementary relation of self and other, in the struggle of human beings to realize—to understand and enact—their nature. In Spinoza, the surprise is a position circumventing the dead ends of nature and supernature, a nature that is the engine of mind and solidarity. In Kant, it is the intimacy of religion and reason as they contend with the borders that keep them in their place and the desires by which they continually transgress them.

Chapter 7, "Modernity as Ground Zero," follows my critique of collective life in chapter 4 with a critique of the epoch of modernity. Chapter 8, "Of Gods, Laws, Rabbis, and Ends," considers the epoch of modernity in light of a few contemporary scenes. Together they bring forward the charge of the book. Insofar as period refers to modifications of history and not also to history's own origination, the principle of history will be occluded. Every change in history presumes the change before it. Every origination is repetitively subject to infinite specificity and infinite generality. The story that modernity is the epoch of innovation in distinction from the epochs expressive of tradition and conservation can always be shown to be false. Novelty was prized in antiquity. Says modernity.

Modernity's confusion is the supposition that novelty in time, the break of epoch, is a break within history and not also the break that is history. Modernity is the name for something that happened in, say, the fifteenth century. Something happened in the fifteenth century, no doubt. Modernity is the happening that is break, creation, novelty, and also the value of these things. But modernity is the paradox that in order to host all changes, history is the one change. It is the one that makes change also one, the epoch of epochs, in refusing the division of the one and the many, the multiples of history as outside any essences.[27] This concept of history's origin is unlike Aristotle's God, the unmoved mover that moves without itself being moved.[28] It is like Spinoza's in being the mover of itself.[29] This epoch, this event, expresses modernity as source not only of "the killer apps" of innovation, as Niall Ferguson names the West's power, but of the novum that is the relationships of two, of reason and history, self and other, the novum of the collective that, in being naturally exclusive, shall also be unnaturally inclusive.[30] This is not to deprive the fifteenth or any other century of monumental happenings or more quiet changes. It is to affirm history as the human story of these things in the light of the commitment that they be of value to tell.

In modernity, confusion abides. Nova are erected. Pasts are denied and reinstated. Criticism is repeated. And innovated. Modernity is never done. But there are two ways modernity is never done, or is incomplete. Modernity is incomplete insofar as modernity requires clarification. Modernity is also incomplete in simply being the principle that one cleave to the work of inclusion, the work to tell the story of human beings working on and against the good in time. This work is never complete.

But if the principle is that this work is the value of human beings in their realities, how could anyone miss it? It may be as Marx had it, that the world is overtaken with suffering, in the light of which one will divide between the world as it is and whatever ideals one holds or hopes for (truth, love, the good). Or as Spinoza observed, that collectives whose borders are absolutized seem the very sign of strength, if only for a time. Each of these distinctions—between the world and the good, between us and them—ensures repetition as a core outcome of the resignation that holds, in defiance or ignorance, that there is no principle otherwise.

Modernity is constrained to the specific rejection of repetition as the fate or meaning of history. What, then, is modernity's specificity? Is it not still, if not even more, the truth that the West's "apps" serve simply to make it a better killer?

It can be stated as follows in beginning. The principle is *of* the global, the inclusive. But it originates in what is called, with what we know is a loaded history, the Middle East, which becomes the West. It is expressed in the writings of the peoples who drew together the stories in and around the Bibles, new and old, that proclaimed, as God says to Abraham, *Lekh lekha*! Go! Leave your homeland for another land that will be shown.[31] Abandon homeland for a home land, two words not one, a promised land founded on equality and freedom, not natural generation: on covenant. That the principle originates will seem false given that many, or all, culture formations have or seem to have some idea of "love your neighbor as yourself." Love all. Be compassionate. What originates, however, is the centrality of origination, historicity, to the principle: that love your neighbor as yourself is both the highest ideal—it is God, for example—and an ideal of history. It is not (the) given but can only be practiced in—being the very principle of—history, as history is the very subject of the ideal. As Hegel puts it, "Freedom as the *ideal* of that which is original and natural, does not exist *as original and natural*."[32] Break with your land, originate your history, not in service to an abstract philosophical ideal but in service to another land, a land of ideals, an ideal history. Begin.

This is to say both that history is the site, the only site, of truth and that truth is nothing other than what history's human subjects are doing in the face of the demand to break with their own kind and love their neighbors as themselves. History shows, to be sure, nothing so much as that this is not for the most part what human beings do. The human story is largely therefore of crisis, as human beings break with their homelands only, alas, to reestablish them in another land, to reestablish, that is, their own kind in the land. In biblical language, the land for which one breaks from one's home is "promised." But this promise is subject to the terms of a covenant, the principle of which is self-rule in concert. It is on the grounds of the covenant's implication in concert (inclusion, solidarity) that Job indicts God for abandonment. It is on the grounds of the covenant's implication in self-rule that Jonah worries about being dominated by God. It is in the terms of the covenant, the principle of self-rule in concert, that it will be mistaken as self-rule in distinction. Even God will get confused. Especially God, modern and primitive both. History is crisis.

So affirm Adam and Eve in being excluded from the illusion of a time when they did not know good and evil. There is no refuge from existence as it is and also as they, with great effort, must originate it. Everything that follows in the Holy Book shows nothing more or less than that this origination is possible; that it is truly difficult and rare; that confusion reigns; that the principle is profaned again and again. It is not, in being the very freedom to profane it, thereby destroyed. As the serpent, Grand Inquisitor of Eden, well knew.

But this is to say no, not the West. Not geopolitical division. Not civilization. Who today could claim that the West possesses some premium on the truth? India is a democracy, an intellectual powerhouse, a critical if suffering emblem of the prodigious experiment of the principle. Africa has its democracies. The Middle East, birthplace of the principle, houses various undemocracies, including, painfully if utterly predictably, in the very land where democracy arose. A country most Western, a West most compromised. Europe is relatively democratic, as is North America. But South America is not uniformly so, a fact that is not unrelated to policies emanating from North America and Europe. Just so do the worlds and economies on all continents struggle with their inextricable relation, their bloody histories, their contests of principle and profanation.

One could say the West is over. It is over as an idea and as an ideal. For now we see that "the West" was built not only on principle, but also on the fear thereof, on the betrayal and resignation thereof. The West, like the Bible itself, is corrupt and corrupting. Each is no less primitive for being modern, consistent with the covenant God makes with Abraham, which proclaims that in Abraham "all the families of the earth shall be blessed," but in which the parties each struggle with the distinctions—the blessings and the curses—that make possible its realization.[33]

One nevertheless affirms, conscious of the threat of chauvinism, Here is the principle. It shall be betrayed. It has been, is being, betrayed. It is confusing and confused. But therefore, Here is what it is not. One continues to state and restate, to qualify, to affirm, and to move forward. Sometimes this means one says West. Sometimes it means no to the West. One worries about not only what has been, but what may still be, with great effort.[34]

2

A History of Religion

We seek
Nothing beyond reality. Within it,

Everything, the spirit's alchemicana
Included, the spirit that goes roundabout
And through included, not merely the visible,

The solid, but the movable, the moment,
The coming on of feasts and the habits of saints,
The pattern of the heavens and high, night air.

Wallace Stevens, "An Ordinary Evening in New Haven"

Descartes to Durkheim

In the opening paragraph of his *Meditations on First Philosophy*, René Descartes makes two observations that signal both the personal nature of what is to follow and its consequence, he hopes, for the history of thought. First, most famously, he writes of his realization that "numerous" of the opinions he has held since his youth have turned out to be false, and thus by implication "how doubtful" are "all those that I had subsequently built upon them." "I realized," he writes, "that once in my life I had to raze everything to the ground and begin again from the original foundations, if I wanted to establish anything firm and lasting in the sciences."

The second thing Descartes observes is that "several years have passed" since he first experienced this realization. He "procrastinated," he admits, until he felt he would be "at fault" were he to "waste the time that remains for carrying out the project by brooding over it." In this spirit he finds the resolve to enact what he calls his "demolition" (*eversio*), the results of which are searchingly detailed in the *Meditations*. Why was Descartes brooding for so long? His resolve, he tells us, takes the form not only of freeing his mind "of all cares," but also of securing for himself "a period of leisurely tranquility" in which he could "withdraw into solitude."[1] Was Descartes just too busy to solve his problem when it arose? If so, busy doing what? Was he simply, as history seems to show, a prosperous gadabout, able to secure leisure for himself as easily as he had avoided it in the first place while completing the mandated spell of soldiering and traveling that fell to the established bourgeoisie in early modern Europe?[2]

Such questions draw attention to the charged images that have accrued in the person of Descartes for almost four hundred years. Although his bold claims about the mind, nature, and God dominate the reception of his work, Descartes is also imagined as the quintessential armchair thinker, an imprecise designation but one that draws together the ambition of his claims, their presumed overreach, and a vague unease concerning his setting and personal fortune. Such images turn a suspicious eye too quickly on Descartes's project of understanding—as if his interest in the philosophical extent of personal questions is itself an unearned privilege; as if, more generally, when we historicize the thinker we need no longer ask whether we are bound by the thought. Let us observe the explanation Descartes himself gives for why he dragged his feet for several years. Quite simply, he notes, "the task seemed enormous."[3]

In taking on religion, I take inspiration from Descartes's sense of enormousness, both insofar as religion poses a question concerning foundations and insofar as it has languished in vaults of procrastination. One might protest, What more explosive topic fills the pages of popular journals? What more vibrant topic exists in contemporary social and cultural theory? The field of religious studies has labored for more than a century to interrogate the nature and parameters of religion in a global context. What I propose is a revision of what Durkheim called religion's "elementary forms."[4] I borrow Durkheim's iconic language while emending his assumption that there are elementary forms of a generic religion at the root of all cultures and ideations. Durkheim is a pivot between religion and its study, identifying a concept of religion in a universal idiom that, in encompassing all peoples, corrects the monstrosity of Western self-regard as reflected in models of scholarship. What the scholarship of his day called the primitive is placed not only at the root of more developed societies, to be surveyed from the heights, but in the very midst of Western civilization. Religion is the idea and practice of community, says Durkheim. The civilized have nothing fundamental to add that simpler communities do not express from the beginning.

It is a brilliant effort. Writing in the early years of the twentieth century, Durkheim worked against many contemporary models that, however invested in cross-cultural understanding, served ultimately to support Western superiority. Durkheim's rejection of this outcome may fairly be considered one of the proudest accomplishments in the history of the study of religion. But it also expresses what it means to say that the question of religion languishes. Religion will repent of its services to imperialist ventures by removing all particular claims and values from its elemental vocabulary. Then and only then can it become an object of study. The question is, What is then being studied?

Durkheim's account of the centrality of social life in thinking about formations of religion is of permanent utility. What remains, however, is to work on distinctions of the social overlooked by Durkheim in his effort to make a unified theory. To say that religion is not an elementary form is to say neither that religion is not a form at all nor that religion is many forms, two well-attested theses in the study of religion. With Durkheim, I contend with the conceptual repertoire that structures religion as a social and intellectual system. But there are distinctions at work in this repertoire, distinctions in social formations concerning the building blocks of worlds, minds, and gods or values. If religion is an articulation and elaboration—a theory—of community as Durkheim held, then it can be enchanting to document all the kinds there are, all the colors and languages and practices. Durkheim had good reasons for wanting the matter to end there. But although he ended there and the field has stalled there, whether in confirmation or in refutation, that is not a reason for readers and citizens to continue to do so. Yes, religion might serve to divide civilized from primitive, West from its others. Division is the very mark, the very totem of community, Durkheim saw, including the community of scholars.

What Durkheim saw only implicitly, however, is that religion can also power the critique of communities whose borders are inclusive only of some arbitrary "we" or, what is the same, a we comprising kin, tribe, and kind. If he is right that the social elementary is one of borders, he did not complete the interrogation of what can count as a border. It might be tempting to respond by flinging open all borders and claiming supremacy over the collectives that cling to them. This is exactly the mentality Durkheim resisted, and rightly so. The point is to understand borders and their different logics.

The power to do so belongs not to a generic religion, but to the distinction of a historical and social topos, a religion, I claim, that can serve as another name for modernity. Religion is modern insofar as it imagines that what theorists like Durkheim help us to see is ordinarily the case—that human beings are communal and political beings—may also be subject to the extraordinary pressure that the border of community be extended. Religion is modern insofar as it holds that what is righteous for one's own kind might be made righteous for other kinds and indeed, perhaps, for all. This religion is a position in the world. It is also a maxim of scholarship. Religion is conceived generically on the grounds of extending its borders to those who conceive and practice it differently. But in addressing only the political struggles that necessarily attend difference, that is, by formulating religion as generic so that it can preemptively include all social formations, the study of religion has evaded the conceptual question of principle, the question of which principles make inclusion possible.

To be sure, religious studies has produced its share of doubt—doubt about its place in the academy, doubt about its object, whether it has one or should have one, doubt about its methods and its genealogies, doubt about its ethics. What it has not doubted adequately is whether a study of religion is possible without the distinction not just of religion, but of the social and conceptual systems this word vaguely points to. Do we know what we study when we study religion? Do we know who we are insofar as we do so?

These questions may be signified by Descartes, the one who, in asking what he knows, also asks who and what he is. Threatened in the second Meditation with the recognition that his mind may be infinitely self-deceptive, Descartes nevertheless asserts that "I am, I exist," then quickly adds, "But I do not yet understand sufficiently what I am—I, who now necessarily exist." He continues, "And so from this point on, I must be careful lest I unwittingly mistake something else for myself, and thus err in that very item of knowledge that I claim to be the most certain and evident of all."[5] Is Descartes's pugnacious confidence in his existence any more striking than his worry that he might just as easily mistake himself?[6] We might similarly wonder whether the "foundationalism" Descartes is perennially saddled with is not belied by the thinker's frank contention with the elusiveness of foundations. What is the value of Descartes's questions? What of his work to establish something firm and lasting—in the world, in himself—must now be razed to the ground?

Descartes is a thinker associated with a modernity dedicated to rethinking inherited ideas about the world. He also comes to signify a modernity of convention, itself needing to be overthrown with each passing generation. In this twin image of criticism and orthodoxy, Descartes might be identified with modernity itself, the ubiquity of his name in adjectival form making it sometimes seem as if modernity begins as a kingdom of one circa 1641.[7] In many quarters of the humanities, Descartes remains alive simply as a position to be "demolished," to turn his own metaphor on him. That he is perpetually in need of demolition, however, signals something about us. Readers seem unable to be done with Descartes. This may mean we have properly kept faith with his impulse to rethink foundations. Or it may mean we have failed to do so adequately, the compulsion to rebroadcast the failed foundationalism of Descartes a sign of our failure to understand.[8] As we will see in chapter 5, on Descartes's progenitor, Saint Anselm, the commitment to existence involves more than it seems to our late modern eyes. The study of religion still has much to learn from this oft-reviled ancestor about its foundations and its procrastinations.

The Study of Religion

To study religion is to enter fraught terrain. There are two research communities who share the terrain, in contrast to those to whom religion matters as either friend or foe. The first research community is the scholarly study of religion, by whose light almost all the sentences one could write to introduce the concept of religion would come under sharp scrutiny. Where does the term religion come from? Whose history does it presuppose? Is religion really a human, that is, a global or universal phenomenon? Does it comprehend everyone, or even anyone? Is religion a term of the religious or of the critic, the insider or the outsider? In scholarly terms, religion may not refer to anything singular, or even to anything at all. It may require explanation in the terms of other discourses, such as sociology, psychology, politics, or evolutionary biology. Scholarship may not need to concern itself with how religious persons describe themselves, especially insofar as it is concerned with the mobility and contingency of the ascription "religious."

The worry is Christianity, and specifically Protestantism, whose theological norms are seen to cling to every effort toward secular study, indeed to the secular as such, and which therefore requires special measures of exposure and critique. This worry also conditions postcolonial studies, which indicts Christianity and the West as historical complexes that have dominated those of other regions and religions, in part by claiming to serve as neutral hosts for an ostensibly expansive plurality.[9] Better, it might seem, to denude religion of any history whatever. Religion would now be undisguised, but also cleansed of identifying features. As a generic concept, religion is both essentially plural—anything can count within it—and essentially empty, neither rooted in history nor possessing any necessary content. From this vantage, to count religion as a generic category is the same as to postulate that religion does not exist. It exists, that is to say, as a function of scholarly investigation and is limited thereto, having little beyond an ideological meaning in the world scholarship aims to understand, and thus constituting a primary site of scholarly demystification.

A reader not well versed in the academic field of religious studies will respond to the term in a more commonsense way. Religion is an ordinary aspect of human social and cultural life. It is a creation of ancients or primitives, of gods or of rabbis. It is on the decline. It is on the rise. It is a topic, as the Pew Forum on Religion and Public Life holds, with a concrete demographic specificity that can be studied with questions such as "How religious is your state?" and surveys such as "Religion among Millennials." Religion, according to this second research community represented by Pew, is an inescapable part of how human beings speak about the world they live in, whether as practitioners or as observers of human behavior. It would not seem to require all that much theoretical or grammatical interrogation. Whatever religion is, it constitutes a prime arena for the business of understanding human affairs both locally and globally. While scholars use research from Pew, and while Pew reflects the scholarly inclination to avoid passing judgment, Pew's interest in tracking, measuring, and disseminating information about religion contrasts with the scholarly interrogation of its formations. Pew is, by its own light, a "fact tank" and accords religion a place as an obvious feature of human life.

Where scholarship is critical, Pew is detached, serving as a "nonpartisan, nonadvocacy organization" dedicated to "discussions of timely issues." While scholarship might conclude that there is no such thing as religion in general, Pew can tell you what Christians, Muslims, and the unaffiliated make of gay marriage, the death penalty, and abortion.[10] For Pew, religion is a simple, albeit diverse, datum. For scholarship, religion is a complex social and intellectual challenge.

I occupy a third stance. My interest is in a history of religion advanced in principles articulated in a critique of religion—an account of the distinctions at issue. This work is different from the work of the Pew Forum in that it probes the frameworks that shape the religious facts Pew studies. Like scholarship on religion, the history of religion is interested in what makes something religious, what counts as religion, and also in why people are religious, thus what social and psychic forces are at play in religion—what it is, in short, that religion refers to. What distinguishes this history is its concern with religion's value, positive and negative. There is robust work in the study of religion that counts as critical of the object, whether to expose religion as a negative force, to identify it as a meaningless but ideologically useful one, or to track its pretenses to escape the tools of analysis.[11] In turn, there are scholars who invest in the value of religion for religious actors or for social systems more generally.[12] The critics will tend to regard differences of religion as subordinate to religion's function in social systems. Those invested in religion's value will tend to be interested in differences, advancing their work directly from within a religious community or with a particular community's resources in mind, or in relation to a particular community as the object of ethnographic examination.

My work pursues distinctions of religion, not in terms of this or that communal tradition but as systemic formations of collectives according to the logic I have laid out in chapter 1. Durkheim's model of religion as a single system is provocative but inadequate. Nor do I follow the level of analysis that accepts the multifarious forms or traditions this system takes.[13] I am indebted to the research to trace the language and logic of world religions, as well as to histories of religion's discovery in early modernity.[14] But my aim is more constructive than these projects of exposure. It is a history and criticism of religion in light of the principle of modernity. The topic of religion divides the broader public between those invested in religion as friend or foe and those to whom it is a matter of indifference. Both scholarship and the Pew Forum attempt to occupy the sliver between these positions. This book hews closer to the public interest in religion as I work now as friend, now as foe. In so doing, I pose the question of what terrain, if any, lies between investment and indifference in order to interrogate the values of both religion and its study. In this the project shares with Pew an interest in values endemic to a flourishing civic life. It thus shares an interest in speaking to those for whom scholarship on religion's viability as a term of art can seem like so much quibbling in the face of the busy mosque down the street. I add to the work of Pew an emphasis on systemic conceptual analysis in deciding what values religion offers to civic life or how it detracts from it.

It is notable that outside the classroom, the scholarly study of religion remains isolated, even from other theoretical communities. It does not easily share its specialized wisdom with ordinary readers, and it relegates the constructive, conceptual approach to religion to other specialties such as philosophy or theology, other precincts such as self-professed religious institutions, and other times such as—to put it bluntly—the past. What the study of religion knows is that the revolution that generates a religion fit for global study is incomplete insofar as Christianity retains social and intellectual power in the West. Until this reality is properly deconstructed, scholarship cannot connect with the person who claims that religion is a source available for ordinary use, simply a form of thinking or truth, even in a plural sense. Indeed, the pluralism of religion—the view of religion enshrined in law and absorbed by a general public—is, from a scholarly standpoint, problematically named, understood, and formulated, even as pluralism reigns in the framework of the field's own practice.

The study of individual communal traditions and more particular topics goes on below the radar of these theoretical anxieties. There are also plenty of theories that presume we just need ever better definitions of religion. What can minimally be agreed on in scholarship is that the study of religion is a form of study and not a form of religion, a distinction that rescues a space for religion not only at the scholarly table but indeed in the realm of the humanities as such.[15] Although the term secular comes under scrutiny as guilty of some of the same things as religion, there is nevertheless an acknowledged common space within which the study of religion is possible, distant from any direct relation to the thing itself. If the garrulous patrol of its borders suggests ongoing insecurity, this is no less a sign that there are securities to protect. We had to stop debating religion in order to understand what religion is. We had to banish God and the gods, in public if not in private, in order to know why on earth human beings believe in them. For this reason, if there were thinkers on the order of an Augustine or a Descartes or a Buber wandering through our contemporary streets, most scholars of religion would on principle seek them out as examples of religion, but not as fellow thinkers in a study of it.[16] This distinction has its rationale. Is it a good one?

Insofar as scholarship on religion avoids decisions, if not questions, of value, it does so by elevating and multiplying its concepts. Religion cannot be evaluated insofar as it is a scholarly construct, not a fact on the ground. Neither can religions be evaluated, since they are each sources of value unto themselves, and in any case the task of evaluating lies outside the scholarly charge simply to understand. The effort to evaluate religion is seen as the crude work of popular opinion and presses. If one does the close reading of scholarship, judgmental questions will simply not arise. At the least, they would need to be indefinitely postponed in the face of the virtually endless mountain of material to master.

The distinction between "religion" and "religions" is a tool to navigate dangerous waters in religious studies. Many scholars use both terms as the need arises. But one can observe a problem in the distinction. If one holds that the designation "religions" is more useful, it is difficult to stop there. Perhaps there are no religions, but only Christianity, Hinduism, and so on: particular formations. But then perhaps even these are too clumsy. There may only be Christianities and Hinduisms, Mormons and South Indians, patriarchs from the Western states and renouncers in Delhi, unto the end of finding there is only x = multiple. One can reach the same conclusion in beginning with the singular. If religion is merely an abstract tool to classify reality, then the object is to attain the most capacious postulate to manage the teeming x = multiple. Yet such a postulate will itself ever be marked as insufficiently abstract, smuggling in its own multiples to render its containing powers suspect. As the formula x = multiple suggests, singularity and multiplicity bottom out in the same question mark regarding which is more basic: the unknowable regress of infinite multiplicity or the unknowable abstraction of infinite subsumption.

In the contemporary academy, things rarely get this deep. Our epoch evinces a marked preference for plurality over singularity, and the study of religion is no exception. But religion and religions both get one there. The concept of religions drives toward increasing specificity, avoiding infinite regress by arbitrarily rescuing some term by which to include multiple, comparative, and historical cases. The concept of religion insists on the bleaching virtues of its generic, the empty condition for all possible cases or any given one. Neither route can raise the question of whether religion is valuable, because neither can get beyond the logic of the one and the many. When Wilfred Cantwell Smith urges readers to discard the term religion in favor of the particular traditions that constitute its cases, he is calling for attention to a lower level of generality/multiplicity while leaving the generic singular intact as what is erased by the multiple instances.[17] When Jonathan Z. Smith makes religion a function of the scholar's interpretive freedom, he makes it a device by which to control, while highlighting, the diversity of human stories.[18] When Talal Asad observes that religion is a term specific to Western theology and a Western canon, he moves readers to suspect its application to non-Western cases while leaving intact its analytic integrity as descriptive of the West.[19] In each of these cases, religion—utilized or discarded—is a term of unity, however delimited, as of plurality, however constrained.

Religion, however, is a historical concept, not merely, as in Asad, a term with a history to which it would be limited or, as in J. Z. Smith, a term by which to pick out historical variation. Religion is a concept used in systemic distinctions in and of history. Generic accounts imagine religion as a sign of primal difference, constituted by such pairs as the sacred and the profane, man and the gods, this world and the next world, the individual and society, chaos and order. Yet in a history of distinctions in (within) religion, religion is not the conceptual container for a difference of this from that. Religion is both productive of and subject to distinction, serving either as the ideological-political conservation of community or the ideological-political engagement with, or confusion of, the principle that the border can be mobile and thus inclusive. This distinction is not without cost. The conception of religion and modernity as key terms whose fates are co-involved cannot support religion as something in general or predicable of the human as such. They therefore have no way of avoiding the offense of privileging particular standpoints.

There has been much effort to avoid this line of thinking. The position that registers the origin of religious studies in the Western recognition of regions outside the West, then imagines a globe within which the West might be merely one history among many, is after the principle and politics of leveling. Religion as an intellectual and social force in the ancient, medieval, and modern West comes to be a term of art for something generically human, a break understood in political-historical terms as the encounter with others and the voyages and projects that made this encounter one of, as it were, demolition. From the perspective of this newly generic religion, religion's former and ongoing promise of a universal history would be untrue in exact proportion to the arrogance and coercion with which it is promulgated. Insofar as Christianity begins as the measure of all religions, let it become the measure of none. Let history suppress, in order to multiply, the particulars of religion so it can be revealed as a social economy supportive of all claims to authority, which claims would call for scholarly deconstruction.

Religion is also, however, a concept in which the historicity of existence is at issue. Religion may be a ubiquitous formation, but it is not ubiquitous as the same thing. We have repented the ages of empire; we have announced the age of the global. But this repentance and this announcement, optimistic though they are, paper over the task of thinking to the edges of our concepts. It is safer, perhaps, to have history take the form of a generic method, the complement to religion the generic concept. If history is conceived otherwise, as itself having a history, with the responsibility then to understand and evaluate its borders and particular content, how could it be deployed everywhere and always? How could it temper the theological impulse to divide?

This is not to deny the power of history in its work to temper dualism. It is to observe that a theology that would be tempered by history is not the same as one rooted in history itself. The assimilation of these gives theology a unified theory, as Durkheim gives religion, consistent with the dualism expressive of the opposition and identity of the sacred and the profane. This theory cannot then take account of a theology rooted in the paradoxes of reality, one akin to the epigraph from Stevens's "Ordinary Evening in New Haven" that observes "not merely the visible, / The solid, but the movable, the moment." In Stevens's inimitable phrase, "We seek / Nothing beyond reality. Within it, / Everything."[20] History in relation to Stevens's "everything" would include the confusions and gaps that are constitutive of the worlds of human beings as they appear, as they exist. Nothing beyond is ruled out so that everything can be ruled in. But "everything" thus paradoxically has a border, a stake, a history. And "nothing" has the extraordinary double sense of what is included—nothing shall now be what we have to confront—and what we expel to a beyond that shall not concern us. "Nothing that is not there and the nothing that is," as Stevens puts it in "The Snow Man."[21] This would not be to disown the methodical dimension of history. It would be to say that history, as the value of "everything," distinguishes itself in toto from a history that parses its topics in opposition to values that are cast as elsewhere. History would be opposed to (this) opposition, not to (all) forms of religion.

It has been some time since Hegel advanced his argument for what he called "the concept" as historical and history as itself a specific concept—history not as method but as thought, thus as some thought, as this and not that. There have been generations of commentary on this argument, together with philosophical and historical work moving, it seems, far beyond it. Hegel is dauntless, however, in insisting that the imperative to historicize applies absolutely provided history is understood to be limited by and to its concept, which is to say, limited by and to the difference that history itself makes.[22]

These reflections place religion and history together as critical terms in order not only to ascertain their value but also to distinguish: within religion and between history and a fateful structure of opposition. This may very well be to wander into loaded terrain, but there is value in doing so. Scholars have long since internalized the unsettling work of tracing the relation between religion and forms of empire and colonialism, formations built on invidious distinction. Such work shows no sign of slowing. The thoroughgoing prejudices at the heart of Western religious thought and politics, the pervasiveness in scholarship of invidious distinctions between us and them, good and bad religion, the West versus the rest, the assumption of Protestant frameworks and metaphysics in contrast with which all else is implicitly deviant, not to mention the perfidy of a liberalism that attempts to solve these ills too quickly or unconsciously—all have been scrupulously documented and exposed. Distinctions of value in or of religion cannot, it is agreed, recapitulate these sins. Now what? It is time to advance to the next move.

Religion is a discourse that manages human struggles with distinction and otherness. This is an observation in recognition of the power of religious formations to mystify and disable no less than to organize and empower. Put differently, human beings will always find ways to mystify and disempower instead of to empower and enable one another. Religion is a way to do both. What is religion such that it is both? What and where is the distinction of religion? It has been easier to multiply the problem out of existence. Here religion is valuable, there it is not. Or this religion is better than that religion. Or no religion is valuable. Or value and religion are not connected. Or just it is all much too complicated to denote with such seemingly simple questions. Certainly religion can be made incredibly complex. Human beings are complex. But there are also plain questions. Once again, Do we know what we study when we study religion? Do we know who we are insofar as we do so?

Scholars in the study of religion have been understandably reluctant to take up the charge of putting themselves in the picture of what they study. They have felt they had to distinguish their study from the practices of religion in a way that scholars of something like literature have not had to do. One might think the best way to make religion at home in the humanities is to treat its issues of interpretation with the same analytic self-consciousness as other disciplines ideally use, giving attention to reader and context of reading as well as to text and its contexts in alternating emphases. But the freight of being a religious insider has seemed much greater than with inquiry in other disciplines; the sense that insider status might fatally compromise the veracity of what one is studying has seemed much stronger—the insider as religious subject, thus as prophet or claimant to privileged knowledge.

The threat of the inside has meant that scholars often seek to occupy an exaggerated outside—outside their subject, to begin with, but also outside any question of who they are in seeing what they see. As Clifford Geertz writes at the conclusion of his essay "Religion as a Cultural System,"

> There remains, of course, the hardly unimportant questions of
> whether this or that religious assertion is true, this or that reli-

gious experience genuine, or whether true religious assertions and genuine religious experiences are possible at all. But such questions cannot even be asked, much less answered, within the self-imposed limitations of the scientific perspective.[23]

Geertz occupies the outside in a complex way. He is both an advocate of the distance he expresses here, distance from evaluations of truth and experience, and also a subtle reader of culture who foregrounds the role of interpretation. He is adept at putting himself in his own picture, at least as educable foreigner to the proceedings.[24] Moreover, Geertz's asceticism toward the "hardly unimportant" truth of the matter might seem moot in relation to the contemporary social scientific avoidance of truth claims altogether, the sense that truth is a word to be used strictly in the plural, where it is used at all.[25]

But his attitude deftly captures a defining position on religion in the academy, whether the position is being affirmed or denied. In the one case, readers follow Geertz in adopting a perspective that locates truth or value outside the frame of analysis and subordinates actors insofar as they are shaped by such things to frameworks they would find unrecognizable. In the other case, readers deny Geertz's distance with reference either to a contextual notion of truth or to the possibility of limited cultural translation. In adopting Geertz on truth, the labor of knowledge would consist in depicting the practices and discourses of a local scene in nonnative terms. In rejecting Geertz's distance, the labor would be focused on the slow work of cultural and linguistic reconstruction, as Geertz himself practices it, with disciplined forays into speculation.[26] What do "they" mean by what they say?

In both Geertzian moves, readers struggle with a question not only of scholarship but also of daily life. What limits knowledge, and what is limited by it? Geertz himself does not appear to struggle with this question. He treats the human actors in his research as manifestly recognizable and locates what is unrecognizable as outside the purview of his thought. This move is endemic to the study of religion, an arena in which the ordinariness of the challenge of knowledge is often taken for extraordinary claims for and against it in a putatively special religious domain. Interest in questions of truth and value—central, one could say, to the encounters, judgments, and difficulties of daily life—are considered specifically theological and ruled out of bounds.

The study of religion thereby serves as the naturalism to religion's supernaturalism, mirroring the dualism of opposition and identity found in one version of religion itself. By contrast, insofar as religion and the secular concern values that emerge in historical existence, including the value of history itself, these formations are critical protagonists and not only inert objects whose truths lie outside the protocols of scholarship. This is to agree with Geertz that neither religion nor secularity is a hallowed space. Insofar as history is the site of value and thus of critique, there is no such space. Critical protagonist is also critical propagandist. The study of religion has made things easy for itself, however, in imagining the religious as fighting out questions of value among themselves and in considering religion the deluded or privileged occupant of hallowed spaces, an intrinsic object of purity, a sacred whose truck with the profane is imagined in oppositional terms. All the better, presumably, to give scholarship the unending task of disciplining and historicizing it. Scholarship thereby simply mirrors its object. Religion may certainly name the attempt at purity. But the relation between history and religion—a history of religion—is better practiced through the criticism of this attempt, in which criticism religion may be participant and not only exemplification. The history that disciplines will be more informative if more difficult, more real if not also more true, if its object is not quite so conveniently opposed to it.[27]

Humanism and Criticism

What then can count as a proper scholarly stance for a history and critique of religion? The question recalls Said's short book *Humanism and Democratic Criticism*, in which he calls for a renewed investment in the humanities as "the critical investigation of values, history, and freedom." This is a renewal that would be as vigilant about the abuses that have been conducted in the name of these values as it is hopeful that the catalog of abuses does not overwhelm the desire to practice them.[28]

Said's call for the humanities to embrace their role in the concourse of value is not disconcerting to most humanistic fields. The study of religion might seem of a piece in accounting scholarly study a humanistic or human sciences work. But in religion this work is understood in distinction from questions of value. Human means what concerns humanity and not divinity, the mundane and not the sacred, the latter objects being left to discourses framed by religious insiders, as with Geertz's concept of truth. The study of religion is unsure of whether or how to join forces with other humanists, whose subjects possess similar stakes in the logics and values of world making. In imagining its opponent as God and his emissaries and in uncoupling human meaning making from divine reference, scholars of religion manage nothing so much as to postulate the

very God they disavow. By contrast, a religion that has no referent outside history makes such an uncoupling unnecessary and indeed impossible. In this light, the study of religion can seem to oscillate between being
a refuge from the concept of God and being its last redoubt.

At the same time, fields outside the study of religion have absorbed a
story that has religion die as a conceptual problem sometime at the beginning of the nineteenth century.[29] Philology, history, and anthropology come to fill the space evacuated by the study of the divine sciences.
These new disciplines support the West in turning its attention to the rest
of the globe and to traditions less buffeted by reformation and enlightenment. To the extent that religion in the West continues apace, it is a topic
for sociology, cognitive science, and perhaps psychology most of all as
elite Westerners settle down to the therapeutic remainder of the god complex. The study of religion becomes the study of why people, these or
those people, are religious; what solves the problem of why there still is
religion—and what it is—given its demise (so-called), the surest sign of
that demise being the very scholarship on religion that asks the question.
Let the field of religious studies take on and represent treasures from the
past and traditions the West ignorantly overlooked, including aspects of
its own past. But what live problems religion presents to contemporary
thought and culture beyond the oddity or offense of its continued existence . . . in the face of this question there is puzzlement.

One of the signal weaknesses of Said's own authorship is his undigested premise that "the humanities concern secular history." Said follows Vico in conceiving the secular as what concerns "the products of
human labor, the human capacity for articulate expression."[30] The "core
of humanism" is Vico's claim that, in Said's words, "we can really know
only what we make or, to put it differently, we can know things according to the way they were made."[31] In the aphorism Said is drawing from,
Vico proclaims his surprise that "the philosophers should have bent all
their energies to the study of the world of nature, which, since God made
it He alone knows," and that "the world of civil society," which "has
certainly been made by men" and whose "principles are therefore to be
found within the modification of our own human minds" should have
been comparatively neglected.[32] We can know history because "we" human beings, not God, have made it. It is a work of the human from beginning to end.

This distinction between the works of human beings and the works
of God does not end the matter for Vico. Said is astute in choosing him
as an intellectual comrade for their shared commitment to history as a
site of human making. But Vico goes further into the matter of God and

the human than Said acknowledges. For who is God? In the humanities, God is simply a name for what stands outside rational and historical knowledge and thus outside the humanities. This judgment has an institutional thrust. For the pursuit of matters divine there are the separate conclaves of divinity. For Vico, however, the realm of human history is also providential, also divine in a sense different both from nature and from some supernatural realm. Said neatly borrows Vico's richest notion—that, again in Said's words, "historical knowledge [is] based on the human being's capacity to make knowledge, as opposed to absorbing it passively, reactively, and dully."[33] Hence the centrality of value to knowing insofar as making involves investment and choice. However, he thereby excises a central dimension of Vico's project: to understand the divine in the terms of history, whose ambition is captured in Vico's multinominal description of his project as a "rational civil theology of divine providence."[34] Said is right that by this Vico means "the secular," but he is insufficiently curious about what Vico's secular fully entails. One has cause to observe in this light that while the study of religion lives uneasily with theology, the humanities live uneasily with religion and its study, neither domain knowing quite how to speak about religion within the confines of scholarly work, neither knowing quite what to do with Said's call for critical thought and human emancipation as parts of the same investigative posture and project.

With Said, I embrace the task of the humanities as involving a "detailed, patient scrutiny of and a lifelong attentiveness to the words and rhetorics by which language is used by human beings who exist in history."[35] Alongside this commitment to what he calls, with Vico, "philology," Said champions an attitude of resistance to cliché and convention—"accepted ideas and ordinary discourse"—as constitutive of the humanist effort to know human beings in other times and places.[36] He is a subtle enough practitioner of the trade to know just how difficult it is to know others in their otherness, skirting the twin temptations of, in Vico's terms, imagining that one's history goes back to the very beginning of the world or making what one knows as old as the world.[37] I join forces with Said when he says that the study of human beings in history is secular and worldly. As he puts it, "Both of these notions allow us to take account not of eternally stable or supernaturally informed values, but rather of the changing bases for humanistic praxis regarding values and human life."[38]

However, Said also regards humanism as a shared enterprise in the service of the texts and worlds that call out for justice. He is therefore in a position to contribute to an enrichment of the very idea of the secular.

Why not also, then, of the religious, in resistance to the "accepted idea" of religion as what he calls eternal stability and supernaturalism, by virtue of which he sets it aside as incommensurable with his project?[39]

In chapter 1, I culled as an epigraph Said's sharp question, posed in his treatment of the Western imagination of the "Oriental" other: "Can one divide human reality, as indeed human reality seems to be genuinely divided, into clearly different cultures, histories, traditions, societies, even races, and survive the consequences humanly?"[40] This question is bedrock. Human reality seems to be divided. One is called to divide it—to distinguish, to apprehend, to conceive. Together in their fierce mutual criticism, these claims constitute the genius and the responsibility of the humanities. Reality will put pressure on our "seems." You will be able to show me, as Said does, that my real is untrue. Yet we are bound to and by a shared real that "seems to be genuinely divided" as we struggle to make our own divisions truthful—supportive of self and other or, as Said puts it, humanly survivable. Our work to do so—to see reality as it is, as we have taken it, shall take it—is ongoing.

Religion, Image and Truth

In an earlier essay, "Sources of History: Myth and Image," I drew attention to Stevens's late, short poem "A Mythology Reflects Its Region" in order to capture a distinction important for the study of religion. Stevens distinguishes between "the image's truth" and what he calls "mythology." It is a distinction between the struggle to contend with reality as it seems, with truth and its images, and the reduction either of truth to image or image to truth.[41] Stevens calls this double reduction "mythology" and observes, "Here / In Connecticut, we never lived in a time / When mythology was possible—But if we had . . ." The question is, What if the study of religion, in failing to make Stevens's elementary distinction, has conceived its object as either the truth without image or the image without truth? In this case Geertz would be more right than he knows, for it would not only be protocols of science that forbid him to speculate on the truth. Truth, but no less image, would, precisely in being opposed, be unavailable to everyone, through any protocol.

What Stevens recognizes is that the claim that God exists, that truth appears, popularized in the person of Descartes but articulated in biblical antiquity, is not (only) a statement of orthodox belief. It is (also) a subversive commitment to a shared reality between what we know and what we want to know, whatever this "what" is or is called. Stevens's poem makes the exile of a truth without image dependent on the recognition that this does not leave us with its simple opposite, image without truth. What one confronts, rather, is the image's truth, and the struggle is to understand both. The struggle, then, is to know equally what the struggle is and is not. For once it is possible to say that the truth is not elsewhere (truth is not without image), it will be possible to say that it is nowhere (there is image without truth) and, even more, to confuse truth and image. If not truth, then science; if not truth, then history. Or as the Grand Inquisitor would have it, if not truth, then my truth and not yours. These claims evade but do not nullify the challenge of the truth being, as it were, dumped into the real where, I am arguing, it requires something of us. What is required is to recognize our very taking of it, and in so doing to commit to its particulars as knowable with others. As Stevens puts it in another poem, description is "A little different from reality: / The difference that we make in what we see / And our memorials of that difference, / Sprinklings of bright particulars from the sky."[42] Religion may pose no special challenge to knowledge. But then it is not that as scholars we cannot ask the question of truth; it is that a study of religion can ask precisely that.

I therefore agree that the attempt to pick out some special dimension of human experience and thought that is uniquely religious is doomed to fail. But I do not agree with the ordinary drift of such thinking, which holds religion to be a "second-order term" used by scholars to analyze pieces of human data, whether or not they call themselves religious. The difference could not be sharper. If the position that religion is a scholar's category holds that religion cannot be found in the world because there is nothing there to correspond to it, I hold that religion can name "everything" and thereby the fundamental challenge of human existence—to contend with or, as Said would say, to survive distinction. Religion is inseparable from art, politics, and ethics insofar as it expresses the principle of inclusion, of the neighbor—the other that human beings struggle to recognize, stabilize, interrogate, or obfuscate. Whereas Bruce Lincoln, echoing Geertz, assures us that "the question of whether spiritual entities exist falls outside my professional purview," I say, with Descartes as with Anselm, God exists as that concept expressive both of what is and of what seems, what is given and what can be made, what I know and what I fail to know, the other in our midst.[43] Religion, then, exists as an act of the mind. God exists as a concept of the inclusion of the other.

Lincoln and I are talking about different things. By God I do not mean what Lincoln means by "spiritual being," so we do not directly disagree. Lincoln and I agree that insofar as there are things outside the purview of knowledge, truths without image, it makes no sense to pursue them. We disagree that scholars of religion must take as their object, must presume as religion, the dualism of opposition and identity, according to which scholarship is responsible only for what is on this side of that presumed outside, namely, "what certain human beings have thought, said, and done at one time or another."[44] It is not that we should ignore what certain human beings have thought, said, and done; it is that we must know what we are knowing when we know human beings. We must know who we are when we do so. We must have a better framework to identify not only the act to place what matters outside, but the act to place what matters here, where it can be known as what challenges both scholar and subject.

There are therefore two senses in which it could be said that religion does not exist. In the first sense, consistent with the first dualism of opposition and identity, religion does not exist because what it names—what Lincoln calls spiritual beings or what Geertz calls truth—is inaccessible to knowledge, or requiring some special, supernatural, or otherwise privileged form of knowledge. What religion names in this first sense forces knowledge of truth to an end in order to redirect it as the pursuit of what appears, what is ordinary in opposition to what is extraordinary and beyond the reach of the knower. Lincoln's commitment to the mundane, and in general the notion of religion as a second-order category, is conceived by the light of this first account of religion. It is an embrace of what can exist—what certain beings think, say, and do—in the light of what cannot exist, whether an object postulated by a believer or a truth outside the system. In this model, truth is both denied (it is nothing) and affirmed as a silence in the framework, a ghost in the system, the place where the scholar says, "I am not in the picture."[45]

In the second sense, consistent with the second dualism of relationship, but also confusion, religion has no existence as a special or ontologically distinct sphere of human activity. It refers to what can be shared—the problems of otherness, knowledge, limit, difference—among the regnant spheres of humanistic investigation, albeit with different emphases. Yet precisely in this second sense, religion (and secularism) is an elementary form of social life tempted by the crystalline illusions of the first sense, in which what matters is pawned off as elsewhere or nowhere.

Each account of religion concerns a concept of duality. The first account concerns the border between existence and something ineffable. The second concerns the border that structures existence as we know and interpret it, the movable border in light of which we might strive for inclusion. Durkheim could be a link between the two accounts, his distinction between sacred and profane structuring the world of experience.

But unlike the second account, which considers what it is to stand in the thing one is also struggling to comprehend, Durkheim manages the dualism of the sacred and the profane as an opposition/identity, replicated in registers both of religion and of its study. The sacred oscillates between being the most different difference there is and the borderless contagion that is everywhere and nowhere, as Durkheim moves between recourse to the social, source of the sacred, and recourse to the natural, source of the social and of scholarship.

Difference, Durkheim's analysis suggests, is hard to hold on to—hard to capture without dissolution and hard to observe without oneself being divided. The elementary forms of religion are elementary to all positions, Durkheim claims. But the elementary dualism of opposition/identity by which this position is riven cannot account for the position that observes it, or rather repeats it. The scholar, says Durkheim, must reject dualistic schemes as fatal to thinking, whether empiricist or rationalist. He erects Hume and Kant as exemplars. Here too is the reviled Descartes, author of the one and the many of mind and body, easily toppled by more historicist or, for Durkheim, naturalist ways of thinking. What Durkheim does not grasp is that it is his naturalism that recapitulates the one and the many, that loses the place of two and thus loses scholarship, as Geertz loses it in failing the reality in which one's own mind is at issue. Durkheim's elementary naturalism endlessly divides without measure. Yet what Durkheim wants is something else: the transposition of nature, the elementary form of religion as society. He rejects the many for the sake of the elementary one. But he cannot find the middle position. Society is natural, he says, with scholarship its witness. As I take up in the next chapter, however, nature will give us a very particular society, and scholarship requires an account of what this is to witness.

In the second account of religion, dualism is the recognition that thinking makes distinctions in conceiving a world doubled between what there is and what we take it as. Here is the Descartes not of minds versus bodies but of minds and metaphors. How will I know that what I take to be myself is not something else? What is self-knowledge knowledge of? What are the principles by which the world, in being taken as a world, is also a shared world? For Durkheim's theoretical heirs, by contrast, for whom the division between mundane and sacred operates as the condition of scholarship, the only question is how to bracket the sacred: how to take the mundane as an end in itself. This mundane alone would then be the site of difference purged of the logic of the one, although the question of how to identify mundane difference then depends on classes of unifying attributes: time, place, color, number, person, position. This unity, suspect, might be modified in taking the attributes for signs of the arbitrary nature of things and concepts—like religion, whose sacred has no content. But this is an ad hoc device to a classificatory scheme wherein the position of critique is edited out.

It is a signal irony not only that the study of religion has been a religious study, but that the religious study it has been cannot see and thus critique itself. The oppositional account of religion cannot conceive of, much less dispute, the religion of history and interpretation, by virtue of which one is in relation to the borders of one's own thinking. The first (oppositional) account of religion would blindly take the second as what is "outside the purview" of thought—which, by the second account, is impossible since there is, as Stevens says, "nothing" outside. The first account of religion does not recognize the second account, assimilating it to itself by distinguishing the scholarly "secular" from the "religious" other and placing the religious in a different ontological space. If (first account) religion names what lies beyond knowledge, then any claim of religion as knowledge (second account) will be taken as authoritative on the beyond and can be included in the scheme only by being excluded in fact, or placed outside. The first account of religion has no concept of difference save for the generic axiom that everything is different from everything, while holding in reserve an elsewhere to which this "everything" is counterposed—empty for the secularists, salvific for the religious.

In the religious version of the first account, this elsewhere would then be beyond difference, or beyond the difference between difference and sameness: beyond thought. But equally, the secular view that everything is different (from everything) commits to a world of change while leaving vacant the space in the system from which one knows what counts as or serves to orient difference. One can see both secular and religious versions of the first account of religion in the commitment to naturalism, which conjures an imagined realm of supernaturalism as fantastical but erroneous counterpart, while leaving silent the place of judgment within its own system. The first account of religion will reject dualism dualistically. It ironically fails to conceive of the place of two: the account of the spiritual beings, the beings of metaphor, that we also are.

I maintain that this muddle, rich in consequence, is what we must begin again. When we say that reason concerns what is human and religion what is divine; when we distinguish history from theology, or a study that must remain outside from a study that is ineradicably inside—when we say, in short, that, in talking about religion we are talking about human beings and not gods, we have said something true. But we are not done. For what is a human being? And what is God or the gods to her?

When we say we want to speak of human beings, we are aligned not only with secular scholarship, but also with the Psalmist. "For what are human beings that you are mindful of them?"[46] And with Shakespeare. "What a piece of work is a man. . . . The beauty of the world, the paragon of animals! And yet, to me, what is this quintessence of dust?"[47]

There is something inescapable about Christianity here, something intransigent within its realms. We have known since the origins of a scientific study of religion that Christianity must be displaced in order to see other religions. Would it be bitter then to recognize that its biblical and poetic sources give us the conceptual armature to perform this displacement?[48] That Christianity and Judaism are deceived, but about their own truth? It could be said that my project of thought takes place entirely within the scheme of a standard Christian distinction, with the first account of religion being one of negative theology and the second account the ontological argument. This would identify Lincoln as a negative theologian, whose historicist commitment to the mundane unavoidably postulates what it also and thereby denies. The second account of religion would be the creation of Anselm and Descartes, who thought that for their part they were merely proving the existence of God. Perhaps the issue is that "merely." As they venture, the existence of God is ineluctably connected to the existence of human beings, or is a name for this existence, alongside those given by poets and thinkers such as Stevens and Said. The entrepreneur, the historian, the critic.

What is named is the site of the humanities, the inimitably complex site wherein we study what we also make, think, and do. In the terms of the Cartesian dilemmas with which I began this chapter, the claim is that scholars are, like the younger Descartes, trading on opinion that is not well founded and are, like him, procrastinating about this fact through the sheer enormousness of the problem the opinions bespeak. The first thing that could be razed to the ground is the opinion concerning Descartes himself, whose demolition of his own earlier positions testifies to his fortitude for self-critique. In continuing to indict him, we not only fail to appreciate the enormousness of this fortitude, we hide from the withering of our own.

It is clear that if the work is to build a better foundation for the study of religion, we can begin by thanking Descartes for standing so long at the origin of modernity and then placing those origins elsewhere, with the principle of reality as distinguished by its "everything": with the principle of collectives as critique. If the truth is neither elsewhere nor nowhere, then there is work to do to realize—to enact—a humanities of inclusion. Thus it is that we will come to understand the content and not only the historical frame of modernity by reconceiving its boundary not as between religious and secular but as between, in Stevens's parlance, truth and image, on the one side, and mythology on the other. In Said's terms, this is to seek the realities we make, and sometimes obfuscate, and by which we are made and sometimes defeated, and to distinguish both from the myth that reality is as it seems, the image that merely reflects its region.

3

Artificial Populations

The centre that he sought was a state of mind,
Nothing more, like weather after it has cleared–
Well, more than that, like weather when it has cleared
And the two poles continue to maintain it

And the Orient and the Occident embrace
To form that weather's appropriate people,
The rosy men and women of the rose,
Astute in being what they are made to be.

Wallace Stevens, "Artificial Populations"

In the history of Western thought, the Neapolitan thinker Giambattista Vico (1668–1744) is known mainly as a precursor of other thinkers and movements: secular history, history of religion, Catholic countermodernity, Hegel, Marx. Said is notable in distinguishing Vico's account of history as central to his criticism. To do so, however, he has to make little of the distinction that actually does distinguish Vico—that between the Hebrews and the other nations. On the one hand, it is a commonplace of believers throughout Western history to regard the Bible as a product of unique revelation, and biblical cultures and peoples as uniquely in command of truth. This is the standard story theorists such as Durkheim and Said are working to combat. But Vico's is not a standard story. The distinction of the Hebrews is of the relation between collectives and the minds that make and study them, not simply, as in Durkheim, in service to their limits, their borders, but also in criticism of them. History is limited to what human beings have made, but then limns the limitlessness of creation. The Hebrews indicate the border that will be transgressed, and as such it could be said that they themselves cannot directly appear.

Still, this will be manifestly unbelievable, that is, offensive. Durkheim at least recognizes that if such stories will not limit themselves to their own borders, it is possible to go below the level of story and repair all the rifts. What sense is there in reinstating Vico's distinction after Durkheim's elementary forms worked to dissolve it? Certainly what Vico called the "one true God" will be misused, just as his concept of secular history will be, the first taken for a substantial privilege, the second for a substantial leveling. Even Vico will be tempted on this score. What Vico's distinction conceives, however, is the principle of what is misused, namely that true privilege is the human achievement of equality and justice, to which history is privileged witness, subject to a critique of its conceits. Vico locates this principle with the Hebrews and their Christian brethren. He equally grounds it in the secular, in the human mind, in consciousness. In Vico, the religious and the secular are each the subject of history.

We must ask, though, How could the path of history be so inaccessible—so dependent on someone's god, someone's text, authority, word? This will continue to be our question as we pursue the distinction of modernity, the distinction that liberates distinctions to include all. The position cannot be presumptively released from the charges it will inevitably provoke—of chauvinism and of ignorance. Spinoza is Vico's proper foil in drily observing that the Hebrews are absolutely ordinary in mind and virtue, their biblical text thoroughly corrupted in politics and practice. Yet, he argues, the Bible, like the mind, contains the principle of its own critique. In following Vico's colorful version of this trail, we will pursue what this is to claim.

I turn first to an exploration of two theorists who, in attempting corrections of Vico's distinction of the Hebrews, find it difficult not to be contradicted by the alternatives. Durkheim will include all positions only to eventuate in the exclusion of his own. Said will reverse the distinction, exiling the Hebrews and their one true God even as he claims Vico's mantle. Each thinker is valuable in the attempt as well as in the failure. Each exemplifies a position that remains seemingly inescapable even as each risks everything in his escape. Like Durkheim's social, Said conceives history as a critical baseline to which the malign mind of Orientalism can be returned.

What neither sees, together with the humanities and social sciences indebted to their work, is that the baseline of history, as of theory, is not expressive of all positions. History is constitutive of a particular theory, of which Orientalism is an ineluctable subversion and from which malignancy there is no natural return. Orientalism is an act to oppress, confuse, make fantastical the sovereign other presupposed in its very precinct. It is the move of the Grand Inquisitor or Milton's Satan—a correction of the good it thereby profanes, outside which there is nothing but the oscillation of nature and supernature. For his part, Said counsels a history of modesty, contingency, secularity. He exiles the dogmatic, the sacred, the impossible. But his thinking, together with Durkheim's, calls for discerning two concepts of the sacred: one a dualism and a fantasy of truth outside history—the eternal truth of the Oriental, the totem of the Occidental social—and the other the miracle of working in concert, the principle (madness, say the Grand Inquisitor and the Orientalist alike) that the eternal is constituted by two in relation, the distinctive structure of the shared real.

Religion and the Theorist

The social realm is a natural realm that differs from others only in its greater complexity.

Durkheim, *The Elementary Forms of Religious Life*

Émile Durkheim's work to connect the elements of simple or tribal societies with those of developed, multicultural ones was among the most influential moves in the twentieth-century study of culture and society. It liberated the prestige of terms such as ritual and the sacred for a variety of generalizable social processes. Generations of theorists in anthropology and sociology have been schooled to elaborate the workings of collective representations in constituting social relation of diverse kinds, and to treat simple and more complex societies with comparable attention. It is because of Durkheim that students of religion can extend the language of religion to instances such as sports events and celebrity culture, tracking social life, then, through structure and function irrespective of how its formations are conventionally named. This is a corrective move. The history of religion that would deny religion to the other is replaced by a theory of religion that can find it everywhere. Durkheim rewrote the presumptive distinction between simple and developed to argue that, whatever their manifold differences, societies can be said to share elementary forms.

But there is a missing distinction in his work. Although all societies make distinctions, not all distinctions are the same. Such is the wager of this book.

The focal point of Durkheim's theory of religion is his elaboration of the totem as symbolic expression of social cohesion. He borrows the term from ethnographic literature on the tribes of North America and the aborigines of Australia.[1] In so doing, he has no pretensions to add to this literature. He is not an ethnographer and has no single case study of his own to unfold. He hopes rather to identify "the most primitive and simplest religion currently known" in order to observe its operations. This is not "for the pleasures of recounting its oddities and singularities." It is "because [such study of primitive religion] seems mostly likely to yield an understanding of the religious nature of man, by showing us an essential and permanent aspect of humanity."[2]

This project arouses contemporary readers' skepticism on a number of scores—the identification of primitive with archaic; the move to set apart the communities these terms are applied to; the aim of discovering "an essential and permanent aspect of humanity." Durkheim is not our contemporary. Over one hundred years of philosophy, politics, history, sociology, and anthropology separate us from the way he thought. Such judgments are not satisfying, however. We may no longer speak in the way Durkheim does, yet his desire to found a study of human beings without assuming a difference in kind between more and less developed is still very much with us, alongside the complementary historicism that would make all differences of equalizable import. In fact, we do need to think beyond Durkheim, though not because he spoke in ways our more sensitized cultural and political awareness has modified. Consistent with Durkheim's own program of study, I invoke his totem not for the pleasure of recounting his theory's oddities and singularities from the safe vantage of having moved beyond it, but to see whether we might observe the contradictions in our own ostensibly essential and permanent convictions as inheritors of Durkheim's leveling resolve.

What Durkheim made inescapable in the study of religion is the investigation of its social constitution. Religion is a social system. It is "a system of notions by which individuals imagine the society to which they belong and their obscure yet intimate relationship with that society."[3] In this Durkheim refuses the supposition that "the main purpose of religion is . . . to provide a representation of the natural world." Religion is not a confused science requiring correction. It is not a "tissue of lies."[4] But neither does Durkheim shift the social far from the natural, where it can be documented and understood. In fact the social and the natural, like his key distinction between the sacred and the profane, are both pillars for Durkheim, oscillating in centrality not just in the lifeworlds he is investigating but also in the way he is investigating them.

Durkheim's view of the relation between the social and the natural focuses on the clan, an entity that lies "at the basis" of the Australian tribes he considered. The word clan comes from the Gaelic word for family, but it typically denotes multiple families that cluster together in the light of a perceived common ancestor or symbol, constituting a subgroup within a larger tribe. For Durkheim, clan is the word that accounts for relations among strangers that are like those of a family. He notes that "the individuals who compose it consider themselves joined by a bond of kinship, but of a very special sort. This kinship does not come from specific blood relations with one another; members of the same clan are kin only if they bear the same name." They are thus "not each other's fathers, mothers, sons or daughters, uncles or nephews in the sense we now give to these terms; and yet they regard each other as part of the same family, either broad or narrow depending on the size of the clan, solely because they are collectively designated by the same word."[5] The family is surmounted by the clan as nature is surmounted by the social. So does the clan become a new family as society takes on a new nature.

On the one hand, then, the clan is a natural form, a permanent feature of social life. "Like any human institution," Durkheim notes, "religion begins nowhere."[6] On the other hand, the origin of the clan is a step out of nature, a constitution not of blood but of name. As Durkheim notes of the Roman *gens* and the Greek γένος, a name might be simply a genealogical designation. In the Australian case, however, the clan name specifies descent by stipulating it. It takes otherwise unrelated people and relates them through the symbol of a third thing, "a definite species of material thing" he calls a totem. As in marriage and religious conversion, a name is definitive of a transmutable social status. It might even be a mark or metaphor of a change of blood. What is distinctive about Durkheim's totem is the movement by which members of the clan are related in denial of blood, yet in such a way that blood is newly valorized. In the sacred of the social, I become a kangaroo, not a Capulet.

Durkheim is careful to point out that this is a symbolic transmutation. Human members of the kangaroo clan are not confused about what they really are in profane terms. The point is that nature shall now be where human value resides. The totem serves to remind human beings that they are not merely natural, to the end of empowering them in the use of nature as their sacral end. In the social that Durkheim identifies, for example, gender is endowed with value not irrespective of natural attributes but in imaginative stabilization of them.

> The human body conceals in its depths a sacred principle that displays itself outwardly in special circumstances. This principle is not different in kind from that which gives the totem its religious character. . . . However, the religious dignity that is inherent, in this sense, in each member of the clan is not equally present in everyone. Men possess it to a higher degree than women, who seem profane by comparison. . . . But men differ too in the way they are marked by their religious nature. Since uninitiated young men are totally lacking such a nature, they are not admitted to the ceremonies. And this religious nature reaches its full intensity among old men.[7]

Durkheim's religion is the constitution of the collective in defiance of mere nature in service to sanctifying the collective in natural terms. Durkheim was right to think he thereby showed something common—the endowment of nature with value, an escape from nature into the glorification of it, whether social laws are endowing men with more power than women, kings with divine right, or the highborn permission to subordinate the lowborn. But this is not what Durkheim thought he had shown in committing to the social as an equalizing—because elementary—power. Indeed, the triumph of one position over others is precisely what he meant to rule out in observing that all societies have the same elementary forms.

What Durkheim did not reckon with is that the elementary form he proffers, the sacred and profane by which the totem refuses mere natural relation, is also a principle of might makes right when seen from the nonelementary standpoint of critique. It is possible to level a critique of nature as value only if the concept of value can be constituted in resistance to nature—not as nature's reformulation in metaphors of subordination but in the postulate, the metaphor, of inclusion. This criticism would be the position of the theorist who strives to include all cases. But one could not then seamlessly join the nonmodern and the modern in the same elementary form, or the natural realm and the social realm, as Durkheim does in contending that "the social realm is a natural realm that differs from others only in its greater complexity."[8] Durkheim is right that the operative distinction is not primitive versus developed. The divine right of kings recapitulates the social hierarchies of the clan and the divine hierarchies of elders, ancestors, and gods. In fidelity to this intuition, Durkheim empowers theory to include all cases in a single elementary form. But the divine right of kings might also be a profanation, a confusion and refusal, of a position it can nevertheless conceive. The position of criticism is to reconceive it.

Durkheim does not distinguish this criticism, and therefore he is not bothered by the connection between what he is studying and how he is studying it—by the fact that his study mirrors the totemic theory of the sacred and the profane. He does not entertain the criticism of this dualism in commitment to the reality of each position, the reality of a social not simply divided or subordinate but equal. Mirroring his subject's standpoint, he sees enough to assert the equality of cases. He finds society natural, basic, elementary, and religion as what comments on and coheres therein. From his point of view, insofar as society is understood as the basic term of religion, religions will be disabused of their temptation to rank themselves, one higher than others. All religions are to be ranked the same, like natural kinds. They are all social logics of integration and elevation. They all divide in terms of the sacred and the profane.

But Durkheim's commitment to nature as both a sorting mechanism in the method of science and an elementary logic in defiance of invidious distinction gets away from him, as nature will. All societies engage the elementary work of subordination—gods over men, men over women, strong over weak, elder over younger, or vice versa. Where does this leave the mind of the theorist? In making the social religion's elementary form, Durkheim fails to see that either the departure from nature concentrates nature's—society's—hierarchies in replicating them or it involves the work to critique them.

Durkheim's theory is lodged in the proposition of a single dualism beyond skepticism and dogmatism, a key to all mythologies.[9] Religious life is "essentially unitary and simple. Everywhere it answers to the same need and derives from the same state of mind. In all its forms its purpose is to raise man above himself and make him live a life superior to the one he would lead if he were only to obey his individual impulses."[10] Contemporary theory will overturn this supposition with the method of multiplication. Religious life is numerous and complex. But Durkheim's move is essential to seeing the limits of this response of manyness to his one. For in fact Durkheim's theory is of a dualism, a "two" with originary powers. This two is in operation in the simplest society, which "exists with all its essential elements from the moment a society is made up of two primary clans."[11] And it is in operation in the human animal itself, which is double, both man and animal, both social and individual, both sacred and profane.[12] Two is how Durkheim can do what he is most invested in—give us the clan as what engenders social and not merely natural relations and therefore serves as the elementary presupposition, the sine qua non, of human communal life.

Yet however perceptive the point is from an anthropological perspective, Durkheim does not make it usable. For there are two twos. Compare Durkheim: "Each individual . . . has a double nature: two beings coexist in him, a man and an animal."[13] And Pascal: "Man infinitely transcends man."[14] The points seem identical. Each gives us the human as doubled. Each is trying to avoid rationalist dualisms that assume human difference without explanation. Each is at pains to remind human beings that, as Spinoza puts it, they do not constitute a distinct dominion within the dominion of nature. Each also wagers that nevertheless human beings are distinct in some sense. Pascal's position is that human beings are twofold. Not twofold as mind and body, or man and animal, but twofold such that, not animal, they are two, either animal or human, either bestial or angelic. The animal occupies two places in the system: animal, and human as animal. In Pascal there are three positions: the position of nature, which is excluded, and humans' struggle to transmute their animality—to become adequate to their image whereby they can love the other as themselves, the position of the divine. As Pascal notes of habit, there are two terms, habit and nature. But there are three positions: habit, "a second nature"; nature, "a first habit"; and the position that would locate humans as either habit or nature in themselves, and in opposition.[15] Like Spinoza, Vico, and Kant on nature and culture, Pascal gives us what twentieth-century thinkers thought they had to invent: the undecidable duplicity of these positions as constitutive of the critique of each.[16]

In Durkheim there are two positions: nature and the social, profane and sacred, the animal and the social self. Unable to ground the position that would surmount the given constraints of the clan, these serve either the position of nonmodernity or the confusion of modernity. Durkheim corrals Spinoza in his defense: "If society is a specific reality, still it is not an empire within an empire." Yet Spinoza, we will see, makes an additional distinction. Nature is the encompassing term; human beings are not an exception to it. But there is a distinction within it. Only in Spinoza's hands does the notion of degree (no dominion within a dominion) also comprehend difference—that the sine qua non of human beings is not what transcends nature, which can just as easily symbolize natural value, but ethics, which enlarges natural law in deference to the other. The power of distinction. Durkheim's thesis that man is double is the thesis that the order of reality splits in two with no remainder. As we saw with Geertz, this presupposition will place scholarship in opposition to religion, expressive of a religious no less than a scholarly dogma—the *b* of an *a/b* system. The missing position is not nondualism (identity), which repeats it. It is the commitment to the doubleness of the actual, the distinction of a history of religion (and the secular), the distinction of scholarship as critique.

Durkheim's distinction between the sacred and the profane cannot articulate its own logic. It is implicitly dependent on one he does not identify. In Durkheim's distinction, distinction cannot be at issue. It just is, written into the scheme of things. So it is with Durkheim's analysis, which, in taking the measure of the distinction, also reflects its oppositional logic. Durkheim will stand outside the distinction between the sacred and the profane just long enough to diagram that there is nothing outside it, that it is natural, found everywhere and always. Durkheim would then be inside the distinction, only to find that it will not stay still, with the sacred now the most different difference and now the contagion that cannot be differentiated.[17]

The question finally is, Does Durkheim speak from the position of the profane or the position of the sacred? It might seem obvious to say that the profane is the position of scholarship and the sacred the quarry of a study of religion. But Durkheim instructs us to see that this is not so. The quarry is the distinction, not the sacred. Religion is distinction. So it is. But if Durkheim does not speak from the profane, where does he speak from? How does he see his distinction, and how does the distinction see, or account for, him? These questions make sense only in reference to the position that is absent in Durkheim—if not entirely so, then finally beyond his accountability. Durkheim begins by recognizing, with Kant, that the signal problem of minds and worlds is not only skepticism—how the mind meets up with the world—but also sociality: What is the extent of the social? What is a mind in a collective? What is freedom? Durkheim goes some way toward an account of freedom in society by casting the human as double, both profane and sacred, both ordinary and extraordinary, both conscious and self-conscious. Instead of delimiting a doubleness that puts pressure on the social itself, however, Durkheim finds society a uniform container for the double, a natural source of doubleness that does nothing but intensify the border, the distinction, everywhere and always. Human beings are double. But in so being they are opposed to themselves, and thus to each other.

In Kant, the sign of the double is critique of the border, the call to extend it, the refusal of its original position dividing self from other. For

Durkheim, reader and critic of Kant, this might have been the ground of a sociology of freedom, in which the tribe's elementary departure from natural relation eventuates not only in ever larger tribes but also in the critique of tribe itself. But Durkheim, fearful of philosophical illusion and wary of theological privilege, roots his concept of the social in nature, losing the double in the process except as what ratifies the natural advantage of a collective life. He thereby loses faith in his tribes, who, having once left nature to form the clan, are then condemned by his theory, as his theory is condemned by them, to take up permanent residence there. This is not insofar as totems cannot become gods. It is that, insofar as totems are gods, they are also nothing but totems, signs of solidarity formed of an us and a them.

So too Durkheim himself, whose scholarly allegiance to natural explanation mirrors the distinction of his tribes, placing the scholar outside what he describes, just as the sacred as the social stands external to the individual.[18] He is beholden to his insiders' continuing to perform their inside separate from his position, while what he describes is effectively his identity with them, scholar and folk mirroring each other's dualism. In this sense there *is* an extraordinary leveling to be seen in Durkheim. But his would not be the elementary form of society—or scholarship—as such. It would only be the elementary form of the version that either opposes or identifies us and them.

Does Orientalism Have an End?

One ought again to remember that all cultures impose corrections upon raw reality, changing it from free-floating objects into units of knowledge.   **Edward Said,** *Orientalism*

The critique of Durkheim is to distinguish modernity from nonmodernity. It is to observe the border by which one may critique all borders insofar as they divide invidiously. Modernity is the critique of divisive borders in support of inclusive ones. Modernity is bordered, then, in being the commitment that they shall be inclusive. Yet once there is modernity as inclusive of borders in critiquing them, one immediately confronts the temptation to erect modernity itself as yet another border. Modernity unleashes the power both to found collectives in enlightened concert and to deform collective life with reference to naturalism or supernaturalism. Although modernity is empowered only in being distinguished from nonmodernity, modernity will need to mind its own decisive distinction. Modernity will need to distinguish the power of the neighbor, with whom I am most powerful, from the power of Orientalism, by which I extend my power only by dominating another in the name of enlightenment. Modernity is mistaken, confused, violent, tempted. But it is not only so. Or it is so, we know, only by virtue of the state of mind that thinks from its center, as Stevens has it in "Artificial Populations." Modernity is and must be self-criticism.

Said is a guide to the distinction mangled by modernity, in distinction from the distinction of modernity. The distinctions are connected, but let us attend also to their difference. Durkheim and his epigones in the study of religion seek to correct the violence of distinction by preemptive inclusion, only to find that there would then be nothing distinctive under inquiry—the dualism of opposition and identity that misses the distinction of modernity. Said will take us to the agony of the violence internal to one's own house—the mutuality of two in betrayal of their relationship.

This is the journey Joseph Conrad depicted in *Heart of Darkness*, a book of signal importance to Said in his own complex journey with Western literature. Like Conrad, Said cultivates interpretations of good and evil that begin and end not with bright certainties, but with the struggle to differentiate them and to enact the difference. His own guide in this endeavor is Vico, whose principles he works to put to use in a world in which the distinction Vico prizes has seemed to name an unending violence. This will be to reconsider the question of where one stands in critique, the question of what is involved in immanent critique—the position of the dualism of relationship. Said struggles with the work of distinction. Does Orientalism have an end in history? Or is it a function of the mind as such? If criticism involves a willingness not simply to identify and cauterize violence, but to move closer to it to see its logic, what will be the way out? How will we find the exit?

Said's *Orientalism*, published in 1978, is a compact treatise on the concept of the Orient in Western literature and politics, in particular the Orient of the Arab world and of Islam as imagined in nineteenth-century Europe and America. Before Said, the term Orientalism referred to the study of the cultures designated as Orient and to the body of Western scholastic material compiled over generations and systematized in the nineteenth century through the formation of the field of Oriental studies.[19] Said retains an interest in the academic connotations of Orientalism as he pursues just what scholars know about the Orient and under what conditions this knowledge was acquired and used. But his survey extends beyond scholarship to what he calls the "discourse" of Orientalism—the way the Orient was conceived and written into cultural narratives from novels to travel diaries to economic and political policies. In Said's words, Orientalism bespeaks "the enormously systematic discipline by which European culture was able to manage—and even produce—the Orient politically, sociologically, militarily, ideologically, scientifically, and imaginatively during the post-Enlightenment period."[20]

The term discourse indicates Said's intention to illuminate what is latent in the practices and mind-sets circulated and naturalized as Orientalism. Said was a literary scholar. But his contribution to the field of literature consists in this work of connecting the literary with logics of production, pursuing conjunctions of ideas, economic relationships, military and political relations, and imaginative representation. By exploring these conjunctions, he reveals the Orient not only as a geography "adjacent to Europe" but as an overdetermined object of fascination and confusion, "the place of Europe's greatest and richest and oldest colonies, the source of its civilizations and languages, its cultural contestant, and one of its deepest and most recurring images of the Other." This instability of the image and the desires it expresses makes the Orient a consistently manipulable entity, possessing enough reality to focus attention on some "there" while retaining the freedom and force of fiction. Simultaneously a place, a fantasy, and a product, the Orient is the *"willed human work"* of one culture in pursuit—of another culture but also of reflections of its own.[21]

There have been several generations of responses to *Orientalism* since its publication. In the preface to the twenty-fifth anniversary edition of the book in 2003, written four months before Said died from complications of leukemia at age sixty-seven, he expressed his "amazement" that "*Orientalism* continues to be discussed and translated all over the world." At the same time, he noted, there is a stubborn irony in the reception of *Orientalism*, namely that a "work about representations of 'the Orient' " should itself be the subject of "increasing misrepresentation and misinterpretation." Upon his death, several of Said's colleagues and friends published a tribute to him, subtitled "Continuing the Conversation," in which some observe how far the disciplines analyzed in *Orientalism* still are from embodying adequate responses to its critique.[22]

An astute criticism of the argument, posed by James Clifford ten years after its publication, is that Said seems confused about what human beings are capable of rectifying. Said is confused, Clifford writes, about whether human beings are "in thrall to a Foucauldian historicist framework," which itself is to blame, or whether they are responsible to pursue a "set of humanistic aspirations that demand agency" and call for revolutionary purpose.[23] Said drafted a response in his short book

Humanism and Democratic Criticism, which argues for a humanism imbued with a historicist mind-set but nevertheless in rejection of passing
responsibility to systems or other nonhuman elements. But the query was
not put to rest.

The question I pose concerns the historicity of Orientalism. Is the argument that this dynamic of asymmetrical power is a function of a particular historical situation or is it endemic to human relations, and even
the mind, as such? Orientalism is very evidently a historical phenomenon. But is it also universal? What would it mean to say "all cultures"
do this? And what is the "this" that all cultures would do? Said speaks
on both levels. He urges us to be mindful that, as the epigraph has it,
"all cultures impose corrections upon raw reality, changing it from free-
floating objects into units of knowledge." "The problem," he continues,
"is not that the conversion takes place. It is perfectly natural for the human mind to resist the assault on it of untreated strangeness." Said puts
the case of Orientalism in the terms of a subspecies of this general rule.
All minds resist the assault of untreated strangeness. He continues,

> To the Westerner, however, the Oriental was always *like* some
> aspect of the West; to some of the German Romantics, for ex-
> ample, Indian religion was essentially an Oriental version of
> Germano-Christian pantheism. Yet the Orientalist makes it his
> work to be always converting the Orient from something into
> something else.

This particular case, then, stands out from the "natural" resistance of the
mind to strangeness in two respects. First, the Westerner is not simply
assimilating what would otherwise be strange. He is recognizing himself
therein and then misrecognizing what he is looking at. The Orientalist
approaches the Orient not to learn who, what, and where but "for himself, for the sake of his culture, [and] in some cases for what he believes
is the sake of the Oriental." One could say the Orient is like the West
and it is this very likeness that is repressed in projecting an exotic other,
which serves to justify the West's elevation. But no less would the Orient
be unlike the West where this very unlikeness is repressed in projecting a
civilization in common, with the West swooping in to fix the flaws in its
reflected partner. The Occident-Orient relationship, intimate, powerful,
is an augmentation of what the mind naturally does in being expansive,
where expansion in this case means inclusion on the terms of occlusion.

The second respect in which the relationship is distinct from a natural one is an intensifying of the general rule. All minds resist the assault

of untreated strangeness. In this particular case the "conversion" is buttressed by impressive discipline: "It is taught, it has its own societies, periodicals, traditions, vocabulary, rhetoric, all in basic ways connected to and supplied by the prevailing cultural and political norms of the West." The West does not just convert the Orient into something knowable, it "schematizes" it, meaning it makes it part of a system in which everything is seen through this single divisive lens.[24]

What kind of distinction is being made between all cultures and particular cultures, between what the mind does in all cases and what the Orientalists did? Do only some minds find elaborate, systemic frames for their projections that bury their origins? In moments, Said seems to imply that the tumultuous dynamics unleashed by the relation of perception, knowledge, self-deception, domination, and named Orientalism are indeed escapable. He allows for the historical loosening of Orientalism's grip even as he laments its continued legacies. He seems to imagine an emancipation from its terms, as Clifford noted. But Said's reference to "all cultures" suggests another line of inquiry wherein Orientalism would concern thinking in relationship as such. Insofar as thinking is perceiving, using, distorting, claiming, and dominating, all selves, all cultures, will be involved in Orientalism.[25] Insofar as Orientalism is understood not only as a historical formation but also as a function of thought or even human nature, what kind of escape could there be? The question is not only how agency is possible. The question is which part of Said's model is historical, and thus contingent and changeable, and which part is constitutive. Does it even make historical sense to speak of "all cultures"? Or does history begin the minute we say "this one"? If so, what kind of a judgment is "all cultures," and what authorizes one to make it?

There are three ways to interpret Said's conception of the relation between Orientalism and what is common to humanity. First, Orientalism could be illustrative of a common human function. There would be no beginning and no end to it. There would be no difference between what all cultures do and what some particular cultures have done, no difference between correction and conversion, except for the details and the degree. Although there would therefore be no escape, the most damaging dynamics could presumably be exposed and strategically ameliorated.

Second, Orientalism might be the historical distortion of a more benign common human function, which function we can reaffirm once Orientalism has been deconstructed. While all cultures know others through a dialectic of investigation and conversion, Orientalism launches this procedure toward destructive ends, and it is this destructiveness that we can target and deconstruct. Whereas the first option collapses the difference between all cultures and particular historical instances, this second option uncouples them. Whether "all cultures" refers to the mind as such in some transcendental sense or whether it refers to what all people can be observed in the main to do, the particular logic of Orientalism would not be inevitable even as we recognize the potentially distorting role the observer plays in knowing anything. One could then imagine returning, as it were, to a conceptual and cultural baseline that is not Orientalist.

Third, Orientalism could be identified as historical without remainder, neither a distortion from some other accessible state nor inevitable or permanent. This identification might seem possible to make in a conventionally circumscribed way. By calling Orientalism a historical phenomenon, one is simply saying it has locatable coordinates and unrepeatable facets. History would refer to the standing method by which to identify this event and these phenomena among countless others.

Said's use of history and universals enjoins a stronger usage, however, along with a different conception of history. To say that Orientalism is historical without remainder is to invoke, in order to resist, what remainder there might have been on an alternative reading—the specter of "all cultures" from which Orientalism would be distinguished as exception. The claim would instead be that Orientalism as historical signifies not only something about Orientalism but also something about history, now not only a method but also a concept, and more pertinently a concept always potentially Orientalist. Rather than history being the automatically larger term within which events and concepts arise—history as a benign and itself value-free perspective—events and concepts would be the terms within which history is comprehensible in the first place. This is to pick up on Said's intuition that Orientalism not only relates to a certain set of individuals and systems in one or multiple times and places but speaks to, is even grounded in, something more basic. However, instead of this more basic thing being "all cultures," let it be history itself.

In this third account, we would not be able to demolish Orientalism without demolishing history, without taking refuge in the natural, a presumptive *all cultures*, where, it must be said, there will be no refuge from domination. This reading holds that Orientalism is neither an illustration of something common, since what is common would itself be historically specific, made not found, nor a distortion of some imagined "all," since the standpoint of history cannot recognize any all but that of its own production. To the extent that history is a distortion, it is a distortion of a standard that it itself has made. Orientalism would be inescapable in the sense that history is inescapable. But its amelioration would not, as in the first account, be merely partial, a tinkering in concession to its inevitability. Rather, because history would itself be a particular conceptual domain, Orientalism, understood as the proposition that the space of other minds shall be filled by mine, could be radically ameliorated, if only based on a competing historical proposition: that each mind shall know others as it seeks to be known. On this account, what Orientalism debases is not some ideal common to humanity as such but the historical maxims that could be offered to contest it. You could escape from Orientalism not into the commonly human but into some other history.

The irony is that Orientalism could be demolished only based on a commitment to its principle of possibility, as Descartes can demolish his truths only in commitment to his work to realize them. Orientalism would coincide with historical beginnings or, as it is sometimes put, the beginning of historical consciousness. It would haunt the historical as what would call for remaking—for progress even—and, as Clifford sensed, for freedom. In this light it is certainly possible to make claims about "all cultures." But it is not possible to do so outside the threat of Orientalism, which would be history's threat. Orientalism would have an end only insofar as it had no end outside history and was thus the persistent and severe consequence of historical thinking. If Orientalism exists, if it has come into existence, if it is historical, then this is to observe that it is the all too common truth of history. The only alternative to the common, if depressing, truth that Orientalism abides would be an ethical commonality, an "all" not naturally assumed but historically fought for—belated, as Vico will show. Such an ethical commonality would count then as the uncommon truth of history insofar as it could come to express what Vico called justice and equality, a possibility that represents struggle and labor, not nature.

This third interpretation is the best way to work through the drift of *Orientalism* in light of Said's interest in both history and culture/nature—his interest in all cultures and in the distinction of West and East, in systems that limit us and in our construction of and therefore our possible liberation from them. It is not quite Said's own position. His writing raises the question of the nature of history, even if he does not directly imagine it as a problem to be settled in the way I formulate the matter. The point is not only to understand Said. It is to understand what he sought to understand and what the humanities work to understand—the relation of mind, history, worlds, commonalities, and beginnings or, as I would put it, the history of the relation of these things, the history of historicity as a way of being in and understanding the world.

Said is at pains to underscore that he is not denying the "brute reality" of the "lives, histories, and customs" that have their "location . . . in the East" and that are "obviously greater than anything that could be said about them in the West." His interest, however, is in the "internal consistency of Orientalism and its ideas about the Orient . . . despite or beyond any correspondence, or lack thereof, with a 'real' Orient."[26] The Orient is systemic: it is not merely a myth that "would simply blow away" when exposed, but a system of ideas embedded and "knitted-together" with durable "socio-economic and political institutions."[27] It is "man-made," an "imaginative geography" that is the product of human beings' dividing the world in a certain way for certain ends. Orientalism thus expresses the "hegemony" of European culture. It is an axis tilting between "us" and "them" that preserves the "flexible *positional* superiority" of the Westerner "in a whole series of possible relationships with the Orient without ever losing him the relative upper hand."[28] In the most basic terms, Orientalism imprisons the Orient, ensuring, in Said's words, that "the Orient was not (and is not) a free subject of thought or action."[29]

Said acknowledges that the West, or the Occident, is no less a construct than the Orient—that they are both, in Stevens's language, "artificial populations." But not on equal ground. As he observes, "it is Europe that articulates the Orient; this articulation is the prerogative, not of a puppet-master, but of a genuine creator, whose life-giving power represents, animates, constitutes the otherwise silent and dangerous space beyond familiar boundaries."[30]

The language of creation raises the question whether we are to abandon not only Orientalism but also its "genuine creator," the West. What is the space outside Orientalism and its Occident? Might the West, in addition to being a creator in a negative sense, also be a standpoint of genuine creativity, thus not only the position of hegemony but also of its critique? Said pursues this question obliquely through the inquiry into what "all cultures" do. And it appears in Said's portrait of the ends of his analysis, wherein he urges readers to free themselves from Orientalist ideology. In the new order beyond Orientalism, "there would be scholars, critics, intellectuals, human beings for whom the racial, ethnic, and national distinctions were less important than the common enterprise of promoting human community."[31] What "all cultures do" from the beginning—correct raw reality, dominate one another—may be transformed into what all peoples can do together in the end.

Said envisions this hopeful projection as a work in progress. Yet by the time he published his book, the Orientalism he investigated was very nearly a thing of the past. The conclusion of *Orientalism* is ambiguous, as attested by Said's parenthetical reference to the present: the Orient was not (and is not) a free subject. How does periodization work in such a phenomenon?

Said appends to the book an epigraph from Marx's "Eighteenth Brumaire of Louis Bonaparte." "They cannot represent themselves; they must be represented."[32] Would the Orient, then, like Marx's "small peasants" under the reign of Napoleon's nephew, be able to "enter into manifold relations" in order to throw off the master and represent itself?[33] Or would it be a matter of escaping the distinction Orient/Occident altogether in favor of "promoting human community"? Will the Orient and all it signifies ever be done with, or will it follow its cultures anew into every present? This is not the question of the long-lasting generational effects of unfree relation, anatomized by Said's precursor Franz Fanon. It is the question of the borders of Said's portrait. His embrace of a human community seems quixotic based on his account of the pervasiveness of Orientalism, the emphatic vagueness of its "where." Does he have an account of "when"—of its ends, its origins—or is this simply the wrong question when it comes to what he calls, following Nietzsche and Foucault, "genealogy"?

The preponderance of Said's argument depends on the question "when" in a standard, if sweeping, historical sense. He finds Orientalist thinking and projects as early as Greek antiquity and observes their flourishing into ancient, medieval, Renaissance, and modern Christian worlds.[34] Dante and his lurid depictions of "Maometto" (Muhammed) in the eighth (second lowest) circle of hell in the *Inferno* are a particular fascination.[35] But the primary locus of Orientalism in Said's analysis is modern European and American experiences of the so-called Near Orient of the eastern Mediterranean.[36] The heyday extends from the late eighteenth century, with Napoleon's invasion of Egypt (1798), to the nineteenth-century and early twentieth-century adventures in scholarship, colonialism, and world making. Said is invested in Orientalism as a function of an imperial past and its vestiges in the present. But in his parenthetical hedge—it is not free—he addresses himself both to a particular history of European and American modernity, which modernity, he sometimes implies, is finally, if recently, concluding its reign, and to a feature of Western thought, and indeed human thought as such, whose end is of necessity provisional and incomplete.

In the final paragraph of the book, Said gestures toward a form of liberation that is possibly close at hand. "The worldwide hegemony of Orientalism and all it stands for can now be challenged," he announces,

contemplating "the general twentieth-century rise to political and historical awareness of so many of the earth's peoples." In the face of this rise,
his book is to remind us "of the seductive degradation of knowledge, of
any knowledge, anywhere, at any time."[37] Said rests his case thus: Orientalism is both a particular, unconcluded history and critique of the West
and a possibly permanent feature of the human project to know.

Said's question about what survives Orientalism can be placed in a
rich history of concern. Once teleology is revealed as the illusion that
what "is" will alone, without the mind, yield the correct interpretation
of itself, then we can conceive of history as a mode of creatively securing interpretation without giving up the idea that there is a difference
between the unendingness of history (what is) and the originating or creative role the mind plays in it (how we take it). More precisely, history
would be possible only in the light of both reality and, as Vico puts it, the
mind that meditates on it and makes it for itself. With the deconstruction
of teleology, history alone and mind alone, like "is" and "as," would
be revealed to be impossible without each other, and just as impossible
would be their conflation.

What is interesting is that if, on this account, history is possible only
once we recognize that the mind is involved, this can mean both that I
can lose my mind in mere history (or historicism) and that history is at
least partly what I think and commit and make. Orientalism could be
both what happens when we resign thinking in history (lose our minds)
and also what we commit to insofar as we dominate the other, even in
trying to know her. That this would be a form of self-domination as well
does not mitigate the responsibility for it, and indeed it underscores the
devastation of the position. Said is close to these truths: that Orientalism is a complex that implicates both of its positions, West and East; that
it is—must be—resolvable, since it is not only there but also made. His
posture is not unlike that of Nietzsche, who begins the third essay of *On
the Genealogy of Morals* with the question, "What is the meaning of ascetic ideals?" Asceticism, like Orientalism, is total, shattering; yet Nietzsche provocatively tacks back and forth between its inevitability and its
contestation and critique.[38]

What, then, is Orientalism? What is the meaning of this ideal? Both
elements of Said's project refer to the act of distinction: that the geography under question is an imaginative one and that what is imagined is
an object of asymmetrical power. Thinking in history distinguishes the
very demand of "as": How do you take things? What Said takes from
Nietzsche is the question, Is it possible to distinguish without dominating? This query leads Said to a second one: Does distinction, dominating

or liberating, refer to the mind as such or to some particular history of it? One wants to insist to Said that his theoretical framework would need to resist any notion of the mind as such, the mind outside history. But since history is so obviously corrupt, this will be the temptation.

Said invokes Nietzsche, Lévi-Strauss, Kant, and Marx on minds and histories. But the thinker he takes refuge in is Vico. It is Vico who ostensibly gives us "all cultures," the world of nations, while still giving us history—indeed, giving us a secular history of all. Said cites the same point in Vico almost each time he mentions him, the dictum that "men make their own history" and thus "what they can know is what they have made."[39] But Said's reference to "all cultures" untethers the question of distinction from the specific Orientalist story, invoking a baseline of the knowledge of "raw reality" that involves domination only in the analogical sense. Is this because Said worries that to truly overcome Orientalism, history, even in Vico's active sense, will not be enough—that the "all" of history, so tenaciously Orientalist, requires nothing less than the "all" of nature, a universal untouched by specific human hands? Does Said's desire for an end to Orientalism cause him therefore to betray his best intuitions about the work of secular history? Let us consider Vico on his own terms before returning to these questions.

History and Origins

Fathers are afraid that their children's natural love may be eradicated. What then is this nature which is liable to be eradicated? Habit is a second nature that destroys the first. But what is nature? Why is habit not natural? I am very much afraid that nature itself is only a first habit, just as habit is a second nature.   **Blaise Pascal,** *Pensées*

Vico's "new science" of the common nature of nations is regarded as one of the first attempts at a theory of religion without recourse to a theological architecture. Yet Vico's main work, *The New Science*, is a wellspring of literary and theological threads. Vico's identity as a theorist of religion undoubtedly begins with his double claim that what drives history is "divine providence," while what drives providence is nothing more than nature and human power. For readers who find in Vico an early ally in the fight against the religious mystification of scholarship on religion, this claim is paramount. Providence is but a theological name for social and political change, wherein God is a character, a human invention like any other.

There is truth in this reading, but an investigation into Vico's contribution to criticism cannot rest there. What is most useful in Vico, albeit difficult, is his insistence, following Pascal, that there is nothing more natural than culture, but then nothing more cultural than nature. Habit is nothing but a second nature, while nature is nothing but a first habit.[40] What does this mean? Vico elaborates a defense of each that insists on the possibility for nature, our nature, to be made into a common culture. What makes Vico such fascinating reading is that although he gives an account of the movement out of nature—the developmental course the nations take to the principle of a common humanity, only to relapse into a state of discord and decadence—he denies this development to the Hebrews, who possess the principle in the beginning. Instead of making this distinction about the superiority of the Hebrews, however, Vico gives the Hebrews their own relapse. They *become* natural—that is, bestial, forgetful, primitive. In the case of the nations, primitiveness recurs in a cyclical repetition; in the case of the Hebrews, the primitive is a primordial temptation.

There are two fundamental insights to be unfolded. First, with the distinction of the Hebrews, Vico reverses the notion of beginnings from what is naturally the case to what is a function of language and work. That the Hebrews possess the principle in the beginning, which beginning is then disavowed, is to say that a common humanity has no natural origin, which makes it precisely vulnerable to confusion with natural exigencies.

Second, Vico's sensitivity to the proximity of truth and error, in particular his observation that the goods of a common humanity—equality and justice—will not eclipse corruption, enables him to distinguish the principle based on which the good is fought for in the beginning from the worldview of fate and recurrence by which nature, however volatile, is made the original measure of culture. With the help of Vico's Hebrews, this is to argue that if nature and culture can develop powerfully toward the good, this can only be because of the good they together express in the beginning, which beginning is a critique of the metaphor of fateful cycles and the cultures that elaborate them. Vico thereby sustains the modern insight that nature, neither enemy nor home, is a site of work, together with the insight that modernity is a work of distinction.

Let us begin with Vico's puzzling claim that history is animated by "divine providence" while what constitutes providence is nothing more than the workings of nature in the human mind. "Man is aided by God," Vico tells us, "naturally by divine providence and supernaturally by divine grace."[41] This distinction between providence and grace appears to underwrite a distinction between cultures. The difference, he contends, between the "natural law of the gentes," the gentile nations he is primarily concerned with in his *New Science*, and "the natural law of the

Hebrews," about which he says very little, is that the natural law of the gentes is granted only "the ordinary help from providence," whereas the Hebrews had "extraordinary help from the true God."[42]

This is a notable distinction. Providence is a natural aid, in contrast to divine grace. It is a natural law by which the gentile nations are formed, in contrast to the Hebrews. Vico's is a science of the gentile nations, a natural history of political change undergone by the gentiles in particular. But he also identifies it as an "ideal eternal history traversed in time by the history of every nation." Religious and secular motifs, not to say motifs of culture and of (all) kinds, are hard to separate here. In the generalizing spirit, Vico's maxim of history, "the first indubitable principle" of his science, is that "this world of nations has certainly been made by men, and its guise must therefore be found within the modifications of our own human mind." If it is unusual to identify the scene of history as the mind, it is no more usual to encounter "our own human mind" just as one is working to appreciate what it might mean to distinguish other ones. Vico temporarily brackets his distinction of gentile and Hebrew in order to make a connection that further obscures it: that the history of the nations is also the history of history. As he puts it, "He who meditates this Science narrates to himself this ideal eternal history so far as he himself makes it for himself."[43]

What precisely is the relation between providence, nations, and minds, and between the ideal eternal history and the historian or scientist who meditates on it? What, further, is the meaning of the distinction between the gentes and the Hebrews, between ordinary natural law and extraordinary natural law, between providence and "the true God"? Vico's use of the term providence might be a theological name for a new (nontheological) science of social and political change. Yet this hardly seems to dissolve the manifold oddities of the position.

Consider the view of religion theorist Samuel Preus, according to whom the Catholic-born Vico was simply using the rhetoric at hand to make the point, unorthodox in its time, that divine providence can be explained away without remainder. For Preus, Vico's move to exempt biblical traditions ("the Hebrews") from his history of the common nature of nations—on the assumption that the former concern the true God and thus do not evolve—is obviously strategic, not to mention wholly unsalvageable. What Vico gives us rather is the secular as a history of human invention dependent on the passage from myth to history, from gods and heroes to men and the nations they build. He thus gives us "the possibility of a science of religion embraced by a universal historical-cultural science of humanity."[44] The Hebrews, distinguished, can simply be edited out, a move that to Preus does not do violence to Vico's predominant intentions.

On the other side, theologian John Milbank embraces Vico's theological language, consistent, it must be said, with Vico's commitment to the conceptual specificity of language and letters.[45] For Milbank, the heart of Vico's work is the Augustinian connection of *verum factum*— the truth is made, or truth is understood in and through creation. This connection bespeaks Vico's abiding ontological commitment to *Homo creator*, the human as participating in the creativity—the work, the making, the labor—of God. Citing Vico in the first edition of *The New Science*, to wit, "subservient to the divine architect, the artificer of the world of nations is human will," Milbank affirms that Vico's providence is really *creatio continua*—that divine essence or force (*conatus*) that is "working through the processes of human making."[46]

This contrast between Preus and Milbank risks being unduly manipulative. Granted it is something of a setup for two strong readings that both comprehend something true in Vico. What is nevertheless valuable in taking them together is that Vico makes a move that only a few thinkers in Western history have likewise made—positing that secular history is providential in having an absolute beginning: that the secular and the religious begin together and, in so doing, distinguish as temptation the contradictory logic that replaces each of them with a dualism of opposition, by which their paragons Preus and Milbank stand in opposition. History is secular in concerning the creativity of human beings. History is divine in coming into existence from nothing natural. It is revealed, if you like. Or equally, it begins creatively. The mind begins creatively. There is no concept for the movement to history and consciousness, but only for the movement from them, whether in progress toward the goods of justice and equality or away from them toward brutishness and force.

This move complicates Vico's own romance with the emergence of consciousness from primitive states, together with the emergence of principles of justice and equality from the heroic logic of might makes right. Moreover, Vico's distinction between grace and providence is confusing in referring to a distinction between beginnings—the Hebrews begin with the truth (grace), the gentes on the way to it (providence)—while also expressing the providential principle that all beginnings share. Preus and Milbank reflect the distinction, with the humanities following Preus in leveling it (religion gives way to the secular) and theology following Milbank in relativizing it (it concerns Christianity alone). But they miss the distinction that would be absolute not in the finite sense of privileging this from that but in expressing the power of beginning in common, neither indifferent cyclical return nor indifferent perennial truth. Vico's distinction of the Hebrews might call to mind the rabbinic distinction between laws specific to Jews and the seven so-called Noachide laws—minimal moral rules—that apply to everyone else. The position I call forth in Vico, however, is the paradox that the Hebrews, in expressing the particular principle of beginning in history, engender a specific history of all.

There is a history of ideas by which it could be said that Hegel, Kierkegaard, and Nietzsche worked out the history of origins and the origin of history with more consistency than Vico. Spinoza confronts these ideas too, as we will see in chapter 6. But Vico makes his own inimitable contribution. In his thinking we see just how odd is the move to make history primary to a study of religion and what convolutions we will fall into before the position becomes clear. Vico is not the champion of the secularity that Preus and Said claim him for, and not just because he was a Catholic thinker struggling with the terms of his inherited tradition. Neither is this to adopt Milbank's position that Vico's project to foreground *factum* (human making) constitutes a kind of countermodernity, "[shadowing] actual, secular modernity" via a "traditional, Platonic, participatory framework."[47] Preus and Milbank need each other inasmuch as each understands, if incompletely, that Vico gives us what I call modernity—the secular for Preus, the divine law of creation for Milbank. Each reader moves polemically in light of Vico's distinction of the Hebrews, and this is preferable to those readers who make nothing of it—who chalk it up to Vico's time or his personal faith, as if Vico does not precisely dramatize in concept the very notion of time and its relation to one's commitments.[48]

What is striking in Vico is his repeated implication that there is nothing more natural than *Homo creator*, the maker of culture, of law, but at the same time nothing more cultural than the "ideal eternal" laws of nature that find their expression in the "common sense of the human race," as perceived in the mind of history.[49] It is through Vico's notion of providence—as both universal and historical, divine and human, given and made—that one gains a sense of his paradoxical embrace of the secular as the site of history. Vico may announce the arrival of the secular in or as modernity. The question shall be, What is the concept of the secular that he has announced?

Two Conceits

Vico's *New Science* (third edition published in 1744) is an extraordinary read, filled with vivid accounts of giants, gods, and heroes, theories of the origin of hieroglyphics and Greek verse, and running commentary on the ancient Chaldeans, Scythians, Egyptians, and Chinese, with lengthy treatments of Homer, Roman law, and marriage and burial rites across cultures. Beyond this wealth of material, Vico is also a great systematizer, and his book is relentlessly structured by threes. The theoretical framework contains elements, principles, and methods; the historical course that the nations run moves from the divine to the heroic to the human; and consequently there are three kinds of natures, three kinds of customs, three kinds of natural law, three kinds of governments, languages, characters, and so on. A first glance at the book and its table of contents suggests an interplanetary collision between Hegel and Jorge Luis Borges. For all its systematizing, it is not an easy book to comprehend, resisting ready access to the fields to which it makes the greatest contribution: the study of religion, philosophy, and history, and especially the study of the relation between these three.

This state of affairs is one that Vico predicts, though he attributes it not to the riotousness of his book but to the failure of philosophy and history (which he calls philology) to understand their first principles, which is to say their relation, both in provenance and in providence. "It is [a] property of the human mind," Vico observes, "that whenever men can form no idea of distant and unknown things, they judge them by what is familiar and at hand." Unlike the ideal historian who makes history for himself in meditating on the history of the nations, in the main human beings crudely make themselves the measure of all things.[50]

This—you could call it—tribal consciousness leads, Vico says, to the conceit of nations and the conceit of scholars. The first names the conviction that a nation's "remembered history goes back to the very beginning of the world," the second names the conviction that what one knows "is as old as the world."[51] These two conceits capture an error endemic to both history and philosophy, namely the supposition that each is capable of entering all realms equally, that each is extendable without limit and, even more, without a concept of limit. Historians, focused on the study of "languages and deeds," "customs and laws," "wars, peace, alliances, travels, and commerce," assume that history is simply the world story instituted at the beginning of time. Philosophers, focused on truths, assume that reason is everywhere and always the same—that ancient humanity can be judged by its "enlightened, cultivated, and magnificent times."[52] Each manifests the error of forming no idea of others, making themselves the measure of all things by casting antiquity in their image, casting their image in antiquity. Each conceit also expresses the failure to learn from each other. Philosophers fail to ground their science historically by taking account of the "languages and deeds" of reason. Historians (or philologists) fail to ground their science philosophically by noticing that the very concept of history is not as old as the world. History is not coincident with the human. Or, as we will see, it *is* coincident with the human in Vico's sense, which concept is not coincident with the natural beginning of humanity.

Both conceits are at play in historical and philosophical reconstructions of what Vico ironically calls "the matchless wisdom of the ancients," by which he means the ancient wisdom Europeans cast as their origin. Europe is understood to begin in Egyptian-Greco-Roman antiquity inasmuch as this antiquity is understood to be, for the scholarly mind, the beginning of history. Antiquity thinks like Europe because, well, it must: what Europe knows is as old as the world.

What concerns Vico is not only the mistake of assimilating the beginning of time with the high culture of Western antiquity, nor is it only to correct the European claim that everyone thinks like Europeans. These are the charge of ethnocentrism, a charge Vico does advance in his way, but one he makes contingent on a distinction that itself sounds profoundly ethnocentric—that of the Hebrews, with their true God, and the gentes, with their more ordinary providence. It is a truism that this kind of distinction is more discordant to our ears than it would have been to Vico's readers, most of whom presumed it or some version thereof. What is not a truism is what Vico means by his distinction.

Consider the conceits. When I assume that my reasoning is as "old as the world," I assume that I am separated from, say, the ancients only by something called history, which, in beginning with time, stands as the condition for a shared wisdom no less than a situated one. I am never really separated from ancients or any other others since, yes, history interposes. But what kind of interposition is this from the standpoint of reason, which finds the transhistorical pattern in the dusty tumult? It might be countered that I am actually absolutely separated from ancients and all others since, yes, reason finds patterns. But what kind of interposition is this in the face of reason's overweening inclination to disregard change? What kind of differences are differences of history and reason—in themselves or relative to each other? Are there two conceits or one?

In the conceit that a nation's remembered history goes back to the beginning of the world, the difference privileged is history as customs, languages, laws, and letters, to which the remembering mind is relative (subordinate). In the conceit that what one knows is as old as the world, the difference privileged is reason, to which history's customs, languages, laws, and letters would be relative (subordinate), the remembering mind made constant. Whereas, says Vico, it is "the constant labor throughout this book to demonstrate" that "the natural law of the gentes had separate origins among the several peoples, each in ignorance of the others, and it was only subsequently, as a result of wars, embassies, alliances, and commerce, that it came to be recognized as common to the entire human race."[53] Both conceits would be wrong then. No one's history goes back to the beginning. There is no single beginning. And no one knows what is as old as the world, since nothing is. Change abides. Reason and history are made, not given in the beginning. They are acts of mind, not recordings of a master plan.

Vico's response seems to be precisely a critique of ethnocentrism. The conceits are slain by identifying them as ignorance of others in the very moment that each claims mastery of them. To which Vico replies, There is not one history but many histories. There is not one mind but many minds. Vico seems thereby to have solved the problem of the conceits and the problem of ethnocentrism in one blow. History is not singular (one, homogeneous), yet minds make recognizable work in it. What is common is not given in the beginning but made, conquered, achieved. Vico's carnival of a book, with its welter of arcana and the militarism of its threes, would contain its own if not quite matchless, then certainly markedly contemporary wisdom.

But let us withhold this judgment. What of the distinction between the Hebrews and the gentes? Right, says Milbank. *The New Science* is a history of God, *the* God, the God of the Hebrews, who makes the Hebrews the center of the world. But then there are Preus and Said. Vico's distinction is a feint. We are all the gentes. If the Hebrews are so central, why does Vico's new science of the nations ignore them or, as Said has it, exclude their religion from the science of history?

These are both true readings, as long as they include each other. The Hebrews appear as an engine of reversal to undercut the naturalism of the conceits, which readily claim beginnings but dissipate them in the fuzziness of always and everywhere. The Hebrews are the standard by which Vico distinguishes history as the meditation on what human beings make and the goad in the system of the gentes' natural law that exposes its conceits. What Vico holds is that in the confusion of mixing and dividing history and philosophy, the conceits express a series of questionable assumptions under the auspices of natural law: (a) that the designation humankind is a class, a homogeneity; (b) that what history marks are temporal modifications within this essential class; (c) that history presupposes its subject, humankind, and begins in the beginning, with the (human) world; (d) that what history is for is the delineation of custom, law, language, letters—experience in time; (e) that for the delineation of what is true, there is philosophy, which, insofar as it pursues what is more durable than history, pursues what is naturally or perennially true.

Vico begins otherwise, with three claims. First, the subject of history is the making of nations, of collectives, tribes, socialities, not the passage of time. Second, this making involves a modification not only of humankind, but of the mind, or "our own mind." Third, the mind in turn modifies the concept of humankind, which is belated, not given.

Vico holds that the origins of the human race were diverse and unknown—as he puts it, "small, crude, and quite obscure."[54] Nevertheless, diverse peoples generated "uniform ideas," that is, uniform institutions such as religion, marriage, and burial. This is evident to such a degree that Vico speaks of human institutions as testifying to "a mental language common to all the nations."[55] But instead of presupposing a uniform human subject who undergoes diverse historical experiences, as Durkheim does, or alternatively supposing that there is no subject of history at all, nothing but diversity, Vico identifies evident historical uniformity as the key question, whose alternative formulation is the question of when history begins.

What interests Vico is that insofar as history is an act of mind, there are borders beyond which history does not extend. The border is not between humans and, for example, animals or other natural entities, but between humans and what Darwin would come to call the origin of the species; the past, to paraphrase L. P. Hartley, insofar as it is an uninhabitable country. Where Terence has "nothing human is alien to me," Vico insists that there are modes of existence that cannot be entered. Sometimes he calls such modes giants, or gods, or heroes, or poets, sometimes simply "ancients." In the terms of this book, the distinction is between modernity and the nonmodern, and the claim is that it is not possible to occupy both positions. It is a key element of modernity that it will confuse itself with the logic of nonmodernity. But this is its own conceit, not a historical reckoning.

What Vico sustains is the insight that what plague both history and philosophy, both history and modernity, are two equally untenable options: either that what is common is what is natural, and thus not cultural or historical (the conceit of scholars), or that what is common is historical and cultural insofar as this assumption entails a perennial history (the conceit of nations). Both conceits depend on the contradiction of nature and culture. When one is asserted the other must of necessity be denied, which makes it impossible to conceive either of the origin of one *in* the other or the origin of one *without* the other. Both positions express versions of providence, a providence of origins and a providence of ends—the natural law that history merely unfolds or the history that lawfully progresses to its inevitable outcome. For Vico, both these versions of providence are misconceived, since, even as each conceit depends on both history and philosophy, each uses one to subordinate the other. A providence of origins subordinates truth to history by failing to account for a change of mind (history as "chance"). A providence of ends subordinates history to truth by failing to account for a change of culture (history as "fate").

In tandem with the critique of the conceits, with its dialectic of history and origins, Vico conceives a seemingly more straightforward scheme whereby humankind moves through ages of "gods, heroes, and men." This is his "ideal eternal history" of the nations, which philologists typically miss in postulating a human subject in the beginning where Vico places only gods. The scheme is therefore progressive. But this alone does not capture its logic. Historians/philologists fail the progression in overriding the nonequivalence these ages express—that the difference between gods and heroes is different from the difference between gods/heroes and human beings, who tell the history. The ages are two, not three. Philosophers fail the logic of a progression that is not in fact progressive—that at issue is the historical mind, the late fruit of the age of "men" that surveys and narrates the gods it once feared. The principal change of history is history itself, in which, to paraphrase Stevens's mythology from chapter 2, it shall have been the case that we have always lived there, even as the "true narration" of gods and heroes knows "we" haven't. Vico tips his hat to this critical proviso through the conceits, which know no distinctions, and the ideal eternal history, which multiples them. For Preus, by contrast, the transition from gods to heroes to men simply narrates the emergence of the secular as that space that substitutes science for providence, expressive of the logic of evolution. For Milbank the transition narrates the participation of the human in its divine origins—*Homo creator*.

When does history begin? The question sounds innocuous on its face but, as will be clear, it is charged. Vico's concept of history is to serve the common law of nations. It is to understand human beings in their diversity and in their patterns. History is a universal discourse, second only to nature, whose author, God, is given notice that his counsel will not be sought. It is inclusive of what human beings make. As we have seen, however, this inclusiveness is dependent on distinctions—between natural providence and the true God, between gods and heroes and men, and between Hebrews and gentes. The distinctions in turn depend on an inclusive providence, supportive of both religion and the secular, these people and those people, God and human beings. Further questions, then: Who tells this history of the universal, the gentes or the Hebrews? Who is the history for? What is it for?

Hebrews and Nations

Vico's ideal eternal history of gods, heroes, and men suggests that the natural beginning of human beings, having given rise to gods as protection from the brutality of the state of nature, is transposed under the guidance of *factum*—making, culture—whereby institutions are created that more and more adequately express the power of human beings to safeguard themselves. From gods to men, from religion to the secular, from inequality and tyranny to justice and equality. Hence "the first law was divine, for men believed themselves and all their institutions to depend on the gods"; "the second was heroic, the law of force, but controlled by religion, which alone can keep force within bounds where there are no human laws or none strong enough to curb it"; "the third is the human law dictated by fully developed human reason," which gives rise to "governments" before which "all are accounted equal."[56] Reason denotes freedom and the universal, the "equality of the intelligent nature which is the proper nature of man."[57]

Vico's idiosyncratic spin on this otherwise familiar genealogy of modernity, his contention that in the beginning there were giants and only eventually human beings, might not appear to mitigate the straightforward developmentalism of the position. This is the developmentalism offered by Hume and many Enlightenment figures, in which monotheism and reason arise from a more elemental polytheism—the position Durkheim's elementary forms sought to eliminate. Furthermore, insofar as Vico departs from this progressive story with reference to the Hebrews, who do not follow the course of the gentile nations, would this not deepen the enlightened ethnocentrism: not only that some single "us" is more developed than some multitude of "them" but that—here Vico's diverse origins surely work against him—there is one history for us and one history for them?

Vico's claim, however, is that humanity is belated—not developed in coming to be rational from a more natural condition but historical in knowing its origins as crude and obscure. Humanity is an artificial population. It is belated in coming into existence as subject not only of a government before whom all are accounted equal, but of a history that can measure just how unequal things might be. Vico's real idiosyncrasy lies not in his giants but in his conception of their genealogy as rooted not only in a crude beginning but in one that itself is belated, made. This is the claim to clarify.

Let us first observe that, together with the scheme of gods, heroes, and humans, Vico makes two key claims about his ideal eternal history. First, the course the nations run—the ideal eternal history that unites all nations despite their diverse origins—applies only to the gentes and not to the Hebrews. Second, *factum*—making—is original and originating. That is, Vico reveals, "gods, heroes, and men began at the same time (for they were, after all, men who imagined the gods and believed their own heroic nature to be a mixture of divine and human natures)."[58] The second claim is not simply that it was "men" who evolved and their concepts with them, it is that there is also no evolution. The evolution, that is, is not within the genus humankind, which would develop from confused ideas to true ones as a germ develops.[59] Nor is humankind for Vico, as in Durkheim, a social container of difference or, as in Feuerbach, the nature whose nature can be reclaimed from illusion.[60] Humans are beings who evolve their images, who make them something (true) from nothing (natural), not necessarily but creatively. They might also, then, fail to do so, confuse their doings, and use their creativity to wreak havoc. "Things do not settle or endure out of their natural state," Vico claims.[61] In nature there is neither simultaneity nor development; that is, neither truth nor history, neither illusion nor obscurity.

This is not simply to substitute *factum* for nature. It is to comprehend Vico's commitment to the transposition of the natural—to the *Homo creator* of natural law. "Legislation considers man as he is in order to turn him to good uses in human society." Out of human vices like "ferocity, avarice, and ambition," law makes "civil happiness."[62] It is law that transforms nature into culture, but law itself must therefore be both natural and cultural. Vico puts it thus: "In view of the fact that the human race, as far back as memory of the world goes, has lived and still lives conformably in society," it is possible to assert that the convictions "law exists by nature" and "man is naturally sociable . . . come to the same thing."[63] There was never a time when human beings were simply natural; but there was never a time when they escaped nature either, for law itself is natural. Durkheim would agree. In the beginning are elementary forms of social-religious life. The question is, What develops the critique of this nature, without which none might be counted equal? What distinguishes the secular, the goods of equality and justice, from the religious, the gods of the patriarchs, and the religious, the divine law of equality and justice, from the secular, the law of force?

Vico's paradoxical observations about law, nature, and society advance the notion that there is no development *from* nature *to* culture, from origins to history—that this movement is inconceivable, and thus unhistorical. It cannot be meditated on, except from the standpoints of history, which presupposes the simultaneity of nature and culture, and of law, which insists nature become human. The very notion of progress presupposes that gods, heroes, and men came into existence together in reflecting a "common ground of truth."[64] That is, development from gods to men is fictional, says Vico—a "true narration," he calls it—in being that by which the mind works to express its image.[65] That we move from gods to heroes to men is not something known to the mind except by the reverse of this order, which is also the recognition of its simultaneity. Preus takes the passage from gods to men at face value—a story of secularization in which the mind comes to see itself as the creator of its gods. But this is only to get as far as Feuerbach and Durkheim. The god is the human fiction of its own distinctness. Missing is the human as she comes to know her image as that of god qua justice and equality. The condition of this recognition, however, is that there is something the mind cannot know, a border it cannot cross. Something, it could be said, that the mind creates in excluding it: nature in itself, or in this case, the time before the mind's image of itself as *Homo creator*. Milbank would have this term signify participation in a scheme greater than human. It may be no disagreement with this signification to claim the principles of justice and equality as those than which nothing greater can be thought.

There are therefore two notions of the gods in human origins. In one notion, gods and heroes express human origins in a restricted sense. Human beings do not develop out of gods and heroes, out of the ideas of gods and heroes. Gods and heroes are the difference of beginning with *factum*, with culture—with human existence or the mind as the origin of (images of) itself. Thinking can never be as ancient as the world because the world as it is is something that thinking originates in knowing it only *as*: truth and its image. This recognition comes to fruition in reason, whose sign is a law before which all shall be accounted equal. This is law as what shall be made natural, where nature is what shall be lawful in being inclusive of all. It is a subject of distinction, in excluding both natural developmentalism (evolution) and its partner, supernatural teleology. It is providential in being rational, true in being historical.

This law of inclusion is expressed through the second notion of gods, that of the Hebrews. On the one hand, the "sacred history" of the ancient

Hebrews is "more ancient than all the most ancient profane histories that have come down to us," the proof of which is that it "narrates the state of nature under the patriarchs; that is, the state of the families, out of which . . . the peoples and cities later arose."[66] The Hebrews in the beginning were human, not divine, not heroic, and their histories thus give us the birth of nations and the principles of an ideal eternal history. On the other hand, Vico depicts a separate genealogy according to which the world was first populated by giant bestial creatures who, "having wandered about in the wild state of dumb beasts and being therefore sluggish, were inexpressive save under the impulse of violent passions, and formed their first languages by singing."[67]

The first men, on this view, were mute, only slowly and gradually making "themselves understood by gestures or objects that have natural relations with the ideas they wish to signify."[68] Indeed, the ideal eternal history instituted by the ancient Hebrews shows that "the nature of peoples is first crude, then severe, then benign, then delicate, finally dissolute."[69] Except the Hebrews themselves? Vico writes, "[The] entire original human race . . . was divided into two species: the one of giants, the other of men of normal stature; the former gentiles, the latter Hebrews. Also that this difference can have come about only as the result of the bestial education of the former and the human education of the latter. Hence that the Hebrews had a different origin from that of the gentiles."[70]

One sympathizes with the desire to distinguish what is usable in Vico from what he could not or should not have meant. But it is not necessary to do so. The key, once again, is the relation between nature and culture. It is "education" that differentiates the Hebrews and the gentiles. It is education that determines which is more ancient, education that unites what is diverse, if it also divides what is united. If education further divides the bestial and the human, this is because education is bound to the conjunction of *verum-factum*. If the truth is made, it may also be unmade, be, that is, betrayed, forgotten, or confused.

The Hebrews come into existence as "most ancient," or in other words as aboriginal, but the gentes *become* more ancient still. According to Vico's story, the relation between Hebrew and gentes can be told via the giants, originally the sons of Noah, who "must be supposed to have gone off into bestial wandering, fleeing from beasts . . . and being scattered over the whole earth."[71] Their very antiquity, which here means their very naturalness, is contingent on something they did, thus on *factum*, on law, on culture. Instead of supposing that in the beginning existence was made lawful from its natural state, where legislation transforms what is into what ought to be, history can only conceive the opposite: that in the beginning existence was *made* natural, now not in the law that paradoxically shall become most natural in being most equal, but in the law that, in constituting the call to equality, shall persistently and dumbly be abrogated. Legislation just as easily transforms what ought to be—human history as the diverse commitment to a common origin—into what is— the natural and brutish existence in which diversity is simply conflict. The latter Vico calls the origin of the gentiles, but, as his genealogy acknowledges, he also follows the biblical genealogy according which the name for both states is Noah.

This genealogy would not exempt a people, "the Hebrews," from being brutish and natural. For either everyone is Hebrew in being diversely human but also crude and obscure in origin, or the Hebrews are not a people but a principle. By the same token, the Hebrews are no one and everyone is the gentiles, identically diverse. No nation begins otherwise than in natural obscurity, where history finds them profaning the image of the human.

If, then, the distinction of the Hebrews is of no distinction, is Preus's reading right to ignore it? Is Said's reading right to exclude the Hebrews' true God as nonhistorical? The argument is clearly no, on both counts. The Hebrews signify the beginning of the good of knowledge, the beginning of history. What human beings can do is not marked in the laws of nature or in the course the nations take without end. The Hebrews are the end of the course in signifying the principle that there is an end, vulnerable always to the confusion and conceit that the end is given in the nature of things. There is no secular history as both thinkers want it without the concept of the human as both maker of history and meditator upon it. As Said affirms, history is a criticism, not only a description. It is content as well as concept.

What "Hebrews" names is the artificial population by which nature is also lawful for human beings, the site of making, history's subject. This name acknowledges the brutishness of natural beginning. What it distinguishes is the beginning that is human, the concept of (human) nature, which then would not be coincident with something designated humankind as such, accessible in its evolution. The difference between the "ordinary help from providence" granted to the gentes and the "extraordinary help from the true God" granted to the Hebrews is that both are visible only in the law of nature taken as "thou shall be equal," the law of reason—ordinary and extraordinary—than which nothing greater can be committed. Let it be said, the Hebrews don't exist. Or the Hebrews are also the gentes, subject to ordinary providence as the immense effort of mind to make common, to make equal, what is confusedly or merely diverse, when it is not assumedly and unthinkingly common. History is the modification of the mind, of our own mind, which comes to itself, as to its others, belatedly.[72] It is then that history is to know the mind wherever and whenever it may be found.

Vico's language of Hebrews and gentiles will tend to imprison him in a Western cliché. Certainly no one would be less surprised than Vico that he cannot escape the history of the languages and letters he himself uses. Just as critically the Hebrews, even if never "Hebrews," have tended to imprison themselves or be imprisoned there, a light unto the nations or its unique scourge. We know what havoc the language of uniqueness wreaks. In the face of this havoc, however, it is inadequate merely to prescind from mentioning it. Vico's thinking remains a way beyond these dead ends, one that is more fruitful than the effort presumptively to stop making distinctions at all, or the oath to make them only from the serene heights of classification, the serene depths of structuralism, or the serene situation of skepticism, which handles and then disavows distinctions pending whoever steps into the ring. Vico is a political thinker in recognizing the foibles of our languages and laws, our conceits. But he makes these foibles apparent in providing their principle. That Vico's own distinction can stand for a bestial history does not make the study of human beings nothing other than an ever-renovated bestiary.

What Vico is elaborating in holding that history is the modification of and the meditation upon our own mind is the mind's history and the mind of history. Following the two conceits, one learns that it is both historically and philosophically impermissible to assume that there has always been mind or always been history. It is only because the mind originates—only because the human image is caused by nothing natural—that history can locate a distinction between itself, what is made, and its other, what is given as nature. It is only because history originates that it is not more ancient still. It is only because it is "most ancient," that is, original, that history is modern, the origin, the difference that is modernity.

For Milbank, the recognition that human making "marks out" not an autonomous "secular" human space but one "open to transcendence" makes Vico's history "counter-modern."[73] What Milbank sees is correct. The transcendence to which Vico's *factum* is open is grounded in his positioning of the Hebrews as the axis of history: that in the face of which the gentes develop, that axis that makes the progress of an ideal eternal history visible as also present in the beginning. But whereas Preus attaches too little significance to the Hebrews/gentes distinction, Milbank makes too much of it in cleaving to the distinction between "natural divine providence" and "supernatural divine grace."[74] Milbank's conception of Vico's countermodernity is founded on the importance of grace to effect the change from nature to culture, from nothing to something, which change secularism would deny.

But Vico denies both this religion and its secular postulate. He gives us the language of grace in a vision of providence that is both ordinary (historical) and extraordinary (true) in identifying the change *not* from nature to culture but from culture to nature—from the space of making (custom, languages, laws, letters) to the space of truth (pattern, principle, reason, equality) and its abrogation. Vico's grace does not transition us from nature to culture, not because he is finally a secular thinker but because the transition is to conceive of both nature and culture as each coming into existence with the other. The beginning, it is clear, is crude and obscure. But it is also provident, where providence means the always miraculous effort to make good on the order of the beginning from which one is, like Noah's brutish offspring, in danger of straying.

Vico puts it like this: "But since without order (which is to say without God) human society cannot stand for a moment . . . providence called the civil order into being."[75] Providence is the simple pattern of history, Vico repeatedly says: the common nature of nations, the ideal eternal law. But it is one that "men have themselves made," and it is this making, "always superior to the particular ends that men had proposed to themselves," that is providential. "It was not fate, for they did it by choice; not chance, for the results of their always so acting are perpetually the same."[76] In the face of which there is nothing more essential than the science of critique.

For Vico, the human is an achievement, one that posits the distinction between itself insofar as it is just and equal and itself insofar as it is crude and obscure. The distinction is not between providence as sacred history and ordinary history as secular. The secular is itself providential; the sacred is ordinary. Both are subject to confusion. The distinction is between providence and the conceits of both philosophy and history, the two conceits that reduce mind to history and history to mind, the recapitulation of one and many. Vico's commitment to the "common" and the "natural," the "made" and the "manipulated," does not commit him to Preus's reduction of providence without remainder. Indeed, Vico is most committed to the remainder of providence in nature and culture alike—the very notion that nature (the big eat the little) and culture (the big get the little to work for them) are present together in the mind as it is tempted to make itself the measure of all things.

The End of Orientalism

Vico is not an easy thinker to do justice to, and he is not easy to think with in the present. The value of attempting both can be stated simply. The fruit of history lies in the commanding image of human beings as empowered to make worlds in common with one another. History is the study not of nature but of human nature. It is thus the study of what human beings make of (their) nature. This image is secular in distinguishing this work as human not godly (supernatural), human not heroic (natural qua might makes right). But it is no less religious insofar as religion authors the distinction between worlds expressive of the common and worlds that reinstate natural divisions and hierarchies. I am arguing in this book that it does not matter whether you call this distinction religious or secular. What matters is the distinction between religion and secularity each taken as the goods of equality and justice and each of these taken as the contradictory doxa of fate or chance. That both religion and the secular can be taken both ways is what Vico's notion of providence helps to illuminate.

Once we recognize that history is the work of the human, it is incumbent on us to recognize the reverse: that the human is a work of history. History is witness to the human power to create in common, and this power is belated. It is modern in principle as what distinguishes between collectives of critique and collectives as ends in themselves; between truths that appear and must thus be taken up and realized in common and truths that are inaccessible or absent.

Vico distinguishes between beginnings that, crude and obscure, cannot be recovered except through the illusion of the conceits and beginnings that are true in being as conscious of what is not knowable as of what is. In this concept of beginning, the development of gods, heroes, and men expresses the secular intuition that the human is the image and the standard of the gods, for these gods and heroes are ours. But no less does it express the religious intuition that the human standard is *a* human standard; that its enunciation is not endemic or natural to humanity but is expressive of a particular—a historical—image. Vico gives us the Hebrews, with their image of God, as what names the principle of the human as *Homo creator*, as cocreator of a common language in the babel of historical existence. That the actual Hebrews were given to wandering off into bestiality only affirms the paradox: that the beginning, absolute in distinction from natural generation, will therefore either be realized in common or be abrogated in violence.

We have learned the painful truth that the distinction between the Hebrews and other nations will itself be constitutive of yet one more violent abrogation of the principle of a common humanity, diverse evils in the languages and letters of infinite histories. But without the distinction between the principle and the nations, there is no way to work on the course the nations must take: to stem the cycles of violence, to activate the power of diverse histories, to conceive and support the common good.

Let us conclude by recalling Vico's aphorism that is most beloved by Said.

> But in the night of thick darkness enveloping the earliest antiquity, so remote from ourselves, there shines the eternal and never failing light of a truth beyond all question: that the world of civil society has certainly been made by men, and that its principles are therefore to be found within the modifications of our own human mind.[77]

For Vico, the question of history is the question of self and other. Since history is made by human beings, it must on the one hand be possible to know even those historical events that are "so remote from ourselves" as to seem enveloped in "thick darkness." This is what is revelatory: that history can be known because we have made it, and this "we" is therefore not simply a figure of speech or an act of discursive expropriation but a herculean work of interpretation across the ages. On the other hand, the "never failing light of a truth beyond all question" is that the mind cannot be laid bare in its principles but rather is "modified" by "civil society"—by, as it were, its own self-production in concert with the others in its time. The never failing truth, then, is that the mind is subject to history as well as a subject of history, which is to say, accessible only through the work of elaborating what it has made and what in turn has made it. History is the effort to know the mind of another. History is the recognition that minds may be (like) ours, even in their patent difference. What follows, however, is that it would never be "all minds" we would be knowing or even all minds that could be known. It is the risk along with the ethics of history that history is itself a modification.

What Said calls Orientalism is a failure of the trial and golden rule of historical interpretation—to know another mind as one would have that other mind know oneself.[78] This principle includes confronting where my knowledge comes to an end. Orientalism is the profanation of the principle that history must include both the mind of the knower and the mind of the known, or must know itself as limited to history. As Vico puts the profanation, we have seen, the human mind, wherever it is "lost in ignorance," makes itself "the measure of all things."[79] This is Orientalism. Instead of the golden rule of interpretation, I make the other in my image. I then rule over this image so that it does not rule over me, or I find myself, lose myself, where I am not. I thereby simulate self-understanding while alienating myself from true self-understanding, which can be constituted only in concert with a historical other. From Vico to Hegel, Marx, Kierkegaard, and Nietzsche, this failure of othering, what Hegel calls the "master-slave" relationship and what Marx simply calls religion, is modernity's intimate familiar.

Said struggles to discern the common source of both history and its profanation. It is because I can know the other in her sovereignty that I can profane her, but then also stand responsible for the profanation. It is because I am limited to history that I can freely—if blindly—dominate where my anchor comes to an end, but then also extend it in inclusion. Both are historical acts. The difference between Said and Vico is that for all Said wants a secular history, he finds history inexorably Orientalist. When he speaks of liberation, he therefore reaches for a set of generics: all cultures, all peoples. Vico makes the mind a historical category, which is to say, he refuses to grant that we can know every mind and culture alike. This principle, the very specter of Orientalism, is also the grounds of its undoing in making the work of inclusion different from a natural fact. Said sees the workings of history in his tale of domination and is then left to speculate about its end. He does not unite the act that distinguishes history as secular with the practices, powers, and distortions of interpretation. But without history, the Occident will be eternal gnostic partner to the Orient, in the light of which the only recourse to these equally dead ends will be to conjure a natural all that is, we have seen, a supernatural some.

In the passage that constitutes a conceptual climax unequaled in the rest of *Orientalism*, Said makes the observation I repeatedly refer to:

> For that is the main intellectual issue raised by Orientalism. Can one divide human reality, as indeed human reality seems to be genuinely divided, into clearly different cultures, histories, traditions, societies, even races, and survive the consequences humanly?

In this brilliantly dialectical sentence, Said captures both the powers of the mind and its limits while venturing the ethical question that is essential to the work of history. Can we survive? How will we avoid dividing in and being divided by violence? Said continues in a more abstract vein:

> By surviving the consequences humanly, I mean to ask whether there is any way of avoiding the hostility expressed by the division, say, of men into "us" (Westerners) and "they" (Orientals). For such divisions are generalities whose use historically and actually has been to press the importance of the distinction between some men and some other men, usually towards not especially admirable ends.[80]

All cultures do this. All peoples do this. History enters to use this general practice of dividing. Or is it that division is "actually" already historical, and the notion of the general is but a heuristic, like the state of nature—useful but not real? Said leaves open the question of how history works on acts of (general) division. But he has already swerved from the model the passage begins with, in which the fact that history has always already been used, reality always already divided, even if into different histories, does not mean we cannot ask how we shall do so, which history we shall tell. Indeed, to find reality already divided, to be divided by it, will be to be enjoined to take responsibility for how we then do so.

Can we think in some way other than through division? Can we divide in some other or better way? Said casts it both ways. Orientalism is a species of thinking and knowing anything. And Orientalism is the hegemonic logic of the thinking and knowing of the historical West. These judgments together can themselves be interpreted in two ways. For Said, that Orientalism is a species of thinking means that thinking without Orientalism would be a function of the "all"—what all cultures do, what all cultures might then refuse. Although Said does not directly conceive a collective human project as an ahistorical one, he does not work through the canon of history outside Orientalism, as if Orientalism is so enormous that it comes to stand for history itself. Although this is indeed my own thesis—that Orientalism tells us something about history in its fundamental contestations—for Said this is just another way of saying there is something (non-Orientalist, non-Western, perhaps) outside history by which we can judge it. Said wants thinking—all cultures—to provide a place of refuge. His partnership with Lévi-Strauss bears this precise fruit:

structuralism has no problem imagining distinctions and classifications that do not have the character of domination.

But Orientalism as a species of thinking can also be a historical judgment. This is the route Vico takes. For Vico, that Orientalism is a species of thinking means that Orientalism is a species of history, and while there would be no escape from its threat, neither would it be inevitable. In Vico's terms, Orientalism would be the illusion of the conceits. One would strive to know when, why, and how this illusion takes hold. In so striving, one would have to be able to imagine forms of thinking that were not Orientalist—that had a different story, a different history. The irony of Orientalism would be that the domestication of the exotic that is characteristic of thinking anything might become nothing more than unmitigated exoticism, the dissemination and then misrecognition of the self in theatrical garb. As we have seen, "the Oriental was always *like* some aspect of the West," an aspect that both lured and repelled.[81] Such an irony presupposes that we would know what the recognition of true otherness was and be able to conceive the history supportive of it.

The movement of the conceits, then, would be not from the human into history, but from a history of mutual recognition into one of obfuscation and violence. The one (recognition) would not necessarily, and indeed would hardly ever, precede the other (violence) in time. Orientalism may be all there is until, sometime in the future, it is replaced by more equitable, more truthful, relation. But the principle of mutual recognition would precede the conceits of Orientalism in concept, as Vico's Hebrews precede their giants. Orientalism would never merely be Orientalism.

Said's reading of Orientalism as a form of thinking mainly alternates between the first and second interpretations I offered in introducing his claims. Orientalism is illustrative of a common human function or is the historical intensification of a more benign common human function, which function we can reaffirm once Orientalism has been deconstructed. According to these interpretations, the mind is in either an original or a secondary relation of domination with reality. There would be no need to discover the origin of Orientalism because it would already be given in the beginning, with thinking or with the Occident, the West. In the beginning is correction and conversion as the Orientalist takes what is "like" himself and makes over the rest in his image and foil. Who knows why the West does what it does or, as in the impertinent question to Augustine's God, what the West was doing before it dominated. That it dominates, and with what methods, is what matters. Since here the West is, as it were, original, the only position from which we could have

descended into Occidentalism is nature—some human nature, recover-
able, Said sometimes seems to hope, from the soiled relations into which
it has fallen. The West would signify the reverse of the Orient and at the
same time "all cultures" insofar as their "corrections upon raw reality"
are bullying.

Let me return to the third interpretation of the relation between Orientalism and what is common to humanity. The best sense of what Said
is ambitiously gesturing toward is that Orientalism is a historical formation that tells us something important about history, the mind, and
their relation. If it is impossible to imagine any human relationship that
is not tainted by the struggles for power imagined, albeit on an immense
scale, in *Orientalism*, then this will have been the gift of Said's book, as
it was the gift of Hegel's work on master and slave. He will have shown
exactly how seriously and consequentially human beings can and will
misinterpret one another and why the reason for this misinterpretation
constitutes the dilemma of human historical existence: that one must
divide, in the light of reality's existing divisions, and one is thus to take
responsibility not only for one's own divisions but for those by which
one is divided. Without this responsibility, otherwise known as criticism,
we will not survive, or our survival will be compromised and our minds
lost, even if we physically endure. Did Said never quite have faith that
this recognition—that there is no relation free from Orientalism—does
not mean all relations are merely doomed to repeat it ad infinitum? He
knew, or he believed, that there is a concept of the collective that empowers equality and sovereignty, not domination and contempt. But it
was as if, since the path there is not clear, the worry that perhaps it is not
there at all was almost engulfing.

It is not there, Vico would remind us, until we make it. We are working, as Stevens says, with artificial populations. Said was drawn to this
thesis. The irony is that he might have been less influential had he committed to it to the end. In connecting Orientalism to ordinary forms of
relation, we could not take refuge in extravagant gestures of repentance
or atonement. This would be to recognize Orientalism's lodging in customs and habits of living and thinking, neither shocking nor quickly
reparable. With this interpretation, Said would be entitled to his concept of a collective humanity only insofar as he abandons the idea of "all
cultures"—only insofar as he recognizes that Orientalism will be with us
as the distinction that also makes its end possible, with persistent labor.

Said began his career as a critic with the aptly titled *Beginnings*,
which opens with a distinction between origins, which lie outside the
compass of history, and beginnings, which must always be begun anew.

Beginnings are contingent and secular; origins are absolute and religious.[82] Said would repeat this distinction throughout his critical texts, championing the secular as what, in exiling the religious, serves as the fundamental contract of the humanities. But like so many theorists, Said does not distinguish between religion as the postulate of an intrinsic truth or god and religion as the work he names the secular—the work to enact the good of history as what human beings make. This oversight is not terminological but conceptual. Said sets aside not just the Forms but also their critique. He sets aside not just the truth that stands outside history but the truth of history. He is right that history's truth must always be begun anew. But his embrace of contingent beginnings cannot account for this "anew" in terms other than repetition. As a result, he cannot be confident that Orientalism can ever end, even as he imagines a world without it. In setting aside religion, Said unwittingly sets aside the structure of criticism: the distinction of modernity from nonmodernity by which the distinction of Orientalism may become something other than the monotonous inevitability of violence.

As Abraham discovered, one leaves the land of Orientalism not for human community as such, but for another land whose sole permanent feature is the struggle to live up to the promise of all. This is beginning, secular and religious. The need to make this promise never comes to an end. But neither can it be forsaken for the resignation that Orientalism has no end. The promise is the principle, the land is the critique of land, the criticism is self-criticism—at the center that is the state of mind of modernity.

4   The Collective

Now the Lord said to Abram, "Go from your country and your kindred and your father's house to the land that I will show you."

Genesis 12:1

Durkheim and Said are valuable precursors. They each wrestled with the question of what it means to be a critic of a nature one is always redoubling. If they do not get further than Vico, who made the God of the Hebrews a secular history, this is because they do not get as far as Abraham, who, in being called to leave his land, is to make a land subject to a promise of freedom. There are good reasons for this failure, among them the terrible legacy of the biblical traditions in relation to the societies of other peoples, beginning with the stories of Abraham. Each critic evidently hoped he could rectify this legacy. Agreed. There is nothing more corrupt than the societies of the Bible. But, it must be added, there is nothing more mindful of its own corruption than the Bible, which gives us not human perfection but the struggle to keep faith with human nature and its critique—the struggle not to be undone by failure.[1]

Said is one of the few twentieth-century theorists to make Vico central to his criticism and the only critic of the West to do so. He is attuned to Vico's uncommon irreverence with respect to pious manipulations of scholarship, finding support in Vico's distinction of the nations for his effort to banish religion from history, to distinguish secular beginnings from sacred origins.[2] This would be to ground a history of the nations that excluded either natural or religious privilege.

Vico is a tough source for Said, however, given that the nations are distinguished precisely from the Hebrews, the chosen of the "true God," surely an Orientalist move.[3] Vico is an ally of Durkheim in working against the developmentalism that pits a primitive origin against a superior outcome, with Vico using the trope of diverse origins, albeit biblically inflected, to achieve an end similar to what Durkheim achieves with a common one. But Vico departs from both Durkheim and Said in using diversity not only in the sense of historicist multiplicity but also to make an elementary distinction between the conditions of historicity and the contradictory logic of natural cycles. In Vico, as in Durkheim, history is also natural. But in Vico we see the missing position whereby the natural that is also historical removes both from the nature of the given—from mere development, from mere leveling.

In the terms of this book, once nature is also history, once one has, so to speak, left it, as Abraham is called to leave for another land, another nature, it will then be possible to restate or "correct" the human project in merely natural, that is, divisive and contradictory, terms. This correction would be what the principle distinguishes in refusing it. Once nature is also history, there is nothing outside the human effort to make, and betray, a better nature. Once nature is also history, there is confusion, but then also the possibility of clarity.

Now the Lord Said to Abram

Modernity is Abram insofar as he leaves his kin and clan, his land, for another land. This event makes him Abraham, father of a multitude. The call is not only that he leave his land, it is that he leave his land for another one. In leaving his land, he is going somewhere and not nowhere, not toward an abstraction or toward the empyrean or simply to wander the earth. But then the new land, the promised land, will be no less subject to the original call—that it not become yet another homeland. Neither, however, is the promise of a land that cannot be shown, of an ideal land whose promises cannot be made manifest. The injunction to leave the land is not only a critique of kin and clan, of metaphors of blood as a social, political, and ethical end. It is a critique of the first dualism, of the notion that there is somewhere other than a land to seek one's ends; that there is no land in which one can do so. Your end is not merely family, the injunction says. But it is not that no one is your family: it is that everyone might be.

Abraham is modern. To be sure, the injunction alone might not seem to make everything about Abraham modern, or even much of anything. Abraham is not, by most accounts, a modern man. But he is called out from natural relation, a call it will take some doing on his part to realize. This call, this realization, is modernity, as the critique of the values of what merely is or what merely ought to be. Realization does not refer to progress, to advancement come what may, a seed becoming a tree, in Hegel's image, as we similarly denied of Vico's eternal history. It is not teleology, as the arrival at an end or the postulate of a beginning given in advance. The story of Abraham's realization of his call is history as the principle, also a value, that neither nature nor spirit alone is ruler of the world—that the world is to be made, that it can be made good. This principle does not rule out evil worlds. It provides only what evil shall be compared with, in taking the name of the good. It provides, thus, confusion. And its critique.

Modernity is the hope for (a) collective life founded on (b) the value of a collective of all, a good whose content is for all. The mark of modernity is this principle and the concomitant identification of a state of affairs before or other than this. Before or other than modernity, there are collectives, and value is either embedded in them or cast outside them. One could call these collectives civilizations, or religions as formations of society, or religio-political entities. Modernity is the uncoupling of value and collective life such that they are neither identified (the collective as of ultimate value) nor opposed (the collective as subject to an ultimate value). The collective in this uncoupling would be that form of life whose value could be realized in a collective of all. Modernity is the creation of a principle, the principle that a collective be principled, that it be in relation to the principle of all. This is not the dissolution of collectives in favor of one encompassing one. It is the creation of a principle in the face of which all collectives will be judged, a set of questions to which all collectives will need to respond: the questions of how inclusive, how many of all, who is excluded and why.

In this account, modernity is a reformation of the collective, the religio-political civilizational mass, in recognition that, taken on its own, the power of a mass is inversely proportional to the resources it needs to shore up its border. Insofar as collectives conceive their borders as the locus of value, a collective is energized to defense of this value but also limited in expending its power there. The reformation that is modernity is the reordering of collective life (value and politics) in refusal of collectives of nature (blood, kin) or spirit (intrinsic truths), thus the invention of a border that, while valuable, is not the locus of value. The locus of value would reside in the concept of all, which locus is therefore localizable but not violent. This concept is the invention of a border that troubles all borders in imagining one in which everyone is allowed in. It would not be to lose more restricted collectives in the absorption of an "everyone." It would be to imagine that a collective rests on values that are not wholly its own, on the value that "one's own" is not ultimate, which therefore critiques the pretense to close ranks in the name of value.

How does modernity originate? One could say that modernity's reformation is of a state of affairs recognized as deformed. It is the recognition both that value might be collective, incarnate, and that collectives might be animated by the value of making something collective and not simply finding it so by the light of nature or spirit. It is the recognition that, if every collective is founded on values and on itself as valuable, collective value will be tyrannical either when wholly confined to the collective's borders or when wholly free-floating, merely ideal. Modernity would be the value that, embodied in collectives, also pressures them to be as inclusive as possible, in a land that can be shown.

But how is this recognition of a deformation possible? It is not. That is, the origin of modernity, neither natural nor spiritual, is made. Modernity is the making of itself. It is the value of making. This is enlightenment, one could say, or creation. Still, it may always be said that the uncoupling of value and collectives is itself the deformation; that only once value and collective life are uncoupled can value float free to serve whatever interests appropriate it. Surely the tyrannies of collectives are no worse than the tyranny of modernity itself.

The danger of modernity is the recapitulation of what it refuses, whether fortifying its all through conquest of others or sequestering its value in some private or privileged realm where it cannot be used to keep collectives critical. The danger of the critique of modernity is that it will confuse modernity with these refused positions, the critique itself then taking refuge in the infinite regress of collectives or of appearances of them, emptied of value or in resignation to value's mere opportunism.

All human life takes place in collectives. The question is how to value them.

In what follows, I elaborate a theory of collective life in the light of these maxims concerning modernity. It might be a theory of religion, but religion is not an elementary form. It might be a theory of the secular, but the same is true there. Throughout this book, religion is a mobile word, whether or not it circulates with its opposite term. Religion is not itself an agent of distinction. It is, indeed, obfuscating of the distinction at issue here: that of modernity, of its principle, and of alternative ways of being in and conceiving the world. Here I use it to name and elucidate the challenges collectives face in negotiating the desire for simplicity, the desire for the integrity of the collective. This is a desire that can be worthy of respect, but it is observed here in the light of the call to Abraham to be faithless to it. Religion is a word that straddles the modern divide, though not with ease. If all human life takes place in collectives, the challenge is to see where this value comes to an end and how to end its most troubling values.

Let us recall the elementary claims from chapter 1, "The Principle of Modernity."

In the model in which truth appears, the refused positions are what opposes truth and appearance and what identifies them. The terms religion and secularism can express either the model or what it refuses.

In the model in which a (single) collective is constituted by and held accountable to a principle of inclusivity, the refused positions are what identifies inclusivity with the collective and seeks either to expand by domination or to exclude by membership and what identifies inclusivity with the erasure of the (single) collective. The terms religion and secularism can express either the model or what it refuses.

The refused positions in the two models are mutually supportive. Insofar as appearance is not where the truth is (appearance is not true) or insofar as truth is merely whatever appears, a collective can only be rooted in and can extend only as far as the representation and conquest of natural or accidental generation: kin/tribe/ethnos/race/empire.

The refused positions structure many frameworks of social and intellectual life. Their refusal is modernity. In the light of modernity, what is refused is or becomes nonmodern. It also becomes the temptation of modernity as it flees from its own principle.

This chapter turns to what these claims involve. In working with religion and its study, I strive to acknowledge long-standing ideas, in particular that religion is an elementary concept, while also laying new ground comprising more fundamental distinctions. The argument is not that religion has many structures together with its many conditions. It is that religion has two structures, whose relation produces further distinctions as principles give rise to their own pitfalls and confusions. Religion is not only a case of the conceptual phenomenon of thinking at odds with itself. It is a name for the particular pitfalls at issue—how thinking alienates itself from its own ideals; how distinctions that make a difference in the relation of self and other are elided or infinitely multiplied in avoidance of the risks and costs of mutual support and freedom. Religion is a name for this avoidance. It is also a name for the principle itself. The work is to distinguish, to make specific which is which, and then to open this work for emendation.

The claims of chapter 1 lay the groundwork. Here I cull theses, ask questions, and give answers, often more than one. This way of working has a variety of models. It borrows something from the geometric form Spinoza uses in the *Ethics*, in which a proposition is stated, elaborated, and cross-referenced. It borrows, too, from medieval question-and-answer modes, as in Thomas Aquinas's *Summa Theologica* and the various catechisms and exegeses in the history of Christianity. At the same time, because I sometimes give competing answers to a single question or proposition—from the mood of "here is another way to look at this" to the maximally blunt "yes and no"—and pose variations on the same question, it may seem rather more Talmudic. I gain inspiration from Pascal and his *Pensées* and from the analysis of free association pioneered by Freud's work on dreams, in which, as in Freud's self-analysis, one serves as both analyst and analysand—here, inquisitor and defendant.

These are weighty precursors. The point is twofold. First, I am interested in the life of concepts and make use of more or less unconventional forms to convey what I mean in cases where commitments cannot be issued without objection and alternative: where the swift and smooth-moving argument form can suppress too much that is inconvenient or clothe an outcome in rightness while the world spins merrily on, deaf to it. Such objections and alternatives are raised to understand exactly what is being committed and when commitments are vague or insupportable or malformed. More Talmud than Thomas, I find multiplicity internal to the principle. But more Spinoza than Talmud, I do not make commentary on what is preemptively principled, what is taken wholesale as sacred. Rather, I propose what is principled in articulating the principle and its commentary, the principle and its versions, the principle and its subversions.

There is, second, the question of one's limits. In the preface to his *Philosophical Investigations*, Ludwig Wittgenstein allows that he would have preferred to write a different book, one more in control of the systematic unfolding of argument. He writes that he finally despaired of arriving at such control, so he brought forth into the world the *Investigations*, ironically taken ever since as a kind of scripture.[4] Or maybe not so ironically. Wittgenstein struggled to speak, mindful as he was of the lure of silence by which he had ended his *Tractatus Logico-Philosophicus*, but determined to give this silence voice by way of offering, he hoped, the conceptual possibility of plain speech.[5] In this he succeeded, at least at the task he sets himself in venturing, "I should not like my writing to spare other people the trouble of thinking. But if possible, to stimulate someone to thoughts of his own."[6]

I take inspiration from Wittgenstein's despair and from his sense of his task. In the trouble of thinking, everyone faces stark decisions in regard to the systems that have given them birth and still hold them aloft. In the trouble of thinking, Kierkegaard advises, everyone must begin at the beginning.[7] But this is already to modify Wittgenstein's task, and perhaps then also his despair. Kierkegaard's addendum, if surely in sympathy with Wittgenstein's solitude, is not only to "stimulate someone to thoughts of his own." It is to make plain that everyone begins at the beginning of where everyone else begins—not absent the system, but called to make of it what one will. Everyone begins at one's beginning, in the plain speech of what one shall make of what one already is (made by). Thoughts of one's own may turn out to duplicate what others have thought, and perhaps thought much better. But this does not excuse one from advancing them, in confrontation both with one's own limits and with those of others. This advance is the only task. One can never be spared it. But in advancing one is not simply alone.

Let my precursors stand as writers who did what they could. I invoke them as an invitation to begin with the theses and commentaries I now turn to.

Theses and Questions

Theses
Religion is a composite term. Its usage includes matters of *politics*, the laws of communal life and their commentary; matters of *society*, the orders of communal life and their commentary; and matters of *art*, expressions of

what appears and what, in not directly appearing, appears indirectly in communal life. I say "communal life" in recognition of the singular interest of human beings to understand and be understood by other human beings. Whatever life human beings have outside some collective or other, they are never outside the collective that this problem represents. But the locution collective life is not merely redundant. Collectives can be destructive of life. They are not its sole measure.

Religion is composite in concerning variations on the concept of two: either the truth appears, and thus the collective may also be principled in being inclusive (though no less may it be confusedly at odds with itself), or these elements, truth and appearance, split, divided in opposition or collapsed in identity. I have called this opposition and this identity dualism—together with the infinitely regressive opposition of opposition and identity itself—even as each asserts that there is only truth or there is only appearance, only collectives (many) or only principles (one). The alternative dualism of the appearance of truth, in which two is relational and not contradictory, could be called incarnational, in reference to the idea that the world is expressive of value. This idea is not exempt from confusions of opposition and identity, together with violence done in their names. The term incarnation risks privileged theological language. The risk is greater, however, in avoiding it in favor of a word, such as religion, that encompasses the very difference at issue. The position is otherwise called simply the principle.

Politics, society, and art appear in both forms of two, relation and contradiction.

At issue in the elaboration of distinctions of religion is the desire for simplicity in the face of (a) the reality of complexity and (b) the value of complexity.

What it is required to see from the outset is also what is most difficult: that the position of nonmodernity—the dualism of opposition and identity, the collectives of expansion, exclusion, and erasure—is recapitulated in modernity as modernity's temptation. It is only in this recapitulation that one can distinguish the nonmodernity that cannot be otherwise. It is only, then, with the principle that the truth appears and can thus be made inclusive, or expressed as inclusion, that this principle can be subverted in all the ways known under the sun. I work to include you, but instead I dominate you. I bask in the joy of the collective, but only if I leave these

and those out. I commit to the truth, but only as long as it stays elsewhere, leaving my own essential givens undisturbed. To paraphrase a line
of Adam Phillips's, if the best thing I do is love you, then the worst thing I
do is pretend to love you when in fact I am doing something else.[8]

The construction is devastating: I know the good; I do otherwise. It is the
structure of what the biblical traditions call sin and what the psychoanalysis that passes from Freud to Donald Winnicott to Phillips recognizes
as the wounds of love. What is shared in both discourses is the recognition that if I am, in knowing the good, however confusedly or unconsciously, responsible for its abrogation, I am also thereby powerful enough
to do it—to love, to care for myself and others. The secular psychoanalysis might seem to blame less, to front care more—indeed, as a concomitant, to doubt knowledge altogether. But this is pure seeming. Both sin
and self-deception share the same construction. I am deceived, powerless,
overcome. But it is I who sees this; I who can do otherwise; I who occupies
both positions, however much I need help to realize this occupation. Both
discourses understand that I land in sin in freedom, even as this freedom is
wholly abstract and compromised by the sin of others, as by my own. Both
understand that love belongs both to me and to those who care for me, to
me and to those have hurt me and are hurt in turn by me and by others.

What is difficult is the distinction between this structure, the temptation of modernity—equally biblical and psychoanalytic, equally secular
and religious—and the structure of the nonmodern, which embodies and
goes no further than the contradiction between truth and appearance,
collective and collective. Even Freud was confused on this score. Oedipus is not the story of the symptom but the story of its impossibility.
Oedipus does not know and thus cannot flee or symptomize the good.
And yet he is done in by what he does not know. This is the distinction
Kierkegaard announces, together with a handful of modern and postmodern thinkers and artists—that sin is unknown in the ancient Greek
literature and philosophy sometimes denoted "pagan." One can abjure
the word pagan and what it justifies. These justifications are precisely
temptations. But one must not confuse the structure. The words alone
do not tell. King Oedipus is confused, ignorant, blind. King Lear is confused, ignorant, blind. But Oedipus is blind to what he does not know.
Lear is blind to what he does know.

I pursue the concomitant to Lear's form of blindness in the next chapter,
in considering the religious and secular truth of Saint Anselm. Lear does

not know what he knows; Anselm knows what he does not know. For now, let me make a set of distinctions in light of the thesis that religion is the desire for simplicity in the face of the reality of complexity and the value of complexity.

Religion, version 1: A system conserving the integrity of a collective where the system extends to the border.

Religion, version 2: A system conserving the integrity of a collective within the confines of complexity (multiple systems). Such a system is consequently a subsociety. In this case, (a) a (sub)society might conserve the integrity of the collective within complexity by affirming the value of complexity. Insofar as complexity is a value, it may come to threaten the integrity of the collective. Or it may mean the collective's integrity becomes more inclusive; (b) a (sub)society might conserve the integrity of the collective within complexity while not affirming complexity as a value, indeed, while resisting or excluding it.

Version 1 is simplicity. Version 2 is complexity. But this distinction alone is not enough. In version 2, simplicity is present as the conservation of integrity and the desire for it, whether inclusive (a) or exclusive (b). In version 1, complexity is present in the impossibility of pure simplicity, no matter the desire. The question in both cases is, What does a collective do with this desire, this impossibility?

The distinction between modernity and nonmodernity and that between modernity and its temptations divide the response to this question in the following schematic way.

I
Version 1: Simplicity
          1a: Greece, for example: truth is other (submission to fate, quest for
              truth).
          1b: Rome, for example: truth is self (conquest of others, submission
              to truth).

Version 2: Complexity (as a value) in the light of the desire for integrity.

II
Version 1: Simplicity

Version 2: Complexity
> 2a: the good of mutuality, the principle in its simplicity as the complex of two.
>
> 2b: the subversion of the principle in the name of its good.

Both I and II consist of the distinction between simplicity and complexity. Both are accurate, but they have different emphases. In I, simplicity has two forms, the two opposite/identical forms of nonmodernity, and complexity has only one form, as a value. This complexity, following my gloss on Phillips, is the good that we know—simple in formulation, complex in enactment. In II, what is most prominent is the distinction not only between simplicity and complexity, but between two forms of and responses to complexity, which are neither identical nor opposed. This is the structure of the good we know but then reject/abrogate/forget/flee, doing otherwise. Sin and symptom. In I, any question about what is valuable can be given a single answer. Complexity is valuable. Complexity is a value that can empower inclusion without destroying the integrity of a collective, as in democracy. But in II, any question about what is valuable is going to confront Phillips's hard truth. It may look like democracy but in fact be tyranny. It may take the name of the good but subvert it in fact—the good that is the complex of inclusion, supportive of self and other. II is the proposition that it is an ineluctable part of the principle of modernity that it can be subverted. It is part of modernity that the Grand Inquisitor, together with Satan, is its most eloquent prosecutor. What is called for, then, is a counterinquisition, as one struggles to ground the good in the midst of its betrayals, conscious that one, too, might be betraying it—and therefore oneself.

Questions

Versions 1 and 2 in Light of Simplicity
Insofar as it is taken as a system of society concerned with the desire for simplicity and integrity, religion is a word that can straddle the distinction between modernity and nonmodernity. Religion is the articulation, elaboration, interpretation, and practice of the values either of a society taken as whole (version 1: simple societies) or of a subsociety in a complex society (version 2). Religion is not identical to values, but values, as modes of social life, are articulated, elaborated, interpreted, and practiced. Religion is a name for these four works. It is a performance of and commentary on social values. In simple societies, in which one might observe

that there is nothing corresponding to the word religion because there is only one system inclusive of society, art, and politics, religion refers to this performance of and commentary on value. Both performance (or practice) and commentary (or articulation, elaboration, interpretation) are constitutive of social life—in the primitive sociality that is the family and its offshoots of kin, ethnos, and tribe, in all forms of subsocialities given and made, as well as in wholes, local and federated. Religion in simple societies (version 1) and in subsocieties (version 2) stands for the preeminent system of commentary and performance, the locus of the (sub)society's voice.

Q1: Given the desire for simplicity, what is religion in a complex society, that is, one in which the performance and commentary of social values proliferate, when, in addition, the idea of proliferation itself might become a value? Can religion in fact be one subsociety among many?

> A1: Religion, notwithstanding the desire for simplicity, is constituted in complexity. Every society is complex insofar as it is composed of more than one family. Every family is complex insofar as it is composed of more than one individual. Every individual is complex. And so on. There is no such thing as a simple society. Society is an entity whose integrity threatens to break apart or change form. A simple society refers to the desire that there shall be as little proliferation as possible. It refers to the desire for unity. Religion refers to the system (commentary and performance) that supports this desire, as enacted politically and socially. Religion is not preeminent insofar as a society is simple. Societies remain (or try to remain) simple insofar as they designate a single system as preeminent. The desire for simplicity will favor societies founded on either natural distinction—family, ancestor, tribe—or supernatural distinction—the concept of a simple elsewhere in contrast to the confusion of nature. The systems of simple societies will tend to be dualistic in terms of opposition and identity, supportive of the quest for the one in the many.

> It is not a rule that simple societies, such as they are, are dualistic as the one and the many. Neither is it a rule that subsocieties in complex societies will embody the principle of two in relation. What determines whether a society or subsociety is principled is whether it takes proliferation, complexity, as a value. Doing

so puts pressure on the society's integrity, where religion is the work to hold it together.

A2: What is religion in a complex society? Every society is complex. But simple societies will work to manage complexity by, as much as possible, expanding and absorbing others through the dissemination of their system of performance and commentary. These others either will be successfully absorbed or will stand in some degree as still other. With enough otherness, even given mechanisms of absorption, the work for simplicity will be called into question. The dissemination of the values of a system is also the system's proliferation. Religion refers to the preeminent commentary and performance of social values. It refers, then, to a system that, in proliferation, might become one among many, notwithstanding its desire.

(I) Proliferation might mean religion is broken into its elements: law, art, orders of life.

(II) Proliferation might mean religion as the preeminent commentary and performance of a system will refuse this deconstruction and take its place alongside its own elements: law, art, orders of life, religion. Religion is a system's desire for simplicity, for unity. So it might make a replica subsociety for itself.

(III) Insofar as a formerly preeminent system moves to the margins by virtue of expansion and complexity, it may have an ambivalent relationship with the center. This relationship may be different between the cases of a new subsociety rendered as such by the proliferation of its own system, and a subsociety a proliferating system has absorbed.

Q2: Why call the preeminent system in a simple society religion?

A1: This is to identify religion not simply with beliefs and rituals but with a society's system of distinctions as expressed in social order, politics, and art. Although a complex society will not have a single preeminent system, the word religion can refer to the desire for simplicity in subsocieties. The word religion, however, is divided by two concepts of distinction.

A2: Religion is a composite of other elements. In a simple society, the composite holds what the elements share, unto a border.

To call this composite religion is both to name a simple system and, insofar as simplicity is compromised, to call for distinction.

Q3: But so: *Can* religion be one subsociety among many in a complex society?

A1: Religion in a complex society may systematize its simple as a dominion within a dominion, in conceptual resistance to its complex host, even if in legal obedience to it, or it may, ~~as it were~~, charge the center, in an effort to decomplexify it. This charge is no less real in being symbolic.

A2: Yes, in that religion in a complex society denotes the migration of a preeminent performance of and commentary on value to a subsociety, to one among many. Or it denotes the emergence of a subsociety. However, religion is not only one among many. It is one of two. It is composite in encompassing society, art, and politics, but insofar as it is divided from simplicity it is divided from itself, void as a singular term.

Q4: Does religion as formerly preeminent have special access to the principles of the social as it becomes complex?

A: Religion is a composite to hold together the simple. Once it is not preeminent to the social at large, not only does it not necessarily have privileged access to the principles of the social, it might have no access inasmuch as the mode of its relation to the social has changed. A society subject to proliferation might fight complexity with the intensifying of the desire for simplicity. Alternatively, it might embrace complexity as the ideal host of plural values or as a value in itself. In the event of the embrace of complexity, social value has no preeminent performance and commentary. It is insusceptible of being performed, and it has innumerable commentaries. No subsociety has privilege, and the projects of commentary and performance are decentralized and proliferated, together with the values they support. This does not mean religion collapses as a system with pretense to preeminence. As society becomes complex, religion is the system of society that resists proliferation. Or/and it names subsocieties that resist in reconcentrating the elements of religion the composite.

Q5: What then when the proliferation happens apace?

> A: Religion would name the system in a complex society that
> acts to conserve simplicity as one subsociety within a larger com-
> plex common (Q3A2) or to siphon energy from the complex
> common and divide loyalty (Q3A1).

Q6: In which identities does religion retain its integrity in a complex
common as the commentary and performance of the social values of one
subsociety among others? In which identities does religion threaten (and/
or is threatened by) the complex common?

> A: The complex common threatens all systems of preeminence,
> that is, all religions. A religion embodying the value of complex-
> ity is not thereby immune to the threat of complexity. Threats
> to the complex common may come either from the religion of
> the common's (proliferated) origin (the preeminent system in
> proliferating dissolution) or from subsocieties either absorbed
> or conquered. But a complex common's original *can* retreat to
> one among many and subsocieties *can* take their place as one
> among many. The image of one among many is a postulate of
> simplicity. In complexity the struggle is for two.

Versions 1 and 2 in Light of Complexity

Religion is a preeminent system that expresses the performance and
commentary of social value in the simplicity of a (sub)society. In complex societies in which complexity serves not only as description but also
as value, the common social cannot be expressed in a religion subsociety
or in any other subsociety. Social value as complexity is, in being insusceptible of performance and constituting innumerable commentaries, inclusive of (host to) all subsocieties. Such value is reducible, as in a constitution, but expansive, as in its emendation.

Q7: In the value of complexity, what would be conserved of religion as a
preeminent mode, a commentary on and performance of social value, a
locus of a society's voice?

> A1: Religion in conditions of complexity will refer (version 2) to
> preeminent systems of subsocieties.

> A2: Religion, insofar as it values complexity, is not conserved.

A3: Insofar as religion is not conserved, the pursuit of conservation takes forms one may call religion.

Q8: What is the relation between religion subsocieties, in having a preeminent system, and subsocieties that do not have one? Why are not all subsocieties religion?

A: All subsocieties may be religion. All subsocieties may possess preeminent systems of commentary and performance. All desire simplicity. The practice of collectives conserves them. You can name this conservation religion. Insofar as collectives take complexity as valuable, they risk dissolution to a greater degree than collectives that do not, although this risk is also a strength that may prove integrative. Simplicity is an element of collectivity, and collectivity will tend to produce preeminent systems that conserve them, which one can call religion. Yet not all collectives do produce preeminent systems. Those that take complexity as valuable cannot easily make a system of it. Just as all collectives, all societies, are complex, even in their will toward simplicity, all societies are unstable. Conservation is a desire, not a fact.

Q9: What is the relation between religion subsocieties and the complex society, its principles, its proliferation?

A1: Religion is conservation of simplicity, and it is preeminence of performance and commentary, whatever else a (sub)society includes. In a complex society, these impulses are constantly being assailed inasmuch as no subsociety can seal itself off either from the proliferating elements of religion deconstructed—art, politics, orders of society, such as opinion, literature, ceremony, economy—or from the complex common, including the value, the principle, of proliferation/complexity itself. Whether religion flourishes will depend on its concept of its complex host.

Religion the commentary and performance of the values of a subsociety may or may not reflect the principles of the complex common and may indeed take a critical stand toward them, whether as the commons' origin, once simple but now disseminated, or whether as an absorbed subsociety. These subsocieties may function quite autonomously—as a series of quasi-simple societies whose only truck with complexity consists in being near other simple societies and being, in the larger order, beneficiaries of and subject to principles other than their own. Insofar as the principle of the complex common is complexity-inclusivity, this should not be a problem. All subsocieties would be included, subject to tolerating if not approving the principle of inclusion, if not of proliferation or even as a stand-in for it. There would be no privileged subsociety, even insofar as a subsociety directly reflected the principles at the center. The center of complex societies wherein complexity is a value cannot host the practices of a single subsociety but only principles inclusive of all of them.

The only principled complex society is a democracy, a society that positively asserts complexity in support of maximal difference, including forms of collective life that maximally conserve simplicity.

But again: The proliferation of what religion is a composite of—politics, art, orders of society such as economy and opinion and entertainment—attacks it as a composite and as preeminent in its own quarters, as do the principles of the complex common. It may respond as (i) charging the center and dividing loyalty, (ii) withdrawing from the center, or (iii) working to transpose the values of the complex common (back) to those of simplicity, notwithstanding factual complexity (Q3A1). Or religion may fight to abide as one among many (Q3A2).

A2: The survival of religion as society becomes complex (host to subsocieties) depends on the relation to complexity as a value. This value threatens religion. Complexity as a value expresses principles that are maximally inclusive and thus cannot be subject to the commentary and performance of a single (sub)society. This might erode the integrity of subsocieties. The composite does not necessarily hold. The common principles proliferate and, in turn, proliferation is added to principles. On the one hand, religion comes to name only the performance of and commentary on principles in subsocieties, where it can continue to be preeminent. It cannot be practiced in common (but neither is there any need to do so). On the other hand, religion can strive to capture the principle of proliferation without being undone by it.

A3: Once again, religion is not an elementary form. It does not necessarily survive.

Q10: Why can politics, art, and economy withstand proliferation and even be its symbols but religion cannot?

> A: Religion is a composite in service of the simple. Its power is preeminence in performing and elaborating social value, in thus reducing complexity even if elaborating it within bounds. Insofar as society is complex in value, religion will be sidelined or simply fade away. Where complexity is description and not value, or where it is value but not fought for, religion can abide in quasi-simple subsocieties.

Q11: What determines whether religion is sidelined or fades away?

> A1: Religion names the desire for simplicity-unity against or within complexity. In being decentered as a preeminent system of a (simple) society, or emerging in complexity itself, it comes into existence as the desire for simplicity within complex society. This is what is meant by the claim that religion is invented in modernity. It is invented as what shall not fade, but it is thereby always at risk of doing so.

> A2: Religion names the desire for simplicity. It conserves the integrity of a collective unto a border or within conditions of multiple borders. This desire can be expressed in performance and commentary whose work is extraordinarily complex. Religion is a will unto the border—one could say, the border of everything. It is the will to contain everything, to make the system preeminent unto the border. There is no byway it will not travel in doing so and no complexity it will leave unheeded. Religion has truck with complexity. Complexity alone, however, does not entail an embrace of complexity as value. Indeed, the desire for simplicity will go to the very ends of the earth to keep itself alive and can seem dizzying in its complex maneuvers.

> A3: The embrace of complexity as a value is not a feature of something called religion, though religion, a preeminent system in conservation of a (sub)society, might name this embrace. It will be confusing to distinguish between the embrace of complexity as a value, which is simple but inclusive, and complexity as boundless multiplication, which is the will to conserve simplicity unto a border. The simplicity of the value of complex-

ity in the principle of inclusion conserves only this principle, and even then not necessarily. Boundless multiplication, by contrast, can serve to defend religion against fading, but only as a distraction. It will seem too big to fail.

Q12: What other forms of society enact the desire for the simple?

A: Strong ties of kin, work, and affinity, such as the nuclear family, corporate cultures, strong minority consciousness, spirituality—that is, popular gnosticisms and mysticisms—and social movements express religion in the appearance of a noncomposite social with sacral borders—borders embodying the value of the collective. Such collectives may in fact be composite in the sense that religion is, deploying a preeminent system of and thus a will to conserve a (sub)society. Most fail to deliver on the desire for simplicity-unity or the will unto the border or the integrity of a collective in its performance and commentary. They might be too eclectic, too nonhomogeneous. Or they might be too homogeneous in failing religion the composite, making the drive for simplicity if anything too simple: merely rules and dogmas in defiance of the commentary and performance that ferment, and not only reproduce, conservation.

Q13: *Will* religion fade away?

A1: Largely, no. The word is knit into the world as elementary concept. For this reason it is essential to emend it in order to see what it conceals. But doing so will reposition it.

A2: The word is knit into the world as desire.

Q14: But *should* it fade away?

A1: On democratic grounds religion persists. Like monarchy, religion's persistence would be:

(I) Memorial, in no longer being the commentary on and performance of common social values while retaining an image of that work as integrating, ennobling.
(II) Illusion, in never having been truly common while projecting an image of that ideal.

(III) Ceremony, in performing without commentary the fantasy of a simple social.

(IV) Tyranny, in the effort to decomplexify = tyrannize a sub-society and surrounding like societies.

A2: Religion is desire, but this desire may require critique.

Q15: Cannot religion be a subsociety in principled contact with complexity as a value, that is, with democracy?

A1: Yes, but it is rare. Complexity is suffered by religion, but is rarely embraced. It depends on a deliberate deemphasis of the redoubts of Q14A1, I, II, III, IV.

A2: Yes. Religion might be one of the subsocieties in principled contact with complexity as a value (democracy) insofar as religion is

Q14A1: (V) Commentary and performance in defense of the other, in resistance to complexity's boundless multiplication and boundless exchange. Religion the composite for the simple might be the simple defense of two, of mutuality, of inclusion.

A3: The condition of A2 is the conservation of simplicity on the grounds of commitment, not identity (birth, clan, tribe, minority). This will no longer be the conservation of simplicity alone, whether in a single (simple) society or in a subsociety of a complex society. *The conservation of simplicity, of the integrity of a collective, will be on the grounds of complexity, which grounds will put it permanently at risk.*

Said the Lord, in saying to Abram, "Go from your country and your kindred and your father's house to the land that I will show you."

This position (A1–3) differentiates itself from the conservation of simplicity on the grounds of simplicity; the conservation of a simplicity of kind; or a simplicity of rank, order, people, or place. The simplicity conserved on the grounds of complexity is relationship: love, politics, art, where these bespeak collectives of inclusion. Without the refusal of the conservation of simplicity on the grounds of simplicity, which refusal need be nothing more than the identification of the refused position, the conservation of simplicity on the grounds of complexity is impossible to conceive, much less to practice.

Q16: Is the conservation of simplicity on the grounds of complexity necessarily religion?

A: No. Religion as the conservation of simplicity on the grounds of complexity is also secular. This is different from saying religion also has secular forms. Rather, religion is also secular. They are mutually supportive in together refusing their opposition, but equally in each refusing opposition as their conceptual structure. This is also to say they are related in refusing their identity, and equally in refusing identity as their conceptual structure. Religion and secular are not what, at bottom, matter, however much these terms denote significance. They are mobile words. What matters is what work they do.

Religion as the conservation of simplicity on the grounds of complexity has as one of its tendencies that it fades away—as religion. But this is not a rule. We can be dumped out of the word religion, but only by nodding at the composite that religion is the desire to conserve unto a border, nodding thereby at:

(I) An atavism, insofar as there is no longer a preeminent system of social values, and the border must be movable.
(II) A value, insofar as the preeminent value of complexity is simple: love your neighbor as yourself.

This is to understand that the conservation of simplicity on the grounds both of simplicity and of complexity can also be secular.

One reserves the good for those formations, secular or religious, that make fundamental contact with the principles of complexity/plurality/proliferation insofar as they are principled—involving, that is, principles of mutuality and inclusion.

Q17: Is the conservation of simplicity on the grounds of complexity retained as a simplicity? Is simplicity retained?

A1: There is a desire for simplicity. In complex societies, the desire may be dissipated and/or redirected. Complexity names two dynamics: (I) the boundless multiplication of the forms that the drive for simplicity can take and (II) the attack on and decomposition of simplicity itself. Complexity thwarts—but also thereby inflames—the desire for simplicity. Insofar as religion fades in some quarters, or should fade, the need, if there is one, for the commentary on and performance of common values remains.

A2: There is a desire for simplicity that complexity might threaten. But complexity need mean nothing more than leaving one's land, refusing natural kinds, even if in so doing one erects a society that is in all practical respects fundamentally simple (homesteaders, for example). The conservation of simplicity on the grounds of complexity expresses nothing so much as the call to Abraham, than which there can be nothing simpler, if also nothing more symbolic of proliferation, and thus nothing more risky.

Q18: Insofar as religion names the conservation of simplicity on the grounds of complexity, is there a reason to commend it as religion and not secularity?

A1: Possibly, if by religion one means the principle as understood in, for example, the story of Abraham leaving the land. If by religion one means a god who institutes the freedom of sovereign relationship through binding herself in covenant, and/or a human being who calls god the love of the other, then, yes. But these things are equally secular. Calling them religion does not go further toward understanding what matters in these propositions. Indeed, religion is mostly obfuscating in encompassing and therefore occluding all desires for simplicity, even as there is a distinction in desire, and simplicity alone is never what makes it. Distinction is two. More fundamental than religion is two different ways of conceiving two.

A2: Yes. It is valuable to see that religion is not intrinsically foreign to freedom and complexity and democracy. It is even more valuable to see that the condition of religion being present to or in these things is the refusal of religion as intrinsically anything.

Q19: Is there a reason to deny the word religion to principles of inclusion, freedom, neighbor, covenant?

> A1: Yes. Insofar as religion presumes the idea of god as the head or totem of a collective, this notion is vulnerable to being tyrannical, consistent with the desire to decomplexify. The good of the idea of god as the head of a collective is dependent on god's being deposed, abrogated, becoming simply sign, if complexly, of the pressure on the collective to be more inclusive.

> Insofar as religion is the story of Abraham as a story in which he leaves his (home)land to join his nation (holy land), where nation means the conservation of simplicity in the light of complexity, but not while embracing it, then there is a reason to deny the word religion to the principle, and to deny the principle to Abraham.

> Insofar as religion means what is holy in itself, separate from the social value of complexity and inclusion, then there is reason to deny the word religion to the principle.

> A2: No. The word religion can be distinguished in both simplicity and complexity, both tyranny and its critique. It cannot alone tell us which, but therefore its retirement is less powerful than its critique.

Modernity is confused. Abraham, but no less his readers, will profane the principle in identifying the land that will be shown with the land he came from. He, but no less we, will oppose the land that will be shown to the land that is promised, holding the one hostage to the supposed holiness of the other. He, and thus also we, will forget that what matters is not religion, or land, or God, or collectives, but the collective and its commentaries that shall be realized in common.

Versions 1 and 2 in Light of Resistance to Complexity

There are nonsimple societies that are not truly complex; that is, they are complex not in principle but in description. All societies are complex; all desire integrity, simplicity. The question is what is practiced, what is elaborated, what is principled. Following the elementary models of (i) truth and appearance, and (ii) collectives—laid out in chapter 1 and worked on here—such nonsimple but not complex in principle societies are what the principle, here democracy, secular and religious, refuses, together with the simple societies conserved unto a border.

To recall, what is refused is what opposes truth and appearance and what identifies them; what identifies inclusivity with the collective and seeks either to expand by domination or to exclude by membership, and what identifies inclusivity with the erasure of the (single) collective. In this chapter I have made the principle and its pitfalls a question of simplicity and complexity in seeking to identify what religion names and where distinction is called for. As my distinction of religion versions 1 and 2 makes clear, the operative distinction is not only between simplicity and complexity but between different conceptions of complexity, between the difference as, I, nonmodernity (version 1) and modernity (version 2a) and as, II, modernity (version 2a) and modernity (version 2b at odds with 2a, version 2 in its semblance as version 1).

The distinction between I and II is difficult to detect. On the one hand, it can be deemphasized. What matters is that in societies that are nonsimple but noncomplex in principle, there *will be* a preeminent system through which the values of the whole society are engaged in commentary and performance. This is unlike a complex society where complexity is embraced as a value, in which this value is insusceptible of performance and gives rise to innumerable commentaries, innumerable subsocieties. Such a nonsimple society might count as a religio-political civilizational mass, as in a theocracy, or it might count as secular, as in empire, where the collective of kin/ethnos/tribe is elevated to the realm of spirit and where affinity becomes yet another word for blood. Between theocracy and empire lie collectives with a majority rule rooted in the majority and not the principle. In all such societies, the preeminent system in service to the integrity of the collective is prejudicial toward nonconforming others in the society and toward outsiders, constituting that system to which other subsocieties must be subordinate. The center will not be host to all elements equally—indeed, to any but a few or one.

Such societies will be unstable insofar as, nonsimple, they contain multiple subsocieties and subgroupings that have interests and that proliferate outside the preeminent system. Proliferation will serve neither as principle nor, except insofar as the system is weak, as fact. But such systems *are* weak inasmuch as proliferation is a current of nonsimplicity, as it is of simplicity, never merely simple. Proliferation threatens preeminence of commentary and performance, preeminence of value. It threatens, one can say, religion or the secular as the conservation of the integrity of the collective through the preeminence of a system of performance and commentary. What societies that are nonsimple but not complex in principle do not know or will is that proliferation, threatening and weakening, is a kind of strength embraced as a value.

Thus again, on the one hand, it does not matter if such a nonsimple society—weak, insensible, despotic as the only imagined route to integrity—is nonmodern or is modernity failing, fleeing, corroding its own principle. On the other hand, it matters absolutely. It is only modernity that can correct itself. It is only modernity that can distinguish between the good—the simple yet difficult covenant of self and other—and the subversions of the good, innumerable under the sun, multiplied without end. This does not mean nonmodernity, such as it is, if and when it is, is forever left out. This move would be the ultimate obscenity of a principle that stands for inclusion. Yet the inclusion of the nonmodern is not possible on nonmodern grounds. It is in service to this recognition that one must work through the principle and its labyrinths.

Q20: Critics of the democratic West regard it and not only, for example, Iran as guilty. Is this fair?

> A1: No. Insofar as the West expresses the value of complexity in principle, it is an example of version 2 in the distinction of I, in which there is only a single modernity—the modernity of principle. There is a single modernity not in being simple but in being distinct in toto from positions that oppose or identify truth and appearance, that conceive collectives unto a sacral border. Modernity is distinct in the identification of these alternatives, and in refusal of them, in critique. Here modernity's own failings are not at issue. To recall and emend:

I

Version 1: Simplicity and nonsimplicity-as-multiplication; complexity unto a border.

> 1a: Greece, for example: truth is other (submission to fate, quest for truth).

> 1b: Rome, for example: truth is self (conquest of others, submission to truth).

Version 2: Complexity (as a value) in the light of the desire for integrity.

> A2: Yes. Insofar as the West confuses the principle, it is an example of version 2b. The structure is: I know the good, I do otherwise.

Although distinct in toto from the good as intrinsically elsewhere or the good as whatever I say it is, modernity is itself creative of a distinction in which it puts itself in question and at risk. To recall and emend:

II

Version 1: Simplicity and nonsimplicity-as-multiplication; complexity unto a border.

Version 2: Complexity
    2a: the good of mutuality, the principle in its simplicity, but no less complexity as two.
    2b: the subversion of the principle in the name of the good; nonsimplicity-as-multiplication; complexity unto a border.

Q21: To what end the critique of the West?

A1: Insofar as criticism of the West is of its subversion of its own good, it is also an affirmation of this good. Insofar as criticism of the West is of its ignorance of what is truly good, the criticism is confused.

The distinction *of* the West is, first, *within* the West, between versions 1 and 2. In ancient Athens and Rome, as in most tribal collectives, the principle (version 2a) cannot be found (version 1). Then, second, the distinction is between the principle and its subversions, 2a and 2b. Jerusalem, let us say (version 2), the principle, will subvert itself, which subversion gives us the confused amalgam "West" in erecting its ideals in the guise of opposition/identity/sacral border (conflation of versions 2a and 2b recapitulates version 1). The very construction Athens and Jerusalem is erected in confusion. What is confused are the moves (i) the value of the collective as the unit of the good (us versus them, domination, membership), (ii) the critique of this value, which critique is then subverted in the reassertion of (iii), the value of the collective as the unit of the good. What is confused is the difference between i and iii, in which confusion the principle, ii, is resigned.

A2: The West is the struggle for simplicity on the grounds of complexity. You can distinguish between Western democracies and, for example, Iran. But take care to make the distinctions beyond that one. A nondemocracy might possess the principle in refusal.

A democracy might arise anywhere. Take care not to make too much of the subversion that is theocracy unless you are prepared to take on the subversion that is the boundless multiplication of consumerism and exchange that passes for freedom in (what passes for) democracy.

Alongside the connection of subversions, there is the difference of them. Ancient Roman colonialism did not have the principle of its own undoing, its own postcolonialism. England, France, Spain, Germany, Holland, Portugal, and America, say, are not to be unduly commended for submitting to this undoing, to self-critique. But submit they have. So, too, may it be, Iran.

It is presumptuous of the West to dictate a polity for everyone. The principle, however, is not presumptuous. It is in existence and for existence. It is to be used—for all, in critique of all.

A3: Insofar as the West refers to an entity that is or has been an empire, and insofar as empire means the forcible (political, economic, intellectual) domination and ruling of others, it is an example of II version 2b. Insofar as the West refers to an entity that hosts subsocieties with aspirations to empire, it is an example of II version 2a. The virtue of I and II is that it enables one to visualize the proximity of good and evil, the power and disempowerments of the good in the world. Truths in appearance, thus the work (and its abrogation) to understand specifics as one extends the truth to all. Collectives in light of inclusion, thus the work (and its abrogation) to include.

Q22: Don't all collectives aspire to be empires? Isn't empire the flip side of the conservation of simplicity?

A1: Collectives may aspire to be empires insofar as they express the conservation of simplicity in the context of complexity. Empire precisely means the work for simplicity in the light of complexity. The work for simplicity means more of what is mine. Empire names and thus signifies the difference between the extension of borders (domination and membership) and borders that are inclusive.

By contrast, the work for simplicity *on the grounds* of complexity will be more of what is mine for you, where you are not mine.

This is not empire, but all relations are threatened by empire. One is never finished refusing it, and critiquing it as one fails to do so.

Collectives might also aspire to be empires insofar as they express the conservation of simplicity on the grounds of complexity. But only insofar as such collectives are confused about their principle.

A2: Confusion about the principle is the norm. Modernity requires ongoing clarification.

By confusion I mean refusal, offense. The principle is that one can be confused only about what one knows.

Q23: Is an empire founded on confusion (of the principle) worse (stronger, longer, more violent, more extensive, more intransigent, more lamentable) than an empire founded on the simple maxim more of what is mine? (Is colonial England worse than imperial Rome?)

A1: No. From the point of view of the dominated, there is no difference.

A2: Yes. The hope for collective life founded on the value of a collective of all, a good whose content is for all, is a hope for peace and for love. Infidelity to these goods in ignorance of them is terrible. Infidelity in the name of these goods is abomination. It is bitter.

It could then be said, biblical (modern) slavery is worse than Greek and Roman slavery. Modern (biblical) misogyny and racism is worse than tribal naturalism.

If you leave the land, Abraham, do not, of all things, gather an army to reestablish your homeland on the body of the other. This will be the difference of your own death, as of ours.

Q24: What is the origin of the principle? In what collective does it originate? In originating the principle of a collective of all, is a given collective necessarily expressive of it?

A1: Modernity is the name for the principle. It names origination, collectives as beginning in principle. Modernity is also confused in taking its beginning for a natural one. Beginnings will be taken as natural, then as infinitely variable, and then as impossible.

A2: Modernity does not originate in a collective premised on the conservation of simplicity on the grounds of simplicity. Nor is modernity simply the complexity that hosts the conservation of simplicity as one subsociety among many. Modernity is the move to make *the value of complexity the conservation of simplicity*. It is the pressure on the integrity of simplicity to become the integrity of complexity. It is the pressure on the integrity of complexity to turn on the simple maxim, Love your neighbor as yourself.

Nothing that comes before this move prepares for it. There is nothing before it. What is before is before only once the move is made.

A3: Modernity begins with Abraham. It begins with Abraham's call. *Lekh lekha.* "Go." But no less with Adam and Eve, and their call to bear up in toil, knowing the good of freedom, struggling with its terrors. So also, then, with the metaphors of creation, good, evil, knowledge, freedom, sin, and work that the biblical books conceive, narrate, exhort, and betray. Modernity begins with the Bible. Whether modernity is unique to the Bible is irrelevant. The claim that modernity begins with the Bible is the claim that modernity is a concept, and not only a generation, of beginning. The concept is, leave your land for one that shall be shown: the conservation of simplicity on the grounds of the values that are plurality, complexity, openness, inclusion. Modernity is this concept of beginning. It begins with this concept, whenever and wherever it is instituted.

Modernity makes possible the distinction between the conservation of simplicity on the grounds of simplicity, whether in a simple society or in the context of complexity, and the conservation of simplicity on the grounds of complexity. Modernity is therefore distinct. This distinctness, this distinction, is not a warrant for empire or a guarantee of privileged access. It is a warrant for inclusion, for peace. But not only does it not rule out confusion (guilt) on this score, it rules it in as the temptation to take distinction as merely "more of mine than yours."

It is thus a temptation of modernity to mistake its temptations for modernity. Modernity requires ongoing clarification.

Reformulations, Clarifications, Augmentations

Neither Religious nor Secular

Position of Simplicity

That in the beginning is community: family, kin, tribe, clan. There is order: frames, rules, customs, ceremonies. Community is also border. The border is good. Everyone needs a land, a place to materialize one's values, one's goods. The border is also bad. It is "they" are not "us." There is no way around borders—in fact or in value.

In a collective that is simple, the border is sacralized; it is the locus of value. This takes two forms: (1) The collective worships itself, often called religion. The border is a fence. (2) The collective is divided from the value of itself, often called philosophy. The border is a ceiling.

The position of simplicity includes, "There is always an enemy." Its content is empty.

Position of Complexity

There is no simplicity in fact. There is complexity. It might have no value. But complexity, given, suffered, might also be valued, principled. This is modernity.

That in the beginning is community: family, kin, tribe, clan. There is order: frames, rules, customs, ceremonies. Community is also border. The border is good. Everyone needs a land, a place to materialize one's values, one's goods. The border is also bad. It is "they" are not "us." There is no way around borders—in fact or in value.

In a collective where complexity and not just collectivity is taken as a value, where complexity bespeaks the collective that might be for all, the border will also be a temptation. This includes borders between self and other, collective and collective, visible and intellectual, this world and some other world.

In a collective in which everyone might, insofar as everyone shall, be included, included means equally so, as measured in the support of each in all. This principle makes some distinctions secondary: for example, individual versus collective, liberal versus conservative, human versus posthuman, Protestant versus global, global versus local. Such distinctions are meaningful in their place. But each side of these secondary distinctions represents the wager that value can be (must be) shared without reference to rank, to spirit as naturalized (naturalism), to nature as spiritualized (supernaturalism). Rather, naturalism and supernaturalism are both displaced by the conception of human beings enacting value in history, and thus in concert with each other. Here nature and spirit are fictions, illusions of the principle. In this light, a border of land is an arbitrary designation, signifying only the practicalities of setting up the rule of law in a land that can be shown. In principle, the more people work together, in not refusing each other, the stronger each is.

The position of modernity introduces the idea of the nonsacralized border, the collective whose borders are arbitrary in being uncoupled from kin, race/ethnos, tribe, clan. It introduces the position that the truth appears in and as history as a covenant of equals.

It is sometimes said that the border of thinking is arbitrary, subject to the whim, the curiosity, of the inquirer (as of, some say, the sovereign). This mistakes the value of the arbitrary. To choose in whim (chance, fate, inclination) is no different from the border that separates minds and worlds, selves and others. It is to mistake the recognition that there will always be a border with the position that the border will always be merely mine. This is to mistake what the nonsacralized (arbitrary) border makes possible: that there is a border that can go not just anywhere but everywhere. That the nonsacralized border is therefore arbitrary is a standpoint available only from the position of its principle, the position that works (or refuses to work) to extend it.

The nonsacralized border, the border that is mobile, subject to the values of inclusion in a land that can be shown, is easy to defeat in practice.

Consider Orientalism.
Consider nationalism.
Consider consumerism.
Consider religion.
Consider class, race, gender, culture.

Q25: Why is not the very idea of the border bad?

A: A border enacts the realization of value. Leave one (given) for another (that shall be shown).

Q26: Does the confusion (conflation, betrayal) of the principle of a non-sacralized, thus inclusive, border with yet another sacral one bespeak the death of the principle, the death of the hope for collective life founded on the good whose content is for all?

A: Why would it? Though, at the same time, why wouldn't it? It is bitter.

The position of complexity includes, "There is always an enemy." Its content is complexity itself.

What the mobile border of truths and collectives requires is

(I) Interpretation. The truth is not given in itself. You have to give a reading in history.

(II) Wager. The truth is not (just) there for you. It requires something of you.

Distinction, in being power, is not of the enemy; it is of the condition of inclusion. The principle that the truth is in history is equalizing. It is consistent with concepts of multitudes and collectives, with power as made, not given, and made in common, not over against one another. Kant says of this good, nothing in the world testifies to it. There are no examples. Spinoza says, the principle is so common as to be on everyone's tongue. Both are right. History largely shows the principle in the breach. But although the principle is not derived from experience, it can be shown that it resides there, that the good is nothing other than what we desire, what we know to be good, in making it so for ourselves and for others.

The principle is the end (aim) of history, which is never then at an end, never done reformulating, clarifying, augmenting.

The principle is that the good I desire for my own kind is fortified in being/becoming unlimited. Abraham is not called to leave his land to sacrifice himself. He is called to sacrifice the premise that he is merely for himself. To say this principle is limited only to history, limited in being history, is to say that the principle does not come down as history's critic. It is not an ideal that historical life can only ever approximate. Rather, the principle otherwise stated is precisely that the good is in the world (already), as the concept of human solidarity, of all, of God and equality, to which human practices may, with great effort, testify and realize.

This is not a new idea. Neither are its formulations merely antiquated. When Anselm of Canterbury notes that God is that than which nothing greater can be thought, he is indicating that the thought of God is no less existent than ethereal, no less real than ideal, and indeed that the ideal to love and create as God does is real for him, a person, a sinner, a mortal man. When the biblical authors give voice to a God who insists to human beings that "the word is in your mouth and in your heart," not in the heavens, not beyond the seas, these authors insist that the work is to live up to what one knows, not to pursue what one does not. When Immanuel Kant finds in reason a categorical imperative to treat others as ends in themselves and when Wallace Stevens enjoins us to perceive everything in reality, these are accounts of the truth in and as history.

They remain revolutionary exhortations. A preponderance of human habit casts the issue as either/or. Either history or truth, either God or existence. Even for the traditions that, consistent with the propositions of the Bible, Anselm, Kant, and Stevens, hold that there is a connection between God and world, truth and history, neighbor and kin, everything and the real, it is nevertheless standard to order these things hierarchically. Human beings are finite creatures. The world only ever approximates its ideals. The ideals themselves reside in an imperium outside history. Or history is unmoored from principle altogether, which would only ever be arbitrary, signifying, then, merely might.

It was and remains radical to say that the truth is that truth is in history, in existence as it is lived. Equally that history is the regime of truth and limited to it. Where there is no principle that the good I desire for my own kind is fortified, if also limited, in being/becoming a good for all, there is no history. This is to conceive history not as what happened or as time passing but rather as the story of human beings insofar as they realize and (mostly) fail to realize their humanity as it *can* be realized and not only given. Or insofar as the question of history is simply what happened, the latticework of evidence includes *what* human beings are practicing in building and managing happenings. It is not only, then, that there is no truth except insofar as it is conceived, embodied, practiced, lived in existence. It is that there is no existence outside human efforts to make existence something of value. History is the story of the work of human beings insofar as existence is valuable. It presumes that this work can be known. It presumes that the work can be realized as what is good for (all) human beings.

As Adam and Eve learn, the obstacle to the good is not their sin—their ignorance, their feebleness, inexperience, confusion: their existence. The obstacle, or challenge, is simply, if not at all simple, the copresence of good and evil for them, knowledge of which is dramatized as a fall into existence. This knowledge inducts them into the possibility of failure, of fear and trembling, in the face of the effort needed to make good on God's admission: that, in knowing good as well as evil, they are "like God," now charged with the responsibility to bring about a preponderance of one in light of the persistence of the other. The fall into existence is this "now": now you are subjects of the principle and not only slaves blindly obeying; now it is yours to realize with and through one another. What is good, then, in this story? The good is the principle, also the process, that reaching for what is good for me involves me in a struggle with you, involves me, then, in work to bring about what is good for us, work that is therefore in common. The good is common relative to the enmity, pain, toil, sweat, confusion, and death that are also our common lot. The good is nothing but the commonality of the good. The good is nothing but commonality. It is part of what is good, then, to see that the good is not a thing that can be passed around, shared or distributed, denied or granted. It must be attained, worked for. It is the very principle that there is a common; the creation, then, of a common. This does not mean there are no individuals, no differences, no goods. It means that these things are involved in producing the common. As democracy is the condition of (individual) freedom. As tempering the instincts is the condition of freely enacting desire.

In claiming that this story is the story of history—that history is limited to just this story and no other—I am, on the one hand, asking, What else is there? On the other hand, what is radical is the address to other images of history: as a method applicable to all cases, as a mode of description and analysis, whatever happens to be under scrutiny, as a response to the question, What happened? The word history may be used in these and other ways. I claim for history, as for truth, a concept, the concept, namely, of existence insofar as it expresses the entirety of human life as it is desired, practiced, conceived, and inevitably also failed and betrayed, repurposed and recommitted. History is existence insofar as it is, in Stevens's words, "everything." This concept of history as everything is in contrast to history conceived as limited, whether to the world of change as opposed to the world that does not change, to the world of contingency as opposed to the world of necessity, to what is as opposed to what ought to be.

What is striking is that even as history, in a philosophical temper, removes itself from the second part of these formulations—there is no ought that history can access, only is; there is no necessity for history, only contingency—it still erects a border that presumes, ghostlike, the unhistorical term. We would thereby learn in the study of history to live without truth, without God, without necessity—to embrace contingency, partiality, reality, change. Does it take a poet to remind us historians and truth-tellers that this is not a real choice—that contingency, partiality, change, reality are visible only with the inclusion of the mind that modifies and is modified in what is included? That can say, everything included? It is not that history has no limits. It is that history is limited to everything and excludes, then, anything that would conceive things otherwise. History is absolutely exclusive—to a concept, a practice, of inclusion, of the good, the common. History is one specific story.

When critics, without this provocation—with, rather, the provocation of the principle—accuse history of being merely Western or Protestant, as leading, that is, only to Western conceptual and political regimes, they might be right. The question is what the West, what history, is taken to include and exclude. If the West, if history, is taken as nothing other than religion version 1, then one would not need to find a way out of it since one would, by that recognition, already have placed it outside. (Though it then may be confusing to identify just exactly where one is standing.) If it is a matter of including within the West values on which it is silent, or of critiquing values that have no value, this is invaluable work. The principle, not identical with "West" or even "history," is of the value of complexity, and so it is open. If history, conceived thinly, needs thickening, let it be thickened. All collectives are ethnocentric, one says, not merely ethnocentrically.

The principle might seem, in its ruthless simplicity, even if in support of complexity, to arrogate all privilege to itself. One will take refuge, perhaps, in insuperable complexity over *against* the principle. But this move is self-defeating. The position of complexity upheld by the principle is simple. It is that the naturalism of kin/ethnos/tribe/clan and the supernaturalism of spirit/Form/idea are the source of racism, classism, sexism, whether these are expressed from the position of simplicity or the position of complexity insofar as it is confused. Does this distinction—of the principle against naturalism and supernaturalism—itself lead to violence? Yes, as confusion. No, insofar as one distinguishes in order to include.

The primary confusion of modernity is violence in the name of inclusion. The secondary confusion of modernity, confusion in the face of the offense that inclusion would itself be violent, is overcorrection for the bewitchment of the double violence: the violence modernity excludes and the violence modernity, in its exclusion, also confusedly if opportunistically enacts. This (over)correction for violence is twofold: presumptive inclusion of all positions, in the name of the all that the principle fails, and presumptive exclusion of the principle, in the name of a postmodernity.

Each presumption erects an uncanny opponent, whether the exclusion of others or the domination of them. In so doing, each presumption recapitulates the positions the principle itself refuses. They thus serve to uphold it, albeit confusedly.

Although it might seem prudent to claim history for the story of humanity as such, the object "everyone" to complement the "everything" that is history's subject, the concept of history does in principle leave much out. The principle that truth is in history, realizable as the good that can be made common from enmity, toil, and mortality entails that history, as the story of this truth, cannot include either what one could call pure history or its opposite, pure truth and its synonyms: whatever is not subject to history, whether called God, the ineffable, the soul, the sacred, the spirit. Although it is unsurprising to say that history is not about truth, it is less obvious to claim that neither is history about history insofar as the latter is taken as what does not involve human value. This all might seem largely semantic, but it is also real. The ancient Greeks had no concept of history—no concept, that is, of truth realizable in and as existence. So says a history of the ancient Greeks, at the border. One must certainly work to understand what happened, to whom, where, why. One can subject any peoples, any events, to history understood as the effort to ascertain what was. But one cannot arrive at the mind of the past outside an engagement with the mind of history, the mind as modified in history. It is this modification that binds the historian in a twofold sense. She is bound to interpret. She is bound to wager, a wager in which she will be modified by decision. One cannot make historical what eludes history. One cannot make decisions about what cannot be decided. History is not visited on human beings; it is a relation with them. There are therefore places—regimes, practices, texts—that history, as the story of the good in existence, cannot go.

> Option I: History is aspirational.

> Option II: History assumes the position of itself. So you *can* tell the story of the ancient Greeks. But you will, in so doing, make them moderns, the conceit of nations and scholars alike. *There may nevertheless be reasons for doing so*, on which Vico was, perhaps regrettably, silent.

There is a critical vulnerability in the principle, as with the covenant that, once it is inclusive of a collective, can become exclusively so. Because truth is in history, and thus not merely identical with what appears or outside what appears, it will always be possible to take the principle Platonically (in itself) or to dissolve it in mere history (= historicism). One oscillates between these: now one is the enemy, now the other, with no sense of how to resolve the question or what the question is. Unlike the difference between liberals and conservatives, in which both are right inasmuch as each corrects for the excesses of the other, both of these readings—that truth is in itself, that history dissolves truth—are wrong. Each mistakes the principle. But the principle will be mistaken insofar as it asks something of us. It asks everything of us.

Both Religious and Secular

Religion

One may call "religion" what is empowered in collectives while being what collectives as clans will need reconstruction to do: take the other as an end in himself (neighbor, stranger). Whatever else human animals do that is unlike other animals, this is absolutely unlike. If the principle is the idea that the truth is in history, in contrast to the idea that the truth is beyond history, it might seem that animals do neither of these things: they do not formulate ideas one way or the other. But the idea that the truth is in history is equally a practice and a command: that *since* the truth is not elsewhere, whatever truth means it means for me; it is a command to me to empower both myself and the others who share my world, my history.

All communities strive to support their fellows as far as such support does not conflict with the collective interests, and even sometimes when it does. There is altruism, it is said, in the human animal and in the non-human animal. What all communities do not do, however, is make commands concerning the mutual: whether a commanded mutuality of all entails for humans all humans or also other animals; whether it means the unborn as well as the born; whether robotics and artificial intelligence are included in the principle's interpreters: these and like debates are important. But the production of such debates does not affect the absurd idea that, beyond one's collective, one's people, however expansive, there is a collective of all that is achieved, not found; a collective of value not identity qua human or qua rational being; a collective of mutuality and not only sacrifice, in which what I want for myself I want for everyone. A collective of "everything."

Human collectives have come up with two ideas: the principle and the opposition, equally the identification, of the principle's inextricable parts, truth and history, ideals and appearances. But of even the collectives that have come up with the principle, it remains an absurdity, a novum, often reviled, refused, remaindered. The mutual is built. At the same time, mutuality is not only the end but also the principle in the beginning, the idea/embodiment of this mutual that makes it possible to work for it—to learn and to understand, to strengthen and to sacrifice.

The mutual has entered into history as our end, where entered means not by nature but by and as history.

The principle can be stated as involving two, and equally as involving all. Two seems a reality, all seems an abstraction. Two is like many, a number I can count. All is like the universal, a number that has nothing to do with counting. Two is the position of intimacy, of love. All is the position of obligation, of ethics and politics, of God. And yet obligation is to the other, to the neighbor. And the neighbor is some particular one, even if also all particular ones. You do not get to all by skipping over the particular. You do not get to the principle by skipping over the one(s) you know: your collective. This is to say, love of one other, whatever else it is in terms of nourishment and pleasure, is also education. It is a training in and for the principle. You can embark on the principle without a beloved. You can do it as a priest or a prisoner. You can do it as simple. The challenge is the same: that in knowing another, in knowing others and oneself as also other, one comes to know the other that one is to include, and by which one is included.

In the terms of the individual, the principle is the self in relation to itself and to another self in such a way that it does not climb up to the other from animality, nor is each erased with reference to a third thing in which they are absorbed. Each is wholly particular and wholly in mutuality, wholly respectful of the other in her/his difference and, in so being, wholly respectful of herself. Each remains also a selfish, self-preservative animal. Sin, says religion; *conatus*, says philosophy. This selfishness never goes away. Indeed, it must not go away. The human self-preservative animal is not finite. She is power. Selfishness is what one can rename the care for the self. The one change is that the care for the self must not abide as the only thing in operation. But indeed the self, on its own, is weak, or rather impossible. The principle states this in strongest terms. Others are not simply a help to you, others are your condition. They cannot, then, simply be a help to further you. They must also come to be those whom you further.

One must come to care not only for oneself but equally for others. This is impossible, says Kant; common, says Spinoza. The first acknowledges how far we are from enacting the equality of another with ourselves. The second recognizes that there is no self to begin with without support from others. We learn to love in being loved as ourselves. So then the task is to become oneself, and this is a paradox, for to become oneself is to become for others. The self that is given is animal, though it is ideally received in love. The paradox is that, in working out of one's animal for the other, in learning to love in being loved, one becomes more powerfully the kind of animal one is, the particular one who one (already) is in being able to be empowered with and for others. This is to be in relation to the other, and not simply in forgetful dependence. To love as one is loved. To be/become the human animal.

Posthumanism, like many overcorrections, casts the principle as a defense of the soul and corrects by leveling to the human animal. It escapes from human specialness to ecosystem. But ecosystem is another word for relation, and relation begins in love/caring/respect.

One may call "religion" just about anything. What one especially calls religion is God, who is especially, says religion, worthy. Like truth, says philosophy. Or neither, says the skeptic to the dogmatist. Let the problem be language, say the two giants of twentieth-century philosophy, Wittgenstein and Heidegger. How many controversies concerning truth and value can be headed off with more elementary thinking beyond vocabularies of philosophy and religion?

What is called for is not beyond vocabularies. It is distinction.

Fear and Trembling, Kierkegaard's Christian theological book providing approving commentary on God's call to Abraham to sacrifice his son, is also the name of a book by Kierkegaard in reference to God's call to Abraham, but this time concerning the first book. What the first book approves, the second book abhors, but not with regret for the first book. Rather, in commendation of it. For it is only, the second book knows, in confrontation with the distinction between these books that *Fear and Trembling* can be a book about Abraham, and not about someone else. It is only in the distinction between them that Kierkegaard can be said to have written a single book. What Kierkegaard conveys is that the religious will tend to mean the vertical triumph of God over humanity. It will tend to signify the subordination of life to some other life, of the human to the divine, this world to the next, the neighbor to the master, nature to supernature. The religious will signify these things even in the book that demands something else. What is the something else?

Readers of *Fear and Trembling* encounter a defense of Abraham's sacrifice of Isaac, in the face of which the tendency to subordinate reverses itself. Is this defense not monstrous? Kierkegaard seems to know that it is, so perhaps Kierkegaard is monstrous. His claim is that Abraham has faith, so perhaps faith is monstrous. Or the structure is the one here: in modernity, modernity will be mistaken. In faith, faith will be mistaken. It will be mistaken, as *Fear and Trembling* is mistaken, as the subordination of the world to God, even in the text in which this subordination is excluded, pinned on Abraham's foil Agamemnon. And why not? What is the space between God and human beings? If God is not vertical, not beyond the heavens and the seas, not beyond vocabularies, what and who is God? Why God? If truth is not vertical, not elsewhere or nowhere, what is it instead? *Fear and Trembling* argues in pseudonym, in contrast to the pseudonymous ideas of the *Fear and Trembling* of Abraham's awesome monstrousness, that the truth appears, and in doing so asks where and what are *you*? It says, "He who loves God without faith reflects upon himself; he who loves God in faith reflects upon God."[9] What is the difference? Faith. What is faith? Not God, not self, not love.

The problem is not language. It is not philosophy. It is not religion. It is existence. What stands between readers and faith, readers and truth is the monstrousness that existence is everything, expressive of good and evil, expressive of the minds that know the difference of the human animal in loving as it would be loved. Faith is that the obligation to the other shall be equal to the obligation to my own self, tribe, nature, collective, God. Faith is a critique of existence in commitment to it. It is the obligation to two: self and other, God and human, truth and reality. The work is a double deconstruction. God deconstructs God in order to say, Isaac, equally. Isaac says, God who? Abraham says, faith is for existence, an imperative I may fail. The principle is not God, who may be just another idol. It is faith, it is critique, where these things stand for the principle that you shall leave the land of your fathers and mothers. For another land.

The Secular

The principle is no less secular than it is religious. What makes the principle difficult for both religion and the secular is its content as beginning and end, its critique of natural beginnings and ends, its transposition of them. I am not only on the way to love of neighbor. I begin with it as my concept, in being loved as myself. The principle, love of neighbor, loves me enough to affirm that this is my human possibility. Just as I am born an animal (ideally) into love, so I am born a lover of my kin/family/tribe into the love that loves me as neighbor.

The history of thought is characterized by the effort to create ever new principles, ever new positions. It must be said, however, that the principle, vulnerable always to confusion, must also be strengthened. Sometimes new positions are advanced because it has simply been too long since we believed there was something permanent that needed strengthening, a "permanence composed of impermanence," as Stevens puts it, permanent in having to be, or failing to be, made.[10]

What is at stake in modernity? Something modernity the conventional period quietly borrowed and then misplaced. This is to restate it. Modernity needs to get its house in order.

5 Images of Truth from Anselm to Badiou

It is not in heaven, that you should say, "Who will go up to heaven for us, and get it for us so that we may hear it and observe it?" Neither is it beyond the sea, that you should say, "Who will cross to the other side of the sea for us, and get it for us so that we may hear it and observe it?" No, the word is very near to you; it is in your mouth and in your heart for you to observe.

Deuteronomy 30:12–14

Metaphors of Reason

In the theological West, the languages for God are poetic ones. God is remote, sovereign, and mighty, but also ardent, jealous, and inconsolable. The case of reason would be different. Reason is that faculty that makes intelligible what is otherwise ambiguous. If the winged philosopher-charioteer in Plato's *Phaedrus* tames the horses of appetite, he does so by rising above not only his own baser truths but also his temptation by the horses of metaphor—rising above even the picture of rising above. This image dominates ideas of modern reason, of reason as refuge against the mad world of multiplicity and interpretation. It is the winged emissaries who shall do our rational talking.

There have been many accounts of Western reason that augment this picture: work on the emotions, habit, practice, gender, race, and other embodiments. I invoke reason's image as what Deuteronomy 30 calls "the word"—the commandment to Abraham to leave the land of his ancestors and go to a land that will be shown; the commandment to love this commandment, to love its author, God, who is equally bound to the covenant of promise. This is a modernity that embeds in the mouths and hearts of those who observe it, not in the empyrean of philosophers and Forms. Descartes is notorious as author of the most purified concept of reason in the modern world: rational certitude, the isolated self, the mind/body split, the quixotic effort to demonstrate God's existence. Yet Descartes's writings contain some of the most vivid depictions of the power he ostensibly settled into certitude, complete with walking hats, melting wax, and evil demons. Descartes plunges equally into reason's powers of demolition and its fragile landscapes, its habits of avoidance, and its lonely passages. In the present age, we conceive reason as conditioned by specificities of social and political life. Reason is an agent of metaphor. But we do not entirely know what it is, in this knowing, that we know.

In 1641 Descartes published the *Meditations* to demonstrate the existence of God and the distinction between the soul and the body. In 1966 another Frenchman, Michel Foucault, published *The Order of Things*, "an archaeology of the human sciences" that comprehends Descartes's demonstration not as an act of reason but as an expression of "the fundamental codes" of his culture.[1] Bookends of a certain modernity, these texts dramatize the distance between the Enlightenment and postmodernity—from universalizing reason to particularizing histories, from the consolation of God's existence to the dissolution of man. Standing on Foucault's side of the modern threshold, Descartes's reasoning, his demonstrations, and his clarities seem alien. Objects of documentary interest and philosophical history, they are no longer ours. It is this alienation that Foucault diagnoses for us, his post-Enlightenment readers. This is our order of things: the story of a Cartesian mind made dim with time.

I am arguing for another story of modernity. Although exciting work in the humanities since the 1960s has happened in proximity to Foucault's studies of the cultural logic of the human sciences, his project, like Durkheim's and Said's, contains a blind spot. This is, first, to reframe Kant's famous question, which also forms the title of a 1984 essay by Foucault.[2] What is the Enlightenment *to us*? For Foucault, the Enlightenment bequeathed criticism, understood as the analysis of the epistemological limits of universal knowledge. Now we must take this attitude and turn it on the Enlightenment itself, using a critical history of ideas—genealogy—to expose the universal as the discourse of a particular epoch. But critique as historical consciousness is the question of beginnings and ends, origins and purposes, not just of the subjects of history but of history itself. This is the question on which work on epochal knowledge tends to fall silent. Foucault gives us "discontinuities in the *episteme* of Western culture."[3] He gives us "the exotic charm of another system of thought," one that exposes "the limitation of our own."[4] But he allows that, although he can diagram such alterations, he is not able to say how they happen.

Foucault's exemplar on the point is Borges, with his story of a list from a fictitious Chinese encyclopedia in which the entries bear no relation to either thing or category: "a) belonging to the Emperor, b) embalmed, c) tame, d) sucking pigs, e) sirens, f) fabulous, g) stray dogs, h) included in the present classification, i) frenzied, j) innumerable, k) drawn with a very fine camelhair brush, i) *et cetera*, m) having just broken the water pitcher, n) that from a long way off look like flies." It is a gorgeous and maddening list, a deconstruction of lists. For Foucault, Borges gives us the image of such incendiary randomness that it "shatters" the "landmarks of thought," threatening "with collapse our age-old definitions between the Same and the Other."[5] It is the discovery of the end of thought. "What transgresses the boundaries of all imagination, of all possible thought, is simply that alphabetical series (a, b, c, d) which links each of those categories to all the others."[6]

In Foucault's image of the boundaries of all possible thought, the boundary is the arbitrary, the position that defeats all principle. But this is yet another version of the many in exclusion of the one. It is a resignation of the fight for two, for truth in and as diversity of epoch as of category and thing. What I am after in the distinction of modernity is what is resigned, the very idea of epoch, of threshold. The epoch of epochs, the thresholds of thresholds, the history of history inclusive of the arbitrary, which is nothing less than the paradox that I don't know what I know. It is a question that takes us not to particularities of epochs, but to the concept and epoch of modernity as expressed in images from the Deuteronomist's heart and mouth to the modern Cartesian subject; from the call to the patriarch Abraham to leave his homeland to Stevens's "Ordinary Evening in New Haven"; from Adam and Eve to Anselm's ontological argument to Spinoza's modification of it. Like Foucault, these figures limn the borders of human knowledge. But they pose the question concerning the principle based on which such borders can be apprehended and criticized.

This is to resist the topos of secularization. It is not a story of desecularization or reenchantment.[7] The metaphors of God and ontological argument are not proffered to expose the religious roots of secular storytelling. Nor are they cited to suggest that our age of uncertainty is another expression of the certainties we thought we had exhausted. The issue is whether those certainties constitute a convincing image.[8] Doubts about knowledge pervade the preface to *The Order of Things*, which promises a meditation on "the stark impossibility of thinking *that*"— the inexplicable incursion of the arbitrary into history. This is consistent with Descartes, who begins the *Meditations* with doubts about what he knows and doubts about himself and concludes with the impossibility of thinking *what* he thinks. While Foucault has his "conditions" that "dominate and even overwhelm" the "perceptive capacity" of the subject, Descartes has demons that deceive him about what seems most indubitable. In Foucault, the concept of discontinuity in history underscores the contradiction of a threshold that ineradicably divides what the historical mind can somehow transgress. Descartes concludes his demonstration of God's existence with the image of the mind touching the very thing it cannot comprehend.

These images, and the distinction between them and Foucault's preferred image of Enlightenment, contribute to a renovation of the concept of modernity. Pascal, Spinoza, and Vico make forays into the labyrinthine dimensions of the rational mind, doubled back on itself, feeling for its own limits, going beyond them, and then returning to redescribe the structure of the quest. So too Kant's antinomies, Hegel's knowledge as a wound, Rousseau's reason bound in chains of its own making, Freud's master demoted in its own house, and, not least, the biblical images of Creation, Fall, and labor, according to which human beings are to become adequate to the good they know together with God—that existence is good only insofar as it can be made in concert, which making will also unleash cataclysms. These dramatic images of reason emerge in materials in which reason's limits are a continual provocation to rethink its identity, its desires, and, as with the Grand Inquisitor, its madness. I have taken continual inspiration from a small selection of the poems of Wallace Stevens, drawing on Stevens's ability to depict the work of the mind to command, without dominating, the world's mysteries—to free the world, as he writes in "The Snow Man," of "nothing that is not there" in order to reckon with "the nothing that is."[9]

Modernity's Mind

I now turn to Descartes's medieval companion, Saint Anselm of Canterbury. Anselm is best known for his argument for the existence of God, enunciated in the second and third chapters of the *Proslogion* (1077).[10] The locus classicus of speculative theology, this argument also has consequences for the history of reason, and indeed for critical work in the humanities overall. Anselm's claim that God is that than which nothing greater can be thought performs more than it seems, placing the absolutely other in the region of human rationality—as absolutely other. Anselm thereby sets aside the Platonic conception of reason absorbed by his Christian, Muslim, and Jewish brethren, according to which the object of thought (the good, the true, the beautiful, the in itself) is opposed to, when it is not identified with, the human being who is seeking what he once knew. Plato's model of rationality, taken up in mystics and rationalists alike, is structured so that, in order to gain the object, one must lose, by transcending, the position of existence, even insofar as existence mirrors the truth. These moves have the effect of ratifying natural hierarchies, which fill the breach opened up by a world of opposition, in which existence is stepping-stones to the truth, and identity, in which existence is mythically sacralized as it is.

For Anselm, by contrast, God may be great, but no greater than what the human mind can think at its very limit. To be sure, Anselm conceives of reason as flawed, inadequate, sinful. God, he says, is right before our eyes, and we can barely see him. But these qualifications only augment the revolutionary premise that the thing human beings shall know, and indeed the thing they most desire, is, however impossible, what human beings do and must know as they enact their ends. The ultimate, than which nothing is greater, is nothing greater than what can be thought, even if thought, but no less what it thinks, is thereby strained to its limit. For Anselm the realm of God is not the realm of the Forms, what is in itself, known only unto itself. It is not, as in Borges, the position that confounds thought for the wonder of what's left over. It is the realm of humankind—the realm of the ordinary, the corporeal, the historical, the sinful. The realm of God is also the realm of the secular.

Part of the surprise of such claims lies in the identification of the eleventh-century Anselm with a revolution in reason and its secular context. This revolution is usually understood to begin with Descartes and culminate in Kant. Partly, too, it is the figure of Anselm himself. Did Kant not pass fatal judgment on what he named "the ontological argument," dispelling once and for all the attempt to use speculative reason to demonstrate theological claims—to confuse truth and belief?[11] In claiming that Anselm's ontological argument is not about confusion but about liberation from dualist contradiction, I am doing more than shifting the origin of modernity back a few hundred years or rehabilitating Anselm as a philosopher. I am suggesting that the revolutions represented by Descartes and Kant can best be understood with the piece of the puzzle represented by Anselm—the spectral presence of his argument in the history of modernity.

Both Descartes's "cogito ergo sum" and Kant's "critique of pure reason" depend on Anselm's distinction between a Platonic rationalism of opposition, the opposition between the mind and what it seeks, and a rationalism of paradox, wherein what is of ultimate value shares the same realm as the one who values it, albeit without losing its otherness. This structure of value and actuality is the condition of otherness as a value. Although Descartes and Kant might seem to exemplify a rationalism superseded by concerns of culture, body, ethnos, and language, such concerns emerge only by virtue of ground cleared by Anselm and then elaborated by Descartes, Spinoza, and Kant over against Plato. It is possible to ask "Whose reason?" or "Which bodies?"—it is possible to root reason in its historical worlds—only if reason is human, historical, and secular in the first place, if reason is indeed coauthor with its others—Gods and neighbors—of its own idiosyncrasies and gaps. It is Anselm, with Abraham, who makes it possible to see the boundaries of reason. It is Anselm, following Abraham, who therefore makes it possible today to investigate what reason habitually ignores.

What, then, is Anselm's move, his "ontological argument," and with whom, exactly, is he arguing? What Anselm shares with Descartes, Spinoza, Vico, and Kant is the question of how it is that the human mind is at once empowered to survey the totality of what appears and also absolutely limited in what it sees. "O whole and blessed truth, how far You are from me who am so close to You!"[12] So writes Anselm in the *Proslogion*, expressing the paradox of the ontological argument for the existence of God: that human beings are close to what is distant (and distinct) from them; that they know, and are known by, what it is they do not know. Yet while Anselm is renowned as the author of the argument that God is "that than which nothing greater can be thought," just as striking is the light this formulation sheds on his concept of the mind.[13] It is the mind, for Anselm, that is truly puzzling and truly awesome, for the mind is able both to see and not to see, to find and not to experience what found: "You are within me and around me and I do not have any experience of You."[14] The mind is both limited and overwhelmed by limitlessness, and thus the mind contains and expresses the central paradox of existence: that human beings are constituted by the desire for what they know. The mind desires and is confused by the very thing that it (also) is.

It is this desire that puts Anselm alongside his modern brethren and distinguishes each from the mind in quest of the being it lacks. In Anselm, God is the other of the mind, the mind of the other, the other that is the mind. God is the name Anselm gives to the difference inclusive of existence. For Anselm and his conceptual interlocutors, the discovery that the self is limited not by the object it fails to see, but by the very thing it sees; the discovery that this limitation is also empowerment, namely, that sight is possible only when there is more than meets the eye; the discovery, finally, that seeing what appears is equally about seeing what does not—this is to tell a story about the mind in and of history through the language of the relation of the human and the divine. It is to tell a story about the mind of modernity.

This is not to claim that Anselm inaugurated modernity or prophesied later movements and ideas, much less to root the secular modern in the religious antique. It is to claim that the conception of history by virtue of which discriminations like those between Western modernity and its others (the Middle Ages, Antiquity, the Renaissance) would eventually gain currency emerges in coordination with the particular conception of the mind as both radically limited and rationally powerful that Anselm quintessentially expresses.

The literature on the history and meaning of modernity has attempted to capture some feature of it—for example, enlightenment, the autonomous self, reformation, political sovereignty, or radicalism—in order to locate this feature in a particular time and place, connecting it to broader historical and intellectual trends. What this book is exploring, by contrast, is the question of what commitments are involved in the very concept that both truth and appearance are history, the question, equally, of how to build inclusive histories and worlds. What Anselm expresses with the ontological argument is that the notion that it is human to struggle with blindness to what is all too present can originate only with a portrait of mind that has already overcome the blindness of fate and chance. This is a notion of the mind that already knows not only that it is blind but what it is blind to, and thus a notion of mind that is powered, not stymied, by its own limitations. Modernity, I claim, is not just the name for a particular concept of mind. Modernity is the name for the idea that minds, but also collectives, can be particular (limited, local, historical) as well as generalizable (empowered, generative, universal). Modernity is the name for the idea of history, and thus for the history of the idea that borders modernity.

What Anselm expresses is the specificity of the notion of history as a discourse that refuses human blindness to its own truths.[15] As we have seen Vico put this refusal, "History cannot be more certain than when he who creates the things also narrates them," and since, he continues, "this world of nations has certainly been made by men . . . its guise must therefore be found within the modifications of our own human mind." What connects Vico with Anselm is the conviction that the project of history is essentially a project of *factum*, of human creation, and that the conditions for this creation originate in the mind as what both knows and can fail to understand what it knows—whose narrations are both truthful and sometimes fictive, both powerful and sometimes illusory. This does not make Anselm modern in any conventional sense, but it grants to his claims about the God and the mind of the Hebrew and Christian Bibles a fundamental difference from what Vico calls the wisdom of the ancients. It situates the creation of historical difference—not just differences in history but the difference that is history—in the concept of the mind's break with itself.

As Pascal would put it some six hundred years after Anselm, "Reason's last step is the recognition that there are an infinite number of things which are beyond it."[16] A century later, Kant concludes his *Groundwork of the Metaphysics of Morals* by observing that "we do not indeed comprehend the practical unconditional necessity of the moral imperative, but we nevertheless comprehend its *incomprehensibility*; and this is all that can fairly be required of a philosophy that strives in its principles to the very boundary of human reason."[17] Still another century later, Hegel writes of the mind in history as the recognition that "spirit is at war with itself; it has to overcome itself as its most formidable obstacle."[18] This is to say that it is reason that knows, but also confuses, what the limits of reason are, and it is reason that is, in this paradoxical logic, unlimited, not as what floats free of existence but as what powers it. For Anselm it is not, as Aristotle would have it, that "all men by nature desire to know"[19] or, as in Plato, that "every soul pursues the good."[20] Desire is for what we know is good, for something or someone close enough to see its very distance and distinctiveness—close enough therefore to contend with and to confound.

This is not only to conceive of modernity in its history, it is to imagine reason as the faculty that has history. When thinkers such as Nietzsche and Freud, and later Heidegger, Foucault, and Said, show that the ostensible universality of Western reason is inextricably wedded to particular social, cultural, political, psychical, and intellectual projects, texts, and institutions, and when they thereby undertake to move the West past its blindness to the limits of its own reason, they are doing nothing less than reviving the ontological argument by which Anselm committed the modern mind to the vexations, if also the enlightenment, of its limits. This is not to say that Anselm is the final word; it is to conjoin thinkers of epoch across historical periods as a way of rethinking the concept of epoch, and modernity as this concept.

The notion that history has an origin like every other human artifact might not seem a controversial idea. History has a genealogy by which it can be shown to have mutated. Yet it is just this recognition that needs scrutiny, namely the sense that *because* history has a history, it can document *only* the temporal and contingent, including its own temporality and contingency. History can commit *only* to the singular, the particular, the local, the constructed. The locus for historical labor, it is therefore thought, can be *only* the specific languages, contexts, gestures, performances, institutions, and social arrangements that are expressive of human life.

But what is historical specificity? How does one think about a plurality of specifics without thinking specifically about the kind of labor and desire this posture enacts? Where does history's power come from? What are the specifics of *its* gaze and *its* decisions? This is to ask more than the historically specific question of when and where human beings began to think about themselves as conditioned by temporality. It is to shine light on the ambivalent reach of history as a discourse that is, however reluctantly, concerned with origins and ends. It is to conceive of history as bound up with the invention of history, and it is therefore to reopen the question of what is the concept of this kind of invention. What is the mind insofar as history is that to which it is ineradicably subject?

The power of history to commit to temporality and contingency depends on the sharpness of its boundaries and the specificity of its "mind": the history of history as the history of one particular way of being in, and seeing, the world. However broad and inclusive may be this "one," it is not infinitely, endlessly, indifferently so.[21]

Traces of History in Saint Anselm

The wax scattered about in fragments, so that the ontological argument had to be pieced together again from the bits.

G. R. Evans

The true or the divine does not get lost.

G. W. F. Hegel

Time will tell.

Alain Badiou

Badiou and the Time of Thought

How much can one think outside one's time? This question has been posed in our time by the French philosopher and political activist Alain Badiou. Badiou's commitments to ontology and to truth stand apart from those strands in Continental philosophy that have made history and contingency central to their vision.[22] Yet few are as acutely conscious as the communist Badiou that "the times" put ineradicable constraints on what it is possible to think, with the exception, perhaps, of readers disoriented by his claim that the time for communism is still before us.[23] The latest, and in his own mind possibly the last, in a genealogy of French thinkers whose concern with the relation of concept and existence dates back, he says, to Sartre, Badiou writes to forestall the judgment that the time has passed for the question of truth.

> Our question will be: What is the dominant ideology today? Or, if you want, what is, in our countries, the natural belief? There is the free market, the technology, the money, the job, the blog, the reelection, the free sexuality, and so on. But I think that all that can be concentrated in a single statement: There are only bodies and languages.[24]

Badiou identifies a certain "postmodern" tendency to fasten on the body's centrality in a drama of finitude—a "biopolitics," to use Foucault's term—in which the object is to "expose the secret" that the human animal is the index of democratic rights with no remainder. There are bodies and there are the languages that express their inextirpable finitude—in other words, "the hard relationship of bodies to the great and indifferent noise of the universe."[25]

Badiou's critique is of this "dogma of our finitude." It is formulated as follows: "There are only bodies and languages, except that there are truths."[26] He aims thereby to mark the distinction between what he calls "democratic materialism," which accepts the totality of bodies and languages, and, as he puts it, "the syntax that disjoins the axiom of materialist dialectics"—the syntax that disjoins truth from its materials. What he is after is the relation of truths to their situations in the world, not their nature in putative isolation. He is after where and what truth is in emerging, and therefore its relation to subjects and their histories.[27] But he marks equally the disjoin. "The structure of situations does not, in itself, deliver any truths." "A truth is solely constituted by rupturing with the order which supports it, never as an effect of that order." Badiou calls this rupture "event." It is a word for a "strictly incalculable emergence."[28] "We admit therefore that 'what there is'—what composes the structure of worlds—is well and truly a mixture of bodies and languages." But then, "truths exist as exceptions to what there is." Truth is neither a "supplement" nor an "addition" to "bodies and languages." There are bodies and languages. "Nothing exists which is a separable 'soul,' 'life,' 'spiritual principle.' " Nor is truth a synthesis of body and language. It is not a discourse or a phenomenology. Rather, " 'truths' is the (philosophical) name of what . . . comes to interpolate itself into the continuity of the 'there is.' " Truth, one could say, is existence insofar as it is creative. It is "novelty," disruption, or again "exception." Badiou reformulates the point in a way that recalls Stevens's twofold nothing. "There is not only what there is."[29]

This question of truth as an exception to bodies and languages is not simply a philosophical matter. To be sure, it involves a conversation whose speakers occupy a certain philosophical marquee: Bachelard, Merleau-Ponty, Lévi-Strauss, Althusser, Foucault, Derrida, Lacan, Sartre, Deleuze.[30] To recognize with Badiou that "truths are without existence" is therefore to traverse a conceptual canon as he makes the next move: "Is that to say they do not exist at all? By no means."[31] On the other hand, the conversation can be given a precise date—let us say, with Badiou in mind, May 1968—and an equally precise demand: that philosophical questions make themselves properly attentive to the times. In 1969, the University of Paris VIII was created to house the radicalism of the student movement and to institutionalize the social and political ambitions of philosophy. For Badiou, the issue is "to have done with the separation of concept and existence—no longer to oppose the two; to demonstrate that the concept is a living thing, a creation, a process, an event, and, as such, not divorced from existence."[32] If truth nevertheless bears an angular relation to existence, the concept—thought as such—founds this possibility in rather than against what exists. There *is* not only what there is. The concept exists.

This might be old news. But how old? European thought internalized, or ought to have internalized, this maxim from Descartes in the 1630s and 1640s. Descartes's account of the existence of God engages the paradox that what there is (God, thought) is simultaneously the condition and the disruption of what there is (existence, reality, myself). The paradox for Descartes is the existence of another: "If the objective reality of any of my ideas is found to be so great that I am certain that same reality was not in me, either formally or eminently, and that therefore I myself cannot be the cause of the idea, then it necessarily follows that I am not alone in the world."[33] Was the proof of the concept of the other not also and simultaneously its undoing as pure concept? Was not existence—I am, I exist, you exist—precisely the reverberating drag on its imperial pretensions?

Badiou claims that it is particularly twentieth-century French philosophy that is driven by the desire to "displace the relation between the concept and its external environment by developing new relations to existence, to thought, to action, and to the movement of forms."[34] He suggests, further, that we do not begin to know the upheaval, the promise, the very precariousness of Descartes's gambit until 1792, and then afterward 1848, 1871, 1917, and so on. These dates and the story they tell are particular to Badiou's communist hypothesis. But the anxiety—and for Badiou the excitement and the novelty—can be elaborated more generally.[35] The question is, What remains of the concept, of concepts, once they have no autonomous or purely intellectual existence? What *is* a concept knit into time? Where is it? Which concepts, if any, do we inherit over time if time is the measure of the concept—if time is the gallows, to put a revolutionary point on it? These questions are equally historical and philosophical. What has it been possible to think then, and then? What shall it now be possible to think—or as Badiou asks, in a Leninist vein, What is required of us now? "What is to be done?"[36]

The guiding postulate of many of the thinkers in Badiou's genealogy—a genealogy he both identifies with (as its "last representative") and also criticizes in its obsession with bodies and languages—is that it is only now possible, indeed now *only* possible, to have a history of the concept, and by extension an economics, a psychology, a sexuality, and so forth—a history of the mind and its temporal, its real, precincts. This possibility is the result of the search for a new relation "between the concept and its environment." It is not only that philosophy, like every other human act, cannot be read without reference to the site of its production. It is that history emerges (in 1630? in 1789? 1792?) as the story of the mind's (not to say the head's) uncertain fate. What is required of us now? What is to be done? History, the Gallic chorus intones. History. Or, as Badiou remarks concerning the legacy of his own concepts, "time will tell."[37]

Given Badiou's political emphases in identifying the rise of historical consciousness, it might seem misguided to linger only momentarily on the dates August 1792 or May 1968, with their images of the barricades, in pursuit of the mistier and seemingly less militant one of 1641, the publication date of Descartes's *Meditations on First Philosophy*. I want to go one better and associate this consciousness with the years 1077–78. These are the years during which the medieval theologian Anselm wrote his *Proslogion*, which lays out his argument "that God really exists"—an argument only slightly more absurd to our ears than Badiou's communist hypothesis.[38] This, again, is not in order to push back the date of modernity. It is not to shed new light on Anselm's charged struggles with the kings William II and Henry I, as intriguing as this would be.[39] In fact, it is these very historical and political postures—of continuity and novelty alike—that I contend with. My interest in Anselm is in his divergence from our own intellectual temperament, informed as it is by the historical and philosophical currents Badiou sketches. It could be said that Anselm is the very exemplar of the premodern—a pious monk and church official who wanted only to elaborate his belief in God and to confess this elaboration to a scholastic audience. Anselm is a paragon of the concept unmolested by its environment.

To be sure, one can imagine dimensions of Anselm's thought and life that twenty-first-century readers might be in a privileged position to appreciate—as a rationalist counterpart, perhaps, to the suggestive connections between modernism and medieval mysticism proposed in recent years.[40] For the moment I want to retain the distance of Anselm's figure in order to consider some of the paradoxes of our intellectual time: historicist, political, postcolonial in consciousness if not in practice, ascetic to a fault in matters metaphysical, ardently antiteleological, and yet so evidently the culmination of the long labor of Badiou's Cartesian concept in and as existence. Which of us does not consider beyond debate what has been so ferociously debated: that time as such—any time—delimits thought? Do we know what this means? Do we know what kind of limitation we thereby conjure, or exactly what is limited? Is there a relation between Badiou's question concerning whether the time for truth has passed and the question of what the past has to do with what can be thought now? What is the criticism adequate to these questions?

Anselm of Canterbury

Let Anselm serve as exhibit A, the perfect other for late modern readers, with his architectonic of reason and the divine. Anselm may offend a maximal number of contemporary scholarly habits of mind, whether historicist, secular, or simply argumentative, without offering the slightest compensatory flamboyance that can make medieval offense—the exotic mystical beauty to the Enlightenment beast—so alluring. He is a resolutely uninspired subject, a cliché, a signpost. How can he be read? Perhaps he cannot be. But this "cannot" represents the challenge of a history of the concept, as distinct from a history of the rationalists who propounded it. In a history of the concept, which—rationality or history—is telling which? When we tell, for example, the history of the concept from 1078 to 1641, will we not have to tell the concept of history from 1641 to 1078 to 1968?[41]

In a textbook for the introductory course in the study of religion, Ivan Strenski observes that we can ask what were the reasons, conditions, circumstances, and conversations that made particular thinkers think the way they do. If their concepts seem unbelievable or even nonsensical to us *now*, we have to work harder to understand why they might have been compelling *then*.[42] No doubt. But although this effort will go some way toward addressing the obstacle to understanding another across time, diminishing incredulity and even generating sympathy, it stops short of taking on the ambivalence when, inevitably, we entertain the argument in our own terms. Historicist protocol will nudge the concept discreetly back into its own terms, or else it will take on those terms as requiring fundamental revision. Understanding why E. B. Tylor thought natives were backward will not liberate me to speak similarly. On the contrary: either I am to suppress my response to the views on their own merits, even as I am empowered to forgive Mr. Tylor, who had his conditions and his reasons, or I am instructed to subject him to the full weight of my outrage as if he were a contemptible elderly relative, where I am attempting, as in Durkheim and Said, to constitute—to correct—the family on better grounds.

Rationalism and our efforts to understand it historically present a distinct class of this ambivalence concerning the confusing brew of distance and value. Without such hot markers as race, gender, class, or sexuality, though strategically reducible to any of these, rationalism, as a subspecies of theology, is the ultimate offense to the coolheadedness of history: not simply something we are encouraged to see in its historical time but history's slightly brutish house guest—the concept as an ill-mannered interloper demanding equal time from history itself. Unlike Tylor's exotic native, we are typically not in the least tempted to entertain it even in its debasement, so it never presents itself except as a sign of warning, a "cannot." It is simply, if invisibly, corrected. Badiou's twentieth-century genealogy throws some names at the work to do so. It is surely why Descartes has always gotten the most ruthless modern and postmodern press. The *concept* exists? By no means. The concept *exists*, and a poor existence it is. There are only bodies and languages. There is only what there is.

To Badiou's crew I recommend the Grand Inquisitor, who, in correcting the prisoner's work, at least knew what was lost.

Badiou, however, follows Anselm, who knows the stakes of the declaration that the concept exists. Anselm is not only exhibit A but also a critic thereof. What does he know? He knows, with Vico, that the challenge of rationalism is to account for itself in historical terms—to map the distance and distinctiveness of the mind and what it can think. In Anselm's argument that God is that than which nothing greater can be thought, we begin with knowledge or thought (*cogitatio*), however confused, not with the Platonic quest that knowledge is what we seek. We thus begin not with the division that separates us from thought but with the paradoxical difference that is thinking.[43] This is to differentiate between knowledge or thought (*cogitatio*), which Anselm's argument presupposes in arguing from existence, and understanding (*intelligere*), which his argument works to establish in existence. As he puts it in the preface, rephrasing Augustine, "I have written the following short tract dealing with this question as well as several others, from the point of view of one trying to raise his mind to contemplate God and seeking to understand (*intelligere*) what he believes."[44] While Anselm is seeking understanding, he chastises his critic Gaunilo for denying what he can think, as if thinking is mere phantasm.[45]

This paradox is articulated in a philosophical register in the *Proslogion*. I can think the concept that is the most distant from and foreign to me, Anselm maintains, and this distance and foreignness call out for my labor. Once again, Anselm's cry, "O whole and blessed truth, how far are you from me who am so close to You!"[46] This cry contains the charge of history, for the very idea that this "blessed truth" is one that "cannot be thought not to exist" *as* what is most distant from me—neither internal nor external to the mind—makes the work of thinking the endeavor to commit to what exists.[47] This is to see what Badiou does in distinguishing between situations, which are "pure indifferent multiplicities," and truths, which "emancipate," "rupture"—which "take place."[48] Truths are not situations, concepts do not exist—until they are and do, at which time what exists is the exception of the exception of the disjoin in joining them. This emancipatory join does not only refer to a point in time where truth meets history; it is a commitment to time. Thought of what exists—the rational, the concept—is at the same time and necessarily thought of the specifics of existence. The "whole and blessed truth" is not the (only) thing we know in Anselm. The truth is the thought, the wager, that makes knowledge of existence, of what exists, the miraculously realizable task. That is to say, existence is not only what is excepted in the event of truth, it is also the exception that gives

us the truths of bodies and languages. There is not only what there is. As
God said to Abraham, leave existence for an existence I will show you.
As Isaac says to his father Abraham, What about existence? As Abraham
says to his son, I commit to it.

But then Anselm knows, too, that the challenge of history is to account for itself in rational terms, to labor in the vineyards of the concept. He knows, in short, that thinking must of necessity happen at the
limits of one's time, for the times alone are inattentive to, or simply uncritical of, their reasons. Anselm therefore knows the difference between
what cannot be read and what it is simply unfashionable to read. He
knows—he is the prophet of what it means to know—what is to be done.

Consider the following fragment.

Like many subjects both medieval and modern, Anselm had a biogra-
pher, a historian named Eadmer. Eadmer's *Life of St. Anselm* (ca. 1124)
recounts Anselm's upbringing, his experiences as a prominent figure in
the communities in France and England in which he taught, wrote, and
served as clergy, and his struggles to come to clarity about his ideas. Anselm himself refers to these struggles in the preface to the *Proslogion*,
noting that

> as often and as diligently as I turned my thoughts [to the question
> of whether there is not a single argument for God's existence],
> sometimes it seemed to me that I had almost reached what I was
> seeking, sometimes it eluded my acutest thinking completely, so
> that finally, in desperation, I was about to give up what I was
> looking for as something impossible to find.[49]

However, finally, Anselm writes,

> when I had decided to put aside this idea altogether, lest by
> uselessly occupying my mind it might prevent other ideas with
> which I could make some progress, then, in spite of my unwill-
> ingness and my resistance to it, it began to force itself upon me
> more and more pressingly. So it was that one day when I was
> quite worn out with resisting its importunacy, there came to
> me, in the very conflict of my thoughts [*cogitationum conflictu*],
> what I had despaired of finding, so that I eagerly grasped the no-
> tion which in my distraction I had been rejecting.[50]

Eadmer begins his narration of Anselm's difficulties by describing Anselm's sleeplessness, distractedness, loss of appetite, and, most worryingly for his subject, inability to focus on worship. Perhaps the drive to find a single argument was the work of the devil, not God. "Then suddenly one night during matins," Anselm's argument came to him. Eadmer omits the language of conflict, giving us "the grace of God illuminated his heart, the whole matter became clear to his mind, and a great joy and exaltation filled his inmost being."

The conflict reappears, however, now not in Anselm's great insight, but in the events that immediately followed. "Thinking therefore that others also would be glad to know what he had found, he immediately and ungrudgingly wrote it on writing tablets and gave them to one of the brethren of the monastery for safe-keeping."[51] It was customary to make first drafts on wax tablets and subsequently to transfer, or have a scribe transfer, the writing to parchment. The tablets were worn in the girdle and carried in pairs, folded toward each other so as not to disturb the wax.[52] Eadmer relates that "after a few days [Anselm] asked the monk who had charge of them for the tablets," but they had disappeared. "The place where they had been laid was searched, but they were not found. The brethren were asked in case anyone had taken them, but in vain. And to this day," Eadmer adds, "no-one has been found who has confessed that he knew anything about them."[53]

Anselm painstakingly "wrote another draft on the same subject on other tablets, and handed them over to the same monk for more careful keeping." This time the monk placed them "by his bed, in a more secret place," likely in a cabinet.[54] In the morning Anselm "found them scattered on the floor by his bed and the wax which was on them strewn about in small pieces." He doggedly "pieced together the wax and recovered the writing, though with difficulty."[55] As Anselm scholar G. R. Evans puts it, "the ontological argument had to be pieced together again from the bits." Needless to say, Anselm was careful the third time around to have a copy made on parchment right away. Yet "it is impossible," observes Evans, "to say how much of the argument, or of the *Proslogion* as we have it, was on the lost or broken tablets."[56]

It would be difficult to overstate the power of this uncannily Mosaic image: the argument of arguments that resolves the antinomy of antinomies—God exists—reconstituted from pieces, perhaps incomplete, certainly belated, a second or third draft. Oh, the reams that could be written on the idée fixe of wax as instrument of scripture, the same substance Descartes would go on six hundred years later to make the very totem of contingency.[57] Oh, the satire that could conjure the concept beheaded by rogue monks. Instead, we have Evans's phlegmatic teaching: It is impossible to say how much was on the lost or broken tablets. How thoroughly unlikely. Which part of "God exists" would be missing? And yet how intriguing that one would be charged with discovering piecemeal what had also to be true in order for this one proposition to be so.

For this is the charge from the *Proslogion* "as we have it," the missing distinction of modernity: that God, but no less the devil, illuminates nothing so much as the conflict of thought in and of the world. God might radiate into Anselm's mind, as Eadmer's version has the moment of truth. But this radiation is concrete—it has a measure, a girth, a waxy mark, a piece. A challenge. As readers of Anselm's rationalism, we know enough of God to know that God is impossible, the very principle of "cannot." But in thinking at the limit, Anselm shows, there is no thing one cannot know. One is charged to know what exists, in defiance of the impossibility that would resign the task altogether, as he almost did. Existence is the thing and it is the thought. Or, since "it is possible to think" that than which nothing greater can be thought, there is nothing greater than to piece it together.[58]

This engagement with thought, conflict, and existence is made vivid in Anselm's debate with his contemporary Gaunilo over the whereabouts of God, appended to the manuscript with Anselm's reply. Gaunilo brings up the glaring objection, Does Anselm's argument not dispose of argument altogether, and his object of all objects? If I know God exists by virtue of thought alone, if thinking and its concepts are equally real, then is this not to say there are no limits to thinking, and so much the worse for existence?[59] Is this not our accusation too, leveled at the ultimate rationalism from which, piecemeal and over the manifold ages, we have now finally recovered? Has the time not passed for thought's concept?

Anselm's response is twofold. First, yes, Gaunilo is right. That I can think of a "lost island" to which no one has access is to ignore the limits of reality. It is, one could say, impermissible or fantastical by the terms of existence, which underwrite the fantasy in the first place, that is, give it shape and form. But, second, God is not like a "lost island." The objection would still be, though, either God is like a lost island, in which case the argument does not hold, or God is not like a lost island, in which case the argument is moot since God would presumably have no existence at all. Either we can think anything, existence be damned, or thinking is limited to and by existence, to and by the times. There is only what there is. The consequence of each alternative is the same: that thought and existence—reason and history—divide the world before collapsing into one. For if thought can think anything, if it is truly unlimited, then thought is nothing more than one lost island after another, time tricked out in the vaporous illusion of the concept.

In Anselm's scheme, however, God is no object, but the concept that names thought in and of existence, the condition, paradoxically, for the anxiety that perhaps they do not ultimately square, that I might and indeed probably do pursue one at the expense of the other. God is the condition for fantasies of the impossible: God the intrinsic object, pure in itself or, what is the same, the conceits of thought and history unlimited by the other, which prohibitions each function precisely as spurs to transgression, for good and for ill.

What Anselm might say to us twenty-first-century readers, anxious especially to fulfill our obligations to the majesty of the date, is that the freedom to think outside one's time—whether to claim the mantle of communism after its failures or to seek the *realia* of 1078—is grounded in the way the mind is in time. The difference between Gaunilo and Anselm, both of whom would discipline thought to what we can know in and as existence, is that for Gaunilo this exercise—ostensibly protective of what really exists—has no way of accounting for the lost islands that do in fact materialize, the lost islands constructed not of idle fantasy but of the improbable labor of thought at its limits. In Gaunilo, as in all skepticisms, all rationalisms, all historicisms, there are bodies and languages, and one wends one's way through these thickets according to their preordained laws and logics. In Anselm one has, if not for the first time, then certainly indelibly, a different calculus of time's cut, and thus the cut of the concept.

The argument is that if we do not think at—or even beyond–our limits, we cannot think with any elasticity within them. If we do not connect thought to what lies as far as possible from it, we cannot see what is present or proximate. Fidelity to time is absolute only insofar as one is conscious of the betrayals one performs as one sets out to master "the ages of time" in their "immensity without limit."[60] In Anselm this fidelity, this betrayal, is God; in Badiou it is truth or event. It is the ontological argument in its pieces. It is the gambit that you cannot do history without ontology. You cannot do bodies and languages without truths, not because the concept, the truth, adds anything substantive to history (it is neither supplement nor synthesis) but because the concept is (of) history itself.

What Gaunilo does not see, together with his modern and postmodern brethren, is that Anselm's argument that God exists is the very opposite of a promiscuous extension of thought where it has no right to go. Indeed, one is, on Anselm's logic, as on Descartes's, absolutely limited by the concept to existence. Gaunilo's mistake then does not consist in conceiving thought as limited. It consists in conceiving these limits as conditioned by the thing we do not know, the impossible of fantasy, rather than by the thing we do know, the concept, impossible except as the power to interrupt what is. I can know God, then, but only as that "present existence" by which I am returned from lost islands to the exigencies and limits of my own conflicted present, "for what . . . has in it something mutable is not altogether what it is."[61] As Descartes puts it, I might mistake myself for something else. Or as Badiou affirms once again, there is not only what there is.

To dub Anselm as much critic as exhibit is to call on him to help us modify our notions of distance. We would do so in the light of a distinction not between thought and existence but between two different ways of conceiving their relation: on the one hand as opposed, by the logic of which they are also identified, and on the other hand as different enough to limit and even, if the situation calls for it, to pass for each other—when it can be permissible to think outside one's time.

This need not be about making Anselm more absorbable by us. Let him remain the ill-mannered rationalist interloper we cannot—or can barely—read. Let us evince no hesitation in showing him the door back to his medieval streets. But—let this be a stake—he is a critic of history as much as of the concept, and this makes him oddly our contemporary, his alienness, our "cannot," also his. One might say that insofar as Anselm is distinguishable by virtue of the intellectual temper identified by Badiou, he is indistinguishable from Badiou himself.

Then and Now

This conceit posits a connection between then and now, between the rationalism that seems to defy its environment and the one that expresses it. The point is also to distinguish. For Badiou, history matters as the discourse that makes his wager for truths necessary again. It might be said that he makes too much of it—that we had to wait until truths had been shown to be merely and trivially possible, history's seconds, to resurrect their radical impossibility, and thus their promise. Or that he makes too little—that history's quarry of bodies and languages is inert. What is at issue is the conceptual relation between Badiou and a conflicted thinker like Anselm. Badiou holds that twentieth-century French philosophy, albeit in conjunction with the apostle Paul and served by his own critique, properly corrects the kind of rationalist-theological excess represented by a figure like Anselm. It reunites the concept with existence.

It is an irony that Badiou then moves to bypass French philosophy and every other kind in search—now, once again—of the intrinsic truths of mathematics and the hushed empyrean of Plato's Forms, by which ontology will be accounted free of the domination of the one. Badiou would dispute the metaphor. For him the virtue of Plato is contained in the maxim from the *Parmenides*: "If the one is not, nothing is."[62] What is gained is the principle that in the beginning is nothing singular; in the beginning, nothing is what there is. What mathematics can capture, consistent with Badiou's Plato, is the not-one, not only as nothing, but as the multiplicity whose "essence is to multiply itself in an immanent manner." Badiou claims this is not to place the many where the one was—that it is to circumvent both one and many with reference to the void, the subtraction, the nothing. The multiple multiplying infinitely and indifferently cannot be thought. Only so can there be event. From nothing.[63]

I do not take up whether Badiou is right about Plato or Georg Cantor's set theory.[64] What matters here is twofold. First, Badiou's concept of event—of creativity, of freedom—works to bypass the logic of the one and the many. Badiou's allegiance to Plato is not in the line of Alfred North Whitehead's claim that "the safest general characterization of the European philosophical tradition is that it consists of a series of footnotes to Plato."[65] It is the opposite. For Badiou, Plato recognizes something the European philosophical tradition mostly does not. What he recognizes is what I show Anselm recognized and what this book seeks to teach anew, that the one and the many is a logic that rules out truths as they might be "militantly" (Badiou's word) realized in history. Second, however, I diverge from Badiou not only in reading Plato otherwise, in which what is, is nothing in relation to one. I tell a different history of what we both see in seeing truths in their disjuncture with history, each of us with our ancient exemplars, each with our saints, but with Badiou convinced, as Heidegger was, that much of modernity got it wrong. Does this matter? If Badiou and I end up in the same place, does the difference of our histories of the concept make a difference? Let me reformulate Badiou's position.

Badiou calls truths that are exceptional to bodies and languages events. What an event inaugurates is a "singular universal," a universal that has a specific, historical site but that is, if not indifferent to this site, then indifferent to the differences that structure it, without seeking to eradicate them. Badiou finds this concept in Saint Paul, whose universalism not only tolerates historical difference but assumes its presence and even its permanence. But he does not settle for it. As Badiou puts it, "*There are differences*. One can even maintain that there is nothing else."[66] What the event brings about, without guarantees, is the "for all," the egalitarian moment in the face of which difference is now open, porous, and unstable rather than structured and closed. It might be as Heidegger describes authenticity: that the event "is not something which floats above falling everydayness; existentially, it is only a modified way in which such everydayness is seized upon."[67] In the event, however, difference would not only be seized upon, it would be *reversed* to the end of producing the creative and laborious inclusion that comes ex nihilo, from nothing given in difference itself.

The difference between a true and a false event is not the standpoint taken toward differences of custom, language, appearance, belief, practice, and so on. The difference is that in a false event, the historical specificity absorbs without remainder the possibilities that follow from it. One nation's revolution will spark a transformation of *its* lifeworld, or perhaps just its vanguard, and those alone. At worst this will be what Badiou calls the "glory of the particular"—the perverse elevation of one element's truth at the expense of all others. At best it will simply be a benign, if still "disastrous," myopia. In the true event, the happening is local but its effects are and must be made universal. This is more than the recognition that difference does not disappear in the event. The claim is that it is only at the level of event that difference can actually be encountered as value and not as mere exchange, duplicity, or indifference.

Badiou's concept of the event is numerically paradoxical. It is a singularity in refusal of the one—in refusal of what Said calls the origin or theorists of religion call the sacred: the positive, the dogma, the metaphysical. Anselm would be guilty here, his reason the postulate of an abstraction suppressive of difference. But as Badiou's concept of event signifies, it may not be enough to identify the one as the enemy with respect to the project to elaborate an open multiplicity of inclusion. Yes, resistance to totality—to law, market, rule—involves the demonstration, if not mathematical derivation, of an irreducible multiplicity. Being is the void, the nothing, the subtraction. *There is* only multiplicity. The one can be shown to presuppose this ontological void, the rift in the structure of things that denies the privilege of the singular in making singularity the pressure of the universal. This order of the multiple and the one is necessary, Badiou argues, to account for the event's possibility and for both its unpredictability and its hiddenness. The point recalls Heidegger's opening to *Being and Time*. Our philosophies have failed to grasp the question at their origins.[68] We need to begin again, for which we need a new language, a new logic, and, as with *Saint Paul* for Badiou, or the pre-Socratics for Heidegger, a new—if ancient—set of exemplars.

As with Abraham. The difference here is that what philosophies have failed to grasp is the exhortation at their origins, in the call to Abraham to leave his land. In this exemplar, it is not recollection or novelty we need, but practice. In the light of my distinction between two dualisms, Badiou's announcement assimilates what are rather two different forms and functions of the one in the history of philosophy, something his own notion of a singular universal suggests. In attempting to retell the history of religion, Badiou charges Nietzsche with the failure to appreciate his precursor in Paul—the failure to look beyond the blighted priest and see the materialist antiphilosopher. But even as he reads Plato as he reads Paul, Badiou can be charged with the same failure in his neo-Platonic reading of the history of Western thought, which misses the broken one, the one that is two, the one that resists the totalizing count of the market in resisting, in my terms, the opposition or identity of truth and appearance, collective versus collective.[69]

If what Badiou calls "the materialist miracle" is a singular universal, why would it be necessary to imagine the one as the opposite of the many? If the principle to be comprehended is the revolutionary conjunction of creation and commitment, why would the primary obstacle be "in the beginning [from nothing] there is one" as contrasted with "in the beginning there is no thing but the multiple"? What indeed *is* the difference between these two statements, unless the one in relation to the nothing has a constitutive dogma about it that the multiple does not have? This presupposition merely recapitulates the unending opposition of one and many. Badiou gives us the mathematics that privileges the multiple as a position beyond one and many, the "inconsistent multiple" multiplying infinitely and indifferently, in contrast with the "consistent multiple, the composition of ones."[70] But if the composition of ones can have its alternative in the multiple, why not in an alternative one?

It cannot be denied that the one can function to close and totalize, to count and delimit. We might be better off beginning without it. But the frozen intransigence of the one is duplicable in every number, even to infinity. For the issue is not number at all but openness versus closure. Badiou claims his is not a dualism but a materialism. There is no substantial thing that we are to wait for or discover. And yet of course his *is* a dualism, committed, namely, to the radical difference between the world and the event: committed to "the divided subject" that rejects the "ethnic" distinction Jew/Greek in favor of the subject "divided in itself by the challenge of having nothing but the vanished event to face up to."[71] This is the dualism of the principle that the truth shall be made actual in the work of human concord. Does it count as dualism if one side of the dualism is the void? The answer could be Anselm's no less than Badiou's. The difference is not between difference (the many) and the same (the one). The difference is between two notions of difference, two dualisms: one that commits to the truth in engendering the event in what is and one that resigns both truth and commitment to the invidious divisions of what is.

Badiou knows that the one and the many will never be timely. Yet insofar as it is the one that is the problem, it is imperative not to erect it as the ghost in the system as you embrace the other side—the multiple in itself, the void. This would not be a matter of suggesting that the one be reclaimed at the origins as the master, the truth in itself. It would be to constitute a wedge in oneness, divided through itself. In modernity one is not one; one is never simply one. The one is free to become one. Freedom is one, in being, in the beginning, two. In the beginning is 1 + 1, the dialectic of self and other, singular and universal, truthful and historical, in distinction from +1 (dogmatism), as from −1 (skepticism).

Coda on Philosophy and History

In the introduction to his *Lectures on the Philosophy of History*, Hegel presciently confronts the skepticism his work would be subjected to in subsequent centuries. Philosophical history, he says, requires "an exposition or justification" different than other kinds of history require, since it will be assumed that "the Philosophy of History means nothing but the *thoughtful consideration of it*."[72] While thought, for Hegel, is "essential to humanity," this way of conceiving of the relation of thought to history supposes that "it is the business of history simply to adopt into its records what is and has been, actual occurrences and transactions," leaving philosophy as what "dwells in the region of self-produced ideas, without reference to actuality": in the position, namely, of a "subordinate to what is given."[73] This is paradoxically to find philosophy both ineffectual and tyrannical, for insofar as history is understood to be "mere passive material," "speculation" cannot be expected to resist the temptation "to force it into conformity with a tyrannous idea."[74] In short, says Hegel, "we seem to have in Philosophy . . . a process diametrically opposed to that of the historiographer."[75]

Hegel sets aside this view of both philosophy and history in transposing them, each in relation to the other. We saw the same move in Vico and his conceits. Badiou also possesses uncommon power on the point. But his history of philosophy stops short of recognizing that Hegel, author of a critique of philosophical history, is an ally. In Badiou's commitments to truth, void, and the infinite, in his focus on love, labor, art, and politics, and in his conception of the singular event that disrupts and orients history, he is practicing Hegel's concept of history. But Badiou distinguishes his own epoch, with ancient exceptions, as uniquely situated to conceive of truth in history. Badiou is writing to renew the question of truth, a renewal that can happen, he holds, only on grounds that recognize why the truth has been forgotten. In this effort, Badiou shares with Foucault and Heidegger an unease when it comes to Hegel. For Badiou, as for virtually every major twentieth-century thinker, Hegel is guilty of the perennial problem of subordinating difference to the "One" or the "Whole," a problem Badiou juxtaposes to his own position on the infinite multiplicity of being—what he calls the minimal difference between a thing and itself and, in a political register, "the axiomatic and egalitarian consequences of the absence of the Whole."[76]

Hegel stands for the inverted image of this egalitarian alternative, the one stable, lawful, interior, ordered being against which there can be no position of critique, no exterior. Badiou intends his concept of the multiple of multiplicities in which "there is no one" to serve as a new history of philosophy.[77] This is consistent with Foucault's account of Jean Hyppolite, translator of and commentator on Hegel who, in 1939, first gave the French a Hegel they could finally "escape."[78] For both Badiou and Foucault, it has seemed necessary to ask, "Can one still philosophize where Hegel is no longer possible? Can any philosophy continue to exist that is no longer Hegelian?"[79] Foucault portrays Hegel as generating "philosophy as a totality ultimately capable of dispersing and regrouping itself in the movement of the concept." Thus the question of critique, whether of philosophy or history, would call for a Herculean response, one that Hyppolite successfully meets, according to Foucault, by "altering" Hegel according to the philosophies of Hegel's "ceaseless [opponents]: Marx, Fichte, Bergson, Kierkegaard, and Husserl."[80] Indeed Hyppolite himself is Hegel's ideal opponent, in Foucault's view. He was close enough to have "an exact appreciation of the price we have to pay to detach ourselves from him" and strong enough to withstand the Hegelian tricks automatically deployed against any "anti-Hegelianism."[81]

These images of Hegel are of interest here insofar as they constitute a history of philosophy that gets stuck on modernity, conceived as an ontology that, in Badiou's words about Hegel, has no exteriority, an ontology in which "everything is intrinsic, since being-other is the one-of-being, and everything possesses an identificatory mark in the shape of the interiority of non-being." The finite and the infinite are "co-engendered."[82] There is no other that is not divided as Jew is divided from Greek, or there is no difference between the same and the same.[83]

As with Plato, I do not enter whose is the real Hegel or what is the real modernity. The question is, What distinguishes what Badiou and I both want? You can call Plato Paul and make both the epigones of Deleuze and Lenin. What are the distinctions that matter? The exile of Hegel in search of a position of fidelity made from nothing given is a symptom of confusion. Shall it be that we rid ourselves of the Whole (+1) or shall it be that we rid ourselves of the Whole (1 + 1)? The difference is the commitment to the axiomatic and egalitarian consequence that the second engenders the one and one in actuality—not as the composed ones of the many but as the event that vaporizes the divided line sequestering the one in the empyrean. Here is the paradox of the resistance to the one—that it requires the one to appear in and as existence. Distinction shall now be of existence, not between it and something else. The one comes into existence. The concept exists. To paraphrase Nietzsche's maxim, one is always wrong, but with one plus one truth begins.

What is two, and why does truth begin with it? Two is the principle that the truth appears, so where is it? It is the principle that the truth appears and so asks something axiomatic and egalitarian of me, in relation to what I share with you. Shall we ferret out wholes and singulars even where, hiding in plain view, they signify what demolishes as much as what is to be demolished—rendered historical, made relational, and universal? Let us instead distinguish what we need for the work to come. This is not to dismiss, but rather to underscore, the requirement to get one's concepts right. It is to say that the concept exists and thus will tend to confound our efforts to be true to it.

Like the materialist and Enlightenment readings of Spinoza I take up in the next chapter, readings of the symptom "Hegel," as of "Descartes," express the inadequacies of the story in which the history of philosophy has been bequeathed. We have worked to excise the one, but we keep reerecting it, in default of the labor for the singularity of concord. In Foucault's words, "If philosophy really must begin as absolute discourse, then what of history?"[84] It is this question that has most bedeviled efforts to devise an adequate relation between philosophy and history. It is the objection with which Hegel begins his lectures on the philosophy of history, one he briskly reformulates in making history and philosophy a common labor. It is not that it is a question of no consequence. For indeed, what *can* be the relation between history and the absolute, where both are vying to depict the nature of existence? Philosophy might simply exclude the absolute from its precincts. But this move, as we saw with Said, is no guarantee of a sound beginning.

What Foucault restates is the problem of the one and the many, a far trickier opponent than the name of Hegel. Badiou is a champion of the multiple in the name of replacing philosophy's one. Foucault is the maven of the one's resolution in the play, the arbitrariness, of disorder. What is required is the one in its distinction as history—the distinction of distinctions or, as in Derrida, the difference of difference.[85] Whatever conceptual, mathematical, and social and political labor is continually called for to retire the one and the many and its perennial dualism, this distinction, the distinction of modernity, is this labor's premise and its principle.

Badiou nevertheless gives us the concept and the conflict. His concept of truth—"there is not only"—in its militant connection to existence— "what there is"—is faithful not to Plato but to Anselm, to Descartes, to Hegel, to Stevens, and to others in time's monastic cabinet whom we, perhaps only now, can see with Eadmer's eyes: the concept pieced together from the bits. This does not make Badiou contemporaneous with Anselm, as if they are having the same argument in gross defiance of time's vicissitudes. It makes them, however impermissibly, at the beginning and at the limit of (their) time. In contemporaneity, one simply says no to distance. In the beginning and the limit, as in the event and the principle, one says yes to it, for distance, time, and history their scribe require that one be true to the paradox Anselm articulates so economically: that thought exists, and thus that history is necessarily—and conflictually—what one shall think.

History is the mind's modification, in Vico's terms, in service to creativity, inclusivity, fidelity. As Badiou puts it, truth is always an exception, not only to bodies and to languages, which are total and complete unto themselves, but to the deadening assumption that the time for truth has passed. Truth must always be recommitted at the limits of body, language, history. The time for truth will never have passed. Or as Hegel says, the true or the divine does not get lost. This is to say that insofar as truth is nothing outside us, we are, like Anselm, always losing it and must always rewrite it. We learn from Anselm and Badiou, together with Hegel, that history matters always and ever exactly in the way one thinks, in thinking at and on, if not also beyond, the limits of what one knows.

6

The Radical Enlightenment of Spinoza and Kant

I'm not finished.

Edward Scissorhands

What Is Enlightenment?

Kant's essay, "An Answer to the Question 'What Is Enlightenment?'" is remembered for his exhortation "*Sapere Aude!* Have the courage to use your *own* understanding! . . . in matters of religion, as in all matters."[1] Although readers continue to find much to do to comprehend Kant's dare in his time, I am interested, it will be clear, in the question, How is it going?

Is this a recognizable question? The Enlightenment is the designation for the complex of claims that nominate reason as a bulwark against human hatred and strife, religiously motivated or not. To be enlightened still has this connotation of insight along with peaceableness, although it stands as much for quixotic desire. The word Enlightenment had different connotations among its original users, not to mention that there are different words for it in the several languages and that many exemplars never used the term at all, the very notion of "it" being ex post facto, with Kant already at the end. These would be the nervous offerings to the secular god history, the god who stands between Enlightenment and the present age. Its devotees find history missing in Enlightenment reason, the sign that it is not an ongoing project. In effect, the Enlightenment is banished to history rather than being a live interlocutor in its conflicts.

Let it be said, reason as bulwark, as good against evil, as the human better against the human worse, as human know-how against divine authority, supernaturalism, and superstition, as the true against the merely contingent—reason has plenty of problems before it worries about the question of history. *Which problems are its history.* Reason in the Enlightenment is a problem. History is one name for that problem. Religion is another. This is to revise the concepts of history and religion, and in so doing to express a longer history, a longer epoch not yet fully in view.

I call up the Enlightenment with an interest in Kant's exhortation as speaking to the powers of the mind in reality. Critics of Enlightenment more than paragons thereof, Kant at the end of the Enlightenment together with Spinoza at the beginning give us among the richest versions of reason as a form of historical thinking; give us, that is, history as a reason to worry. They nominate reason's work as the contention with otherness, whether natural, political, theological, or psychical, and thus as constituted by contested relations. Reason, like religion, is not alone with itself. It is divided, division, distinction. This Enlightenment would be a radical one, but its fruits have yet to be fully realized. In the words of Edward Scissorhands, eponymous protagonist of filmmaker Tim Burton's revision of Frankenstein, whose inventor dies before he is able to give his creation hands, it is not finished.

What is thought to be most radical about the Enlightenment is its critique of religion—idea, institutions, and social power. The Enlightenment is the promotion of a commanding human reason in the face of considerable hostility and entrenchment. These images resolve into one. Religion shall be subject to reason alone. The inheritance of, and resistance to, the Enlightenment derives from this image.

But as with religion, because of religion, there is unfinished business in this signal Western epoch, which wobbles in standing for the larger one, modernity. Religion is an energized and troubled aspect of our contemporary worlds, confined in the West, if imperfectly, to the protected locations where some Enlightenment epigones, in the name of reason, deposited it. The question What is Enlightenment?, together with the dare to use one's own understanding in matters of religion as in all matters, recovers and reexamines the deposit.

This is to recall the centrality of the concept of God to Spinoza's and Kant's projects—to their critiques of a theology, but no less a philosophy, that confuses the orders of nature and freedom. Both thinkers, whether they are taken as radical or as moderate, were critical of theology and religion as they were typically promulgated by churches and synagogues, priests and rabbis, ordinary believers and intellectual adepts. But they were not critics of theology and religion as such. They were critics of thinking that now in religious, now in political, now in philosophical form divides human nature: in Spinoza, divides humans from their nature, which, as Kant puts it, divides them from reason's critique of nature. Such divisions obscure the distinctions that make ethical and political life peaceable and free.

These critiques, together with the Protestant and scientific revolutions, ostensibly augur a secular age. What needs clarification is that this secularism would then represent a secularization simply of the religious form of what Spinoza called inadequate thinking and Kant called antinomy. Religion taken in itself. The intrinsically sacred. The true in itself. The supernatural. The theologies confusingly asserting these values as the end of nature—teleologies—would be set aside, but no more than the tyrannical politics and philosophies that do the same.

The confrontation is with the conceptual and political dimensions of why peace and freedom are so difficult, why the Enlightenment was so uneven in its achievements. A critique of religion is hard to prosecute, its work and subject easily lost in broadsides, distinctions unplumbed or caricatured—the sacred captured for the interests of the day, which such a sacred will both mirror and contradict. This unevenness is inclusive of our own confusions about religion, reason, and history. And it is inclusive of our indecision regarding the Enlightenment as a construct outside a certain temporal period. Although we know the Enlightenment as a populous and quasi-fictional entity from times past with innumerable competing voices and visions, and although we are sophisticated in our conception of its threads, emphases, and limitations, we also sense it as our problem, even if we don't agree on what that problem comes to.[2]

A study of religion comes to a dead end without the work to plumb the history of modern thought. One needs a thinker like Anselm or his more familiar heir, Descartes, thinkers who reply to their stock characterization as exemplars of invidious Western dualism by articulating the very terms of such a critique. The problem, these thinkers show, is not distinction per se but which distinction is in operation. The Descartes who exemplifies a modern dualism of soul and body is critiqued by Descartes himself, who commits rather to a person's ineluctable contest with distinction as she struggles to make adequate—to act on—what she knows: that thinking and existence, reason and history must be, because they can be, affirmed together.

As Kant and Spinoza likewise argue, the problem is not the body or nature, as the Stoics would have it. The problem, in Kant's language, is the human being insofar as she is free, or striving to use her freedom, and her battle is with both the limits she finds in her (in)capacity as an individual and those she erects as forms of self-denial and domination. Since nature is absolute—it is law—a person faces herself not as other than natural but as creative of, or failing to be creative of, what is given to her. In Spinoza's idiom, this puts her in contest not with nature, which is incontestable, but with herself and others as she strives to become powerful enough to make nature also for others: to make her nature an ethical one, which Spinoza casts as the love of God, as of reality. The struggle is not between nature and freedom, but between nature, human nature, and the discontentedness of their relation in and as history. Each of these thinkers is concerned to understand this discontent, and each struggles to master the concept of nature in the widest sense—reality—that such an understanding implies.

Anselm, Descartes, Spinoza, and Kant give us a modern subject implicated in the dualism that is the freedom to realize the principle of the mutual relation of self and other—in Burton's gothic figure, the freedom that is in one's own hands, finished with the help of others. This subject is in refusal of the competing dualism that erects enlightenment as the one, the master of nature, the totem and the telos of the many. Both dualisms might invoke "God." Both are religious or secular, neither religious nor secular. The words do not tell you which. Both might be postulates of subjects or postulates of scholars.

The question is, What of modernity in its conventional periodization? If these thinkers are the inheritors of God's call to Abraham to leave the land, if they continue that call in criticizing it, in making land the very subject of criticism, then is the break of modernity secular or religious? We can see in reason the same struggle with otherness and fragmentation as we see with the concept of God. We can see in religion the same struggles as in reason to reduce what we know of the other to a dualism that divides between (or identifies) us and them, as between ideal and real. To deploy either reason or religion is to struggle with which they shall be. Kant's account exemplifies the effort to conceive reason and religion each as the contest with the other in together being the commitment of otherness. To read Kant alongside Spinoza is to apprehend the common effort both commit to making religion and reason a question not of God's or reason's mysterious whereabouts or separate nature but of the charge, no less rational than religious, to make the world adequate to what we know of it.

Insofar as religion bespeaks the contention with otherness that works to enact a common life of mutual recognition, it is of value. But these qualifications are significant. Obstacles to this recognition come directly from religion itself, including ideas of otherworldliness or transcendence in a Platonic sense of being unavailable to an embodied intellect; or the use of religion to divide—to oppress or neglect others; or the idolatry of assuming that religion is the thing itself rather than a common human task, both rational and creative, to work for more sustaining and inclusive worlds. Reason is no less equivocal. Kant reveals the extent to which reason gets tangled in fantasies equally of grandeur and self-erasure as a constitutive part of knowing self and other.

Kant remains a valuable resource for thinking about religion, reason, and history. But he is no good to us if we place his notion of reason in a secular framework, according to which the Enlightenment critique is of *religion* rather than of all forms of thinking that oppose or identify what matters with what exists. It is equally confused to include Kant or Spinoza in a genealogy of philosophical-theological rationalism in the tradition of Plato and Aristotle, whether Christian, Jewish, or Islamic.[3] Just as Descartes is a critic of the Cartesianism twentieth-century hermeneuts erect in order to deconstruct, Kant is a critic of the Kant he became, an exponent of purified reason in harmony with or external to religion. In my formulation that the truth appears, and is thus neither reducible to nor the opposite of appearance, Kant is the author of a practical reason that puts both reason and religion to the test of the actual. Spinoza is likewise a critic not only of religion but also of the secular radicalism that was foisted on him, whether by religion's fellow critics or by its exponents. The true radicalism of his work to show that a collective might be constituted by and held accountable to a principle of inclusivity is not yet clearly visible.

In the light of these claims, it is useful to invoke Nietzsche, standing between the Enlightenment and its twentieth-century revaluations. His critique of Kant centers on the charge that Kant saves freedom only by the construction of a "doer behind the deed," a rational realm of freedom in opposition to the actual one.[4] Nietzsche shares with Hegel, Marx, and Kierkegaard the conviction that, after reason has had its say, we recognize that all reason is someone's or some epoch's reason—that interpretation and historicity are fundamental to what and who reason is. Yet these thinkers also understand that it is no less true that interpretation and historicity themselves have reasons and are thus not without their own conceptual structure and limits.

Nietzsche is significant because of the degree to which his ideas are received as pointing directly away from Kant and toward the century in which psychoanalysis, historicity, phenomenology, hermeneutics, and deconstruction work their way through reason's passages. But if Nietzsche is seen as the beginning of the end of the life of reason as it had been hopefully (or hubristically) construed in an earlier age, he is also the thinker who, in disrupting reason's pretenses, recalls us to the role of abruption in Kantian reason, to reason not as a bare faculty but as a specific event or act that is no less historical than it is rational. If Nietzsche nevertheless swings his ax at his great Enlightenment predecessor, if Hegel claims credit as the thinker who contends with the historicity of the concept against Kant, if Kierkegaard in turn gives us a Hegel who cannot think the incommensurability that is reason in history, it is readers of these thinkers who must navigate the shadowboxing to identify the elementary work at play in all of them.

In sum: If Kant, or even Anselm, knows what Nietzsche knows in committing to a history that is the realization of truth, if Nietzsche is not a correction to but an interpretation of what Kant held in holding reason to be a form of (self-)criticism, the twentieth-century critique of "metaphysics" needs reformation—reformulation, revision. Just as significant, if Nietzsche knows what Kant knows in committing to a truth that is realized in appearance, then we have to rethink the Nietzschean maxim that all is interpretation by which Said's heirs continue to slay the zombie Orientalism. We have to move the ineluctability of interpretation from a position of skepticism to an articulation of the contest of reason in its histories. Although this contest may seem nothing more than the power by which one interpretation is disempowered by another, this disempowerment profanes the alternative, the contest for the "two" that, in neither opposing nor identifying its elements, forges a common history.

One could say that for all that the Enlightenment was confused about enlightenment, the beating that religion took from a wide array of its thinkers, together with the criticisms of Marx and Nietzsche among others, was valuable, if no more so than the critiques of monarchy, of tyranny of all kinds, and of a purified rationalism impervious to embodiment, gender, or history. A critique of religion involves the desire that religion disappear in its standard forms—not only pick up its wares and go private, as it did in the political Enlightenment, but disappear, dissolve, deconstruct. Self-critique. Think itself to its end in becoming collectives of thought and life, protective of nothing in itself but the human struggle to liberate self and other psychically and politically. Some religions preach this message with impressive force. Few do so without a set of mysterious or canonical conditions, even as, under pressure from critique, these conditions are reconceived as options or accidents. This would be a true radical Enlightenment, one different from the historical thesis that goes by that name in being interested in the critique of religion as one of religion's main projects, one of its principal values.

This prospectus for a radical Enlightenment launches the question not just of whether religion, but of which religion. The difference of religion is not marked either by an indefinite pluralism or by an us and them. Rather, religion, like reason, can mean two things, the principle or what it refuses. And it therefore involves two distinctions. Religion is subject, first, to the distinction between modernity and nonmodernity, history and nonhistory. Insofar as religion is conceived historically, it can have value as a meditation on otherness, including the otherness of history itself as the work of specificity and relationship. Religion is subject, second, to the distinction between two uses of history, one to dominate or be dominated by the other, and one to liberate and be liberated by the other. Said's work is useful in dramatizing this second distinction. Orientalism, I have argued, is a result not of being ignorant of the other, but of using whatever knowledge we have to dispossess him. Orientalism is an abrogation of the other's sovereignty predicated on a historical concept of her. It thus presupposes its other, the neighbor, a knowledge of the other that can be liberating.

Both uses of history are to be distinguished from a relation to the other that is predicated on the dualism of the one and the many, of opposition/identity: the truth that cannot exist, the collective that is merely itself in infinite replication. This dualism is possible only in specific conceptual regimes—what I am calling nonmodernity, although it appears as a fantasy in modernity insofar as it resigns the work of two. Modernity has boundaries. These boundaries are not merely markers in time, they are markers in the mind and in the other and in their relation. What readers and thinkers struggle with is the relation of the second distinction, which presupposes modernity and its confusions, to the first distinction, the missing distinction of modernity. Without the first, the distinction *of* modernity, it is impossible to identify, and thus to rectify, the confusions and violence of the second—of self and other, truth in history.

I enlist Spinoza and Kant in this work. I have argued that the common does not abide. It is not there to be discovered. It is to be distinguished, postulated, made. So Spinoza and Kant argue, and so too do I employ them in my readings. I use them insofar as they help us plumb this common work, however much this agrees or disagrees with how they have been taken. In launching these readings, I recall Vico's distinction between "the Hebrew religion" and the "gentile nations." Vico, we have seen, levels a complex defense of each, predicated on their distinction. The Hebrews serve as a goad to the nations to avoid the conceits by which they prop up their certitudes, their borders. If the Hebrews do not stand alone, if they are in themselves just another nation, just another idol, this recognition is in fidelity to the principle of inclusion by which "the true God" is shown to be simply the idea—if never simple—of inclusion, of the equality of all before the law. The distinction of critique is that by which the all is made common. But the all is no sovereign abstraction. It has no land of its own. It is, as promised land, the distinction of two, the openness of self and other over against the dualisms that would reduce the all to the collective or elevate the collective to the all, the dualisms of the one and the many.[5]

Spinoza, son of the Hebrews, and Kant, son of the gentiles, together show the limits of both Judaism and Christianity insofar as they confuse the distinction of the principle with the one and the many. This confusion takes the form of the dualism of supernaturalism and naturalism. It takes the form of the dualism between this world and another world, or between religion and reason, revelation and the mind, God or what is beyond God and human beings. Ironically, Spinoza and Kant are often read as exemplars of these dualisms, whether in haste to get beyond them or in defense of the virtues of one side or the other—Spinoza the naturalist, Kant the rationalist. As they both show, however, without the critique of the dualism of one and many, there is nothing but the dualism of competing monisms by which collectives are taken as ends in themselves in subordination to ideals they cannot actualize. What Spinoza and Kant know is that this position cannot be critiqued on its own terms. Hence distinction, the distinction that distinguishes critique, with its confusions, from the mere replication or oscillation of positions. This critique, this commitment, is modern, biblical, deconstructive, and rational. There is nothing beyond it. Within it, everything.

I turn first to Spinoza to pursue his naturalism by distinguishing it from two strands of interpretation: historians of the Radical Enlightenment and materialist theorists of the multitude. Each strand circulates a "new" Spinoza, bringing his work fruitfully into conversation with desiderata in the present. But each in turn misses Spinoza's true radicalism, his identification of the distinctions in operation in nature by which human beings can come to practice freedom and solidarity. I then turn to Kant, whose concepts of religion and reason constitute what I have called the principle of modernity—the relation between principle and actuality, the single idea of human concord: love your neighbor as yourself, interpret the other as you would be interpreted, practice freedom for others as you would for yourself, and indeed as much as possible for all others.

Together, Spinoza and Kant identify this principle as what is power, in which as much as possible means the more so, the more power to do so. Each thinker is mindful that insofar as this single idea is realizable, the actual is history as the principle's realization, but no less betrayal. History has the principle as its principal subject. The idea is realizable in history insofar as the idea is of the idea realized, human concord attainable, attained as what is and may be actual. The distinction, we continue to see, is of the principle as what is actual from positions that oppose or identify—principles and actuals, selves and neighbors. There is no principle in history without this distinction of the principle that is history. There is no concord without setting aside opposition and identity, no love of neighbor without identifying, suffering, what are other ways of construing love and neighbor. In Spinoza and Kant we conceive a radical Enlightenment, a radical modernity. They will show our confusions and our mistakes in recommitting us to understanding and thus rectifying them.

Spinoza the Radical

> Whether a man be wise or ignorant, he is part of Nature. . . . Yet most people believe that the ignorant violate the order of Nature rather than conform to it; they think of men in Nature as a state within a state. They hold that the human mind is not produced by natural causes but is directly created by God and is so independent of other things that it has an absolute power to determine itself and to use reason in a correct way.[6]

Much of what is considered radical about the Radical Enlightenment concerns religion. If the Enlightenment "marks," in the words of Jonathan I. Israel, "the most dramatic step towards secularization and rationalization in Europe's history," indeed "no less in the wider history not just of western civilization but, arguably, of the entire world," its radical exponents differ from their more moderate brethren in being more definitive in their critique of inherited religious regimes.[7] The distinction of a Radical Enlightenment underscores how more moderate voices forged common cause with the institutions and theological norms of the churches (and in a few cases synagogues). Israel identifies René Descartes (1596–1650), Nicolas Malebranche (1638–1715), Jean Le Clerc (1657–1736), John Locke (1632–1704), Isaac Newton (1642–1727), Christian Thomasius (1688–1728), G. W. Leibniz (1646–1716), and Christian

Wolff (1679–1754) as thinkers who, whatever else they were committed to in the period of "Scientific Revolution," also "sought to substantiate and defend the truth of revealed religion and the principle of a divinely created and ordered universe."[8] Not so Spinoza and the others of the Radical Enlightenment, who followed Descartes and Newton in propounding a world knowable through the agency of science but who did not hesitate to deduce from that world a revised theological view.

The main tenet of this revision was a negative one: there is no God, at least as this concept had traditionally been understood. From this followed a further set of propositions. What can be called God is not separate from the universe, thus is not supernatural. There are no miracles or revelation because nature is inexorably lawful and, again, there is no God separate from nature to bring these things about. Spinoza asserts, perhaps in an attempt at diplomacy, that the regularity of nature is a far greater sign of God's greatness and power than miracles would be. Indeed—though here his diplomacy seems to end—the idea of God as associated with the suspension of the laws of nature has rather the effect of casting "doubt on God and on all things."[9]

The list goes on. No revealed Bible. No immortality of the soul. No risen Christ. No punishment and reward from God. No prophecy. Israel's scope seems right. These claims were surely among the more important in, as he puts it, "the history of man," and certainly the intellectual history of the Western man who had heretofore held variants of the positions now denied.[10] In this light one cannot but observe the incompleteness of the Enlightenment—how much religion survives and even flourishes; how many theories of this survival compete for our attention; and how radical Spinoza would remain today.

Still, the focus on Spinoza's critique of miracles and metaphysics will tend to be less attentive to what is positively the true miracle for him, the true sign of reason and God alike: the power to understand reality in common and to form communities of justice and charity, notwithstanding innumerable obstacles. Spinoza's commendation of the power of thinking in common is situated in the context of his examination of human natural existence—appetite, bondage, causation, and determination. Nature is total in this portrait. There is no escape from it. Yet nature as a totality does not rule out what he calls freedom or, as he also puts it, ethics: the union of self and others such that each is more empowered. Understanding what this ethics, this freedom, has to do with Spinoza's critique of religion is a much needed dimension of understanding what the Radical Enlightenment, insofar as Spinoza is identified with it, bequeathed the "history of man."

Spinoza's concepts of nature continue to confuse readers who, in seeking an ally in the release from supernaturalism and its history, are at a loss for how the opposite, naturalism, can support the goods one wants from such a release: universality, equality, democracy, the dynamism of social movement contra natural rank, and the freedom of the people. My treatment of Spinoza is conceived in relation to contemporary materialist readings of him. These readings reflect and celebrate the portrait of Spinoza made prominent in the concept of the Radical Enlightenment, accentuating his philosophy of nature and his commitment to egalitarian politics. Spinoza was, and remains, an incomparable radical. The question today is whether we yet know what Spinoza's radicalism truly consists in.

The Materialist Spinoza

In the past two generations, Spinoza's social and political thought has given rise to a number of strong, divergent interpretations. Leo Strauss's jeremiad in *Persecution and the Art of Writing* stresses Spinoza's absolutist state, his elitism, his conception of religion as a sop to the masses, and his use of equivocal language.[11] Steven B. Smith recommends the *Theological-Political Treatise* as "one of the great documents of Enlightenment liberalism."[12] Israel gives us a Spinoza of the Radical Enlightenment, whose "prime contribution to the evolution of early modern Naturalism, fatalism, and irreligion . . . was his ability to integrate within a single coherent or ostensibly coherent system, the chief elements of ancient, modern, and oriental 'atheism.' "[13] Materialist readings such as those of Louis Althusser, Alexandre Matheron, Antonio Negri, Étienne Balibar, Warren Montag, and Hasana Sharp depict a Spinoza committed to the power of the multitude and a posthumanist politics.[14] All four interpretations make Spinoza's critique of religion central to his significance, with the second two, that of the Radical Enlightenment and the materialist, connecting this critique to Spinoza's work on the concept of nature. Having taken on the first two approaches in an earlier essay, here I work to supplement the second two in their attention to Spinoza's concept of nature as a cornerstone of his critique of religion.[15]

Materialist readings give us a Spinoza whose contention that human beings are "part of nature" signifies a revolutionary portrait of the human condition " 'beyond' the tradition of bourgeois thought," as Negri puts it; beyond the humanist, liberal individual divided between thought and practice, private and public, personal freedom and political sovereignty.[16] As Sharp puts it, "Even if humanism typically rejects a supernatural order in favor of human community on earth, from the perspective of Spinozism it relocates supernaturalism within the human mind."[17] Materialist readings, by contrast, stress Spinoza's deconstruction of an exceptional human mind, together with the conceptions of transcendence and teleology that undergird it. They stress his commitment, then, to immanence, to the mind not as master of a bodily house but as an expression of embodiment. The mind is the very idea of the body, as Spinoza has it. Although this claim—that "the object of the idea constituting the human Mind is the Body"[18]—is hardly simple, it has been galvanizing for those who work to conceive an integrated subjectivity in the context of a philosophy whose primary reference is politics.[19] In a history of critical theorists from early modernity to the present, Spinoza exemplifies for such readers the radical materialist extraordinaire.

Materialism, however, is a potentially misleading way to describe what Spinoza puts in place of a human-centered universe manned by a God who, as Spinoza depicts the teleological illusion, "directs all things" for their use.[20] Materialism may express one aspect of nature in Spinoza, illuminating his reshaping of reason through the language of *appetitus* and *conatus*. But what is matter? As Margaret C. Jacob observes of the materialism of the eighteenth century, it "had many origins and faces." There is the version that emphasizes "the mechanical and self-moved properties of matter." There is the "pantheism" that emphasizes "the vitalistic, spirit-in-matter qualities of nature," which "tended inevitably to deify the material order." It is this latter move, "the deification of nature," Jacob notes, that is "most obviously associated" with Spinoza.[21]

Spinoza does not use the term materialism. His terms for what had been called "matter" are extension (*extensio*) and corporeal substance (*substantia corporea*), both ways of expressing God's infinite and indivisible existence. In the generations after Spinoza, materialism (or materialist) was a term of rebuke, used of those like Spinoza and Hobbes who diverged from the teleological universe and its concomitant conception of the human soul as an entity set apart from the operations of the natural world.[22] Spinoza's reply is the centerpiece of his posthumously published masterwork, the *Ethics*, in which he writes that such conventions "seem to conceive man as a dominion within a dominion," disturbing rather than following nature's order.[23] How, he asks, could such a picture account for the patent inability of human beings to quiet the overwhelming fact of being affected in innumerable ways, which serve now to increase and now to decrease our power of action?

Spinoza poses such questions not to denigrate human beings, but to advance their peace of mind and indeed their power by seeking to understand them as they really are.[24] To readers like Pierre Bayle (1647–1706), however, Spinoza's philosophy as it appeared in the *Opera Posthuma* (1677), emerging from the striking doctrine that there is one substance, God or nature, and all else is a modification of it, constituted "the most monstrous hypothesis that could be imagined, the most absurd, and the most diametrically opposed to the most evident notions of our mind."[25] Or, more simply, "all those are called Spinozists who have hardly any religion and who do not do much to hide this."[26] For Bayle, Spinoza's crime is the heresy of substance monism, a position that eclipses a God who, creator of the world, is himself not subject to the world. Materialism would count as the name for the doctrine of the one substance insofar as it is taken in a theologically deflationary sense, although, following Jacob, readers could just as well take the same position as the deification of nature. The question is whether there is any difference between these positions and whether either captures what Spinoza is doing with nature.

In the nineteenth century, materialism comes to attach to the name Karl Marx, and it is in light of Marx's philosophy of economy and history that it is reclaimed in the twentieth century as a term of approbation in the description of Spinoza by students and colleagues of the French philosopher and political theorist Louis Althusser. In the 1997 edited volume *The New Spinoza*, it is largely the materialist reading that accounts for what makes Spinoza new. The claim is that an appreciation of Spinoza's critical contribution in his day involves the apprehension of a new Spinoza in ours, new in replacing the Spinoza received through the Enlightenment, new, that is, in radicalizing it. Spinoza is made new for contemporary readers in stressing his commitment to the primacy of bodies, power, and practice. "Spinoza's materialist metaphysics is the potent anomaly of the [seventeenth] century," Negri proclaims, both founding "modern materialism in its highest form" and constituting a radical alternative to bourgeois modernity to this day.[27]

Such readings might be slyly juxtaposed to Spinoza's demurral at the close of chapter 14 of the *Theological-Political Treatise*, to wit, "My purpose in writing these chapters has not been to introduce innovations but to correct abuses."[28] Or it could be said that novelty is given a new valence in materialist readings of Spinoza's work: not what categorically breaks with what came before but what transforms it—novelty as immanent critique. On this view, the difficulty of understanding Spinoza's thought is rooted neither in the challenge of retrieving his seventeenth-century context nor in the arcane protocols of the *Ethics*'s geometric method but rather in "the opacity of the present to itself."[29] Readers today are still blinded by the mystifications—metaphysical and political— that Spinoza so prophetically challenged.

It is intriguing, this invocation of Spinoza's "paradoxical and unsuspected contemporaneity."[30] It is as if the post-Enlightenment critiques of reason, religion, and economy finally created the conditions by which we can read the writings of an early Enlightenment critic; as if Spinoza can come into focus only once he is seen to be a radical critic of the very Enlightenment he supposedly inaugurates; as if, in short, we can see just how "anomalous" Spinoza is only when we place him not simply in his time but also in our own. Is it that we had to wait for Marx, Nietzsche, Freud, Max Weber, the Frankfurt school, Foucault, Althusser, and Deleuze—we had to wait until the critique of modern rationalism had attained critical mass—to appreciate a Spinoza who might have saved roughly two hundred years of conceptual illusions? The point is that we see Spinoza now; we are ready for him precisely insofar as we see that his difficulty is political as much as philosophical. We see therefore exactly why it took so long.

In sum, then, the materialist reading of Spinoza stresses his commitment to, in Althusser's words, "the necessity of the factual stripped of every transcendent guarantee (God) or transcendental guarantee (the 'I think')." Althusser puts the point in an extended metaphor:

> An idealist philosopher is like a man who knows in advance *both* where the train he is climbing onto is coming from *and* where it is going: what is its station of departure and its station of destination (or . . . as for a letter, its final destination). The materialist, on the contrary, is a man who takes the train *in motion* (the course of the world, the course of history, the course of life) but without knowing where the train is coming from or where it is going. He climbs onto a train of chance, of encounter, and discovers in it the *factual* installations of the coach and of whatever companions he is *factually* surrounded with, of whatever the conversations and ideas of these companions and of whatever language marked by their social milieu (as the prophets of the Bible) they speak. All that was for me, or rather became little by little, as if inscribed in filigree in Spinoza's thought.[31]

In eschewing first and final causes, Spinoza gives us facts, languages, singularities, bodies; encounter, companionship, exhortation. Nonmaterialist readings of Spinoza, it follows, violate these emphases, confusing his language of God, man, and mind for modern philosophies and anthropologies of consciousness and individualism. Such readings reduce Spinoza to one more bit player in the unfolding drama of modernity, missing his prescient critique of this drama and the entire "subterranean history" whereby Spinoza and his heirs challenge readers to finally liberate themselves from the domination of superstition internal to the modern.[32]

The Doer and the Deed

> Since human power should be assessed by strength of mind rather than robustness of body, it follows that those in whom reason is most powerful and who are most guided thereby are most fully in control of their own right.[33]

The materialist reading of Spinoza coheres in many respects with the Spinoza retrieved by historians of the Radical Enlightenment. Each emphasizes social, religious, and philosophical reform in the service of populism and a mobile pantheism, to use a term specific to Enlightenment literature.[34] It is also possible to identify classically liberal, Enlightenment principles that do not contradict materialist ones. Spinoza's political thought is no more invested in the power of the multitude than in the sovereign powers of the individual, even if such powers are only ever realized in concert with others. Indeed, it is Spinoza's singular accomplishment to show how the apparent rift between the standpoint of the individual and the standpoint of the sovereign is rectified only when sovereignty is at once absolute and democratic.[35]

Materialist readings are faithful to Spinoza's corpus insofar as they recognize that if, as Montag reminds us, "there can be no liberation of the mind without a liberation of the body," it is no less true to say that there can be no liberation of the body without a liberation of the mind.[36] The materialist vantage could be a matter of emphasis, gaining force from the shock of its contrast with the portrait of Spinoza as a paragon of contemplative rationalism, provoked to generate a political theory only in order to shape the public sphere within which philosophy might go on undisturbed.[37] In reading Spinoza's philosophy, by contrast, as dynamic, critical, affective, practical, immanent, embodied, and political, materialist readers return us especially to parts 3 and 4 of the *Ethics* ("On the Origin and Nature of the Affects" and "On Human Bondage, or the Powers of the Affects," respectively) and place the *Theological-Political Treatise* and the *Political Treatise* at the heart of Spinoza's oeuvre—not simply the political arm of his philosophy but key expressions of it. If one now insists that the political texts by which one works through the metaphysics of the *Ethics* must themselves be worked on in and through the metaphysics, one is perhaps enabling the materialist readings to come to fruition. The Enlightenment Spinoza, whose investment in mind, reason, and, with the moderates, God is the same Spinoza as the one invested in bodies, affects, multitudes, and sovereigns.

Yet the question is whether the materialist readings of Spinoza, together with Bayle's image of the substance monist and the Radical Enlightenment's pantheist, do not obfuscate a set of distinctions Spinoza makes *within* the natural or the material in his work. Spinoza is less a critic of eighteenth-century Enlightenment *avant la lettre*, or even of Descartes, than he is a critic of Platonism and its neo-Platonic theological epigones—in the Renaissance, in antiquity, in the Middle Ages, and in our own modern and postmodern worlds. Spinoza's critique is of immaterial rationalism, along with the political elitism that is the counterpart of the conception of the mind as a "dominion within a dominion." But this critique is in the service of better distinctions, ones that would structure the reality that is inclusive of minds and bodies both. Thinking would be an intervention in the world we are a part of, not the consideration of or the ascent toward a realm transcending this one. As Spinoza puts it, reason "demands nothing contrary to nature."[38] It involves the cultivation of what we use and depend on. This is to say, he writes, that "if we consider our Mind, our intellect would of course be more imperfect if the Mind were alone and did not understand anything except itself."[39]

To comprehend this critique of the solitary, transcendent mind, however, we need to differentiate between the world from which this concept has been evacuated—a pure materialism, it might be said—and the world insofar as it expresses values such as solidarity and democracy, which, while natural, are also rational. Spinoza and Descartes share the ontological argument whose target is the Platonic divided line according to which thought (the "intelligible" realm) and existence (the "visible" realm) are structurally opposed.[40] By this structure, Spinoza's great axiom, "man thinks," is impossible except insofar as we rid ourselves of the fleshly obstacles of the first term.[41] Even for Descartes, who would have us "join" mind and body, there exists a concept of mind that is powered in and by materiality. When Descartes discovers in the *Meditations* that he can be sure only of thought alone, it is with the paradoxical recognition that thought is itself multiply constituted through the full range of affective media: "But what then am I? A thing that thinks. What is that? A thing that doubts, understands, affirms, denies, wills, refuses, and that also imagines and senses."[42] Far from separating the subject from the world, thinking is of the world as sensed and imagined, as encountered.

These claims aim at the following questions. What if, in seeking in Spinoza the correction for mind-body dualism, the materialist Spinoza overcorrects toward the body by failing to distinguish between two concepts of mind: on the one hand, materialism's opposite, the ethereal mind that would cleave to the Forms, or to God, Platonically conceived, and on the other, the mind torn by its confusions in and as the body? It is not only Spinoza who anatomizes confusions of mind as body. This is the obsession of postbiblical metaphysics, from Paul and Augustine through Descartes, Hobbes, and Kant, according to whom the obstacle to enlightenment is not the body in some animal sense but the body's mind.[43] What is *this* concept of mind in its relation with Spinoza's mind-body unity? From which intellectual and political error, the Platonic or the Cartesian, would Spinoza's materialist anomaly be saving us?

If it is the Platonic notion his materialism is directed to, then this materialism is not in the least anomalous, even if certainly outstanding, putting the materialist Spinoza alongside some unlikely theological and philosophical bedfellows. For again, Spinoza's is the work of the ontological argument, the signature of his critique of ancient Greek reason— not that thought can bring about existence, but that thought exists and is of existence. If, by contrast, Spinoza's target is figured as Descartes, who shares with Spinoza an appreciation for the embodiment of thinking, what could be conserved in materialism but the contradictory embrace of bodies as ends in themselves?

What materialism can do at best is expose the extent of Spinoza's antisupernaturalism: his insistence that reality is perfection and not a reflection of or moved by a more perfect (more rational, spiritual, soulful) realm. Reality is subordinate to nothing, compared to nothing, sovereign.[44] Yet these claims do not make Spinoza an antidualist, for distinctions pervade his work—what is divine and what is human, what is in itself and what is in another, what is natural and what is social. If Spinoza's materialism unequivocally rules out supernaturalism and the hierarchy of mind over matter quintessentially found in ancient Greek philosophy, there are complex separations and relations that it thereby very much rules in, above all those found in the relations between nature, religion, reason, and the *civitas*. It can be fruitful to read Spinoza through the lens of Marx, with his subordination of consciousness to life, or by implication Nietzsche, with his erasure of the "doer" behind the "deed."[45] Both thinkers pave the way for a materialism that attends to the social powers by which subjectivity is constituted. Read alongside Spinoza's language of power and striving, they shed light on his social and political, not to say metaphysical, commitments to freedom.

What is confusing is the conflation of the opponents, the identification of all rationalisms with those that bear the structure of the ancient Greeks, whether they are dubbed Christian or Enlightenment or modern. This conflation of the two dualisms is a confusion from which neither Marx nor Nietzsche is exempt, nor are their readers. After Nietzsche's invocation of "that little changeling, the 'subject,'" by which "the popular mind" inserts a fictive soul behind the existence of "the deed," it is a challenge not to take all rationalist and theological precursors as subject to the same popular mind, and Spinoza as thus heroic for refusing the bait.[46]

What structures Spinoza's thought, however, is not just nature but human nature: not just the bare life of sovereign natural right wherein big fish eat little fish, but the sovereign power of human society as bulwark against impotence and ignorance.[47] This is a story, to be sure, about nature and the primacy of material existence, but it also concerns the human power if not to transcend nature then to transform it. One becomes, in so doing, "most natural," as Spinoza expresses the paradox of democracy in the *Theological-Political Treatise*. One becomes, unlike fish, free.[48] Spinoza knows that the word freedom (*libertas*) has served many illusions in philosophy, but that does not keep him from utilizing it. If one rules out reason, or God, as the first and final cause of reality in order to place reason, or God, rather in the midst of the real— "the course of the world, the course of history, the course of life," says Althusser—then the operative question is how to turn the world to one's purposes, together with those of others: how not to be overwhelmed by the world's power. In Althusser's train in motion, that I know neither its origin nor its end may be less important than that I would presumably have to know how to avoid falling off—how, in short, not to get flung off by the very forces that got me on.

Spinoza's rationality, his materialism, it is true, is an embrace of deeds, a rejection of phantom doers. But, as in Nietzsche himself, there is no simple reversal here, no deed alone if this means the natural counterpart to the supernatural illusion. Spinoza's critique of the soul serves a concept of rationality constituted by the movement from nature, whose adjectives in reference to human beings include ignorance, finitude, contradiction, and passivity, to civil life, where human beings gain power in relation to one another. This movement is impossible, as we saw with Vico, from the standpoint of nature insofar as it is conceived through the metaphor of natural law—the "right and established order" whereby "every individual thing" is "naturally determined to exist and to act in a definite way."[49] No one is exempt from this concept of nature. In Spinoza's parlance, none of us is God, understood as the totality of what is.

The necessity of existence binds all in exactly the same way. The mind is the body seen from a different angle. Consciousness and free will are illusions.

Yet collective life is a relief, if not from nature then from its logic of might makes right. The movement of the collective, the movement of reason, is of a nature enacted in common.

Spinoza's not only is a warning against the hubris of transcendence, it is also a call to understand, to the end not of serene contemplation but of empowerment. In the *Ethics*, Spinoza distinguishes between God (*natura naturans*) and God's attributes (*natura naturata*).[50] He distinguishes between what is "in itself" and what is "in another."[51] Although human beings must be said to be "in another," in God, in what exists or part of existence, the distinction is not simply between infinite and finite. Human beings may either be confused, at odds with, and limited by one another or they may be expressive of God's infinite essence through adequate ideas, and thus freely in concert. In the *Theological-Political Treatise*, the distinction is between a nature in which all are determined and a nature that, in determining all, is also itself determined. Spinoza rejects first and final causes as overlays onto nature's indifferent operations. But he is absolutely interested in the origin of nature—in the operation whereby what exists increases in power, to put it in terms of degree, or brings itself into existence, to put it in the terms Spinoza reserves for God, or nature, of which we are all a part. It concedes too much to Spinoza's opponents to remove first and final causes only to continue to use the language of finitude and chance to describe what is, as it were, left over.[52]

In the *Theological-Political Treatise*, nature is discovered only insofar as one's nature begins to be realized in and through the "pact" of social and political life rather than forfeited to another who is stronger. This realization is painstaking to say the least, for "men are . . . by nature enemies,"[53] subject to "strivings, impulses, appetites, and volitions, which vary as the man's constitution varies, and which are not infrequently so opposed to one another that the man is pulled in different directions and knows not where to turn."[54] Here is Spinoza's challenge. We are too natural to find it easy to be civil. We are too dependent on civility to be able to survive without it.

Two Natures in Spinoza's Political Thought

> As we have said, men are by nature enemies, and even when they are joined and bound together by laws they still retain their nature.[55]

I pose two questions in the light of these reflections on materialism and nature in Spinoza, both pursuing the issues raised in reading Vico. First, how is one to understand the relation between nature and culture, nature and the *civitas*? What kind of a distinction is this if in fact the *civitas* is natural and nature is not forfeited in civil society?[56] Second is the question of origins. Althusser and his readers insist that Spinoza grants us knowledge neither of the "station of departure" nor of the "station of destination," which is correct insofar as it means that in nature we do not get to the unmoved mover or *telos*, because there is neither. Spinoza's interest in the origin of social and political life in other terms, however, can be seen in his repeated references to the story of Adam and Eve, whose "fall" from nature Spinoza takes as illuminating just the opposite: that the first man was "like us . . . subject to passions."[57] It can also be seen in his accounts of the origin of social and political life in the *Theological-Political Treatise*, in part 4 of the *Ethics*, "On Human Bondage, or The Powers of the Affects," and repeatedly in the *Political Treatise*, beginning with this declaration:

> since all men everywhere, whether barbarian or civilized, enter into relationships with one another and set up some kind of civil order, one should not look for the causes and natural foundations of the state in the teachings of reason, but deduce them from the nature and condition of men in general.[58]

There have been several ways of understanding the relation between the various accounts Spinoza gives of the origin of social and political life. The views cluster around the observation that the *Theological-Political Treatise*, concerned as it is not only to give a defense of "the Freedom of Philosophising," as the title page has it, but also to explain the proper role of religion in the state, has recourse to the model of two original pacts, one between humankind and God and one among humankind: "For nobody knows by Nature that he has any duty to obey God" or to live in a state.[59] The *Political Treatise*, by contrast, dispenses with pacts altogether. In this account it is proper, as the "Schoolmen" say, "to call man a social animal," that is, a being who finds himself within the multitude, and hence the *civitas* in some loose sense, from the beginning.[60]

In the *Theological-Political Treatise*, then, Spinoza uses the language of *pactum* to refer to the action of human beings both to stand before God and "to unite into one body."[61] Since he gives up pact language in the *Political Treatise*, his last (unfinished) work, one might regard its importance for his thought as immature or mistaken. Just as religion looms as a problem in the *Theological-Political Treatise* only to be sidelined in the *Political Treatise*, so Spinoza's political interests seem to shift from questions of origin to the power and freedom of the multitude as it has always existed. Steven Barbone and Lee Rice frame the shift this way in their introduction to Samuel Shirley's translation of the *Political Treatise*:

> If the TTP [*Theological-Political Treatise*] knocks political authority off its former scriptural and ecclesiastical foundations, then the TP [*Political Treatise*] must offer some other basis on which to found any and all civil right. . . . It is no wonder . . . that Spinoza roots political organization not in God, the Bible, any sacred promise, nor even any long past historical event, but in the human metaphysical condition that finds humans are everywhere and always in a civil state.[62]

Spinoza does not, however, dismiss the Bible in the foundations of the state in the *Theological-Political Treatise*. The Bible's "dogmas" of justice and charity, he holds, are crucial to founding a state that is truly secure and peaceful.[63] This is not only because human beings require social and political laws to ameliorate their impotence and ignorance, as in the case of the Israelites in the desert.[64] It is also because security and peace require those laws that will enable human beings to live in obedience to their "nature," that is, freely in concert with others. Spinoza considers the Bible a document specific to its time and place. But this does not prevent it from articulating a concept of God consistent with what he calls in the *Ethics libertas humana*: the knowledge and love of God as true religion and freedom.[65]

It is equally inadequate to characterize the *Political Treatise* as the finally fully secular working out of political thought made possible once Spinoza has dispatched the problem of religion in the *Theological-Political Treatise*. The problem of religion, Spinoza is clear, is the problem of superstition—ignorance, passivity, dependence, enmity. And superstition is natural, found in any and every state as its greatest challenge. Insofar as Spinoza depicts religion as a problem, he means this ecumenical concept of superstition, its constitutive power to trouble political life anatomized in the *Ethics*, parts 3 and 4. Insofar as religion is not a problem for Spinoza, it counts as the universal divine law of justice and charity, whose philosophical expression attains exquisite concentration in one of the key philosophical-political propositions of the *Ethics*: "man is God to man."[66]

Let us consider the pact imagery, focusing on the problem it solves—and perhaps also creates—for him. The pact effectively dramatizes the conflict at the heart of every polity, every multitude. It represents Spinoza's attempt to capture the tension between divine universal law and human laws—between the laws of justice and charity, on the one hand, and the laws of peace and security on the other.[67] This is the tension, in my terms, between the principle of inclusivity and collectives that are constituted with the pressure to be inclusive but that are tempted to make their borders sacral.

What both the *Ethics* and the *Theological-Political Treatise* make plain is that the difference between divine and human laws is *not* the difference between God and human beings, wisdom and ignorance, power and impotence, adequacy and inadequacy. It is not the difference, moreover, between truth and its shadows or replicas, or between absolute and contingent goods. Human laws can be just, charitable, and liberating, hence natural, adequate, tenacious, and salvific, to use four of Spinoza's honorifics. By the same token, divine law is simply "the rules for living a life" devoted to the "knowledge and love of God . . . insofar as he exists in our minds."[68] The pact, or rather the two pacts, the one God enters into with human beings (the origin of religion) and the other enacted between human and human (the origin of the civil state) have the effect of uniting the divine and the human, the universal and the singular, in their differences.[69] The pacts serve as the mark of principle. Each law, divine and human, is a law "which men lay down for themselves or for others to some end," in the one case concerning "the supreme good" inclusive of all and in the other case concerning the "safeguard[ing] of life and the commonwealth."[70] What they share is a "transfer" (*translatio*), a passage, a movement whereby what is natural qua ignorant, passive, unfree becomes natural qua free, active, rational.[71]

The movement the pacts signify, then, is from nature to nature, a paradox Spinoza expresses in considering the biblical story of the first human beings. What he allows is that Adam and Eve, "like us," begin in ignorance, impaired in their ability to use reason, confused by the command to choose the good "from love of good, and not from fear of evil."[72] This is, on the one hand, a rejoinder to those who depict the story as a fall from a more perfect state. Human beings are part of nature and hence are driven by appetite while being, for the most part and certainly in the beginning, unconscious of the causes of this appetite—and thus utterly destabilized by it.[73] On the other hand, God's prohibition with regard to the Tree of Knowledge announces the salience of good and evil in the constitution of the human condition. In Eden, human beings do not yet know the good that is their desire. They do not know or know how to affirm that desire is good, conjuring a good outside themselves rather than a law they themselves can lay down—a law that is "most natural." Nevertheless, Eden is already an economy of transition. The command is to "acquire a virtuous disposition" even if, Spinoza notes of all human beings, "a great part of their life has gone by" before this can be accomplished.[74]

The struggle with good and evil at the origin is the sign that, although human beings are not "born free," freedom exists in the beginning as the fruit of the hard labor of living according to one's nature, which turns out to be possible only with the support and structure of law, if not also of prohibition.[75] As Spinoza observes, "A man who is guided by reason is more free in a state, where he lives according to a common decision, than in solitude, where he obeys only himself."[76]

The story of the Fall shows that, mutatis mutandis, there is a before (nature) and an after (freedom), although they are not sequential and not opposed. It is not that, since we are born and remain in the natural state, the point is to expose the Bible illicitly creating an origin story for a fictional doer behind the deed that can now be retired. It is that, on the contrary, the Fall has already happened and is always happening in our nature. We are already, originally, deceived; we are already, originally, "subject to the passions." We are not the cause of ourselves or our condition. And yet this *causa sui* is exactly what desire, the law of human nature, lays down in the heart of the illusions and the passions— the incipient power to enact something "of which we are the adequate cause."[77] Spinoza notes that theologians compound the confusion with talk of original sin, for this assumes that "our first parent" was of fully "sound mind and master of his own will," when in fact "it was not in the power of the first man to use reason aright."[78] And yet it is possible to credit the language of original sin with the same dialectic Spinoza has in mind: that to awaken to a choice between good and evil is already to have made (the wrong) one.

The Fall names for Spinoza this curious conjunction of nature and freedom. It names the difference between the minuscule power with which nature endows individuals and the power of freedom they can achieve, albeit with great effort and cooperation. This is a movement within nature itself, although no less is it a movement within freedom. It is a movement, as Spinoza puts it, "from a lesser to a greater perfection,"[79] an "act in accordance" with one's nature.[80] The model is Spinoza's God, who, "as he exists from the necessity of his own nature, so he also acts from the necessity of his own nature; that is, he acts from absolute freedom."[81]

This is a solution of a kind to the problem Spinoza raises in using the language of nature to refer both to the regime of fish and physics and to the human attainment of freedom in solidarity. Like Hegel's idealism, Spinoza's materialism—his conception of nature, reality, actuality as the very site of enlightenment—is both a critique of the world as we find it and an affirmation of its fundamental value for us. There is no difference between the world as we find it and what Hegel and Spinoza both call reason except the difference this very recognition makes, together with the practices to realize it.[82] Insofar as I see that this is the only world there is, I immediately thereby create another *this world*—I am reordered, one might say, in my relation to reality and thus I reorder it. Insofar as I see (and experience) that human beings are part of nature—ignorant, impotent, conquered by things outside their control—I am no longer simply part of nature in the sense of turtles, for example, which are ignorant that they are ignorant. At that moment my eyes are opened, to use the biblical imagery. I have simultaneously become natural and must realize (achieve) my nature:

> But the main thing to note is that when I say that someone passes from a lesser to a greater perfection, and the opposite, I do not understand that he is changed from one essence, or form, to another. For example, a horse is destroyed as much if it is changed into a man as if it is changed into an insect. Rather, we conceive that his power of acting, insofar as it is understood through his nature, is increased or diminished.[83]

But is it right, then, to speak of a *moment*? Does not the concept of the pact—with its connotation of two worlds—betray what Spinoza is trying to illustrate, namely that nature for me is not natural: that I was never "in nature" to begin with, for I am always naturally civilized, moving from a lesser to a greater—and unfortunately just as often from a greater to a lesser—potency, from superstition to truth, from ignorance (impotence) to knowledge (empowerment) and vice versa?

It is best to say both yes, the concept of pact betrays Spinoza's conviction that human life, impossible in the state of nature, begins and ends with "some kind of civil order," *and* no, the pact expresses a distinction fundamental to Spinoza's metaphysics and politics.[84] The distinction would not be between nature and the *civitas*. Human nature is civil—civil society is natural—from beginning to end. Just so are materialist readings authorized. There is no human nature outside civilization, history, making, no spirit above the letter, no doer behind, before, or in service of the deed. Equally, then, the *civitas* is not simply a rational or philosophical entity but a practical one—"bodies, masses, power," as Montag's title iterates. Spinoza's allusions to Machiavelli in chapter 1 of the *Political Treatise* loom large in these readings.

But the pact expresses the distinction between two natures—between natural law, on the one hand, and human and divine (natural) law, on the other: between the realm of God insofar as it expresses "a universal law governing all bodies" and the realm of God insofar as it expresses "a rule of conduct which men lay down for themselves or for others to some end."[85] God is one, Spinoza strenuously shows in the *Ethics*, part 1: infinite, free, necessary, and unique. Human beings, "necessarily subject to the passions" and the "common order of Nature" to which we "accommodate [ourselves] . . . as much as the nature of things requires," are also capable of singularity and of freedom.[86] Insofar as human beings are torn, conflicted, and contrary to one another, they express the way they are part of a nature that is sublimely unconcerned with their well-being and to which they are accommodated. But insofar as human beings strive to be useful to one another in seeking their own advantage, they find that "there is no singular thing in Nature that is more useful to man than a man who lives according to the guidance of reason."[87]

Nature, then, is not indifferent to human beings except insofar as human beings are indifferent to their nature. Once Spinoza expresses his critique of nature (and God) as the source of the good, he can then turn to the good as the source of nature (and God)—the good that is "the model of human nature that we set before ourselves."[88] The *Ethics* culminates in parts 4 and 5 with the passage from nature (the passive affects that make us contrary) to nature (the active affects that express our free relationship with each other). The realm of nature is also the realm of human nature, now hostile, now indifferent, now a source of pleasure, desire, and companionship.

What this means is that nature as it exists "in itself" separate from human nature (the body in Plato's "Phaedo" that simply traps and imprisons the mind) does not appear in Spinoza except in the breach.[89] This absence underwrites the way nature in itself is always a danger for human beings—the backdrop to the human fantasy of being the apex of the natural kingdom, the imagination that might makes right. It is the pact that marks the limit of this fantasy, a fantasy that is confused regarding the difference between nature's "eternal order . . . of which man is but a tiny part" and "the laws of human reason, whose aim is only man's true interest and preservation."[90] The distinction to underscore is not between these latter two versions of nature—the common order of nature that, with fish, we follow and to which we are subject, and human reason (civility). The distinction at issue is between both of these, whose fraught relation characterizes the human condition, and the nature—matter, material—in which humankind has no part, the complement of the soul in which we have no part. It is this distinction that the pact, like the notion of an original multitude, marks: that (human) nature is movement within reality, within the *civitas*, within "perfection." By giving this movement a beginning (the *Theological-Political Treatise*) when this beginning has always already happened (the *Political Treatise*), Spinoza is suggesting that the difference of the human in nature—the difference of human nature—is the possibility of this movement, this *translatio*, at all.

Spinoza the Modern

> So when we say that the best state is one where men pass their lives in harmony, I am speaking of human life, which is characterized not just by circulation of the blood and other features common to all animals, but especially by reason, the true virtue and life of the mind.[91]

Spinoza's most fundamental critique is of a God, but equally a truth or an idea, that contradicts what materialists call the material order and Spinoza calls reality. His critique is of the entire conceptual economy: not only the soul of religion or theology but also the nature of materialism and atheism insofar as these are understood to be opposed to the first terms—the economy, in ancient Greek terms, of the one and the many. It is above all in these terms, from either a materialist or an idealist starting place, that human beings are conceived as a dominion within a dominion, as constitutively divided soul from body, mind from matter, truth from shadow, ruler from ruled.

Materialist readers of Spinoza have assumed that Cartesian and, later, Kantian rationalisms, along with other philosophies of the subject and of consciousness, are expressive of the view Spinoza rejects. As Montag fearlessly puts it, Spinoza diverges from "a thousand years of theological and philosophical arguments that an immaterial soul or mind transcends the corporeal existence that ties it to and sets it in perpetual conflict with the natural world."[92] But the worldview at issue is that of Plato's dialogues, whose inheritance in Western philosophy and religion is pervasive but hardly total. Spinoza's critique is rooted in the ontological argument that thought and existence are on the same side of the divided line. While it took Spinoza to rid us of the maladroit "join" between mind and body, Descartes, like Anselm before him, is committed to the first principle that thought exists in and as sense, body, emotions, will. Even in Descartes there is no going back to a time before materiality was a problem, for to go back as far as God is to go back as far as the mind that can think God as well as doubt, will, affirm, sense, and imagine the world that constitutes this thought.

The construct of the pact cannily performs reality's limit once there is no line to divide soul and body, and thus neither soul nor body to be divided. Once God, but then reason too, is figured not outside the pact but simultaneous with it, once we recognize, says Spinoza, that "God has no special sovereignty over men save through the medium of those who hold sovereignty," then the very notion of materiality is disrupted—by the mind in and as the world.[93] Materiality is to rationality what the natural is to the civil: overcome in being fully realized. In other words, *pace* Bayle, religion, God, mind, and reason survive in Spinoza. They are not absorbed, though neither do they stand alone, any more than nature stands alone. The postulate of the pact holds, on the one hand, that there is nothing before nature, nothing before the *civitas*. But this image presupposes, on the other hand, that each, in expressing the other, is an achievement.

One may depict the scene, again courtesy of Althusser. Although Althusser's metaphorical train leaves us with an un-Spinozistic choice between motion (change, chance) and inertia (the foreknown, the previously concluded), he nevertheless gives as an example of the factual others I might chance upon on my journey "the prophets of the Bible" who make justice and charity, Spinoza holds, the journey's content.[94] Althusser is recalling Spinoza's insistence that we take account of the prophets' circumstances as we interpret them. This attention to history is itself a form of a justice. Perhaps Althusser indicates thereby that the train has no beginning or end but the ones we give it—its beginning for us as we take on the burdens, and not just the caprice, of the ends that constitute reality for us.

This emendation of the materialist Spinoza revises Spinoza's place within the Radical Enlightenment, as indeed in modernity. Both Israel and Jacob give us a familiar Spinoza—secular, scientific, materialist, relentlessly reasonable, explosive in applying the power of reason to disrupt ecclesiastical authority, political hierarchy, and superstitious thinking. Spinoza the oddball pantheist in the margins is interpolated into the central plotline of modern history. In moving Spinoza there, Israel and others have suggested that he and his radical cohort stand singularly against a more moderate tide. Materialist readers put this more sharply. No one but Spinoza truly understood the roots of illusory thinking and tyrannical politics. Only Spinoza articulated formulas of liberation from them. In the slow struggle to bring these formulas to fruition, no one would be less surprised than Spinoza to discover how long it has taken—or is taking even today.

In emending readings of Spinoza that emphasize his radical materialism, I stress that his voice on the roots of illusion and tyranny, powerful and distinctive as it was, was not alone. This is not only to place him in a cohort that would include Descartes and Kant, the thinkers who are for some readers his perfect opposites, it is also to challenge the account of his thought that places him as an anomaly in the first place. Spinoza is radical not simply in killing off illusions dear to political and religious elites at a time when the risks of doing so were not few. He is radical in the ideas he replaced these illusions with, ideas that ironically reconnect him to, among other acts of thought and practice, the richest sources from which religious illusion is fed: the Bible, together with theologies faithful to its complex depiction of human natures.

There is no value in identifying Spinoza as a biblical thinker if this is taken as an invalidation of what he worked so hard to accomplish in his critique of Platonist theologies, whether Jewish or Christian, and their preemptively sacral biblical text. Spinoza had no investment in saving religion per se, which he united with the realization of political goods. What portraits of him as simply vanquishing religion miss, however, is Spinoza's concepts equally of religion and of nature. The nature that makes it possible for human beings to be free, to be unified, collective, universal, and democratic is not what is left over when you strip away religion or the supernatural. It is a realm made and tended in sharp contrast to the natures we are born with, ignorant of the causes of things. This third position, neither nature nor supernature, is the realm of the modern: of ethics, striving, achievement, and failure. It is a human realm divided from other beings not by (super)nature but by work—work to understand, to relieve oneself of illusion, to join with others in common projects, to teach and share. This makes it also a realm of the sacred, consistent with Spinoza's declaration that "nothing is sacred or profane or impure in an absolute sense apart from the mind, but only in relation to the mind."[95] The sacral object would then be nothing other than the quotidian work with and for other minds.

The recognition that the sacred is a principle of inclusion is only the beginning of what it shall mean to work in common with others without being undone by the ignorance and tyranny of making nature our end without distinction. But let us not for all that be confused about what it is one is working for.

Kant and the Worlds of Reason and Religion

In Kant, as in Spinoza, one encounters an uncommon commitment to the elaboration of what is common to human beings, in defiance not only of what divides self from other but also of what would presumptively unite them. The work of the common is complex, rife with distinctions, embattled not only by opponents but by the very powers of mind that serve as protagonist of such a project.

Kant did his most important work in thinking about religion—that object that reason is preeminently to clarify and, whatever is left, to set aside. Kant did not eradicate religion, and he did not settle debates about its nature, but he did bequeath it as among the fundamental problems of thinking. Kant's critique of religion is incisive in deconstructing illusion, yet it also invests human beings with powers of mind and practice that take us to the very limit of the human. His critique of religion is also a defense—of religion and of the mind that loses itself therein. Nevertheless, there is confusion about what we are to learn from Kant's concepts of reason and religion. Readers get bogged down, as they do with Spinoza, in contending with dualism—the semblance of one, the distinction of two.

Surely This Commandment Is Not Too Hard

Kant's most complex book, the *Critique of Pure Reason*, is a book with a claim on you. It begins with this:

> Human reason has the peculiar fate in one species of its cognitions that it is burdened with questions which it cannot dismiss, since they are given to it as problems by the nature of reason itself, but which it also cannot answer, since they transcend every capacity of human reason.[96]

Within a few more lines, Kant has underscored reason's unavoidable perplexity, its "fall" into "obscurity and contradictions," its mindfulness of "hidden errors" that it nevertheless cannot dispel, and its emplacement on a "battlefield" of controversy called metaphysics. Once the queen of the sciences, metaphysics is now "despised on all sides; and the matron," as Ovid has it, "outcast and forsaken, mourns like Hecuba."[97]

Few works of philosophy begin so dramatically; fewer still alert the reader from the outset that the work's intractable problems will be hers as she tries to read it.[98] There is no creation narrative in Kant's first *Critique*. We begin, it might be said, in Genesis 3, when the serpent enters

Eden. But Kant's book is a bible, or like the Bible, in two senses. It arrives with finality as a completed account of its protagonist, reason, and it completes an account of the strangeness of this protagonist without diminishing its strangeness.[99] Kant does not solve the problem of reason's "peculiar fate" any more than the Bible solves the problem of sin or idolatry. What he does is invite readers into reason's multifarious dimensions, which also happen to lie at the heart of the thing they themselves are. This is to make reason—and not only sacral books—a monumental work and Kant's an invitation to this work, an invitation to us.

As we ask whether this invitation of itself makes something biblical, let us recall Kant's story: How reason burdens itself with questions it can neither answer nor dismiss. How it makes its own identity a maelstrom of confusion and desire, careening at images, teetering on foundations made insecure by "all sorts of passageways as moles might have dug, left over from reason's vain but confident treasure hunting."[100] How reason assumes its dignified place at the head of an ordered cosmos only to forfeit this place repeatedly, "the light dove, in free flight, cutting through the air," in search of a paradise of its own.[101] How one man commanded us to stay both vanity and fear, calling attention to the simple shared fact that "I need not seek far beyond myself, because it is in myself that I encounter" reason's principles, and thus its appetites, its manners, and its worlds.[102] It is difficult to be indifferent to the heroism of this message, no matter the immense work it puts before us.

The passage in Deuteronomy I used as an epigraph to the previous chapter on Anselm is instructive. As he so often does, God is instructing the Israelites to obey him "by loving the Lord your God, walking in his ways, and observing his commandments." In that chapter, the work was to conceive of transcendence as what calls forth the labor of historical reality, involving the mind in the concepts of God and history as it encounters its limits. This was to read Anselm otherwise than Kant did when he made Anselm's argument into a supernaturalism—reason going where it has no support to go, an image without truth. It was to read Anselm as consistent with Kant himself. Let us bring forward this same passage to bear up the connection.

> Surely, this commandment that I am commanding you today is not too hard for you, nor is it too far away. It is not in heaven, that you should say, "Who will go up to heaven for us, and get it for us so that we may hear it and observe it?" Neither is it beyond the sea, that you should say, "Who will cross to the other side of the sea for us, and get it for us so that we may hear it and

observe it?" No, the word is very near to you; it is in your mouth
and in your heart for you to observe.[103]

The passage is notable for God's anticipation of the Israelites' perception
of their task and for God's refusal of that perception. In the episode of the
golden calf in Exodus 32, the people of Israel become impatient with Moses's absence when he is up on Mount Sinai hearing the commandments
from God. In judging this absence unacceptably long, the people recruit
Moses's brother, Aaron, saying "Come, make gods for us, who shall go
before us; as for this Moses, the man who brought us up out of the land
of Egypt, we do not know what has become of him."[104] Aaron duly col-
lects gold from the people and shapes it into the image of a calf. The Israelites are doubly confused, however. It was God, together with Moses,
who brought them out of Egypt; and insofar as they recognize this fact, in
proclaiming of the calf, "these are your gods, O Israel, who brought you
up out of the land of Egypt," they do so in suppression of Moses, whose
leadership makes good on the exhortation to go.[105] The golden calf, in
short, is an idol of both God and Moses in confusing the pact of freedom
out of Egypt, even as the commandment to have no other gods is what
keeps Moses away so long, and thus one their impatience postpones.

In Deuteronomy 30, the temptation is not other gods; the temptation
is God himself, conceived as something too great, too difficult. The idol
of distance in contrast to the idol of proximity. The idol of greatness in
contrast to the idol of ease. The commandment that is "not too hard for
you, nor is it too far away" is, Observe the commandments. But what
is a commandment? What is not too difficult or too distant? What, in
short, is the word of God?

There is a Kantian peculiarity to the instruction from Deuteronomy.
God warns the Israelites not to mistake their work with reference to either opposition or identity. God's word is not in the heavens, nor is it to
be worshipped as it is. It is to be observed, "with all your heart and with
all your soul."[106] But like Kant's reason, which heedlessly vaults into the
theoretical gaps it knows cannot be filled, and like Vico's Hebrews, who
will lapse into bestiality, the command recognizes that the Israelites will
be mistaken on precisely this paradoxical point. How could they not be?
The word is not too distant, says God, from a distance. Or the distance
is yours, not mine. It is you who make me distant, then resolve to span
the distance—achieve holiness—by magnifying it in taking the word as
a prohibition, as Adam and Eve did in (nevertheless) knowing good and
evil. As the Israelites do in embracing the piety of rank, God in the heavens. As Said does in delimiting distinction per se as violence.

The mistake would be that the Israelites assert the piety of distance (it is too hard for us) by suppressing the ground of the difficulty—not that it is God who makes the request (it is not too hard), but that the request—that they know God's word—involves their own mouths and hearts. They do not want to know what they know in God; they refuse to know themselves, either in distancing themselves or in abrogating that distance on command. In their haste to observe the protocols of the possible—to love God, to bridge the distance, to fill the gap, they would misplace the work of the impossible, climbing to the heavens and crossing seas without knowing the miracle of the pact in mouth and heart. The word of God has the peculiar fate of being, like reason, already disputatious. The word of God is to love God, which act is already to risk the betrayal of God's injunction not to send off to the heavens. This act is already to have pressed beyond the boundaries of nearness that the word enjoins, and already to have raised the question of "who" has done this, and from where.

Kant's opening lines frame just the paradox that God puts before the Israelites: that reason finds itself insecure precisely as it tries to secure itself; that reason is mistaken about what will secure it; that this mistake makes impossible the order and the obedience that reason also calls for; but that if it were just a matter of obeying the word and contending with what can be answered, there would be nothing to obey and no questions to be asked, beginning with the first one Kant poses to himself of the "secure path of science" he seeks: "Is it perhaps impossible?" Kant responds in the manner not of God but of Job:

> Why then has nature afflicted our reason with the restless striving for such a path, as if it were one of reason's most important occupations? Still more, how little cause have we to place our trust in our reason if in one of the most important parts of our desire for knowledge it does not merely forsake us but even entices us with delusions and in the end betrays us! Or if the path has merely eluded us so far, what indications may we use that might lead us to hope that in renewed attempts we will be luckier than those who have gone before us?[107]

Here lies the beginning of Kant's invitation. He knows it will not be a matter of luck. What he will unfold introduces the figure of reason in its essential character—desirous, afflicted, deluded—within whose modes he will work to identify reason's power in the worlds it inhabits. And what are those worlds? This is God's question too, when he insists that the human burden, or birthright, is the confrontation both with God and with our idea of God: both with ourselves and with our idea of ourselves, with the life we come to through knowledge, and with other lives this knowledge sets before us. To begin, then, Where is it that we live? What is the word and the world of life? What is the word and the world of reason and its realms? If, as Kant says, "I need not seek far beyond myself, because it is in myself that I encounter" reason's principles, then, as Descartes asks, What and who am I?

The answer, we have seen, is that I am the being who, in concert with others, both makes and profanes modernity, as I am made and profaned in relations with others. The question has been, How is it that critique, in the service of its principle of self and other, is confused by what it criticizes? How is it that critique, instead of serving the common, serves violence? We have observed that it will always be and have been true, as it were as a function of a human nature, that when the truth appears, we will be confused—will be, so to speak, in offense. Why confusion? Because truth appears, so then where and which is it? Why offense? Because, in appearing, truth asks something of us—to wager that this shall be it and, in so doing, to act. This is to underscore the power of distinction. The principle that is modernity is hard enough to discern. One needs to know what it is not. But then, too, the principle that is modernity, in announcing that principle shall be in this common, all too common world, is hard enough to enact. One needs to refuse the positions that exile or nullify it—by imagining it cannot be nullified.

Religion and Reason Are a History
A few pages into the final chapter of his *Groundwork of the Metaphysics of Morals*, Kant offers a tantalizingly brief précis of his earlier work on reason. In this third chapter, Kant takes on the last and most difficult piece of his argument concerning the nature of morality. The first two chapters lay out the elements of his theory over against competing philosophies. Kant argues for the integrity of a single moral law, to which all human beings, as rational beings, would be bound. His argument in the first two chapters is that *if* human beings can be moral, if indeed morality is an obligation of human existence, then it has the force of a single command to act on the maxim that one's will accord with the will of all others: put otherwise, to treat all others as ends in themselves—to make the sign of the good what is good for all.

In the final chapter, however, Kant faces the challenge, But *can* human beings be moral in this sense? Does morality address subjects who can, and therefore must, live up to its command, or is the moral law merely a fiction disseminated by a trickster overlord, whether God or reason or the imagination? Is the moral law genuinely lawful? Put differently, What is the relation between human beings and their ideals, given that such beings are clearly in the business of formulating ideals they also quite radically fail to meet? Kant's position in the third chapter is that this failure, along with this formulation, is precisely the point. Morality, together with rationality, presupposes freedom. It therefore presupposes the abrogation and the obfuscation not only of the moral law but also of freedom itself, the abrogation and obfuscation of the command to use it for the good and therefore, as Spinoza shows, for empowerment. This is not the first we hear of freedom in the *Groundwork*. From the beginning, Kant conceives morality—the will to take the other as an end—as an exercise of autonomy, in contrast to the will to use the other, or be used by the other, for ends that subordinate self to other or other to self. But whereas in the earlier chapters he focuses on the principles of a moral law, in the final chapter he freely exposes the vulnerability of his theory. How can we know that we are indeed free, thus free to be both moral and immoral? How do we know that immorality is immorality, and not just necessity or nature or destiny?

Kant is not afraid to build gaps into his system. The vivid and hungry protagonist that is reason in his work twists restlessly in its flaws no less than in its ambitions and its genuine power. Kant insists he cannot prove we are free in the way his system seems to require. Instead, he offers the striking claim that "every being that cannot act otherwise than *under the idea of freedom* is just because of that really free in a practical respect, that is, all laws that are inseparably bound up with freedom hold for him just as if his will had been validly pronounced free also in itself and in theoretical philosophy."[108]

Is this argument or mere assertion? Does it indicate the fictional status of the idea of freedom, or is it simply agnostic on the fact of the matter? Readers of Kant's "theoretical philosophy" know the fruit of Kant's limitation of freedom to practical reason, the power of ideals that are realized in relation with others in contrast to those that are known in themselves in opposition to what exists. But the statement is still shocking—*just because of that really free*. This comes at the beginning of a chapter in which Kant does not abjure the question of proof. He does not simply assert that human beings are free. What he does is make freedom expressive of the architectonic of reason and its critique, whose paradoxical signature—the sign of critique in the bulwark of system—is the insufficiency of the system to master its quarry. "All human beings think of themselves as having free will," he writes. "Yet this freedom is no concept of experience, and moreover cannot be one, since it always remains even though experience shows the opposite of those requirements that are represented as necessary under the presupposition of freedom."[109]

It is to address this tension between freedom as an idea fundamental to how human beings think (of themselves) and freedom as that whose possibility is insusceptible of explanation that Kant turns in his work on morality to a summary of what he has shown about the nature of reason in the first *Critique*. Is the claim of freedom legitimate? Is it not perhaps dangerously circular, as we at once "take ourselves as free . . . in order to think ourselves under moral laws," while "we afterwards think ourselves as subject to these laws because we have ascribed to ourselves freedom of the will"?[110] "One resource," Kant promises, "still remains to us," and this resource takes him back to the work he did to elucidate the "different standpoints" by which one can regard a human being, now as free and now as the effect of causes "we see before our eyes."[111] As Spinoza would put it, freedom is not a departure from nature but the same thing from a different angle.

There are three elements of interest in Kant's passage on these different angles. First, Kant introduces the summary with the claim that "no subtle reflection is required to make the following remark, and one may assume that the commonest understanding can make it," albeit, he says, "by an obscure discrimination of judgment which it calls feeling."[112] Everyone, in effect, is a dualist. This move of Kant's to identify his work as something everybody knows, or can easily know—something common—is a fundamental aspect not only of his sense of how his work can be taken and who can take it but also of the content of that work, its analysis of what is common, collective, ordinary. In the compactly argued *Groundwork* alone, Kant insists several times that, if the severest difficulty of morality lies in living up to its commands, the idea that I am free, and thus obligated to use my freedom morally, while also being subject to the laws of nature, which exclude this freedom, is an idea whose deduction "common human reason confirms," from the lowest "scoundrel" to the most exalted philosophical treatise.[113] Indeed, Kant is wont to credit the scoundrel over the philosopher, who is hampered by "the monopoly of the schools" which propound innumerable philosophical confusions.[114]

For this reason, Kant ventures that "there is something splendid about innocence." The philosopher, "though he cannot have any other principle than that of common understanding, can easily confuse his judgment by a mass of considerations foreign and irrelevant to the matter and deflect it from the straight course."[115] It happens that practical (moral) reasoning possesses over theoretical reasoning the fact that, while each avails itself of what human beings ordinarily think, "if common [theoretical] reason ventures to depart from laws of experience and perceptions of the senses it falls into sheer incomprehensibilities and self-contradictions, at least into a chaos of uncertainty, obscurity, and instability." In "practical matters," by contrast, "it is just when common understanding excludes all sensible incentives from practical laws that its faculty of appraising first begins to show itself to advantage."

In the terms of this book, theoretical reason is liable to confuse the dualism of two, the truth appears, with the dualism of opposition and identity, wherein the truth is either sought elsewhere than in existence, like the Israelites in being tempted to the heavens and across the seas, or resigned altogether, as the Israelites do with the golden calf. Practical reason is Kant's name for the principle of self and other, the principle that principles are the work of two. In practical reason the confusion is of collectives that enact the good through inclusion of others with collectives that patrol the good of the border, the "sensible incentive" of us over them. Each sphere of reasoning is founded on something Kant names the common. What is "bad" about innocence is that "it cannot protect itself very well and is easily seduced."[116] What is bad about common human understanding is that it does not always stop before it alienates itself from "what every human being, even the most common," is bound to know and to practice.[117] In each case what is called for is critique. In each case this is to resolve what the mind enacts in its commonalities.[118]

The second element of interest is the first *Critique*'s central gambit—the position that Kant thinks requires no subtle reflection. Everyone knows (or senses or "feels"), he says, that "all representations which come to us involuntarily (as do those of the senses) enable us to cognize objects only as they affect us and we remain ignorant of what they may be in themselves." This means that "even with the most strenuous attentiveness and distinctness that the understanding can ever bring to them we can achieve only cognition of *appearances*, never of *things in themselves*."[119] Kant's terminology here, with its narrow window into the scope of his project in the first *Critique*, is likely why readers have not made much of Kant's insistence that these things are commonly understood or that they draw on common experience.

But what he is saying bears further scrutiny. Whether the right locution would be "human beings are aware that . . ." or "thought typically produces the idea of . . . ," Kant holds that we arrive sooner or later at "a distinction, although a crude one," between what he calls "a world of sense and the world of understanding." We come to this distinction, he thinks, because we notice the difference between "representations given to us from somewhere else and in which we are passive, and those that we produce simply from ourselves and in which we show our activity."[120] These latter indicate reason in its "spontaneity," its ability to generate ideas far beyond what sensibility "can ever afford it."[121] By virtue of this power of reason, and in light of the notable, but hardly obvious, fact that the human being cannot even claim to cognize herself as she is in herself, one "must necessarily assume something else" lying at the basis of what appears; one must assume an other lying at the basis of one's own self.

Is this an obscure observation or an ordinary one? By ordinary, Kant may simply mean that we observe in ourselves the capacity to think what we want, in defiance of the limited materials we are given to encounter. Thinking escapes the confinements of the world; it seems to gesture to other realms, other lives. Although Kant, following Anselm's reply to Gaunilo, will show that this escape is not nearly as thoroughgoing as it boasts, certainly his "crude" distinction is evident to anyone who imagines, fantasizes, or experiences something else or other to existence than what appears plainly evident. One might dismiss the metaphor of depth Kant is employing. Do we really need to "admit and assume behind appearances something else that is not appearance, namely things in themselves," or could the varieties of existence be accounted for strictly through surfaces—through differences of perspective and interpretation? Perhaps everyone knows the world is not only as it seems. But does this knowledge commit us to the admission that appearance presents something that is central to the structure of the whole?

These questions are those Kant himself poses to reason's ambitions, as he seeks to make plain the conditions under which reason's spontaneity is truly generative—the dualism of practical reason in which truth appears in the good of self and other, collective and collective. This is in contrast to the conditions under which reason and its hopes for its quarry are foiled—confused, opposed, identified.

What is notable is that Kant's summary of what was quickly to become notorious in the history of philosophy—his theory of existence as distinguished by appearances and things in themselves—barely alludes to one of the theory's most arresting dimensions. This is not the fact (or the thought) that existence is divided. It is the activity of reason in its role both as purveyor of the unity of appearances and as restless pilgrim for what is beyond them. Kant notes that "we resign ourselves to being unable to come any closer" to things in themselves than the bare assumption of their existence or, better, the bare assumption of the distinction. We resign ourselves, he says, never "to know what they are in themselves." And yet such resignation is little in evidence, either in ordinary life or in Kant's philosophy thereof, in which reason is consistently ambitious to a fault. Kant suggests that our resignation is what gives evidence of the distinction in the first place. Human beings tacitly acknowledge something true in itself only to give it up, and it is this giving up that grants Kant the license to explain why common reason is wise in doing so. It is simply that Kant is also the thinker who shows us that reason is just as reckless as it is wise, just as wild as it is resigned and docile, leaving things that cannot be known to their own counsel and then prodding its dark materials into being despite its own avowals.[122] Every being that cannot act otherwise than under the idea of freedom is just because of that really free in a practical respect.

This brings us to the third notable aspect of Kant's foray into his theory of reason in the midst of his treatise on morality: the concept and the problem of God. Having reviewed in short order his theory that the world is a world that appears to us; that this appearance is not a totality, for totality does not and cannot appear; that, nevertheless or therefore, human beings must assume that the world of appearance does not comprehend everything there is to comprehend about existence simply because "the human being can never think of the causality of his own will otherwise than under the idea of freedom," an idea ruled out by appearances, Kant returns to his claim that not only must "a reflective human being . . . come to a conclusion of this kind," but indeed that even "the most common understanding" will arrive at something of this notion. How and why so, we ask? In thinking of oneself as free, he has said. But also, Kant says, because the common understanding, "as is well known, is very much inclined to expect behind the objects of the senses something else invisible and active of itself."[123] It expects, one might say, God.

Is this a criticism of religion or a commendation of it? Kant's allusion to God follows his use of the concept of freedom and the thing in itself. "No subtle reflection" is necessary to see that if freedom were justifiable in the world as it appears to us, it would equally refute itself. Human beings are not, as Spinoza put it, a dominion within a dominion. Any claim to the contrary can easily be deconstructed with reference to natural law, than which nothing in the world is greater or more efficacious. Freedom *is* justifiable, Kant holds, but we must allow that the world as it appears to us is not the only way of taking the world. It is not that there is *another* world, but that this world (*the* world) can be accounted not only in its appearance but in the dynamism of what appears. Everyone "knows" this wager in taking themselves as free.

God names this same wager—that there is something invisible and active. But which God—the one who rules nature (many) as its telos (one) or the one in prophetic critique of natural and supernatural idols alike? The picture is of reason working to keep faith with its spontaneity, its "self-activity" as an engine of borders and their mastery, if also as an agent of their obfuscation. There are metaphors at play: that existence is layered; that it deconstructs its own apparent solidity. Such metaphors help us augment the reading that would have Kant simply catching common wisdom in the desire that there be something salvific behind the curtain. We know, meanwhile, that this—naturalism and supernaturalism—is the temptation.

Kant's division of the world is within existence. The division between the world and something else is what his critiques criticize, even as we do not know what exists in finite totality. Although Kant criticizes the ontological argument for its use of existence as a predicate, insisting that concept and existence cannot be patched together by fiat, his approach to the division between appearances and things in themselves retains *what* appears as a part of the system, part of existence, in contrast to letting it float free in some special realm in the manner of the Platonic Forms. God and freedom are part of the system. But what part? And in what way?

This is the both the promise and the delicacy of the project. Certainly the image of God behind a curtain is what Kant is relying on when he both locates God in the place of freedom and then also shows that the concept of distinction tempts us to want an illicit more: to make objective what is fundamentally creative—an act, not a thing. The commonest of the common, he seems to be saying, is the view that there is something invisible and active of itself behind the world. No less common is the temptation God notes of the Israelites: that God will then be taken as a thing to be located rather than a commitment to be practiced. Thus, although God might name an empowering version of the structure of mind and world, God is also the sign of the mind's confusion. For God shows us in a vivid way that the moment when "the most common understanding" correctly perceives that there is "something else invisible and active of itself," it "spoils this again by quickly making this invisible something sensible in turn."[124]

In the space of the *Groundwork*, reason appears as a disciplined and rigorous faculty, in contrast with the afflicted and vaulting actor in the first *Critique* that sometimes seems bent on nothing so much as its own destruction. In the *Groundwork*, reason is that capacity by which a human being "distinguishes himself from all other things" and, most impressive of all, "distinguishes himself even from himself insofar as he is affected by objects."[125] Reason knows both itself and its others. Reason is other than or more than merely itself. This characterization of reason is at the center of Kant's concept of morality, as reason creates for itself, from itself, the conditions of a law grounded in the other. It is only in the passage on the mistake that is religion—on the other that is God—that reason in the *Groundwork* shows its more undisciplined or driven side. We get religion right only to get it wrong, because we "want to make it [what is invisible and active] an object of intuition, so that it [the common understanding that rightly senses the other] does not thereby become any the wiser."[126]

One wants to ask Kant, What do you expect? What virtuosity of asceticism would be required to appreciate that truth appears, to ascertain what is valuable "at the basis" of the world, and to prescind from thinking anything further about it?[127] In wanting to make it, God, an object of intuition, do I not thereby show unequivocally that the nature and structure of things Kant is elaborating are very far from what common human reason normally does? What could follow from Kant's recognition of our incapacity to hold thought free from sensible intuition if not the cliché that religion is but an archaic form of thought that is ultimately transcended by reason?

Yet this is precisely what Kant is not saying. Religion is right. Until it is wrong. Religion would simply be wrong were it not also right. Religion bears the form of a world, or a mind, divided and thus dramatizes well the consequence of division for the mind that encounters it. Kant seems to make the issue a temporal one: first "a reflective human being" concludes that there is something invisible and active, then this same human being spoils it by making the invisible visible. But the most accurate expression of Kant's position is more paradoxical than either this rendering or the division of the world in an oppositional two suggests. In the very *act of being right*, Kant is suggesting, religion is—also—wrong. We run aground in our powers of spontaneity, by which we also recover the good of our desire.

What is required here, a theory of religion or a theory of reason? Is it religion that is at issue, or is it reason in its Janus-faced role as both stolid purveyor of unity and restless pilgrim of the beyond? Is not the language of the invisible made sensible merely a faith-baiting way of saying what Kant says of reason in the first *Critique*, that reason is not merely mistaken or confused about what lies beyond its purview but actually expresses principles that "incite us to tear down all those boundary posts [supplied by possible experience] and to lay claim to a wholly new territory that recognizes no demarcations anywhere"—the drive from the intelligible to the sensible and then back?[128] And again, one could ask, as with religion, would this be a criticism of reason or a commendation?

My intent is to observe the conceptual proximity of religion and reason in Kant's thought in seeking his assistance to refound both. As the title of his book on religion announces, Kant seeks religion within the boundaries of mere reason.[129] It seems to be the ultimate Enlightenment credo, the submission of the miraculous and the mystical to rational investigation. Certainly Kant has been received as the thinker who tried to squeeze all the power and interest of religion into the bare bones of thinking. For some critics of religion this makes him a hero. In the main, however, this has been one significant arena of Enlightenment knowledge where common human understanding, not to mention rarefied scholarly presumption, typically rebels.

But let us ask again what is involved in Kant's title. Religion within the boundaries of mere reason. The refractory religion controlled by right rational modes. Yet is not reason itself a refractory power? If religion is within the bounds of reason, what binds reason? Does Kant not show that reason is always slipping its bonds, confronting its limits, and then either powerfully extending them, as it does in assisting the empirical work of the understanding, or gleefully flouting them, as it does when it takes as merely another object the most generative, but also most potentially illusory, of its ideas? Did we somehow forget to ask what kind of chaperone reason would make for the domestication of religion?

Kant never suggests that reason can finally be purged of its wildness. It can be critiqued. It can be deconstructed and then redeployed as a critical agent of freedom and (self-)knowledge, but reason's system is not a closed or final one. Its epoch cannot be over. How could it be, when, as critical agent of freedom, reason brings about the one thing the known and knowable universe is set against, from the heavens to beyond the seas? As we have seen him claim, with Deuteronomy, reason is what I encounter in myself and not far beyond it. It is therefore mine to know. It is also what will urge me far beyond what I seem to myself, a facet in which reason rejoins forces with ordinary human understanding, which has no difficulty "transferring" the human being "into an order of things altogether different from that of . . . the field of sensibility."[130]

Is this to say that Kant's confrontation with reason's aspirations and its antinomies renders the title of his book on religion absurd? What is required is to reconsider Kant's terms for reason—to see that they share something of the creaturely universe of Anselm's theology, Stevens's poetry, and Dostoevsky's novels as much they do the exertions of some of Kant's rationalist contemporaries and epigones. Mere reason is a circus of happenings, the madness of lost islands as much as the madness of the Grand Inquisitor in his work to sequester what he knows. This is to see that religion can take its place squarely within the confines of reason only insofar as reason acknowledges the centrality of religion to its own projects: its quest for the heavens and the seas; its estrangement from and astonishment at its own "mouth and heart," its power, its gaps, its mistakes.

Such claims return students of religion to a period before the questions were, Which religion? Whose culture? Why reason? What can it mean to rescue religion and reason bare of further specification when these questions have hewn so many fruitful paths, closer to the ground, so to speak, in search of lifeworlds and outliers, languages and exceptions, practices and their histories? What Kant reminds us to ask is, Is there religion at all? He means this question not in the contemporary worry of false coherence. He means, Does not religion, gesturing toward totality, also critique totality? Is not religion, then, its own critic, or might it not be? Might it not be critical of itself precisely insofar as it forgets itself and becomes . . . religion? Is it not also, though, right, as thinking and living reach beyond themselves to worlds we know as more tremendous than they seem?

In "The Sail of Ulysses" Stevens writes, "We come / To knowledge when we come to life. / Yet always there is another life, / A life beyond this present knowing." Where do we stand when we say such things, when we wonder whether we all somehow know this? "We know it," Stevens says, "one / By one, in the right of all."[131] Stevens gives us the relation between knowledge, history, and ethics—the elements of modernity. Kant, with Anselm and Spinoza, helps us see that there are two ways of asking about the "life beyond this present knowing": one takes it as a claim about another world, and one takes it as a claim about this world—about the invisible and the active, the other, the all. One makes holiness about imitating a God, and one makes God a concept and practice of holiness. This is not Euthyphro, that either the good is subject to the gods or God is subject to the good. It is that the subject good is God, the good of self and other, the dualism of mutuality. God is the subject of the good insofar as we recognize that the good of self and other is inconceivable without the desire of reason to vault beyond the known, to create what does not yet exist, and to submit to no borders but its own, by which it is also deconstructed.

Religion and reason belong together. They are partners in critique. Religion does not require philosophical proof. Philosophy does not need more evidence that its ends are also beyond it, like the psyche as it fails to seal its gaps. Each is a provocation to otherness, including its own. Each is nonexistent, irrelevant, without this recognition. Custom, language, culture, art, ritual, history—all of these are the purview of a study of religion. But there is more to say on the thing identified as religion, more to say on what makes it common. Religion is a history with mistakes, wrong turns, extravagant gestures. We can be, in our center, also confused, like the Israelites with the thing closest to them. Commitment and its revisions. Critique and its interpretations. Enlightenment and its radicals.

7

Modernity as Ground Zero

"Yesterday morning I was still contained inside the single golden fruit hanging on my tree. At noon it burst and fell open, and there was I, newly hatched. In my tadpole stage I was delivered to Metron Ariston and transmogrified, and here am I. My name is Sporos, by the way, and I do not like your thinking names like mouse-creature and shrimp-thing at me. *Sporos*. When I have finished this phase of my education—if I finish—with one of you for a partner, I will root myself, and Deepen. After an aeon I'll send up a small green shoot out of my kelp bed, and start growing into an aqueous deciduous spore-reproducing fruit-bearing coniferous farandola."

Calvin looked horrified. "You're mad. I've studied biology. You're not possible."

"Neither are you," Sporos replied indignantly. "Nothing *important* is."

Madeleine L'Engle, *A Wind in the Door*

The Epoch of History

In his introduction to a collection of essays by social theorist Niklas Luhmann, *Theories of Distinction: Redescribing the Descriptions of Modernity*, editor William Rasch tells a story of "the Western Philosophical tradition" according to which it burns out in the modern confrontation with history and science.[1] In this story, modernity marks a loss of faith in reason, the "unblemished reason" that "afford[s] a comprehension of the whole," the totality, the nature of things as they are. In modernity this majestic reason, having imbued human life with "purpose and meaning" by accessing the order of things, is replaced with a more cramped scientific rationality at work in an "immanent, partial, and severed world, the posited world," the world in which human autonomy "takes center stage" and human knowing takes merely itself as object.[2] As Rasch puts it, "The whole that is modernity is the whole that strains to see itself and thus a whole that forever divides itself with every observation into more and more 'facts.'" Luhmann's account of this reflexive state of affairs is that reason is removed from "a foundationalist 'first' philosophy" to "a 'second-order' philosophy of observations of the observations of self and other."[3]

Although Luhmann's vocabulary of distinction might suggest him as a partner to the work of this book, his conception of social cognition as "a processing of differences" encapsulates the views of history and philosophy—as of modernity—that this book sets aside.[4] Like many twentieth-century thinkers, Luhmann conceives modernity as the understanding that the old orders are gone—not in one fell swoop, perhaps, but slowly, through corrosions of science, industry, idealism, Marxism, the death of God, and phenomenology, it dawns that the attempt still to access the whole must be given up, however reluctantly.[5] One must finally "renounce ultimately foundational unities."[6] In Rasch's narration this means the recognition that there is no "absolute that is *prior* to distinction" but only "the absolute *of* distinction."[7] This is Luhmann's work—to map the distinctions that constitute the self-determination, or self-positing, of social systems, systems without grounds in something outside them.

The problem with the story Rasch and Luhmann tell is that it imagines that the lost thing—reason, order, cosmos, whole—is the thing against which history, fragmentation, and observation are juxtaposed. History will be the recognition that the order of orders is gone and will curb its own ambitions accordingly, albeit, for Luhmann, in deference to sociology, which can properly be purged altogether of ambitions for wholes.

But unlike Anselm's argument for God, which is recovered in pieces, the ordered cosmos that stands outside history cannot be broken. It can only be erected as an idol generation after generation, as thinking is confounded by what it means that time is a concept and not only a context—that wholes may be historical too. The order that is the cosmos is erected generation after generation as the thing that sober minds know must be given up. It is erected, then, generation after generation as the fantasy that it was once otherwise than it is now. There was one; now there is only many.

To reject this move of the generations is not to submit that history and loss are all we ever have. It is to reckon with the history of the concept that would escape history, in service to the concept, the missing distinction, that history also is. History names something specific, even as it typically serves, like religion, as a generic. The specificity of history resides in its very commitment to specificity, to experience, to reality. In this commitment to specificity, history ostensibly abides as a generic panorama able to include all cases. History is a method. What else would it be? The question is, What else is there?

The two candidates that present themselves are Luhmann's wholes, nature and reason. Each raises potentially insoluble problems, as we saw in thinking with Anselm, Spinoza, Vico, and Kant. In the first instance, something is historical as opposed to natural. History is that dimension of reality that expresses the human story, in contrast to nature, of which human beings are a part but which, considered as what exists in the widest sense, is a system in which human interests are null. Human beings might affect the natural order to the point, we now realize, of our own self-extinction, but this order is not interested in this fact.

By contrast, human beings make and are made by history. We participate in shaping a reality that is also formative for us, the metaphysical version of citizens in a democracy. This image of the human being as *Homo historicus* raises the question of exactly how the regimes of history and nature would then be related. Is history a dominion within a dominion, to use Spinoza's language, a distinct domain within nature but with its own rules?[8] Or is history subordinate to the order of nature and thus finally eclipsed by it? The first leaves in doubt the very reality history needs to secure by presuming a phantom division that its work in the soil of things would not be able to sustain. The second makes history a modal construction—the duck of discourse assimilable to the rabbit of nature.[9] This ambiguity can be seen in the temptation to treat history as a kind of science, simply in pursuit of the most accurate state of affairs. But the phantoms cannot be suppressed. Accurate by what measure? By whose standard?

In the second instance, history stands in contrast to reason. History is reality insofar as it involves a specific past, where reason is understood to access what is universal or generalizable. But note: If nature is the more encompassing term inclusive of history, then reason and history would belong together in the same quandary—both expressive of human interests, both taking up residence in a natural order that is inexpressive of such interests. Indeed, one finds the contrast between history and reason mainly in the breach. There is no ahistorical reason, or, as one hears in the humanities, no one any longer believes in eternal truth. But it also underlies the formation of history as a separate discipline. There are many things to consider about the human being in the world. History is only one of them, specific in requiring training in method. Yet what aspects of human beings would lie outside history? Would bringing history to philosophy be bringing the methods and manners of the professional historian, reminding philosophy that its problems have coordinates (who, what, where, when, why)? Or would it be bringing the very experience that is history—humans making and being made by what they live through—in which case history's interests would seem to coincide with those of philosophy?

In the first contrast (with nature), history would be a part of the human and social sciences over against the natural sciences. It would consider human beings insofar as they have agency, however limited or quasi-predictable, and the world insofar as it bears on and bears up in such beings. In the second contrast (with reason), history stands not for agency but for detail, cause, concreteness, location, attribution. It will tend to leave questions of agency to the philosophers and take on the thicker brew of the myriad aspects of existence by which human beings are shaped and buffeted—what we call context or conditions or simply chance. History, the discipline, possesses the discipline to look beyond or behind rhetorics of reason and agency to the collective processes, struggles, accidents, and fortunes that constitute the innumerable elements of existence in particular places, times, and languages. In so doing it will tend to depict nonhistorical ways of approaching existence archetypally, without necessarily thinking through its relation to them. Is it even possible to conceive reason as unhistorical? Does the discipline of history need it to be?

These questions raise yet another contrast. Insofar as history stands distinct from pursuits of reason, it is also ineluctably a theological combatant. History would be the stable and worldly science over against the flights of the divine. If the battle to root the humanities in history over against divinity presumably was won long ago, meaning that the contemporary university rarely imagines divinity as a conversation partner, much less a threat, the victor history is nevertheless given to assimilating the claims of reason with theological claims in carving out its own space. Not consciously, perhaps. Reason has its proper academic provenance and use. But what a historical or social scientific humanities imagines reason to involve can seem bound to the assumption that reason, unmoored by historical method, would eventually float up into the empyrean. History is "secular." By its good light no one in its precincts believes in eternal truth anymore. History is reality insofar as it does not preexist or transcend the human hand.

But what does preexist or transcend the human hand? Surely not even the God whose story theology tells, much less the reason by which any telling transpires. Or, less obviously, what doesn't? Can we identify the coordinates, the epoch, of history itself?

History can seem not as contentious and confusing an idea (or a field) as religion. History is pervasive and agnostic, a solution to many intellectual and even political ills. But history *is* strange. Consider history's image as the study of change over time. History would then be demarcated from other scenes of change by the concern with time. But what other kind of change is there? Time abides. One wonders whether the conjunction of change and time signifies what, despite change, can be picked out over time, time serving as the Trojan horse for the forging mind that makes it possible to observe change in the first place. This mind would need, though, a theory of its significance to the practice of history if it is not, courtesy of time, to render history the mere accidental modifications of a substantial self.

When we speak of something like the Renaissance or the Enlightenment, we are using the notion of epoch or period, a conceptual device that calls attention to clusters of changes. History will be thought with the help of such devices, whether named by the historical actors or by the scholars who study them. Let us try out a distinction between period and epoch. Let period refer to an entity bound by dates, however contested, and let epoch denote an entity whose dates, in cutting into the world, are nevertheless questions of concept. Let date be shorthand for the temporal along with related coordinates such as place and language. The distinction between period and epoch operates on the intuition that there is something different in historical degree if not also kind between something like modernity and something like the Cold War. Each can be dated. Each is also ideas. With something like modernity, however, it can seem not quite historically serious to ask about a date. Would not modernity be too grandiose for such delicate work? The dates of something like the Cold War, by contrast, are called for, however rife for contestation. Historical thinking about this entity will be conditioned by where they are placed. Indeed, historians will take a lot of trouble on this score. The date is a site of historical innovation. Here the question of date and the question of concept would be ineluctably joined.

In the case of modernity, date and concept would also be conjoined. Historians and theorists have gamely provided dates for modernity, and there continues to be exciting work in this area.[10] The question remains, however, what it means to subject modernity to a date without also conceiving the date as subject to modernity. Modernity is like the Renaissance and the Enlightenment in collecting a variety of attributes that ostensibly separate the contemporary world from something that came before. It is unlike the Renaissance and the Enlightenment in effortlessly encompassing them. It is possible to say that this is because modernity does not mean anything, or means anything one needs it to. It is unquestionably a polemical concept, a value as well as a state of affairs. However, the problem of modernity is not that it is maddeningly vague. It is that once it is, it will always have been. Modernity has an absolutely decisive relation to its date, which shall then be absolutely mobile—irretrievable in its original mandate, unspecifiable as a moment in time. Modernity will have to be remade, redated over and over again, not because it means nothing but because it contends for the epoch of everything.

Modernity is the contention of concepts and dates. In this case the characteristic shrug of the scholar regarding the origins of concepts is self-defeating. It may be, as with Wittgenstein giving us philosophy in ordinary language, that concepts are just what certain people do and say in certain times and places. No origins necessary. But this limitation of concepts to minds and times is itself a concept. How will we identify its origin? Perhaps the word origin, too, is used in ways that require criticism. The fear of origins, essences, beginnings is the fear of being faithless to contingency, detail, change, and more covertly to pluralism, toleration, inclusion, difference. But who said they were opposed? The opposition of essence and change is a concept, and modernity's concept is otherwise—that there are no essences and origins outside changes; no changes that are not inaugurations of concepts. The work to understand these relations is conditioned by the change (date) of the announcement (concept) that holds these things together—as history. This makes history the refusal both of nature, insofar as it denotes time in itself, and reason, insofar as it denotes concepts in themselves. History announces that these positions are unthinkable, unhistorical. History is both natural and rational in holding that, if concepts are true only in being limited to nature, to reality, this limitation is a concept, whose inauguration empowers nature to include not only what is but also what is desirable, achievable, good (and evil), inclusive (and exclusive).

In the case of the Cold War, I do not need to call the series of things and events conventionally included in this classifier by this name. I can call them something else, or redistribute them, re-count them in such a way that the "thing," the Cold War itself, disappears. The so-called

Cold War, I then write. Or just "the Cold War." In the case of modernity, there is nothing there to be named or reclassified. Nothing, that is, but concepts, or rather the concept of dates as expressive of concepts. But the concept of modernity, therefore, far from being a grandiosity that floats above the serious business of temporal concern, is entirely interested in and dependent on temporality—on events and happenings and conditions and choices and accidents. And minds and decisions. It is a historical concept, *but it is also a concept of history*. Modernity is not only something history conjures, only to worry whether it is really there. History is something modernity conjures in saying "now begin." Or, as Pascal exhorts in the wager, commit, for you are already committed. You have already begun in history. Now comprehend your beginnings, so that you can begin again with ever more power in if not also over your end.

Insofar as modernity is a concept of history, then, and not only a historical concept, it is bound by concept and not only by date. In history it is not only dates that do the binding. This is epoch. But because modernity can be, and must be, dated, it is also period. Epoch and period coincide, as they do with the Cold War. But note: It is not that modernity's dates depend on what you consider modern and what I do. What is at issue is not the mobility of the word or the attempt to freeze it in place. The distinction of modernity arises whatever it is called. Moreover, it is not that modernity's dates cannot be located with finality, pending further evidence, or that modernity is a flimsy ascription, an empty classifier. One can assert either of these, the position of positivism or the position of positivism's denial. But such assertions practice without giving an account of their history. Modernity names the cut of concepts into the world, neither absent but for evidence nor merely empty, precisely not empty in bringing into view the details of everything in the world. Modernity's history, then, is a confrontation with the extent to which the dates given will be wrong without reckoning with this cut, with the principle of principle realized in and as the world, the principle that the good of (understanding) the world is also the good that the world can make. Something *like* modernity is, then, nothing. There is nothing like it. Everything else is unlike it.

What is powerful about history is that it is an act of interpretation. We demand a degree of stability in the past no less than in the natural world, although we sense—at the borders of vision—how each realm teems with creaturely motion. Insofar as period concerns chronology, it is a mode of orientation, like lines of longitude and latitude on a globe, the word Tuesday, or the numeral 42. History is our periodical walking

stick, carved on or knocked over, shattered and reglued, pointed elsewhere or used to prop open the cellar door. There were no Middle Ages.
The Reformation was about grain, not religion. Homosexuality began
in 1890. In 1968 (or 1492 or 2001 or 0 or yesterday or just now), the
world changed irrevocably. You cannot do without chronos, and you
cannot stop refashioning it. Am I not now and now and now subject to
and the subject of infinite changes? Is not the first period the one I coauthor (as) myself so that I stay put long enough to see what else there is?

This does not mean that anything goes—that the Middle Ages, the
Reformation, homosexuality, Tuesday, 42, or I can mean just anything,
or everything. History is the act of interpreting the world insofar as it is
shared by other human beings. You have to be able to make your story
stick. Let us say religion is a modern invention, the West is anti-Semitic,
the Enlightenment is radical, the peasants knew more than we assume,
the aborigines are not aboriginal. These are not only the fruits of more
extensive and astute research. It is all some concept of ours, mine, yours,
hers. We cannot think history without period, without interpreting what
is otherwise the absurdity of temporality, its equally micro and macro
incomprehensibility. But period is a concept that history would always
have the power to dissolve. History may dissolve any given period,
though not the very notion of period. Period may condition any history
subject to the period that is history. History is an epoch, a period.

Perhaps we say change over time in rebellion against a concept of
change that is good, as the Catholic catechism has it, until the end of
time.[11] Change over time would speak back to revelation, referring to
change insofar as it (change) changes, the doubling necessary to inter-
pose change between time and the end. It is difficult to avoid paradox in
either case. The change that endures until the end of time, at which point
it changes by not enduring. The change that is over time, at which moments it is either its (unchanged) self or another (change).

Modernity is a name for the challenges of holding together time and
concept.[12] It is a name for history's queer reasons.

The Epoch of Modernity

This book is an experiment. Modernity, I am arguing, is impossible, in
being a call to begin from nothing natural. This is to refer to, in order
now to modify and advance, the distinction employed in thinking with
Anselm, Spinoza, and Kant. In all three thinkers, religion as supernatural is impossible and therefore to be distinguished from what is a source
of power and knowledge. Yet Madeleine L'Engle captures their great

announcement: That nothing important is possible. That everything important is impossible. Hence one must distinguish. In L'Engle's dialogue between the paragons of impossibility, the impossibility that is (human) existence (as an end) itself, she expresses the absolute difference between two impossibles: the one we cannot achieve, in dualistic opposition to or identity with us, and the one we can and must, the one, Sporos notes, we already have and already are: mutual creation. Creature of just one day, in stunned dialogue with himself as much as with the boy Calvin, Sporos declares that, having "hatched" and "transmogrified . . . here am I." He is ready to finish—"if I finish"—this "phase of [his] education." Like Edward Scissorhands, Sporos's existence calls for modification. Like Abraham, he stands forth for the job. What Sporos is after is to become himself, to become what hatching alone cannot yield. In this endeavor he needs "one of you for a partner," someone with whom "I will root myself, and Deepen." Grow. "After an aeon I'll send up a small green shoot out of my kelp bed, and start growing into an aqueous deciduous spore-reproducing fruit-bearing coniferous farandola." "Not possible," says Calvin.[13] Indeed.

I have indicated that modernity is a concept. I have indicated that its concept is a principle: the enactment of truth in history as the realization of inclusivity, plurality, and equality, the realization of collectives that, in being collective, are yet not simply homelands. By realization I do not mean telos. I mean work, the work of interpretation in asking what truth is the truth I realize and the work of wager in asking what the truth demands. This is the call to Abraham, a call that he, like his readers, will misplace. But it is his call nevertheless, and it resounds in the experiment of modernity unto today.

I now turn to modernity insofar as, a certain concept, it is also epoch. Modernity is a break in all the ways conventional periodization has suggested. Something happens. Modernity is a name for something or plural somethings, conceived as a congeries of events and ideas in certain parts of the world roughly fifteen hundred years after the events marked as year zero in the Gregorian calendar.

This more conventional concept of modernity offers an opportunity to think about what is being claimed: the very idea of history in which something of the magnitude of modernity can happen, the particular time in which modernity is identified, and the "what" itself—what it is that happens at base. There are countless answers to these questions. I counsel a refusal of countlessness, however, as what bypasses the paradox of history—that only in beginning is history endless, countless. Only in beginning is it never-ending. Not finished. But then only in beginning can its ends be made, and not simply given, attained, recalled, lost. Beginnings must be conceived to be liberated in and for this work.

I argue for a dual conception of modernity as both a break and a recapitulation. This is not to say, then, that modernity is simply to be dated earlier, or that its origins are elsewhere than the convention. It is to mark the doubleness of modernity as a revolution consistent with the revolution that time and history can bear the beginning, can be "in the beginning," as Genesis has it. This is beginning in the sense Said misplaced in taking beginnings (versus origins) as what are contingent as opposed to absolute, secular as opposed to sacred. Said's distinction is expressive of what modernity refuses, in which origins—sacred, religious—are conceived in opposition to history in order for beginnings to be merely identical with history.

Modernity is rather the beginning of the absolute value of history, thus of beginnings expressive of the good. Origins and ends, naturalisms and supernaturalisms, bugbears of religion and secularism, history as mere contingency are equally revealed as fictive, fantasy, confusion. Modernity is the revolution of its very idea. It begins with the story of Abraham, who is called to leave his land for a land that will be shown. It begins with the story of Adam and Eve, in which beginnings involve the recognition that whatever history is—a vale of tears, a site of toil, conflict, and ignorance, a condition of shame—it is also the site, the only site, in which to enact change for the good. Modernity is the good—and not only the pain—of change. One is therefore never finished beginning. There is no natural condition, no origin, no intrinsic truth, no telos, but also no contingency that rectifies or rescues from this profound critique of all simple givens, whether origins or ends.

Modernity is ground zero. It is the origin of everything human, before or behind which there is nothing (that can be known), the origin of history as the home land of work, of minds, and of collectives, as distinct from natural homeland. The work of history in this light is to mark the changes that human beings make and suffer in time. But it is equally to recognize that part of what is always and ever changed is what we see and how we interpret. History is interpretation. So we have never been modern.[14] Or modernity happened in 785 CE. Or it was situated in Asia and not in Europe. It was tyrannical. It was good. This is the work that history is to make, to suffer, and to judge. To wager. This is modernity, the change that initiates and, so to speak, sacralizes, change itself as work, as commitment to others, and as ours.

I make good on these claims by introducing a brief story of Western origins. These origins involve doubleness. There is, first, the doubleness of modernity as what begins in biblical critique and is recapitulated—articulated, elaborated, interpreted, and practiced—in the critiques of supernaturalism that we dub secular. Modernity is an innovation in both of its "times." It is the innovation that everything can be new under the sun in commitment to the creative work of collective life in history. This doubleness of two modernities requires scrutiny. The modernity of the secular will misapprehend its origins. It will advance a critique of supernaturalism while failing to contend with the naturalism that springs from the same head. The modernity of biblical critique will fail to connect with secular innovation. Called to the promised land, it will reerect the homeland of gods and fathers rather than the good, no less religious than secular, of land for all. These confusions call for scrutiny of a second doubleness, of faith and reason, theology and philosophy, as they respond, together and separately, to the double of human beings as they become who and what they are.

I recall and augment the propositions from chapter 1, as I did in chapter 4.

In the model in which truth appears, the refused positions are what opposes truth and appearance and what identifies them. The terms religion and secularism, as those of theology and philosophy, can express either the model or what it refuses.

In the model in which a (single) collective is constituted by and held accountable to a principle of inclusivity, the refused positions are what identifies inclusivity with the collective and seeks either to expand by domination or to exclude by membership and what identifies inclusivity with the erasure of the (single) collective. The terms religion and secularism, as those of theology and philosophy, can express either the model or what it refuses.

The refused positions in the two models are mutually supportive. Insofar as appearance is not where the truth is (appearance is not true) or insofar as truth is merely whatever appears, a collective can only be rooted in and can extend only as far as the representation and conquest of natural or accidental generation: kin/tribe/ethnos/race/empire.

The refused positions structure many frameworks of social and intellectual life. Their refusal is modernity. In the light of modernity, what is refused is or becomes nonmodern. It also becomes the temptation of modernity as it flees from its own principle.

Throughout this book, the invocation of doubleness is always of this dense thicket. Two ways of taking the two elements of truth and appearance. Two models of the elements of modernity, one concerning truth and one concerning collectives. Two versions of the two ways of taking the elements of truth and appearance as of collectives, the one making central the distinction between what cannot be otherwise and what can— the distinction between nonmodernity and modernity—and the other making central the distinction between the principle of modernity and its subversions, the distinction expressive of the structure of both modernities of this chapter—the modernity of Abraham and the modernity of innovation. Chapter 4 worked on the model of twos embedded in the concept of the collective, whose pitfalls have the common names imperialism, collectivism, exclusion, triumphalism, abstraction. In this chapter I work with history as the concept of truth in appearance, and now I consider the conceptual work of theology and philosophy as they alternate between the principle and its refusals, between modernity and its temptations, and between modernity and the nonmodernity it delimits and sets aside or confuses—the pitfalls of naturalism and supernaturalism.

The proximity of so many distinctions can seem insuperably complex. These are words, not equations. I rejoice, however, in the challenge of words while aiming to communicate as clearly as I can. That human beings are doubled in embodying a truth that appears is a motif in many philosophies, theologies, sociologies, and anthropologies. I make specific the concept of doubleness, of two, in a history of ideas in which what matters is relation—what is possible between ideas, persons, positions. The power of distinction is the power to differentiate between forms of distinction that liberate each side of a duality for each other and forms of distinction that suppress or dominate one side. These forms are at the base of most human conflict. They are periodized and named and circulated and recirculated. My aim throughout is to see as much as possible at the elementary level: how societies and scholars conventionally divide and what these divisions make possible and obscure. The question is what it means to differentiate between dualities in which domination and submission are elements of an inexorable division in and from existence and dualities in which domination and submission can be rectified by principles present in their profanation. The aim in this chapter is to contend with the epoch of this difference.

One acknowledges that the modern as "West" has enough problems of its own making to last indefinitely, without giving us again a preeminent West, a sublime modernity. But it must continually be said that there is no modern West outside the challenge of comprehending its borders and its ideas of borders: its exclusions, blindness, violence. This challenge is equally to state anew what is inclusion, what is freedom, what is the standard of critique. In a democracy, all substantial subcollectives can be shown to be merely strategic in the context of the condition of their possibility, which is the very idea of collectives of affinity and commonality over against privilege and natural rank. Yet it is a truism of the practice of democracy that this clarification will need to be made again and again—that at times democracy and its cultures will serve simply as one more substantial subcollective calling for critique.[15] The repetition or perhaps compulsion of domination abides. But then critique will be most powerful when it itself is not simply repetition or compulsion—when critique takes on the task of modernity's substantial reformation.

In the reformation that is modernity, there is work to do to bring together what we know and what we forget, what history we like and what history we'd prefer to avoid. If I am more inclined to deemphasize the crimes of modernity in favor of those elements of self-correction internal to it, this is because its principle—the principle of critique, of democracy, of interpretation—must be brought forward anew for each age, for individual readers to make of it what they will.

Questions

On his 2017 web page at the Department of History, University of California, Berkeley, intellectual historian Jonathan Sheehan lists courses he has taught or is teaching in his capacity as a professor of early modern European history. Four of interest include:

> *The Substance of Things Unseen: Matter and Spirit, 1650–1800*
> Between 1650 and 1800, matter, spirit, and their relationship, became subjects of unprecedented attention in Europe. Mechanism, the development of a science of forces, new forms of religious imagination, new spiritualisms, the rise of sensationalist psychology, the development of an aesthetics of the sublime, fascination with legal and political abstraction, new materialist ethics, the discovery of "real" immaterial things (public opinion, society, the economy, e.g.): all of these together fundamentally structured what we might broadly call modern immanence and transcendence. Primary readings will likely include: Descartes, Hobbes, Newton, Bekker, Hume, Diderot, Rousseau, Smith, and Kant.

Thresholds of the Modern Age
The period between 1500 and 1800 was the staging ground for many of the formations characteristic of what we understand to be European modernity: science, capitalism, social leveling, secularism, the disciplines of knowledge, and much more. This research seminar will offer students interested in the period a semester-long opportunity for intensive primary research and the writing of a substantial work of historical analysis on a topic in the field. It will also serve as a complement to this semester's History 280 "Substance of Things Unseen: Matter and Spirit, 1650–1800."

European Intellectual History from Renaissance to Enlightenment
Between 1500 and 1800, European thought helped to build the foundations of modern culture, politics, economy, government, law, and religion. This course will introduce students to this transformative period in intellectual history. It will showcase the interactions of ideas and their wider cultural contexts. Its content will range from the Renaissance rediscovery of antiquity to the Scientific Revolution, from the theological innovation of the Reformation to the new forms of political theory that accompanied both French and American Revolutions. Readings will consist principally of primary texts from the period, and will range among a series of writers, including: Erasmus, Martin Luther, Niccolò Machiavelli, John Calvin, Michel Montaigne, Thomas Hobbes, Benedict Spinoza, René Descartes, Jean Jacques Rousseau, and others.

The Reformations of Christendom
Christianity as we now know it has its origins in the European Reformations of the sixteenth century. These Reformations splintered an older Christian world into competing Protestant and Catholic confessions, and fundamentally reconfigured the political and cultural landscape of Europe. This course will focus on the long history of these reformations from 1500 to 1800. It will address the innovative theologies of the period, and their impact on people, churches, and the wider society. And it will particularly highlight the connection between the religious events of the period, and the formation of modern political society. Internal conflicts between Catholics and Protestants, attempts to suppress and repress religious heresy, efforts to impose Christianity on

New World peoples: these bloody battles—we will discover—
were key to the development of the economic, military, and political institutions of modern governments. By understanding
them, we will seek to understand the complexities of our modern
world.[16]

Sheehan's outlines promise to show exactly how uncommon our common notions of modernity are. Yes, capitalism and Reformation; yes the
rediscovery of antiquity and the Scientific Revolution; yes, heresy, inter-
necine conflict, and imperialism. But what are these things? For Sheehan,
an introduction to modernity is an introduction to the question Stevens poses in "An Ordinary Evening in New Haven." What is the history and meaning of reality once reality is all there is? Once reality is—
everything? Sheehan's answer in these courses is not just to underscore
"the complexities of our modern world." He shall be guide as well to the
occult qualities of complexity, as things seen and unseen come to emerge
paradoxically into view: public opinion, society, the economy, the invisible hand that becomes the principle of self-organization.[17] And less directly, the course, the primary reading, the renaissance of criticism, and
not simply bloody battles and heresies.

In recognition of Sheehan's ingenuity, I pose the question whether
there is not a supplementary course to be taught that can fortify students as they make sense of these queries. Stevens does not say whether
his ordinary evening in New Haven is one with a demythologizing intent. Might it mean, "We used to seek beyond reality for everything, or
at least something worth having. Now we seek nothing beyond reality.
Within it, everything"? Is Stevens's wager a history? It is difficult not
to read it as such. In "The Snow Man" Stevens distinguishes between
"Nothing that is not there and the nothing that is," the devastating perception—Is it?—that the loss of God shall not excuse us from the work
of making out what Sheehan calls "the unseen."

Q1: What, though, would be Stevens's history?

> A: The revolution that is the reality of the unseen, the unseen of
> reality, begins, as Stevens begins, with the mind, with God, with
> the poem at the center of things: with the "vulgate of experi-
> ence," the ordinary transposed, with, in short, the moment when
> we can say, with "The Poems of Our Climate," "The imperfect
> is our paradise."

Q2: When is that?

> A: "Pain is human," Stevens writes in "Esthétique du Mal." "This
> is a part of the sublime / From which we shrink." And yet, again in
> "Poems of Our Climate," "Note that, in this bitterness, delight, /
> Since the imperfect is so hot in us, / Lies in flawed words and stub-
> born sounds."

Q3: When is modernity?[18] When was the moment when we knew, "except for us, / The total past felt nothing when destroyed"? When is the
past ours, our destruction? When is this bitterness that is also delight?[19]

In chapter 1, I summoned the Grand Inquisitor and his diabolical maxim:
I have corrected your work. The Grand Inquisitor speaks to the silent
prisoner, whose call to leave homeland for promised land, to enter into
the wager of freedom, to make what is good for you also thereby good
for others, is too difficult. Correction of this principle will entail subversion of it. This is not the glorious subversion that finds the way to freedom in upending what cynically passes for the good. It is the subversion
of resignation. There is no good. I will not get that far.

We saw too that, in claiming not to get as far as the good, the Grand
Inquisitor dissimulates. For he can resign only a good he knows. There
can be no correction of this truth of the proximity of good and evil. Or
there can be only the corrections of its continual clarification, if not its
obfuscation.

It is in this spirit that I enter into the question of when is modernity,
correcting Sheehan's presuppositions as a form of clarification. Is it possible that, in failing to reckon with, in simply presupposing, the question of when, one will misplace "what," misplace the concept? Precisely.
But then no less is it true that, in obsessing about when, one might very
well become deaf to the relevant call, which is to practice, in the fields
of bitterness, the history, if not the rectification, of pain. The total past
destroyed, felt, if only by us. Get on with it, Sheehan would say. Get on
with the projects of history.

So but, yes. Here is what this might mean, following Kant's lead that all
is history except for the conjecture of its beginning; following Nietzsche's
conjecture that "perhaps the past is still essentially undiscovered!"[20]

Modernity is a revolution consistent with an origin that is both past
(came into existence) and present (must continually do so). It is at the
same time the refusal, not simply the retreat, of dualisms of the opposition and identity of truth and appearance, supernatural and natural, self

and other, collective and collective. In modernity, it shall not be as it was in Homer: that it is more honorable to slay another unless and until one is slain by him, or as it was in Plato: that it is better to suffer injustice than to do injustice.[21] Modernity is the refusal of these choices. It is the principle that one is honored in giving honor to the other; that one suffers injustice precisely in doing injustice; that, knowing good and evil, one is forever recused from the recusal that it is one and not also the other—recused, thus, from the choice between them without the choice of them both, in the face of which one can either commit to the good of self *and* other or be in offense. Modernity is not only the wager that the good is not pure, that no good can come of seeking purity. It is the wager that, in the refusal of purity, one cannot, one must not, take refuge simply in impurity, in the world as it is, corrupt, given, animal, violent. One is called, as Abraham is called, to leave all that—to take the world instead as it might be taken, a world of pain that can also be a paradise of equals, of readers, of poets.

At the same time, modernity is the confusion of the dualisms of truth versus appearance, supernatural versus natural, dualisms that, refused, will not retreat. Modernity is the fantasy and the rebellion of their return.

There is a missing distinction in modernity. The perennial dualism of the one and the many embedded in thought and politics is actually two dualisms, two twos. The distinction, I have shown, lies in the relation of the terms that constitute them. In the one case, the terms of the dualism are either opposed or identified. In the other case, the terms are in mutually constituted relation. Only one of the dualisms, the one that refuses relations of either opposition or identity, is creative of human power. But thinking will tend to assimilate these dualisms—to see only one. This assimilation *is* the move of the dualism of opposition/identity and misses the structure of mutual relation. This is so even as the structure of mutual relation is the dualism based on which the very distinction between the two dualisms can be ascertained and the powerful one brought forth. It is missing, then, but present. It is present but must be activated.

Although this observation is dealing in abstract relations, the missing distinction has profound consequences not only for how we think but also for how the world is organized. Dualisms of opposition and identity are the operating system for social and personal dead ends and violence. The claim is not that one is fighting such dualisms with the missing kind. The claim is that in modernity the missing dualism, the dualism of mutual relation, is the very condition based on which such a fight may be launched, as well as betrayed. It is already, so to speak, in the operating system. It is already operating. The work, then, to pick it out—to promote and cultivate it—is the work of criticism, whereby one observes the confusions at play, confusions such as the refusal of the dualism of one and many in favor of the many or the one, or the ineffable beyond one and many, or the dualism of one and many presenting itself as final.

The epoch of modernity is the wager of critique. Once it is possible to constitute two in mutual relation—self and other, Orient and Occident—it is then possible to subvert mutuality, resigning the work to support each side in deference to opposition (they are merely different and can thus be ranked) or identity (they are merely the same and can thus be assimilated). This resignation recapitulates the logic of the one and the many. But it does so—and we can perceive and critique the corrupt move—because of the very self and other that something like Orientalism also profanes. This is as it is in democracy, wherein the critique of natural privilege (divine rights, dynasties, ethnic and racial ranking) gives rise to its recapitulation in terms given the patina of modern right. And it is as it is in religion, where God and neighbor are articulated together, only to serve as yet another instance of the one outranking the many.

In the epoch of modernity the dualism of opposition/identity presupposes the dualism of mutual relation. But then mutual relation is haunted by the other dualism insofar as collectives and persons flee the task to make good on what is possible for them—the inclusion and support of others as the condition of our own inclusion and support.

Modernity is paradox in beginning with the absolute end of mutuality. It is paradox in beginning absolutely.

Freedom is a preoccupation of modernity. But this preoccupation is a paradox. What is the history of freedom? The historian leans in to diagram its change over time. But would freedom not have always been in the world, as the standard against which its defilements can be measured? Would it not have emerged simply as a function of the human animal? Or a function, in keeping with the mood of our age, of the illusion of the animal called human?

Modernity is the recognition that freedom, together with truth and the good, is made, as politics is made, in confrontation with the limits of the human imagination of its law. Modernity is the paradox that the project of the human animal originates.

Q4: Does freedom originate always and everywhere?

> A1: Yes. But first it has to become possible. Like good and evil, it is the cause of itself.

> A2: Therefore no. Freedom has an origin in history. History is the origin (of the) story of freedom. *Lekh lekha.* Leave the land of your fathers and mothers.

God is a preoccupation of modernity. In modernity, God recedes, religion recedes. But what recedes? The God who is the master of nature, only to be mastered by it. In modernity, God is the concept of, in being subject to, a shared reality that grounds, in expressing, human freedom.

Modernity is not only the separation of the mind and God as, The mind knows nature (science) and not (only) God. It is not only, Nature is the realm of science, and the mind knows nature and itself (science). Modernity is also the connection of the mind and God over against their division. God is what the mind can practice even as, Anselm and Descartes bewail, they can but barely touch. Nature in turn is not outside the mind. They are not opposed. Nature cannot be thought outside the person who also enlarges it in taking it some particular way. The law of the neighbor is not in nature. But it must be exercised there; it is for there. There is nowhere else.

In holding that there is nowhere else, modernity is the primacy of labor.

In the primacy of labor there are two modernities, the one an innovation (science, industry, revolution, secularism) and the other a call to the work of continuity (freedom, love, promise). These modernities, in their diversity, are not opposed.

The innovation of the period modernity is real. It is important in social, political, institutional, economic, and artistic respects. In concept, however, there is no break but the one in the beginning, the break of—the epoch of—freedom from the land of one's ancestors, freedom for the land that is promised.

The break of postmodernity is either skepticism of the value of the break of modernity as social, political, institutional, economic, and artistic innovation or conviction that the modern break is illusory, subordinate to an error it does not interrupt that reaches back to some earlier point in time. In this case, the break of postmodernity will identify the modern break and its ancient beginning with respect to some problem in the beginning (philosophy, theology, politics) that the break did not solve. In the light of which postmodernity will solve it.

Postmodernity is confused inasmuch as the problem the break of modernity did not solve is simply the problem that is its continuity with its beginning, which institutes modernity as incomplete in being impossible in Kant's second sense—requiring labor. Postmodernity cannot solve this in instituting yet another break. Indeed, in so doing, postmodernity manufactures a problem, the positive (one), that only it, the negative (many), can solve. It happens, however, this this manufactured problem is but a repetition of the dualism of opposition/identity that both the innovation of modernity and its beginning refuse. Postmodernity refuses dualism too, but it also reduplicates it. Consistent with postmodernity's confusion of its work, it will sometimes claim that only premodernity knows what it knows, solves what it solves, forging an alliance between a manufactured problem and a manufactured period, with modernity the emblem of error.

Postmodernity is modern in its inventiveness. Modern, too, in its rebellion.

Readers and moderns have noticed that the innovation of modernity, the invention of the secular, carries over things from "before," whenever and whatever that is. The argument is that theology is carried over. Christianity is carried over. Violence is carried over. This observation has value in reference to the beginning of freedom, modernity the epoch, which the innovation of modernity the period both enacts (activates) and profanes.

In Kant's language, the break of freedom is modernity's "rational" origin, liberating both good and evil for the story, the history, of all origins, changes, and breaks, violent and otherwise.

Postmodernity is sometimes taken as what happened very recently, for example, in the 1910s and 1920s or the 1960s and 1970s. Postmodernity is indeed the coming into existence of modernity as modernism, as critique in principle, even if it confuses the question of authorship. Postmodernity is a reformation. It is intensification, remaking, and reframing.

What postmodernity confuses is not only that it itself is not a primary break. It confuses the novum that there can be such a thing as a break in time, which novum does not happen in time taken in itself (the date) but is the origin of (its) history, the concept and value of dates.

Postmodernity announces its work as making history the central *topos*, but it only shows thereby that history, as modernity, abides.

On the one hand, postmodernity thereby recapitulates the problem from which the innovation of modernity also suffers, in confusing its beginning. It (postmodernity, modernity) does not understand it (the beginning) in erecting its own beginning as novel. On the other hand, postmodernity is more confused than modernity. It is, so to speak, confused twice over, first, in taking for a nonbreak the innovation of modernity, which already "knew" (even if it confused) its innovations as continuous with the principle, and, second, in missing what *was* the break of modernity in its social, political, institutional, economic, and artistic significance; in missing the principle × two in quest of something else, something behind appearances. Reformations are good. But the destruction of the past is ours.

In the break that is modernity, consistent with the beginning of freedom, there is a struggle that confuses where is the truth, where is God, where is nature, and where is the mind. In the multifarious, not to say endless, varieties of positions that pit these elements for and against one another, the position that holds them together—how it does, what it means that it does—stands alone as the principle that the good I desire (God, truth) shall be made (mind as work) in a nature that includes both you and me. It shall not be a matter of imperialism to observe that it was Abraham's God who changed the terms of Plato's—from opposition to mutual freedom. Indeed, since there can be no movement from opposition to freedom, there is no credit but to the call, the movement from freedom to freedom, from the departure from the land of the ancestors to a land that will be shown. And yet we know imperialism abides. The land that will be shown will confound freedom, recapitulating the homeland.

Q5: Athens and Jerusalem, philosophy and theology, the secular and religion: When and where does philosophy begin (and end)? When and where does religion begin (and end)? If philosophy begins in ancient Greece, is it thereby modern? If religion begins in Jerusalem, is it thereby ancient?

A1: Philosophy begins as the question, What is good, true? This might also be, What is divine? But when, for example, Nietzsche, late to the change of modernity, says "God is dead," philosophy, which recalls that it knew this, becomes (returns to being) something that can be applied to the question of the divine. Or not.

Theology begins as the question, What is good, true? What is the divine? It begins as apparently indistinguishable from philosophy. But after, for example, Nietzsche, theology is still the question, What is the divine?, a question it now pursues (resumes) either without philosophy or in exceeding it.

A2: These are conventions.

Q6: What is the change that is the removal of philosophy?

A: There are three answers, and the question needs augmentation.

Q6a: What is theology to begin with? Does theology begin without philosophy? If so, when would philosophy be added, and what is its principal difference?

A1: Theology begins as religion (Jerusalem, Bibles) without philosophy (Athens), and philosophy begins as reason without religion. Philosophy (Athens) is added to theology (Jerusalem) as theology's handmaiden, to prove its claims and/or to effect a synthesis between reason (mind) and revelation (mystery). Philosophy, in becoming handmaiden to theology, takes on theology's question of God, but in philosophical terms. The philosophy of religion. The principal difference between theology and philosophy is that theology seeks God and philosophy seeks truth. The one would remain mysterious, the other would become rational. But since philosophy, in seeking truth (the one), seeks a truth that transcends the world of appearance (the many), there is no difference between them. The philosophy (the truth) of religion (revelation) is that they are the same. Thus various medieval syntheses, whether philosophical or mystical.

With the death of God at the end of modernity (Kant or Nietzsche), or in the Renaissance (the discovery of the Greeks), philosophy is cut loose, returning to its original state apart from theology, if not different in relation to its goal. The change for philosophy in being cut loose from theology is that the divine is no longer the name of its question. The change for theology in having philosophy cut loose is that it must become, as it were, philosophical on its own, if always ambivalent with respect to philosophy, which now does not recognize it, theology, as philosophical. (Theology is dogmatic. Philosophy is skeptical [of this dogma].) Theology, for all its ambition, allows this to happen in failing to convince philosophy (or itself) that the question of the divine is not "religion" only, not dogma in relation to which philosophy is argument or question.

The term continental philosophy is designed to house those for whom God did not die and philosophy did not split off. But the opposition between philosophy and theology cannot be evaded, that is, their oppositional relation to each other in terms of the identical object.

A2: God dies four times in modernity.

1. In the biblical traditions God dies as a Form outside existence in being/becoming the form of existence in light of death.
2. In the rational and mystical syntheses of the biblical traditions with Platonism and Aristotelianism, the God who dies as a Form (1) dies in being resurrected as the opposition (and identity) of Form and the form of existence.
3. In Kant's critique, the resurrected God (2) dies in turn in the recognition that the death that is the resurrection of Form is merely a confusion (of 1).
4. In the nineteenth and twentieth centuries, God dies in and as the confused apprehension of (1) and (3). If (2) is the position that kills the God of life and death in bringing God back to a life opposed to death, (4) is the position that worries that the God in (1) and (3), dead, is yet not dead enough–a legitimate worry given (2). Thus "God is dead. God remains dead," says the madman. "And we have killed him."[22]

A3: Theology (Jerusalem, Bibles) does not begin without philosophy (the death of God). Theology is not dogma to philosophy's

argument or question, not gods/revelation/mystery to philosophy's reason. It is the principle of enacting the good of realizing
for others what you would realize for yourself. It is the divine law
that collectives shall be founded on the principle of inclusion, not
domination, extension, or membership. Theology is the abrogation of God as the head of natural law, the death of God as the
abrogation of truth outside history. Philosophy is the principle
that truth appears. Theology will call this principle God, neighbor, faith. Philosophy will say reason, thought, history. They
practice the same principle.

Therefore insofar as theology begins with Jerusalem and its bibles, theology and philosophy begin together there and then. Insofar as theology as the question of God, or truth, begins there,
philosophy as the question of God, or truth, begins there too. It
would take over from its Athenian identity exactly nothing. For
in Athens the question of God, or truth, cannot be posed outside
the opposition and the synthesis of Form and form. In Athens
theology would be in service to the good, or truth, that the gods
love, in contradictory identity with the service of philosophy to
the good, or true, that is loved by the gods.

The question of God—that is, self and other without contradiction, freedom for one and all, truth in and as history—is the
beginning that is philosophy. It is the beginning that is modernity. You can place this beginning in Descartes, or in the Bible,
or in any of the thinkers and artists who understand, with Kierkegaard, that you begin at the beginning only to find, as Said and
Vico teach, that one must begin again. God is one name for this
beginning. Modernity is another. Go! is another. Freedom is yet
another.

Q6b: But are philosophy and theology, then, two discourses or one?

A: The difference between theology and philosophy insofar as
they come into existence together cannot be finally or constitu-
tionally established. The difference between philosophy and theology can be seen only when they attempt separation at the ostensible end of modernity or attempt synthesis in the ostensibly
premodern. Theology would retain its interest in the question
of God, but it would concede that this interest requires belief or

confession. Philosophy would extrude the question of God, and likewise assimilate faith to belief, in favor now of truth—of language, logic, argument. Now God would be either an obstacle to understanding the world rightly (philosophy) or a royal road to it (theology). The difference between philosophy and theology, then, insofar as they begin together but attempt (or fantasize) separation, is what each asserts in being separated from each other. One says, my God. The other says, there is no God.

Insofar as theology and philosophy begin together, the difference between them is what they share—that each needs reformation with reference to the other.

Q7: What does it mean, then, to grant religious freedom?

A: *Lekh lekha!* Go!

Homeland: what is mine, genetic value, collective as an end in itself, totem.
Home land: the collective that makes possible, in also expressing, inclusion, openness, egress.

Promised land: yet another (now intensified) homeland (terror).
Promised land: the constitution of a home land (faith).

Abraham leaves.
Adam and Eve leave.

Abraham leaves homeland (ancestors) for promised land.
Adam and Eve leave homeland (Eden) for promised land.

1. From religious (Eden, ancestor) to secular (history, politics, violence, rectification)
2. From secular (nature, fathers) to religious (covenant, promise, violence, rectification).

The distinction of modernity is of what is open, supportive of complexity, critical, yet also liable to confusion. In each of 1 and 2, the second is modernity, both religious and secular, neither religious nor secular. But one moves, as Adam and Eve show, not from nonmodernity to modernity but from modernity to modernity: From the land as sacred in itself to the land that shows we never lived there, but then also reinstates it—the sacred in itself. From homeland to home land. To homeland.

Adam and Eve are modern in being tempted by homeland as the refuge of (their) nature, with God as head. They are tempted by order as hierarchy. This order is not nature as big fish eat little fish. It is nature as the value of natural order. In Judaism and Christianity, this order puts God

> 1. as head of state (divine right)
> 2. as outside the state (in itself)

But Adam and Eve fall, they begin, in recognition that each of these premises shall be refused. They begin in recognition that they are like their God in knowing the good of mutuality, not hierarchy, the order of freedom, but then therefore work, toil, labor, suffering, madness. Adam and Eve, together with God, are thereby modern in enacting covenant in place of ignorance and mere mastery. They are, together, modern in leaving Eden, in leaving what postmodernism manufactures as the positive, confusedly attributing it to modernity and religion: the in itself, indisputable, blind assertion of and subjection to (nature as the) good.

Q8: What is Abraham's struggle with Isaac? Why do Adam and Eve leave home?

> A1: Abraham and Adam and Eve are the same. To leave one's home is to inaugurate the modern of working in concert for the good of live and let live.
>
> A2: Abraham and Adam and Eve are different. Modernity distinguishes itself
>
> > 1. from homelands (Abraham).
> > 2. from the myth that there is a homeland (Adam and Eve).
>
> Modernity is a fight with the temptation to make homelands and to take itself as one.
>
> For Abraham and Adam and Eve home is not evil, but it must be deconstructed. It is not an end in itself, an absolute border. Nature

is not evil, but it cannot be home. It is, as the story of the Fall has it, temptation. What must be refused is not nature but

1. Human nature insofar as it takes its nature as its only (given) end.
2. God insofar as God stands as the head of nature.

In so refusing, or, for Adam and Eve, falling, they become like God, but no less God becomes like them, issuing promises to which God is subject instead of blind decrees that are subject to no one. The relation with God and with each other becomes for Adam and Eve, as for all human beings, the sign of what they can betray but not exclude: knowledge of the good of knowing one's nature as also neighbor. It is then that, insofar as human nature takes the other as its end, in leaving the value that is my nature as an end in itself, its nature is/becomes a home land.

The promised land that is a home land will not prevent the confusion/temptation of nature, the desire to have one's ends given, to remain in one's home.

A1 and A2: Abraham and Adam and Eve are the same. But insofar as they are different, Abraham is the sign of the distinction of modern and nonmodern and Adam and Eve are the sign of modernity and its confusions (temptations). The first distinction (Abraham) establishes the principle of modernity, the principle of inclusion, of egress. But once modernity is distinguished, it hosts all distinctions. All is modernity and its confusions.

Q9: In modernity, or once modernity, what becomes of the nonmodern?

A1: Abraham before Adam and Eve reverses the biblical order. Abraham's beginning begins in distinction from all others. The distinction is *of* beginning, of leaving home.

Meaning 1: Abraham has no attributes as important as this one.
Meaning 2: If all others begin likewise, then Abraham is different from no one, distinct only in, himself, beginning. Adam and Eve's beginning shows the double

distinction: from others, from our myths (of others). Abraham and Adam and Eve can each be first or second.

A2a: The attempt to avoid using the modern (qua West, Christianity) as the standard of knowing others—the danger of the subordination of the nonmodern to the modern—begets the effort to know the nonmodern

1. as nonmodern, but even
2. as the content of the modern—to subordinate, but in the opposite direction, as Durkheim does in making the primitive elementary. This is like the effort to know Greece as the origin of modernity, to subsume West in Greece or to bifurcate West as Athens and Jerusalem.

A2b: This move is based on the convictions that

1. the claims of the West/Christianity about the other, in being formulated in domination, are incorrect, and
2. the West/Christianity dominates others, but it is just like them, just another other, as measured by an elementary form that contains all but is not specifically any.

A3: The West and Christianity are inarguably formations that are confused, opportunistic, dominating. But neither the position of the nonmodern nor the position of the elementary form that contains nonmodern and modern is tenable.

1. The nonmodern, together with theories thereof, expresses a dualism of opposition and identity, of inside and outside, sacred and profane, natural and supernatural, truth versus appearance, collective versus collective. It is the position criticism refuses in committing to the collective that is also open, the truth that, in appearing, deconstructs the truth as it would be in itself.
2. There is no elementary form inclusive of nonmodern and modern. The only elementary form is the distinction of the nonmodern from the modern—the distinction of (a) the position that is distinguished from, in being critical of, its border (modern) and (b) the position that merely expresses border (nonmodern).

3. Religious studies and anthropology each include the effort to isolate the position of the nonmodern and, in some cases, to make it the condition of the modern, in response to domination. They are presumptive inclusion in the face of presumptive exclusion. Philosophy names the effort to derive the modern from nonmodernity without distinction between them. The first (RS and A) mirrors nonmodernity while tying off modernity in the name of representing it—as nonmodernity. The second (P) reads nonmodernity (ancient Greece) as just like modernity.

A4: The critique of nonmodern formations begins with their refusal and ends with their inclusion. Refusal is not domination. The critique of nonmodern formations begins with the temptation to dominate them and ends with the deconstruction of this temptation, the critique of modernity.

Q10: Is the conservation of simplicity on the grounds of simplicity (non-modernity) possible, then, in the social setting in which religion is version 2, the conservation of simplicity in the context of complexity?

A1: Yes. The conservation of simplicity in the context of complexity is not necessarily modernity, which is the conservation of simplicity on the grounds of complexity. Once modernity, however, all simplicities are in the presence of complexity as a value, which puts pressure on their simplicity. This is the value of freedom of religion. Insofar as religion is unfree, it is pressured or reformed by the value of freedom.

A2: Freedom of religion requires that freedom, in turn, be about religion qua principle, that is, supportive of difference, not a freedom that runs over everyone as the price of inclusion.

A3: Freedom of religion helps to reform religion, but thus also itself, insofar as each is conceived and fought for in and through the other.

Q11: Which religion needs to be reformed?

A1: Religion is a system conserving the integrity of a collective

1. unto the border
2. as a contestation with borders

Freedom is to reform 1. But freedom, says Kant, is the same as religion insofar as religion is the constitution of democracy, the principle of ethics = 2.

A2: Once there is modernity, the nonmodern is in relation to modernity. There is nothing outside modernity, not because modernity has no borders, but because its borders = inclusion, critique. Modernity, then, insofar as it is not inclusive, is nothing other than the betrayal of its principle. The freedom of religion is to pressure both nonmodern (unto the border) and confused modern (unto the border).

A3: Insofar as freedom is commitment (host, complexity as a value), not instrument (coercion, contradiction), it reforms religion (collective) insofar as it is unfree. It allows collectives to abide. It is the larger term. The elementary term. Freedom of religion is a critique of religion insofar as freedom says to the collective:

1. Be as you are.
2. In and by means of inclusion not opposition.

(1) + (2) can be taken as warrant for domination. This is confused. The principle of pluralism is a principle, not just a plural. Pluralism has conditions (2). Yet it is easy to confuse pluralism, together with liberalism, for domination. This is not only because pluralism has conditions (2). It is because insofar as pluralism is taken as mere complexity, it *is* domination; that is, there will be nothing to stem might makes right, whether of the collective or against it.

Q12: Whither freedom of religion?

A: Freedom of religion is essential precisely insofar as it is impossible. Religion is the conservation of simplicity. It needs critique.

Q13: One asks Abraham, What? Why?

> A: In leaving home, one finds, on the one hand, simply more of what one left. The world is not different by my leaving. Why would it be? My leaving is for another land, albeit one that shall make good on the principle: *leave your homeland*. One, then, that does not set up another homeland, much less one in the name of the promise. The promise, rather, is of critique. It is a promise of a home founded not on the fathers but on persons, one that can include all, not as converts but as themselves.

> What is the world? The world = systems and the words to justify one's spot in them. Critique is, What is the border of the system you are in (self, collective, corporation) so as to include?

> Inclusion not expansion. Inclusion not domination. It is not to envelop another in your system. It is egress in the system. It is system in support of persons, without whom it is nothing.

Critique is abrasive, perhaps, and disruptive. But critique is also, Affirm what is. What is, alone, cannot do this. Confusion abides. (Evil, be thou my good.) To do it, to affirm the real, you have to see it as you would be seen, know it as you would be known. History and/as ethics. This is the response to what might be confused, wrong, evil. Commit to know— know to commit—as much as is in your power, which commitment, which knowledge, in the distinction of good and evil, enacts the good. In criticism, as in canon, one's beginnings are never arbitrary.

> 1. Grand Inquisitor: It is hard to be for the other, not simply dominating or being dominated.
> 2. Satan: It is even harder not to be.

Q14: How does change happen, then?

> A: This is the one change. The act of reading; the act of knowing the good of the other. Sometimes critique is a sword, but always constrained by knowing and committing to the other.

Q15: Modernity is the principle that is the death of the collective as an end in itself. It is the other(s) as an end in themselves. It is critique of systems that operate without persons to engender them. It is the system by and for persons. Democracy would be principled but, like freedom of religion, it will be confused. Is the point to allow us to be as we are (affirmation) or to reform us (affirmation)?

> A1: Principle is affirmation. The system of freedom, the process that is principle, has as its consequence that not only will it host the unfree entities that are betrayals of it, it will betray itself. It is too hard for us.

> A2: Education/understanding/interpretation is nevertheless and therefore in praise of the tenacity to bear up under the difficulty and to struggle for you as for me.

This is to offer a course supplementing those of Jonathan Sheehan. It is to hold that modernity is not finished, not only because the grand schemes that modernity inaugurated—science, capital, industry, printing, heresy, reformation, antiquity recovered and lost—have left a terrible mark, such that to know them is to know the total past, destroyed. It is not only because we might recuperate something from the mess that is yet realizable. Modernity is not finished because it is built on principle, not on schemes. It is incomplete, impossible, not in being futile, quixotic, but in being fundamental, originary, but hence true to the insight from Stevens that modernity's principle, together with the pain of its enactment, is "part of the sublime / From which we shrink." From which we will not simply be destroyed. This is ground zero—ashes and their history.

8

Of Gods, Laws, Rabbis, and Ends

It is paradoxical that what exempts people is the ground for their inclusion.

Adam Phillips, *Equals*

The Religion of Freedom

In the conclusion to *The Impossibility of Religious Freedom*, Winnifred Sullivan argues that religious freedom is not a value that can be upheld in law. The book examines the Florida case of *Warner v. Boca Raton* (1999) concerning the display of prominent religious memorials at a city cemetery. Although it is "about what counts as religion, legally, in Boca Raton, Florida, at the beginning of the twenty-first century," Sullivan demonstrates what she calls the "opacity" of the languages of religion and law to each other.[1] After an account of these languages in sometimes tortured confrontation, Sullivan's conclusion is that it may be time to jettison the idea of religious freedom. She writes:

> The evidence in the *Warner* case could be understood to suggest that what is sought by the plaintiffs is not the right of "religion" to reproduce itself but the right of the individual, every individual, to life outside the state—the right to live as a self on which many given, as well as

chosen, demands are made. Such a right may not be best realized
through laws guaranteeing religious freedom but by laws guaranteeing equality.[2]

Sullivan's concern is the difficulty of identifying what religion is from
a legal standpoint. But it is also the question of whether the effort to do
so is unnecessary in light of a more encompassing right. This would be
to say more than that courts are ill equipped to manage the complex object religion. It is to strike at the usability of the term as such in order to
direct our attention to more identifiable, if not also more pressing, questions of equality and the realization of life outside the state, as Sullivan
puts it. Outside, that is, the regulation of the state's representatives in the
name of a falsely subtractive common sphere. One thinks of teenagers
in France getting arrested for sartorial threats to the secular. Or, in Sullivan's material, debates over the size and tastefulness of objects to mark
a loved one's grave. Surely the commons has no interest here, she urges.
At the least, in cases where religion names something seemingly obvious,
such as the display of a crèche in a town square, are we not overdue to
converse in public about what scholars of religion have striven to make
manifest, which is that the "thing" the freedom of religion is supposed
to protect may have long since migrated to other social and discursive
arenas?

What does freedom have to do with religion?[3] Might it make sense to
declare a failure the constitutional experiment to protect a separate right
called freedom of religion? In addition to the charge of opacity, there
is the question of whether this freedom is self-defeating, foisting a particular concept of religion on a plurality of phenomena only to find that
the plural realizations of it cannot be clearly recognized. Sullivan's line
of questioning opens up the possibility of revisiting a foundational issue
through questions of equality, plurality, and guarantee.

In support of this work, I have asked the reverse: What does religion
have to do with freedom? The question is, How might religious freedom
be affected by the supposition that freedom includes a concept of religion? Freedom is the determination of one's own ends, says Kant, which
singular practice presupposes, he argues, the ends of others. Kant's concept of freedom is also an expression of religion insofar as religion is an
expression of equality, the relation between self and other.

How relevant are these connections to thinking about religion in
the contemporary world? One response might be that by religion Kant
meant Christianity. Therefore his religious content to freedom cannot
be extended to a plurality. Freedom in a constitutional context has no

such content. The word Christianity, however, is not prima facie indicative of what Kant is trying to do in holding the terms religion and freedom together. The same is true of the word religion itself, whose mobility can be obfuscating. What is at issue is the social and plural value of substantive notions. What if the value you are enacting is the value that values be enacted? Would this be the position of freedom or the position of religion? As we have seen, it is not clarifying to assume that value (or truth or the sacred or reality) is something intrinsic or self-contained, to be put into practice or freed while remaining complete unto itself. This notion may be precisely the problem with the freedom of religion, since a self-contained value is a contradiction. Once you assert it, it is uncontained and requiring interpretation, which interpretation would then, by its logic, dissolve it.

Nor is it clarifying, however, to position critique as merely the observation of this contradiction. The question is what the observation is to serve. What is it to take the stance of the partner to the intrinsic object, the negative of procedure to the positive of substance, or, as we saw in chapter 2, the negative of history to the positive of religion? Will this relation not reduplicate itself regardless of what is under scrutiny? The move to imagine religion as other than religion-the-object is to ask what kind of relations critique specifies and to connect this question to the very thing under scrutiny: religion. Although it may behoove modern liberal democracies to rid themselves of the tenets of a specifically religious freedom, such societies are presumably not free to jettison freedom itself and thus, on a certain reading, are stuck, it might be said, with religion. If the courts have been inept on the question of religion, we scholars or simply moderns have been no less perplexed about what freedom entails.

Reading Sullivan alongside a similar article by Michael J. Sandel will clarify the stakes. In *The Impossibility of Religious Freedom*, Sullivan argues that law cannot protect religious freedom in contemporary America at least partly because secular law cannot recognize the pervasive kind of religion in circulation, a religion that consists as much of local and family customs, improvised ritual borrowing, and voluntary association as it does of authoritative bodies, classic texts, and historically continuous traditions and dogmas.[4] *Warner* shows that the court, looking for something more traditional, or at least stable, was ill equipped to deal with the realia in front of it.

In "Religious Liberty: Freedom of Choice or Freedom of Conscience," Sandel argues just the opposite: that American law, from its sources to the present, presumes and supports a liberal subject for whom religion concerns a set of voluntary behaviors. Such law, then, cannot acknowledge, much less protect, the subject for whom religion is not voluntary but obligatory. This would be the subject who seeks not the freedom to be religious but the freedom to have been always already under the obligation of religion, which is to say, to be unfree. By this account the courts trivialize religion, whether they are protecting the right to display nativity scenes in public or restricting the wearing of yarmulkes in the military.[5] Sullivan acknowledges as much when she notes the "Janus-faced quality" of religion in the late modern period, either associated with the irrational and sequestered or rendered invisible as a set of Jeffersonian ideals about the proper republic.[6]

These versions of the religious self, as unencumbered and as encumbered, not only have a common history, they are variations of the same concept of history. The one (unencumbered) places the self in a neutral civic space within which she has a set of rights to self-expression that include the right to practice this or that religion (A). Critics of this self and this neutrality will often say that both are religious objects, conditioned by a Protestantism that lurks in the structure of the American secular public. The other (encumbered) places the self in some set of fundamental traditions, narratives, and obligations without which it cannot be understood to be in possession of any rights whatever (B). Critics of this self will note the authoritarian dangers of this position and worry about its incompatibility with democracy and its culture, including the values of toleration and equality.

The positions are variations on a concept of history understood as what gives birth to unbounded differentiation (periods, selves, positions) and the differentiation of bounds (just these and not those). Each position emphasizes one more than the other. But both, in their opposition, are inadequate. They are not inadequate descriptions of religion understood as what people do and believe. No doubt Sullivan and Sandel accurately depict the two dominant performances of religion in contemporary America as conditioned by the maxim freedom of religion. They are, rather, inadequate in failing to plumb what they share, in clinging to a distinction whose logic neither side plumbs and whose mobility produces the repetition of infinite versions of opposition.

It is possible, I have shown, to use the concept of religion in service of a distinction and a history that is more generative, more attentive to the terms of inclusion. Freedom of religion, impossible as religion is impossible, might also be simply redundant. This would be to take religion as what some Enlightenment thinkers called *vera religio*, true religion, or what the biblical prophets called *mishpat u'tzdakah*, justice and righteousness, that is, concerning freedom in equality. The divine law in these traditions is the law that holds, as thinkers like Hegel and Marx put it, that each is free if and only if all are free. One nation under God. To be sure, God as head of state will be to position a totem at the head of a collective for opportunistic purposes. But it might equally be, as Spinoza had it, the position of democracy, the principle before which all are equal.

What is typically denoted religion in freedom of religion includes those things that are determined to require limitation: the institutions and rites whose values do not necessarily coordinate with a commons, a public. Critics of this premise remind us that the common might itself be an opportunistic event of a particular totem. But they miss the critique that conceives religion as a name for the form at the root of freedom, "impossible" in being the critique of nature, of our nature. This is the critique of religion that is equally a critique of reason, a critique of existence. Kant is exemplary on this score, declaiming two impossibles, consistent with the two dualisms, the distinction of modernity: one that is thinking's downfall and one that is included in the power of thought. The first, the dualism of opposition/identity, includes theologies of God as the master of nature, naturalism and supernaturalism; the second, the dualism of mutual relation, includes the concept of freedom, but also religion insofar as it is expressive thereof. Kant's distinction differentiates the two impossibles, but it is also makes one dependent on the other. The second impossible (of freedom, of religion) is what the first impossible (God as head of nature) confuses. Insofar as religion denotes the second impossible, it requires not protection but clarification and commitment. Insofar as religion denotes the first impossible, it requires critique, not protection. Religion forms the ground of its own critique. There is nothing outside it because it is the human condition "at war with itself," to employ Hegel's locution again.

Consider the "king's two bodies" on which both politics and religion in the Middle Ages were written: the natural body, by which the king was understood to be properly mortal, and the body politic, by which he was proclaimed eternal.[7] This divinized politics whereby blood is elevated to the status of the gods through the body of the monarch is one the nation-state categorically rejects, marking its end as modernization, secularization, whose signs are parliament, the rule of law, the multitude, the transposition of the monarch into symbol, into "flag." Politics is modernized in being separated from the blood of religion. Durkheim observes, to be sure, that flags and multitudes are religion by another name; that religion is not blood but clan, and thus totem—the collective that is engendered through the sacred border. But Durkheim's insight, we have seen, is also a suppression of the specificity, the distinction, of the modern.

The distinction that is modernity is not flags where once there were gods, which now are revealed as interchangeable. It is multitudes whose laws are gods in refusing clans: the end, but of course never the end of the fantasy and temptation, of blood, thus kin, ethnos, tribe as ultimate value. The problem with religion from the standpoint of modernity is not kings and gods but nature. The news of the truly radical Enlightenment is not that religion can be reduced to nature.[8] It is that this reduction is not news, for religion is all too natural: not natural as birds and bees are natural, but natural as only human animals can be—in making nature as it seems in itself their sole nature. The collective absolute in totemic splendor. It is not, then, as Durkheim would have it, that religion is an elementary form. For it might mean blood or it might mean its refusal. The elementary form is modernity, the name for the refusal, which itself then will be ritually refused.

The question of modernity and religion is, In the light of the modernization of politics from, as it were, slaves to subjects to citizens, would not religion also have modernized? Could religion be not the thing that needs protection but the very framework determining the bounds of what needs protection, the framework determining the bounds of rights and freedoms?

The question of whether religion modernized yields two responses, two stories.

> A1: Yes. Religion modernized. It became, for better or for worse, disenchanted in detaching from cosmos and kingdom. It may still be of value. Or it may be of negative value—the story of the unencumbered self, the liberated self in novel thrall to the engines of innovation, singularity, and capital. It is Protestantism and its orderly mass world, whether overtly a prelude to the rise of consumer culture or clandestinely a smuggling of the sinister collective of blood, modernity itself, that is, Christianity, ethnos by another name, visible only in the demonized others, the Jew, the Muslim. Visible only in blood itself, impossible to escape precisely in making it metaphor.[9] Once religion is detached from the body of the monarch, where it constitutes the glorious and heinous marriage of church, state, and nature/cosmos, it retreats into the shadows, where it dawdles and sputters when it is not plotting its return or hiding its tracks.

A2: No. Religion remains an undigested scandal, for better and for worse. It remains tied up in the blood of the divine king. Naturalism, supernaturalism.

Is it inconceivable that religion, released from blood, that is, equipped precisely to name it, is now encumbered with nothing so much as the task Adam and Eve faced: simply to live up to this release—to keep faith with it, to refuse the lure of enchantment and disenchantment both? Religion the fruit that is thus neither indigestible nor tasteless nor secretly rotten? Religion, then, as what is supportive of persons and collectives as they make "their solitary way" in worlds of toil and strife, free at least from the rank waters of a pregnant cosmos, free at least to found collectives on other grounds?[10]

We are stymied in comprehending that our business with religion is unfinished because the Enlightenment and we its epigones were so successful in banishing religion according to the dichotomy in Sandel and in Sullivan, reflected in Jefferson's deistic opposition of religion as mystery and religion as reasonable. This banishment would not be a problem if the unfinished business with religion concerned merely religion. If it did, we could simply go to where religion has been banished and keep talking about it (as in departments of divinity) or keep on banishing it (as in departments of religious studies). But the unfinished business with religion does not concern merely religion. It concerns the founding of good collectives, as it did with Adam and Eve. Instead of making this difficult labor central to religion and its critique, we cling to religion the totem, whose Enlightenment "critique" did nothing so much as establish it. This critique brought with it an ethic of tolerance that, after having been too restrictive (disingenuous), came to be free of all restriction: live and let live. Tolerance as, I don't know what you do but you are free to keep doing it, for the most part, until you break the law: a law that does not understand you. Enter Sullivan. What alternative is better? Perhaps tolerance as, I know what you do and we differ, but we do so based on a fundamental agreement. Yet this latter version of tolerance has been charged with contradiction, the very concept of agreement diverting from the thing at issue—genuine difference.

These are important challenges, but they are not insoluble either intellectually or politically. They do not require tomes of disputation or generations to study the problem further. The Enlightenment critique of religion was confused on the questions both of religion and of critique. Spinoza and Kant, exceptions as well as exemplars, are unusual to this day in refusing the contradictions and hypocrisies in which this discourse draws energy. (Which does not mean they are perfectly contemporary in sensibility or indeed perfect at all.) Given the "impossibility" Sullivan brings up to date in looking at contemporary legal decisions, an impossibility founded on a diversity of ends, a diversity of concepts, and a confusion of purpose, the Enlightenment attempt to critique religion was its failure—that is, it failed to advance adequate criticism. The consciousness of the legitimate claims of diverse citizens merely determined that the heirs to this legacy would turn on the messenger, declaiming Enlightenment reason itself merely a masquerade for violence in the commons. The solution has been to grant religion, external to what is common, freedom to be exactly itself, what it was, what it is always tempted with: the attachment to cosmos, kin, and clan.

Is this all modernity can manage?

The thing that begins Enlightenment is not the religion of reason, which would have been no match for the religion of blood. It is the religion of the impossible, religion as a critic of itself, a critic of the romance of blood in exposing the matrix expressive of divine might makes right— whenever and wherever that has been. Modernity forgets itself.

In the study of religion, scholars are careful to describe and delimit and reframe. Religion is complicated. We therefore do not do what the judges in *Schempp* or *Warner* do. Should the Bible be read in the classroom? We say we know how it can be done consistent with the law. But if the law does not understand what a Bible is? If the law is not merely inconsistent but actually incoherent on the question of what religion is? How can we be in accord with it? If we are not in accord with it, because one cannot be, *what* then are we in accord with, and whose standard or law is this?

When it comes to religion in society, to the question of religion's role in a good or better society, we lay our scholarly cards down with impressive speed. The multiplication of scholarly complexity is for what social purpose? Freedom *of* religion, end of story. End of what story? End of the story of complexity, for one thing. Religion shall mean what the religious say it means. It shall mean, in other words, what the constitution needs it to mean: the individual under a set of obligations by which she understands herself as unfree (B) and/or the individual who is first and foremost free to be anything she wants (A). (B an object of respect or fear; A one of skepticism.) We will strive to understand how it circulates; we will track it, pummel its certitudes, and observe its workings in the social and political spheres it appears in. But is religion of value? Should we require it to be of value or study what value it is not? My grasp of its complexity, such as it is, will not equip me to answer these questions. End of the story, therefore, of progress. Why would, or how could, re-

ligion then be anything other than an endless site of definition, redu-
plication, and confusion? Why would, or how could, it ever be a site, a
source, a critique of common value?

To accede to "freedom of religion" is to surrender the task of ensuring that religion concerns freedom, the common task of taking the ends
of others as our own, which religion—its defenders and critics alike—is
uniquely equipped to obscure. For either religion is a form of criticism
or it dwells in the confusions of collectives. Either it is the principle of
taking others as ends in themselves or it is the boast of a collective to be
an end in itself. When we walk away from the precincts of confession in
order, perhaps, to study them, or simply to let them be, do we not abandon the problem, the problem that is politics too, namely how to ensure
the value of competing values? Religion—not freedom of it, where the
"it" is in vacuous, because irresolvable, question, but religion as the novelty and impossibility of freedom. Religious freedom may be impossible,
then, not only because religion is impossible, but because freedom is.
Which is why we must fight for it.

This, at least, is what a cohort of modern thinkers thought. They
linked the question of political modernization to the question of religious modernization, not imagining that they were the first to do so but
insisting that the time for asking religion to become (again) adequately
modern was propitious. They may not, by our lights, have understood
enough religion to make this demand. They were comparatively primitive on the question of what could count as religious objects; they were
blind to the prejudices of the religions they themselves inhabited. Have
we progressed at least in this? May we now ask again—Is religion free?
Ought it to be free? Or has all of our understanding, all of our scholarship, shown us nothing so much as that the question cannot be asked?
Did scholars, thinkers, and moderns, then, *decide* it could not be asked?
Or did we just forget, or somehow repress, the question?

I began this book with an interest not only to belabor what is wrong
with the humanities and its worlds but also to renew the commitment
to what is right: to search out such majesty as can be found, to recall the
Stevens fragment this study begins with. I have worked with Stevens,
Said, and many others to make it clear that this commitment cannot
be exercised separate from distinguishing forms of thinking to which
one is not committed. To that end, I have been dedicated to overcoming
the proposition that, as I once heard it said, "at the end of the day religion must still be standing." No less am I dedicated to overcoming its
opposite—that religion must be vanquished, or has been vanquished. I

have taken a stand on this question not merely in deference to a doctrine of pluralism, and certainly not from agnosticism on the terms in question. I stand rather in defense of critique and in service to the principle of inclusion, consistent with the maxim of Adam Phillips that inclusion is "an exemption." An exception. Critique is a position, I have argued, that might just as easily be advanced by religion as trained on it.

Both positions—that at the end of the day religion must be standing and that religion must be toppled—are incomplete and potentially fallacious. What critique is for is to sort out what value a concept and formation like religion possesses and to remain alert that one does so in intimate engagement with the conceptual structure of the thing. At the end of the day, we stand shaped by the principles imbuing our concepts. It is therefore never adequate to absolve oneself of the responsibility to think their implications to the end, again and anew. This is not a neat trick of academic argument. It is a wager for the value of thinking without oppositions such as that between religion and the secular, or between religion and criticism—without oppositional logic as such, but not without distinction.

To advance this wager against and for religion, I have learned from sources that lay more adequate ground for inclusive, differentiated, invested humanistic thinking—from Stevens to Vico, from Kant to Anselm, from Edward Scissorhands to Spinoza to Madeleine L'Engle to the God of Deuteronomy. I invoke God no less against our anonymous defender of religion; against the piety of the divine. No one knows better than God that God has, in Spinoza's words, no special sovereignty outside the commitments human beings make in God's name. There is nothing to stand on save the promise to make them good ones. Let God be another name for this promise, and for its betrayal.

I have called this principle, this promise, modernity, in recognition that modernity too is incomplete and potentially fallacious. The religion that modernity claimed needed reformation—the investment of nature with (super)human value—made room for a secularism that works identically. In modernity, we still confuse natural accident with value. We still inhabit and invest in the barbarisms of sexism, racism, and ethnocentrism—diabolical confusions all. We still use religion and secularism to disempower others, in defiance of principles of the common. We still proliferate distinctions to no end but division. Modernity's critics are right that it is barbed. The Enlightenment is barbed. The West and its religions and secularisms are barbed—hypocritical, uneven, confused.

What is of utmost importance in these laments, however, is to distinguish between positions, formations, and principles that betray themselves and those that merely oscillate between one position and its opposite. I have distinguished the latter as the distinction of the one and the many, the position of nonmodernity—the duality that cannot hold on to the truth of two positions. It is the position in which one's ideals (the one) are only ever opposed to, or identified with, reality (the many): the position in which two (self and other) are therefore identically, but never differentially, in relation. In this position the source of truth is elsewhere, in the face of which both self and other fall short, or it is nowhere, identical with the natural relation closest to hand. In this position, then, the end is the beginning and the beginning the end. One is resigned to the asymptote of the good, or stuck with the good as whatever the mighty make of it. In the West, this grim state of affairs is elaborated in Plato, but not critiqued there. Indeed, in the Platonic world there is a lofty beauty to the metaphysics, a beauty that nevertheless does not survive exportation. Philosophy no less than religion must come to be able to distinguish itself in refusal of Platonic dualism—in refusal of the contradiction that is this concept of reality. The West must be refused as a totality, as it must be refused as a tyrant.

Modernity is this refusal. It is this distinction. It cannot be said to be birthed in nonmodernity, for the contradiction of the one and the many has no end. But modernity, in coming into existence, does so as the refusal of nonmodernity, a position it will forever after mistake for its own. In the principle of modernity, betrayal and confusion are precisely the sign that there is work to be done. The power of the formation in which I can betray you is the principle of the good we share but can also resign in frustration, confusion, fatigue. Modernity will pass itself off as nonmodernity. We will treat each other as animals, as occasions for distinctions of domination. But, as one learns from Pascal, "man transcends man." The human being is more powerful than her given positions. She is dual, animal and angel, only in recognition that beginnings are never purely one or the other. Our origins are twofold—the truth is actual, the self does not contradict the other—in distinction from the third, the one, the many, where we never lived. Again, Nietzsche: "One is always wrong, but with two, truth begins." Therefore the work is to commit to collectives and their critique. Commit to the distinction of inclusion, for you are already committed one way or the other.

I write in protest of the resignation of this work as much as I join forces with those critics of modernity who emphasize its perfidy. There is something unloosed in modernity's first principle, the call to abandon kin and homeland, natural rank and eternal goods-in-themselves. This something requires fidelity, of each in her own way and her own time.

Modernity happens. It is a break. It happens in the West. It is distinctive, but it is incomplete. It is not then that the West has a right to say of everyone else, you must become like us, such that the West's critics can then say, we are different.[11] It is that insofar as the West treats others in betrayal of the principle of modernity, of inclusion, it is in betrayal of itself. It is not only that others must not be subjected to Western models, it is that the West must be liberated from itself. We have mistaken the West's confusion and failure on this score for the principles themselves. We have confused the very idea of principles with Platonism.

These dynamics of distinction concern religion, a concept requiring distinction. In Kant's terms, insofar as religion means God, it refers either to a confusion of reason or to a principle of lawfulness, inclusive of those laws that human beings can propose to and for themselves. God is subject to criticism, not to clear the heavens, but to remove a signal obstacle to law, which obstacle might equally be figured as law itself insofar as it is given in the nature of things (natural law) or by God (supernatural law).[12]

When it does not refer to the concept of God, religion refers to the practices, ideas, and myths of community—religion not as the postulate of an object but as a border. Durkheim gives us God in community as that entity whose boundaries are sacralized—that is, absolutized. On the one hand, a community is just a bounded entity—this one and not that one, from the smallest scale of the family up to the human or posthuman community taken as a whole. On the other hand, inasmuch as Durkheim's supposition is that all communities naturally have the same elementary form, he cannot ask, What of the distinction between boundaries that suppress principles of inclusion and those that might be modified by this principle? Under what conditions might a collective absolutize a border that is not only its own, in distinction from collectives that naturally absolutize their own? What is the distinction of the border that criticizes borders? If Durkheim helps us understand the collective as the concept of religion, Spinoza and Kant help us to ask which religion, but no less which philosophy, founds its collective in a critique of collectives.

Three Examples

The Rabbi and the Fossils
I have found popular accounts of religion useful in reflecting on its ends. Three examples to conclude. In a 2005 article in the *Atlantic*, Yale psychology professor Paul Bloom asks, "Is God an Accident?"[13] The article begins with an anecdote about Bloom's rabbi during his teenage years,

who, he recounts, "believed that the Lubavitcher Rebbe, who was living in Crown Heights, Brooklyn, was the Messiah, and that the world was soon to end. He believed that the earth was a few thousand years old, and that the fossil record was a consequence of the Great Flood. He could describe the afterlife, and was able to answer adolescent questions about the fate of Hitler's soul."[14] Bloom stresses that, although his rabbi's beliefs were not common in the cultures he was raised in, such beliefs are common not just in America, with its high percentage of believers in God, angels, and devils, but worldwide.[15] As Bloom later adds, "Most people I know believe in a God who created the universe, performs miracles, and listens to prayers."[16] The header for the article announces: "Despite the vast number of religions, nearly everyone in the world believes in the same things."[17]

Bloom's thesis is that the belief in God as an incorporeal entity in relation to the corporeal world is a function of "a distinction between the physical and the psychological [that] is fundamental to human thought."[18] Even babies will distinguish the world of rocks and trees from a social world that includes desires, beliefs, intentions, and goals. Bloom analogizes these two systems to "two distinct computers in a baby's brain" that "develop at different rates" and that help children to "anticipate and understand—and, when they get older, to manipulate—physical and social entities."[19] The catch is that, although "both systems are biological adaptations," "these systems go awry in two ways": they make it possible for us to conceive of soulless bodies and bodiless souls, leading to beliefs in gods and the afterlife, and they lead us to "overshoot" our social knowledge, "inferring goals and desires where none exist."[20]

Despite these sometimes inconvenient postulates, however, very few members of the world's population believe in Darwin's theory of evolution, which would rule them out, including not least babies and children.[21] We are, in short, "natural-born dualists" and creationists, given to structure the world in this way regardless of the particular content.[22]

Bloom gives a scientific account of the dualism of the one and the many, of identity and opposition. Humanists might tend to reject Bloom's pretense to offer a scientific explanation for religious and philosophical thinking. But my work affirms what Bloom sees, consistent with Kant's observation that minds are "inclined to expect behind the objects of the senses something else invisible and active of itself."[23] Most cultures, minds, persons, myths think like this.

My difference with Bloom is that, like most humanists, but unlike Kant, he sees only a single dualism in operation. The word religion, I have shown, will tend to short-circuit the question of religion A or religion B, not as traditions or regions but as concepts; not as a pluralism of concepts but as two concepts, two concepts of two. Like Durkheim, Bloom leans on the power of natural explanation to solve seemingly intractable rational dilemmas, observing that religion mischievously ratifies the mind's inclination as dualist, as a dominion within a dominion, while obscuring its truth in the material monism of evolution. To see what Bloom and Durkheim see—I call it God, you call it accident—is to realize that a reasonable person should know how to keep religion's lures at arm's length. Bloom says, God is an accident of our adaptive powers, a natural confusion. Religious faith is inevitable, but it must not be confused with making true claims on the order of science.[24]

Yet science does not dislodge religion's work, not only because of the intransigence of illusion as evolutionary overreach. In negating one side of the soul-body dualism in order to occupy the other side, science holds the opponent in place as a ghost in the system while closing down other ways of thinking about the mind in the world.

I am calling for a criticism sensitive to the proposition that natural dualism is not simply natural, the imagined alternative to supernaturalism. Natural dualism is also a confusion of reason, a ratification of natural existence as a site of value. This is not to position reason as opposed to nature. We learn from Durkheim, as from Spinoza and Pascal, that humans are animals. What enables human beings to flourish is collective life, the ones we are given and the ones we critique and enlarge. Insofar as reason in its disputations and its extravagances conceives its nature as inclusive of others, it empowers itself in transformation of the nature it is given. The confusion of this transformation with the reinvestment of natural hierarchies (God over human, soul over body, reason over nature) is what modernity refuses but then fantastically replicates— that the truth is merely what is actual; that the truth is opposed to the actual. Both positions reflect what Bloom might identify as natural illusion. But he resigns us to their ceaseless oscillation. Like Feuerbach, like Durkheim, like Geertz, or more recently, like Stewart Guthrie, whose *Faces in the Clouds* tracks the human tendency toward anthropomorphism, Bloom knows that religion can bespeak a confusion, a projection. It reflects, as Bloom puts Guthrie's discovery, the extent to which "we see intention where only artifice or accident exist."[25]

I have pursued what it would mean to supplement this dualism, including the scholarly resignation to dualism that hunkers down in one of its parts. The supplementation I have been after is the identification of a second dualism, a concept of two that bypasses the rigor mortis of endless contradiction and reduction. It is a standpoint neither science nor the humanities can strictly identify in being a movement, not a standpoint—a function of a system at war with its own dogmatism and skepticism.

Bloom is nevertheless a valuable partner to the study of religion in puncturing the structure of a generic that contains all positions. Bloom goes further in holding, with Durkheim and others, that human beings consistently produce religion in a singular way.[26] The one thing he does not go so far as to see is that this very production might have already deconstructed. In the story of the golden calf, the Israelites are chastised for the natural-supernaturalism of their idol. Why? Not because God is a more super supernaturalism, but because the Israelites are confused about what God is for, in betrayal of their promise to constitute a righteous collective. Durkheim held that the scholar knows something the religious person does not know, which is that her icons are representations of society, not of gods.[27] But once I know what the religious do not, that the sacred is social, I might also come to know what the scholar does not, which is that the social, given, like scholarship, to the production of a natural-born dualism, may also be critiqued, which standpoint is a different kind of scholarship, a different commitment to the social.

The Rabbis and the Afterlife

In the course of interviewing radio personality Ira Glass on his podcast *Here's the Thing*, actor Alec Baldwin raises the question of the relation between personal views and work.[28] Glass, host of Chicago Public Radio's *This American Life*, observes that he sometimes feels the need to state his views when he believes listeners assume they already know them. He says, "We've done so many stories about God, at some point I went on the air and said, look, I don't believe in God" so that listeners can then properly contextualize the documentary work. "Truth in packaging," Glass says.

Although the drift of Glass's comment concerns journalistic credibility, Baldwin takes Glass up on the content. "When did you realize you didn't believe in God?" Glass says what Bloom says: "teenager" plus "rabbis." "At some point it just didn't add up for me, like you know you're in love or you're not in love. There's another explanation for everything around me which makes more sense than that there is a big Dad who created all this." He recollects arguments he had with his teachers at Baltimore Hebrew College, "these old rabbis," with whom Glass wanted to take up ideas from *Chariots of the Gods*, a popular nonfiction book he was reading at the time. The book and its sequels hypothesize that the Bible records contact between humans and an alien race.[29]

"I remember arguing in Hebrew College with my professors there. They were not, they did not buy it." Baldwin riffs on the young Woody Allen getting slapped by the rabbis in his movie *Radio Days*: "How dare you mention this!"

Glass then turns the tables: "Are you an atheist?" Baldwin: "No. I believe, I don't know what I believe in terms of the specific. I had a Catholic priest once say to me, I believe in a piece of many religions." Jews have something to say, Buddhists, Hindus. "The joke is that the reason to be Catholic is simply because they have the best real estate." Baldwin then becomes more serious: "I believe in a God—I mean something had to be responsible for this."

So far, Glass and Baldwin are Bloom's exemplars, respectively, of nature's scientists and its fools. Baldwin continues: "And I also believe, oddly enough, as a result of some stories I have heard on your show. Life itself and stories make me believe there is something behind it—this is my belief, not a fact." Glass jokes that his atheism is evidently not coming through in his work. But he adds that he treats religion as extensively as he does because it is not handled well in the media. The religious are depicted cartoonishly, he says, as inflexible and doctrinaire, whereas Glass himself wants to tell the stories of the type of thoughtful and compassionate Christians he himself knows. Baldwin concurs with the need for this correction, relating the story of a friend, an actor and a devout Jew, to whom he posed the question, What is Judaism to you? Baldwin was "leveled" by the friend's reply. Religion "is the study of how we as human beings distinguish ourselves from the animals." "I'll take that," says Baldwin.

Baldwin brings up two further elements of his belief: his emotional connection to his late father and to historical-political events like the Kennedy assassination, and his interest in the reality of love. He asks the question a natural-born dualist will ask: Is this life it? Does emotional energy and investment just dissipate? Is there something else, somewhere else where it survives? Glass recalls a poem by Billy Collins called "The Afterlife," in which everyone goes to the afterlife he or she believes in. "You go to the place you always thought you would go, / The place you kept lit in an alcove in your head."[30] "And so I worry . . ." Glass trails off. Baldwin counters that to him the afterlife is very simple. You go into a screening room, and God shows you what you want to know— what really happened in Kennedy's assassination and which woman really loved you. "You get your answers," joins Glass. Baldwin: "You get your answers."

Notwithstanding their bonding over Collins, however, Baldwin and Glass neither agree nor disagree about religion and the afterlife. Like contemporary culture more generally, they are confused about what they are talking about. Glass, with Bloom, says, Darwin, not God. Baldwin asks, What does love look like? And what is real? Glass is the deflationary, if strictly correct, Bloom via Durkheim. Baldwin, with his Jewish interlocutor, is Pascal, Kant, and Badiou: not just a counter to the "old rabbis" but a best version of them—after something else altogether.

What is the human animal? "There is not only what there is," says Badiou. Let us also borrow from Jonathan and Daniel Boyarin in asking, Given what is, what is? The brothers Boyarin open their book, *Powers of Diaspora*, with French historian Pierre Legendre's definition of humanity: "Man is 'What is?' "[31] Legendre sources his definition in a story in the Babylonian Talmud (Tractate Hullin 89a) that connects God's love for Israel to its humility, putting the language of Abraham, "I am but dust and ashes," and of Moses and Aaron, "we are nothing," together with that of God, who "hangeth the earth upon nothing."[32] For the Boyarins, these commitments to nothingness constitute the human animal as the one who questions what is, a position secure in being "compounded of all the questions of our ancestors" while also mindful that "everything is permanently at risk." The "paradoxical power of diaspora" is the conjunction of these two components—genealogy and contingency—in support of a collective of stories and questions.[33]

Baldwin and Glass agree that religion need not mean dogma, together with Bloom, who credits the sympathetic religious. "Who can object to the faith of Martin Luther King Jr. or the Dalai Lama?" Bloom asks, adding the qualification, "at least as long as that faith grounds moral positions one already accepts."[34] But therefore between Baldwin and Glass-Bloom the words God and religion are obfuscating. For the questions of which woman really loved you and what is the meaning of your relationship with your father are not items one already accepts. Can God answer them? In the story in Tractate Hullin, the tractate of "ordinary or profane things," one imagines God is the warrant to ask for such answers.

This is to hold, on the one hand, that "religion 'does a lot of different things,' " as Karen Armstrong puts it. Religion has no single essence and in particular, for Armstrong's worthy purposes, no single violent essence. "Identical religious beliefs and practices have inspired diametrically opposed courses of action."[35] Religion has, in other words, no single value. I have argued further that the essence religion does not have as it splits into its many variations concerns a distinction that the manyness of it will tend to obscure. Armstrong is right that all religions can be violent; she is right, too, that all religions offer critiques of violence and injunctions of ethics and peace. Human beings vacillate between the poles of aggression and generosity just as surely as they overreach their cognition and postulate a dualism of souls and bodies.

But there is a distinction between formations, whether religious or secular, that articulate a principle of human concord as a struggle to be realized and those that postulate this principle as unrealizable in this world, from which the most ethical response will be fatalism or withdrawal, however compassionate or curious. Baldwin, for all his talk of the afterlife, poses questions alert to the struggle for concord; Glass, notwithstanding his commitment to the more scientific explanation for "all this," sounds a fatalist note. His good-humored worry about whether the poet Collins is right about his afterlife might be a deeper recognition of what stories of God are good for. But Glass's own story of his rejection of his rabbis on the grounds of their skepticism about aliens in the Bible suggests they may know this better than he does.

Bloom grants that religion might agree with what one already accepts, but he neglects the position that transmutes acceptance into critique, by which morality and religion stand for what might be made in and of our nature. Whatever one calls this neglect, and whichever religions or secularisms count as guilty of it, it is distinct from the principle of modernity, if only in being modernity's confusion of its principle—which principle constitutes, in Baldwin's terms, the miracle of stories, the emotional investment of true relation, and the commitment to reality subject to the interpretation of self and other: the critique that commits to a reality inclusive of everything.

The Rabbi and the Matzah

I bring this book to an end with my own anecdote about a rabbi—or rather, an anecdote about a rabbi's anecdote. The anecdote is not about a rabbi's belief in a God who does supernatural things, as in Bloom and Glass. It is not concerning the position we still need Kant, but no less the Boyarins, to rearrange. This one is Durkheim's bailiwick: community, sacral borders.

A rabbi gives a homily right before Passover on the topic of matzah. Not matzah the food of liberation or the bread of affliction. Not matzah the food of resourcefulness, of salvation. Rather, the homily is on the *kashrut* (kosher laws) of matzah. He prefaces his story by enjoining congregants to remain alert during this time of preparation for the festival, which involves removing all leaven from the house in commemoration of the Israelites' having to leave Egypt in extreme haste. It happened, he told the congregation, that a couple, having faithfully met their *halachic* (Jewish legal) obligations with respect to removing leaven and preparing for the seder, the festival meal, had unwittingly brought home from the grocery store a box of matzah that was not kosher for Passover. Some grocery clerk had not noted the absence of the Passover stipulation on the box and had carelessly placed it in the Passover section of the aisle. Such matzah will bear a kosher insignia, but it will not say "kosher for Passover." The drama of the story was that the couple had come very close to using this matzah that was not kosher for Passover for their seder but were saved at the last minute by a more perceptive guest, who noted that the guarantee was absent. The moral of the homily was, Be careful when you buy matzah that you buy the kind that is kosher for Passover. The matzah that is sold year round should not be assumed to be, and gentile grocery stores will not note the difference.

The story was pitched as gently instructional for a relatively knowledgeable congregation. What is striking is that the rabbi dwelt at length not on the fulfillment of the obligation to eat matzah on Passover, but on the potential for devastating confusion on the point. He did not consider the oddity of worrying about matzah that is or is not kosher for Passover.

Is not the very idea of matzah a creation of Passover and, a fortiori, the laws of *kashrut*? Could it be not the grocery clerk who is confused but the rabbi and his hapless Jewish couple, who came dangerously close to . . . what? Eating matzah on Passover, as they are commanded to do?[36]

There are, to be sure, answers to the question of the difference between matzah that is kosher for Passover and matzah that is not. They have to do with the degree of stringency of ensuring that no leavening has occurred, from the harvesting of the wheat, to the grinding, packing, and transporting of it, to the cleaning of the machines, preparation surfaces, utensils, ovens, and the timing used to make the matzah.[37]

But therefore the distinction of kosher for Passover matzah resembles Glass's response to his "old rabbis" and not Baldwin's and his devout Jewish friend's response to the problem of God—factual and natural, not metaphysical and self-critical. The implication seems to be that the commandment to observe matzah needs reinforcement. But what kind? There is a handmade matzah you can buy for Passover called *shmura matzah*, matzah that is watched, guarded: observed. Extra precautions are taken. It is an ethos that redoubles the commandment to observe the laws concerning matzah, right down, in the rabbi's homily, to the observance of the perceptive guest. But like the absurd God Bloom and

Glass do not believe in, whom Baldwin's and Collins's God might easily expose as a golden calf—a mere naturalism, a mere supernaturalism—this distinction evaporates what it asserts. The commandment to observe matzah is basic to its nature. The redoubling of observance would then be nothing so much as the fateful admission that there cannot be matzah at all—the recognition that the observation, and thus the observance, would always fail.

Whither the rabbis? It might be concluded as follows: The biblical story of the Exodus that Passover remembers concerns the vicissitudes that begin with the call to Abraham to *leave* his homeland, including above all the dangers of landing in a homeland where there is no such call. The closure of a self-identical system, in contemporary parlance. The rabbinic tradition conceives the Exodus as the urgency for Jews to make a *new* home—not, of course, in a land, readers like the Boyarins are at pains to note, but, it seems, in the sacral borders of home writ in the laws of chemistry. This could be a liberation from the travails of state formation. It could be a reminder of the necessary labor of the desert, wherein community constitution will ever be contingent. But the horrors of territorial state formation are relative to the community erected, relative to the concept of boundaries enacted.

When Spinoza insists that "God has no special sovereignty over men save through the medium of those who hold sovereignty," he is addressing the role of religion in society.[38] Let it not be a dominion within a dominion. Let religion be the practice of the common. He is also arguing that it is only in conditions of sovereignty—social and political existence ratified in a land—that the sovereignty that is democracy can be enacted and critiqued. It is only in a land that God can be lived out as the good of the common and critiqued as the warrant for might makes right and natural privilege, the devils of invidious distinction. So the call to Abraham to leave his land for a land that will be shown. It is only once we risk the creation of human laws that can bring harmony in our borders that we are subject to the divine law of human concord that is the critique of all borders as ends in themselves. It is only once we risk subjection to the divine law of human concord in a land that will be shown that we have the opportunity to observe the ways our divine laws will trade on natural advantage and fantasies of home. It is therefore only then, in the presence of our human and divine laws in the land, that we can engage in the work of critique and reformation—to make a home land subject to the law of inclusion.

The rabbis give us something else.[39] What they give is not a substitute for this critical democratic sovereignty. Indeed, it is the rabbis who must not set themselves up in a land. Their law is designed as a fortress in exile, and it draws on the natural as a boundary, an operation, visible in the matzah, that is recapitulated in the ethnic statehood to which it symbolizes opposition. Opposition, but not necessarily critique. Judaism seems poised between both of these impulses—to redouble the natural certainties of home, to leave or otherwise confound them. In both Judaism and Christianity, distinction is paramount. From the beginning that is Genesis, God separates the heavens and the earth, the holy and the ordinary, Israel from the nations. But therefore it remains a diabolical challenge for readers to work through the meaning of these distinctions and their impact for communities and others—to resist profaning the divine law of human concord by splitting it between us and them.

What, though, of the split between the thing and itself? The matzah presents a signal case of something, the homeland of the law that reminds Jews of the danger of eating even their own symbolic foods. Would this be the intra-Jewish logjam that while the biblical matzah shall be observed, the rabbinic codes show it cannot be? Would it be a distinction that disrupts the thing in such a way that it short-circuits observance altogether? Or something else?

A key blessing in observing Jewish law is the Havdalah (separation) blessing, which serves to mark two distinctions: one between the Sabbath day and an ordinary work day/week and one between the Sabbath day and a day of festival. The first is "Blessed are you, Lord, our God, king of the universe, who separates between holy and ordinary." The second is "who separates between holy and holy."[40] This distinction between the holy and the holy recalls Badiou's "divided subject" who rejects the "ethnic" distinction Jew/Greek in favor of the subject "divided in itself by the challenge of having nothing but the vanished event to face up to." It recalls, too, the Boyarins' Talmudic Tractate in which God and humans find and make a world founded on nothing. It would be the power of the event and its stories, a non-self-identical system, a work of the collective and the future.

We have seen that the question is whether the vanished event one is to face up to also resolves to critique its own vanishing—by making it present as the ordinary work to be done. As Žižek puts it, the work of the event is not revolution. It is what happens the next day.[41] So, too, with the creation of worlds and laws, with the exodus from slavery, with the achievement of the promised child, the promised land. How will you distinguish the event from the bodies and languages—the norms—that don't recognize it, that will thus assimilate it to what is merely given and even use it to ratify domination and death? The matzah shows that this drama is not yet the final question. It is not only fidelity to the event that is to be distinguished. The question is also, How will you distinguish fidelity to the vanished event from the event as vanished in the multiplication of distinction without end?

The question is whether the impossible matzah is the nothing of the Boyarins, by which the holy is distinguished from the holy as what must be continually remade, or the nothing of Durkheim, the end of the sacred as it divides to no end. This latter might equally be the hyperrationalism of scientific description, the cultural confusion of a humanities of guilt, or the bureaucratic rules of the state no less than a Judaism torn about what is the urgent question of Passover. The rabbi's homily, although it risks being a distraction from this question, is working with it—the mind in its distinctions, the powers of distinction.

The question has been, What is distinction—distinctness—insofar as it realizes the principle of inclusion: the single idea of human concord, the dualism of two in mutual relation, the principle of modernity? There is a critique of politics in this principle, as in all images and theories of community as an end in itself. This is why it should be difficult to go after the rabbis of the Talmud. The rabbis are the ones without homeland, living in fantasy, practicing diaspora. One has digested the point of their antinationalist heroism, together with the significance of a Jewish critique of Judaism as mere self-identical norm.[42]

The question now is whether the matzah can bear up the point—whether, even, its impossibility might constitute critique itself, for which we need both it *and* the grocery clerk's error, as we needed both events of the law tablets from Sinai, or whether the matzah is merely impossible because contradictory, non-self-identical in its self-identity.

This is to count Judaism an example of a formation whose value is dependent on the identification of the dead ends it faces in its struggle with its own principles. I observe, in saying this, that one might get stuck in the worry that one cannot criticize Judaism as Judaism—that to do so would be ethnocentrism, racism, colonialism, Enlightenment prejudice, antiritual, anti-Talmud, Protestant. Anti-Semitism. Anti-Judaism. As important as these worries can be and have been, they leave (this) religion on weak ground.[43]

So stands postcolonial studies—that the work to escape the thinking of empire will risk romanticizing the colonies, thus failing their desire to be something else. Subaltern studies and their next generations take on the stakes of this comparison in working on the virulence of secular and religious nationalisms in South Asia and elsewhere as only one among possible responses to theological-political domination. The Jewish question might be inspiration here as these thinkers note the dead ends of various political solutions to communal minorities, the dead end of the very notion of minority.[44] What can be said is that it is an open question whether communities do not require critique more than salvation. This is one of the most difficult questions of all.

Acknowledgments

An earlier version of part of chapter 5 first appeared as "Traces of History in St. Anselm," *Method and Theory in the Study of Religion* 20, no. 4 (2008): 371–84. An earlier version of part of chapter 6 first appeared as "Spinoza the Radical," in *Reassessing the Radical Enlightenment*, ed. Steffen Ducheyne (New York: Routledge, 2017).

I am grateful to interlocutors and mentors. William Arnal, Ehud Benor, Constance Furey, Tomoko Masuzawa, James Robson, and Winnifred Sullivan invited talks and panels that led to some of this work and serve as critical companions in it. Michel Chaouli, Jonathan Elmer, Jennifer Fleissner, Joshua Kates, and Benjamin Robinson have been comrades in high-energy metaphysics. Charles Mathewes extended an invitation to write an essay that this book finally finishes. Jonathan Sheehan's generosity and example have been a goad for me to get the work done. Noreen Khawaja is partner in experiment and incomparable reader. Kenneth Reinhard is inspiration, whose practice of this kind of work makes it possible to join it. Thanks to colleagues at Williams College, who made an intellectual commons, colleagues at Indiana University, with whom the ideas were tempered over years of debate, and colleagues at Yale University, who offered time and support to complete them. Special thanks to Emily Bakemeier, Tamar Szabó Gendler, Christine Hayes,

Amy Hungerford, Mary Miller, Sally Promey, Skip Stout, and Kathryn Tanner.

Alan G. Thomas has been an exacting editor and guide throughout the process of publication. I am grateful for his support, for the stewardship of Randolph M. Petilos and Erin DeWitt, and for the criticism and suggestions of the three readers for the University of Chicago Press. Alice Bennett's editorial assistance was invaluable. Many thanks to Susan Hernandez for assistance with the index.

I have benefited from the opportunity to publish short pieces and reviews on the Social Science Research Council blog, *The Immanent Frame*. Thanks to colleagues there for sustaining this network of ideas.

I am indebted to the students of all ages and life experience with whom I teach and learn.

For essential companionship and counsel in all things, I thank Avron Kulak and Terri Kulak. For the bulwark of friendship I am grateful to Nancy Hiller and Mark Longacre, Miryam Segal and Wolfgang Müller, Janet Gyatso and Charles Hallisey, Martin Kavka and Tip Tomberlin, Daphne Brooks and Matthew Frye Jacobson, Phyllis Granoff and Koichi Shinohara, and Ellen Cohen and Steven Fraade. And to Brayton Polka, for this life of learning. Special thanks to Paul Bloom and Jon-Jay Tilsen, whose ideas I sample in these pages; to Kati Curts, Marko Geslani, and David Walker for spirited conversation; to Jennifer Connerley and Leeza Meksin for your art and your kindness; to Jason Earle for reaching out; to Eva Robertson for endurance; and to David Bleecker, for help with beginnings and ends and all the rest. Finally, I thank Susan and John Lofton, and Lauren Lofton, Dave Zero, and Brian Lofton for affinity and care, and my family, Aasta Hjertholm Levene, Sam Levene (1936–2016), and Julie Levene (1964–2012), who have been the bedrock of these questions of collective life.

Kathryn Lofton is the one without whom this book would not be. It is dedicated to her and to Kinneret Levene Magid, the two with whom— everything.

Notes

CHAPTER ONE

1. The allusion is to Kierkegaard's ironic proposition that "in our age, everyone is unwilling to stop with faith but goes further." See Søren Kierkegaard, *Fear and Trembling*, trans. Howard V. Hong and Edna H. Hong (Princeton, NJ: Princeton University Press, 1983), 7.

2. Each of these locutions references a veritable library. The first is captured by Michael Allen Gillespie's *The Theological Origins of Modernity* (Chicago: University of Chicago Press, 2009), the second by Guy G. Stroumsa's *A New Science: The Discovery of Religion in the Age of Reason* (Cambridge, MA: Harvard University Press, 2010).

3. Plato's position is that Forms—truths in themselves—elude knowledge unless and until we can transcend bodily existence. Until then, "I will not even allow myself to say that where one is added to one either the one to which it is added or the one that is added becomes two, or that the one added and the one to which it is added become two because of the addition of one to the other" (Plato, "Phaedo," in *Five Dialogues*, trans. G. M. A. Grube [Indianapolis: Hackett, 1981], 136). For readings of the difference between biblical and other ancient concepts of reality, see Erich Auerbach, "Odysseus' Scar," in *Mimesis: The Representation of Reality in Western Literature* (Princeton, NJ: Princeton University Press, 1953); Marcel Gauchet, *The Disenchantment of the World: A Political History of Religion*, trans. Oscar Burge (Princeton, NJ: Princeton University Press, 1997); Robert Kawashima, *Biblical Narrative and the Death of the Rhapsode* (Bloomington: Indiana University Press, 2004); Nancy Levene,

"Athens and Jerusalem: Myths and Mirrors in Strauss's Vision of the West," *Hebraic Political Studies* 3, no. 2 (Spring 2008): 113–55; and Brayton Polka, *Rethinking Philosophy in Light of the Bible: From Kant to Schopenhauer* (Lanham, MD: Lexington Books, 2014). The distinction is central to concepts of reason in Kant and Hegel and of faith in Kierkegaard.

4. My work engages issues in common with Lacan-influenced contemporary social and political thought—the neighbor, critique, the universal. See, for example, Slavoj Žižek, Eric L. Santner, and Kenneth Reinhard, *The Neighbor: Three Inquiries in Political Theology* (Chicago: University of Chicago Press, 2005). It must be said, therefore, that I do not draw on Lacan in this or other of my writings. When I say, for example, "not all," I mean this as a distinction of the position of inclusion and not the Lacanian "not-all" that functions to interrupt universals, though there are undoubtedly fruitful overlaps. The "all" will be a central concept in this book, in its false forms—as a generic, a unity, an act of domination—and in its true form as inclusion, openness.

5. T. S. Eliot, "The Love Song of J. Alfred Prufrock," in *The Waste Land and Other Poems* (New York: Harvest Books, 1934), 4.

6. Søren Kierkegaard, *Works of Love*, trans. Howard V. Hong and Edna H. Hong (Princeton, NJ: Princeton University Press, 1995), 225.

7. Fyodor Dostoevsky, *The Brothers Karamazov*, trans. Richard Pevear and Larissa Volokhonsky (New York: Farrar, Straus and Giroux, 1990), 246–49.

8. Ibid., 250.

9. Ibid., 260.

10. Ibid., 255.

11. Ibid., 260.

12. John Milton, *Paradise Lost*, book 4, lines 105–10 (http://www.paradiselost.org).

13. Søren Kierkegaard, *Philosophical Fragments*, trans. Howard V. Hong and Edna H. Hong (Princeton, NJ: Princeton University Press, 1985), 35.

14. Ibid.

15. This proposition follows Marx's comment that "men make their own history, but they do not make it just as they please; they do not make it under circumstances chosen by themselves, but under circumstances directly found, given and transmitted from the past." Karl Marx, "The Eighteen Brumaire of Louis Bonaparte," in *The Marx-Engels Reader*, ed. Robert C. Tucker (New York: W. W. Norton, 1978), 595.

16. Alternatives to the humanistic appreciation for cultural difference, the Marxist notion of inheritance, and my principle of distinction are the social and natural sciences insofar as they hold that the soldering of community and inclusivity and the doubling of truth and appearance are an amalgam of nature and culture. For psychology, see Paul Bloom, *Just Babies* (New York: Broadway Books, 2014). For cognitive science and anthropology, see Pascal Boyer, *Religion Explained: The Evolutionary Origins of Religious Thought* (New York: Basic Books, 2002), and Maurice Bloch, *In and Out of Each Other's Bodies: Theory of Mind, Evolution, Truth, and the Nature of the Social* (Boulder, CO: Paradigm, 2013).

17. This has been the work of a history of religions, from Mircea Eliade's sentiment of "the emergence of Asia into History" and the "spiritual and po-

litical awakening of the 'primitive peoples'" (*The Two and the One*, trans. J. M. Cohen [Chicago: University of Chicago Press, 1962], 10) to J. Z. Smith and Bruce Lincoln's work to level the research field of religion by assuming the comparability of all cases.

18. In response to the reply that "the right thing is not to wager at all, Pascal says, "Yes, but you must wager. There is no choice, you are already committed" (*Pensées*, §418).

19. The first is from Plato, "Phaedo," 103. The second is the position of Kant in the *Groundwork*—that the human being, as a being of sense and inclination, must, insofar as he is also rational, "in all his actions, whether directed to himself or also to other rational beings, always be regarded *at the same time as an end*" (*Groundwork of the Metaphysics of Morals*, trans. Mary Gregor [Cambridge: Cambridge University Press, 1997], 37). For Kant's critique of Platonic dualism, see Kant, *Groundwork*, 65–66, and idem, *Critique of Pure Reason*, trans. and ed. Paul Guyer and Allen W. Wood (Cambridge: Cambridge University Press, 1998), 129.

20. See Tomoko Masuzawa, *The Invention of World Religions* (Chicago: University of Chicago Press, 2005). This argument is developed in chapters 5 and 6. For a history of the "Semitic" as it informs the moves of Orientalism, see Jeffrey S. Librett, *Orientalism and the Figure of the Jew* (New York: Fordham University Press, 2015).

21. See most recently Stephen Greenblatt, *The Swerve: How the World Became Modern* (New York: W. W. Norton, 2011), which gives us a modernity grounded in the rediscovery of the ancient Roman writer Lucretius's work, *The Nature of Things* (trans. Frank O. Copley [New York: W. W. Norton, 1977]).

22. Plato, "Euthyphro," in *Five Dialogues*, trans. G. M. A. Grube (Indianapolis: Hackett, 1981), 15.

23. Deuteronomy 30:19–20. *The New Oxford Annotated Bible*, ed. Bruce M. Metzger and Roland E. Murphy (New York: Oxford University Press, 1991). All biblical quotations are from this translation.

24. Ezekiel 20:25.

25. For a recent critique of the "pathological dualism" that divides human beings into good and bad, us and them, see Jonathan Sacks, *Not in God's Name: Confronting Religious Violence* (New York: Schocken Books, 2015), 51. Sacks identifies monotheism as the alternative position that can handle the "complexity" of good and evil without pathology (53). What I call modernity, however, associates all oppositional dualisms, including those of many Jewish and Christian "monotheist" positions, both philosophical and mystical, which trade on Athenian logic and have commensurately pathological outcomes. Similar to Sacks, Yoram Hazony, in *The Philosophy of Hebrew Scripture* (Cambridge: Cambridge University Press, 2012), defends Judaism's uncommon handling of the relation of reason and revelation, distinguishing the Jewish tradition as a source of philosophy comparable to that of the Greeks. At the same time, Hazony assimilates Greek and Christian positions in delineating that of the Hebrew (see chapter 8, "Jerusalem and Carthage"). The position of modernity, by contrast, refuses the Hellenist dualism in both Judaism and Christianity on the grounds of what the biblical traditions, secular and religious, share.

26. Wallace Stevens, "Artificial Populations," *Wallace Stevens: Collected Poetry and Prose* (New York: Library of America, 1997), 474.

27. For a related argument see Avron Kulak, "Kierkegaard, Derrida, and the Context of Context(s)," *Philosophy and Theology* 17, nos. 1 and 2 (2005): 133–55.

28. Aristotle, "Metaphysics," in *The Complete Works of Aristotle*, ed. Jonathan Barnes (Princeton, NJ: Princeton University Press, 1984), 2:1694.

29. Benedictus de Spinoza, *Ethics*, in *The Collected Works of Spinoza*, vol. 1, trans. and ed. Edwin Curley (Princeton, NJ: Princeton University Press, 1985), 408.

30. Niall Ferguson, *Civilization: The West and the Rest* (New York: Penguin Books, 2012), 12.

31. This is the line with which Genesis 12 begins: "Now God said to Abram, 'Go from your country and your kindred and your father's house to the land that I will show you.' "

32. G. W. F. Hegel, *Lectures on the Philosophy of History*, trans. J. Sibree (New York: Dover, 1956), 40.

33. Genesis 12:2–3.

34. Needless to say, I do not agree with Marx that "the Tradition of all the dead generations weighs like a nightmare on the brain of the living" (Marx, "Eighteenth Brumaire of Louis Bonaparte," 595).

CHAPTER TWO

1. René Descartes, *Meditations on First Philosophy*, trans. Donald A. Cress (Indianapolis: Hackett, 1993), 13.

2. For details of Descartes's life and setting, see Desmond Clarke, *Descartes: A Biography* (Cambridge: Cambridge University Press, 2006). For Descartes's intellectual journey, see Stephen Gaukroger, *Descartes: An Intellectual Biography* (Oxford: Clarendon Press, 1995).

3. Descartes, *Meditations*, 13.

4. Émile Durkheim, *The Elementary Forms of Religious Life*, trans. Carol Cosman, abridged and annotated by Mark Cladis (New York: Oxford University Press, 2001).

5. Descartes, *Meditations*, 18.

6. One thinks here of Oliver Sacks, "The Man Who Mistook His Wife for a Hat," in *"The Man Who Mistook His Wife for a Hat" and Other Clinical Tales* (New York: Touchstone, 1970). Sacks was a contemporary Descartes both in his humane commitment to the right of all minds to be understood and in his restless desire to get to the bottom of his own ignorance.

7. In *Cosmopolis: The Hidden Agenda of Modernity* (Chicago: University of Chicago Press, 1990), Stephen Toulmin tracks both the Descartes of this extravagant image and more subtle ways of deploying his identity in relation to other momentous characters and events in the stories of modernity.

8. I draw inspiration in my reading of Descartes from Avron Kulak, "Descartes and the Infinity of the Other," in *European Culture in a Changing World:*

Between Nationalism and Globalism, ed. Daniel Meyer-Dinkgräfe (Cambridge: Scholars Publishing, 2003).

9. See, for example, Dipesh Chakrabarty, *Provincializing Europe: Postcolonial Thought and Historical Difference* (Princeton, NJ: Princeton University Press, 2000); Rajeev Bhargava, ed., *Secularism and Its Critics* (New York: Oxford University Press, 2004); Saba Mahmood, *Politics of Piety: The Islamic Revival and the Feminist Subject* (Princeton, NJ: Princeton University Press, 2005); Richard King, *Orientalism and Religion: Postcolonial Theory, India, and the Mystic East* (London: Routledge, 1999); David Chidester, *Empire of Religion: Imperialism and Comparative Religion* (Chicago: University of Chicago Press, 2014); Talal Asad, *Genealogies of Religion: Discipline and Reasons of Power in Christianity and Islam* (Baltimore: Johns Hopkins University Press, 1993); Webb Keane, *Christian Moderns: Freedom and Fetish in the Mission Encounter* (Berkeley: University of California Press, 2007); and Masuzawa, *Invention of World Religions*.

10. See http://www.pewforum.org/Pew-Forum/About-the-Pew-Forum.aspx.

11. Bruce Lincoln, *Discourse and the Construction of Society: Comparative Studies of Myth, Ritual, and Classification* (Chicago: University of Chicago Press, 1989); idem, *Holy Terrors: Thinking about Religion after September 11* (Chicago: University of Chicago Press, 2003); Timothy Fitzgerald, *The Ideology of Religious Studies* (New York: Oxford University Press, 2000); Russell T. McCutcheon, *Manufacturing Religion: The Discourse on Sui Generis Religion and the Politics of Nostalgia* (New York: Oxford University Press, 1997).

12. Robert Orsi's studies of Catholic life in America are exemplary in taking on the value both of the religion he studies and of the study of religion. See most recently *Between Heaven and Earth: The Religious Worlds People Make and the Scholars Who Study Them* (Princeton, NJ: Princeton University Press, 2006).

13. For a theory of religion in its plural forms that foregrounds the dynamism, embodiment, and localities of both religion and theory, see Thomas A. Tweed, *Crossing and Dwelling: A Theory of Religion* (Cambridge, MA: Harvard University Press, 2006). A related approach is taken by Manuel Vasquez, *More Than Belief: A Materialist Theory of Religion* (New York: Oxford University Press, 2011).

14. On world religions, see Masuzawa, *Invention of World Religions*. On the discovery of religion, see Stroumsa, *New Science*, and Hans G. Kippenberg, *Discovering Religious History in the Modern Age* (Princeton, NJ: Princeton University Press, 2002).

15. The distinction between teaching religion and teaching about religion comes from the First Amendment Supreme Court case of 1963, *School District of Abington Township, PA v. Edward Lewis Schempp et al.* The Court upheld the district court's ruling finding unconstitutional a Pennsylvania statute requiring public school children to hear and read portions of the Bible. Toward the conclusion of the majority opinion, Justice Thomas Clark writes: "Government must inevitably take cognizance of religion, and indeed, under certain circumstances the First Amendment may require that it do so. And it seems clear to me from the opinions in the present and past cases that the Court would recognize the

propriety of providing military chaplains and of the teaching about religion, as distinguished from the teaching of religion, in the public schools" (School Dist. of Abington Tp. v. Schempp, 374 U.S. 203 [1963], 61). J. Z. Smith makes much of the significance of this distinction in the preamble of his essay "The Devil in Mr. Jones," in *Imagining Religion*, 103–4. Two more recent conceptions of *Schempp* in relation to religious studies are Sarah Imhoff, "The Creation Story, or How We Learned to Stop Worrying and Love *Schempp*," *Journal of the American Academy of Religion* 84, no. 2 (2016): 466–97, and Winnifred Sullivan, "Teaching Religion: Refusing the *Schempp* Myth of Origins," posted on *The Immanent Frame*, the blog of the Social Science Research Council on Secularism, Religion, and the Public Sphere: http://blogs.ssrc.org/tif/2016/08/15/teaching-religion-refusing-the-schempp-myth-of-origins/.

16. Amy Hollywood, Elliot R. Wolfson, Thomas Carlson, Martin Kavka, and Tyler Roberts are among the most skillful in employing religious figures for theory. See Amy Hollywood, *Sensible Ecstasy: Mysticism, Sexual Difference, and the Demands of History* (Chicago: University of Chicago Press, 2002); Elliot R. Wolfson, *Language, Eros, Being: Kabbalistic Hermeneutics and Poetic Imagination* (New York: Fordham University Press, 2004); Thomas Carlson, *Indiscretion: Finitude and the Naming of God* (Chicago: University of Chicago Press, 1999); Martin Kavka, *Jewish Messianism and the History of Philosophy* (Cambridge: Cambridge University Press, 2004); Tyler Roberts, *Encountering Religion: Responsibility and Criticism after Secularism* (New York: Columbia University Press, 2013).

17. Wilfred Cantwell Smith, *The Meaning and End of Religion* (Minneapolis: Fortress, 1962). Other examples of the will to discard the term include William E. Arnal, "Definition," in *Guide to the Study of Religion*, ed. Willi Braun and Russell T. McCutcheon (New York: Cassell, 2000), 21–34, and Timothy Fitzgerald, *The Ideology of Religious Studies*. See also William E. Arnal and Russell T. McCutcheon, *The Sacred Is the Profane: The Political Nature of "Religion"* (New York: Oxford University Press, 2013). Whereas W. C. Smith thinks that religion cannot apply to anyone in particular, both Arnal and Fitzgerald think there is something incoherent about the very idea.

18. See Jonathan Z. Smith in the introduction to *Imagining Religion* (Chicago: University of Chicago Press, 1982), xi–xiii.

19. Talal Asad, "Toward a Genealogy of the Concept of Ritual," in *Genealogies of Religion*. See also Daniel Dubuisson, *The Western Construction of Religion: Myths, Knowledge, and Ideology*, trans. William Sayers (Baltimore: Johns Hopkins University Press, 2003).

20. Wallace Stevens, "An Ordinary Evening in New Haven," in *Collected Poetry and Prose*, 402.

21. Stevens, "The Snow Man," in *Collected Poetry and Prose*, 8.

22. Readers of Hegel from whom I draw inspiration include Robert Pippin and Slavoj Žižek. On Hegel on religion, see Thomas A. Lewis, *Religion, Modernity, and Politics in Hegel* (New York: Oxford University Press, 2011), and the essays by Jeffrey Stout, Molly Farneth, Thomas A. Lewis, and Adam Y. Stern in *Journal of Religion* 95, no. 2 (April 2015).

23. Clifford Geertz, "Religion as a Cultural System," in *The Interpretation of Cultures* (New York: Basic Books, 1973), 123.

24. Geertz's essay "Deep Play: Notes on the Balinese Cockfight" is exemplary in this regard (*Interpretation of Cultures*, 412–53).

25. Asad critiques Geertz's essay in taking up the history of religion in "The Construction of Religion as an Anthropological Category," in *Genealogies of Religion*, 27–54.

26. In the rejection of Geertz's distance, the works of Jeffrey Kripal and Robert Orsi are exemplary. See Jeffrey Kripal, *Esalen: America and the Religion of No Religion* (Chicago: University of Chicago Press, 2008), and Robert Orsi, *The Madonna of 115th Street: Faith and Community in Italian Harlem, 1880–1950* (New Haven, CT: Yale University Press, 1985). For the problem of context and truth in the study of religion, see J. Z. Smith, "I Am a Parrot (Red)," in *Map Is Not Territory* (Chicago: University of Chicago Press, 1987). For an overview, see Nancy K. Frankenberry and Hans H. Penner, *Language, Truth, and Religious Belief: Studies in Twentieth-Century Theory and Method in Religion* (Atlanta: American Academy of Religion, 1999), which includes essays from such philosophers as Ludwig Wittgenstein, A. J. Ayer, Donald Davidson, and Richard Rorty alongside those from philosophers of religion such as Frankenberry and Penner, among others.

27. Bruce Lincoln's "Theses on Method," first printed in *Method and Theory in the Study of Religion* 8 (1996): 225–27, exemplifies the oppositional logic in question.

28. Edward Said, *Humanism and Democratic Criticism* (New York: Columbia University Press, 2004), 13.

29. There has recently been interest in the humanities and social sciences to subject religion to new scrutiny. The blog *The Immanent Frame* (http://blogs .ssrc.org/tif/) was inspired by Charles Taylor's *A Secular Age* (Cambridge, MA: Belknap Press of Harvard University Press, 2007). See also Talal Asad, Wendy Brown, Judith Butler, and Saba Mahmood, *Is Critique Secular? Blasphemy, Injury, and Free Speech* (Berkeley: University of California Press, 2009); Craig Calhoun, Mark Juergensmeyer, and Jonathan VanAntwerpen, eds., *Rethinking Secularism* (New York: Oxford University Press, 2011); Michael Warner, Jonathan VanAntwerpen, and Craig Calhoun, *Varieties of Secularism in a Secular Age* (Cambridge, MA: Harvard University Press, 2010); and Philip S. Gorski, David Kyuman Kim, and Jonathan VanAntwerpen, *The Post-secular in Question: Religion in Contemporary Society* (New York: Social Science Research Council and New York University Press, 2012).

30. Said, *Humanism*, 15.

31. Ibid., 11.

32. Giambattista Vico, *The New Science of Giambattista Vico*, trans. Thomas Goddard Bergin and Max Harold Fisch (Ithaca, NY: Cornell University Press, 1948), §331.

33. Said, *Humanism*, 11.

34. Vico, *New Science*, §342.

35. Said, *Humanism*, 61.

36. Ibid., 82.

37. Vico, *New Science*, §§125–28.

38. Said, *Humanism*, 61.

39. Said can be more capacious on the point, citing in one instance the Islamic notion of *isnad*, "interdependent reading" of the Koran, as a practice exemplifying what he is after (*Humanism*, 68–69).

40. Edward W. Said, *Orientalism* (New York: Vintage Books, 1978), 45.

41. Nancy Levene, "Sources of History: Myth and Image," *Journal of the American Academy of Religion* 74, no. 1 (2006): 79–101.

42. Wallace Stevens, "Description without Place," in *Collected Poetry and Prose*, 300.

43. Bruce Lincoln, *Gods and Demons, Priests and Scholars: Critical Explorations in the History of Religions* (Chicago: University of Chicago Press, 2012), xi.

44. Ibid., xi.

45. The locution is taken from Gilbert Ryle, who popularized the phrase "ghost in the machine" as a critique of Descartes's mind-body dualism. See Gilbert Ryle, *The Concept of Mind* (Chicago: University of Chicago Press, 2000). I use the term instead to mark the confusion of oppositional dualisms, which cannot be overcome on their own grounds.

46. Psalms 8:4.

47. William Shakespeare, *Hamlet* (New Haven, CT: Yale University Press, 2003), 75.

48. I advance a related argument in Nancy Levene, "Does Spinoza Think the Bible Is Sacred?" *Jewish Quarterly Review* 101, no. 4 (Fall 2011): 545–73.

CHAPTER THREE

1. Durkheim, *Elementary Forms*, 76–83.

2. Ibid., 3.

3. Ibid., 171.

4. Ibid.

5. Ibid., 88.

6. Ibid., 9.

7. Ibid., 107.

8. Ibid., 20. In *We Have Never Been Modern*, Bruno Latour pioneers a new set of arguments for Durkheim's contention. See Bruno Latour, *We Have Never Been Modern*, trans Catherine Porter (Cambridge, MA: Harvard University Press, 1993). See also Latour, *Politics of Nature: How to the Bring the Sciences into Democracy*, trans. Catherine Porter (Cambridge, MA: Harvard University Press, 2004).

9. George Eliot, *Middlemarch* (Boston: Houghton Mifflin, 1956), 206. The ambition is that of the Reverend Edward Casaubon, the older scholar Eliot's heroine Dorothea marries.

10. Durkheim, *Elementary Forms*, 309.

11. Ibid., 126.

12. Ibid., 104.

13. Ibid.

14. Blaise Pascal, *Pensées*, trans. A. J. Krailsheimer (New York: Penguin Books, 1966), §131.

15. Ibid., §126.

16. See Michel Foucault, *The Order of Things: An Archaeology of the Human Sciences* (New York: Vintage Books, 1970), 377.

17. For the sacred and profane as the most different difference, see Durkheim, *Elementary Forms*, 38. For the sacred and the profane as liable to contagion, see 237.

18. This is a point Durkheim makes repeatedly throughout the book—that the social/sacred is external to the individual but equally, as the soul, internal to the individual. The sacred is society, the thing that supersedes individuality, and the sacred is the soul, the route this externality takes in the individual. For the first, see chapter 7, "The Origin of These Beliefs," in *Elementary Forms*, especially 170–74. For the second, see chapter 8, "The Notion of Soul," in *Elementary Forms*, 183–202.

19. Said, *Orientalism*, 43.

20. Ibid., 3.

21. Ibid., 15.

22. Homi Bhaba and W. J. T. Mitchell, eds., *Edward Said: Continuing the Conversation* (Chicago: University of Chicago Press, 2005.

23. James Clifford, "On *Orientalism*," in *The Predicament of Culture: Twentieth-Century Ethnography, Literature, and Art* (Cambridge, MA: Harvard University Press, 1988). See also Akeel Bilgrami, "Interpreting a Distinction," in *Edward Said: Continuing the Conversation*.

24. Said, *Orientalism*, 67–68.

25. Compare Durkheim on the social at the root of thought in *Elementary Forms*, 10–21.

26. Said, *Orientalism*, 5.

27. Ibid., 6.

28. Ibid., 7.

29. Ibid., 3.

30. Ibid., 57.

31. Ibid., 328.

32. Marx, "Eighteenth Brumaire of Louis Bonaparte," 608.

33. Ibid.

34. David Nirenberg's *Anti-Judaism: The Western Tradition* (New York: W. W. Norton, 2013), also on a deforming distinction, has a similar, almost unbelievable sweep.

35. Said, *Orientalism*, 68–71.

36. Ibid., 17.

37. Ibid., 328.

38. Friedrich Nietzsche, *On the Genealogy of Morals*, trans. Walter Kaufman (New York: Vintage Books, 1974), Third Essay, §1.

39. Said, *Orientalism*, 5.

40. Pascal, *Pensées*, §126.

41. Vico, *New Science*, §136.

42. Ibid., §313.

43. Ibid., §349.

44. J. Samuel Preus, *Explaining Religion: Criticism and Theory from Bodin to Freud* (Atlanta: Scholars' Press, 1996), 78.

45. This principle is scattered through the book. But see, for example, Vico, *New Science*, §§428ff.

46. John Milbank, *The Religious Dimension in the Thought of Giambattista Vico, 1668–1744* (Lewiston, NY: Edwin Mellen Press, 1992), pt. 2, 10.

47. John Milbank, *Theology and Social Theory: Beyond Secular Reason* (Oxford: Blackwell, 1990), 4, 12. The question whether the Platonic intelligible realm is one in which there can be participation depends on how one understands Plato's concept of relation. See Plato, *Republic*, trans. G. M. A. Grube (Indianapolis: Hackett, 1992), bk. 6, 178: "You've often heard it said that the form of the good is the most important thing to learn about and that it's by their relation to it that just things and others become useful and beneficial. You know very well now that I am going to say this, and besides, that we have no adequate knowledge of it." To participate in the good is to have access to it, however limited. This, I hold, is the position of the ontological argument. It is not the position of Plato, for whom one can love and pursue the good only insofar as one is not able to access it.

48. Hayden White's reading of *The New Science* stresses Vico's commitment to the relation of speech and consciousness and to the coordination of forms ("tropics") of discourse with forms of life. In so doing, he reflects the developmentalism that Vico attributes to the gentes without accounting for Vico's position on the Hebrews, which White relegates to an uncritical piety (216). White, that is, notes the distinction of the Hebrews but makes nothing of it. See Hayden White, "The Tropics of History: The Deep Structure of the *New Science*," in *Tropics of Discourse: Essays in Cultural Criticism* (Baltimore: Johns Hopkins University Press, 1978).

49. Vico, *New Science*, §348.

50. Ibid., §122.

51. Ibid., §§125, 127.

52. Ibid., §123.

53. Ibid., §146.

54. Ibid., §60.

55. Ibid., §§144, 161.

56. Ibid., §§922–27.

57. Ibid., §927.

58. Ibid., §446.

59. The image is Hegel's in *The Philosophy of History*, in which he compares the development of Spirit and the development of a germ. Both develop and produce themselves. But "that development (*of natural organisms*) takes place in a direct, unopposed, unhindered manner," whereas "in relation to Spirit, it is quite otherwise." It must work with but also against its nature—against what is natural. As Hegel puts it, "Spirit is at war with itself: it has to overcome itself as its most formidable obstacle" (55).

60. Ludwig Feuerbach, *The Essence of Christianity*, trans. George Eliot (Buffalo, NY: Prometheus Books, 1989).

61. Vico, *New Science*, §134.

62. Ibid., §132.

63. Ibid., §135.

64. Ibid., §198.

65. Ibid., §408.

66. Ibid., §165.

67. Ibid., §230.

68. Ibid., §225.

69. Ibid., §79.

70. Ibid., §172.

71. Ibid., §301.

72. I am indebted to Avron Kulak and Terri Kulak for this use of the concept of belatedness.

73. Milbank, Theology and Social Theory, 4.

74. Vico, *New Science*, §310.

75. Ibid., §1100. In *The Myth of Ham in Nineteenth-Century American Christianity: Race, Heathens, and the People of God* (London: Palgrave Macmillan, 2004), Sylvester Johnson explores the history of racism associated with myths concerning Noah's son Ham. Although Vico imagines all of Noah's sons together and places the gentes there, it is prudent to consider Johnson's history given Vico's proximity to racist discourse.

76. Vico, *New Science*, §1108.

77. Ibid., §331.

78. The conceits would also describe the skepticism foisted upon Nietzsche by readers who take his theory of interpretation for the justification of might makes right.

79. Vico, *New Science*, §120.

80. Said, *Orientalism*, 45.

81. Ibid., 67.

82. Edward Said, *Beginnings: Intention and Method* (New York: Columbia University Press, 1975), xv–xvii.

CHAPTER FOUR

1. On violence and monotheism see Jan Assmann, *Of God and the Gods: Egypt, Israel, and the Rise of Monotheism* (Madison: University of Wisconsin Press, 2008); Moshe Halbertal and Avishai Margalit, *Idolatry*, trans. Naomi Goldblum (Cambridge, MA: Harvard University Press, 1992); and Regina Schwartz, *The Curse of Cain: The Violent Legacy of Monotheism* (Chicago: University of Chicago Press, 1998).

2. Said, *Beginnings*, xv–xvii.

3. Vico, *New Science*, §167.

4. Ludwig Wittgenstein, *Philosophical Investigations*, trans. G. E. M. Anscombe (Oxford: Blackwell, 2009), 3.

5. "Whereof one cannot speak, thereof one must be silent." Wittgenstein, *Tractatus Logico-Philosophicus* (London: Routledge and Kegan Paul, 1922), 189.

6. Wittgenstein, *Investigations*, 4.

7. Kierkegaard, *Fear and Trembling*, 63, 121.

8. Adam Phillips, *Equals* (New York: Basic Books, 2002). The paraphrase is of the opening line of the book: "If the best thing we do is look after each other,

then the worst thing we do is pretend to look after each other when in fact we are doing something else" (xi).

9. Kierkegaard, *Fear and Trembling*, 37.

10. Stevens, "Ordinary Evening in New Haven," 403.

CHAPTER FIVE

1. Foucault, *Order of Things*, xx.

2. Foucault, "What Is Enlightenment?" in *The Foucault Reader*, ed. Paul Rabinow (New York: Pantheon Books, 1984).

3. Foucault, *Order of Things*, xxii.

4. Ibid., xv.

5. Ibid.

6. Ibid., xvi. See Jorge Luis Borges, "John Wilkins' Analytical Language," in *Borges: Selected Non-fictions*, trans. Esther Allen et al. (London: Penguin, 1999).

7. For an intriguing reply to this topos, see Jeffrey L. Kosky, *Arts of Wonder: Enchanting Secularity—Walter de Maria, Diller + Scofidio, James Turrell, Andy Goldsworthy* (Chicago: University of Chicago Press, 2012).

8. A searching entry into this question with nineteenth- and twentieth-century sources is Noreen Khawaja, *The Religion of Existence: Asceticism in Philosophy from Kierkegaard to Sartre* (Chicago: University of Chicago Press, 2016).

9. Stevens, "The Snow Man," in *Collected Poetry and Prose*, 8. I am indebted to Brayton Polka, "The Ontological Argument for Existence," in *Difference in Philosophy of Religion*, ed. Philip Goodchild (London: Ashgate, 2003), 15–32, and idem, "The Image's Truth: Wallace Stevens and the Hermeneutics of Being," in *On Interpretation: Studies in Culture, Law, and the Sacred*, ed. Andrew D. Weiner and Leonard V. Kaplan (Madison: University of Wisconsin Press, 2002).

10. Saint Anselm, *Proslogion*, trans. and ed. M. J. Charlesworth (Notre Dame, IN: University of Notre Dame Press, 1965).

11. Kant, *Critique of Pure Reason*, 563–69.

12. Anselm, *Proslogion*, 137.

13. Ibid., 117.

14. Ibid., 137.

15. I differentiate history in both Anselm and Vico from a concept of "sacred history." But this does not leave us only with secular history in Said's sense of what indiscriminately exiles the sacred. For the standard usage of the vocabulary of sacred history, see Katherine van Liere, Simon Ditchfield, and Howard Louthan, eds., *Sacred History: Uses of the Christian Past in the Renaissance World* (Oxford: Oxford University Press, 2012).

16. Pascal, *Pensées*, §188.

17. Kant, *Groundwork*, 66.

18. Hegel, *Lectures on the Philosophy of History*, 55.

19. Aristotle, "Metaphysics," in *Complete Works of Aristotle*, 2:1552.

20. Plato, *Republic*, bk. 5, 179.

21. This is a claim I launched in Nancy Levene, "Sources of History: Myth and Image," *Journal of the American Academy of Religion* 74, no. 1 (2006): 79–101, and bring to completion in this book.

22. Alain Badiou's major work is *Being and Event*, trans. Oliver Feltham (London: Continuum, 2005).

23. Alain Badiou, "Must the Communist Hypothesis Be Abandoned?," *Yearbook of Comparative Literature* 55 (2009): 79–88.

24. Alain Badiou, "Bodies, Languages, Truths," talk delivered at Victoria College of Arts, University of Melbourne; http://www.lacan.com/badbodies.htm (2006), 1.

25. Ibid., 1.

26. Ibid., 1–2.

27. Ibid., 2–5.

28. Badiou, *Being and Event*, xii–xiii.

29. Badiou, "Bodies, Languages, Truths," 2–5.

30. This is Badiou's order of the thinkers who characterize what he calls "the adventure of French philosophy," those who define a "new moment of philosophical creativity" that is "both particular and universal," bookended by Sartre on one side and at the end of which he places "myself, maybe." See Alain Badiou, *The Adventure of French Philosophy*, trans. Bruno Bosteels (New York: Verso, 2012), lii.

31. Badiou, "Bodies, Languages, Truths," 2.

32. Badiou, *Adventure*, lxi.

33. Descartes, *Meditations*, 29.

34. Badiou, *Adventure*, lvi.

35. Badiou, "Communist Hypothesis," 82–86.

36. Badiou associates Lenin's pamphlet of 1902, *What Is to Be Done?*, with the dominance of the question of time to the second historical sequence of the communist hypothesis that begins in 1917 with the Russian Revolution, ends in 1976 with the end of the Cultural Revolution in China, and includes the militant movements around the globe starting around 1966 "whose epicenter, from the point of view of political innovation, was May 1968 in France" ("Communist Hypothesis," 83). The first sequence begins with the French Revolution and culminates in the Paris Commune of 1871. The second sequence is no longer "about formulating and experimenting the communist hypothesis"; the question is "about realizing it," and thus about how to endure, how to survive time, and how to survive over time (84).

37. Badiou, *Adventure*, lii.

38. Anselm, *Proslogion*, 103.

39. G. R. Evans, "Anselm's Life, Works, and Immediate Influence," in *Cambridge Companion to Anselm*, ed. B. Davies and B. Leftow (Cambridge: Cambridge University Press, 2004), 17–24.

40. See Hollywood, *Sensible Ecstasy*, and Bruce Holsinger, *The Premodern Condition: Medievalism and the Making of Theory* (Chicago: University of Chicago Press, 2005).

41. See Richard Rorty, Jerome B. Schneewind, and Quentin Skinner, *Philosophy in History: Essays in the Historiography of History* (Cambridge: Cambridge University Press, 1984). In early modernity, this question is posed by Vico.

42. Ivan Strenski, *Thinking about Religion: An Historical Introduction to Theories of Religion* (Oxford: Blackwell, 2006), 2.

43. Anselm, *Proslogion*, 185.

44. Ibid., 103.

45. Ibid., 177.

46. Ibid., 137.

47. Ibid., 177–79.

48. Badiou, *Being and Event*, xii–xiii.

49. Anselm, *Proslogion*, 103.

50. Ibid.

51. Eadmer, *The Life of St. Anselm Archbishop of Canterbury*, ed. R. W. Southern (Oxford: Clarendon Press, 1962), 30.

52. Ibid., 30n2.

53. Ibid., 30.

54. Ibid., 30n3.

55. Ibid., 30–31.

56. Evans, "Anselm's Life," 12.

57. Descartes, *Meditations*, 21–24.

58. Anselm, *Proslogion*, 137.

59. Ibid., 163–65.

60. Ibid., 143.

61. Ibid., 145.

62. Quoted as the epigraph to Badiou, "Meditation Two: Plato," in *Being and Event*, 31.

63. Ibid., 33–35.

64. See Badiou, *Plato's Republic: A Dialogue in 16 Chapters*, trans. Susan Spitzer (New York: Columbia University Press, 2012), which is a creative translation and rewriting of the text. On Badiou's Plato, see Kenneth Reinhard's introduction, "Badiou's Sublime Translation of the Republic." On set theory and event, see *Being and Event*.

65. Alfred North Whitehead, *Process and Reality* (New York: Free Press, 1978), 39.

66. Alain Badiou, *Saint Paul: The Foundation of Universalism*, trans. Ray Brassier (Stanford, CA: Stanford University Press, 2003), 98.

67. Martin Heidegger, *Being and Time*, trans. John Macquarrie and Edward Robinson (New York: Harper and Row, 1962), 224.

68. Ibid. "This question [the question of Being] has today been forgotten" (21).

69. Gillian Rose works through a related point in her Hegelian reading of the West, *The Broken Middle: Out of Our Ancient Society* (Oxford: Blackwell, 1992). Emmanuel Levinas means to differentiate between two kinds of one in *Totality and Infinity: An Essay on Exteriority*, trans. Alphonso Lingis (Pittsburgh, PA: Duquesne University Press, 1969). But he cannot see his precursors through this distinction, assimilating Plato, Descartes, and Hegel. This failure muddies the distinction itself. See Gillian Rose, "Angry Angels: Simone Weil and Emmanuel Levinas," in *Judaism and Modernity: Philosophical Essays* (Oxford: Blackwell, 1993).

70. Badiou, "Meditation Two: Plato," in *Being and Event*, 35.

71. Badiou, *Saint Paul*, 58.

72. Hegel, *Philosophy of History*, 8.

73. Ibid., 8–9.

74. Ibid., 8.

75. Ibid., 9.

76. Alain Badiou, *Theoretical Writings*, trans. Ray Brassier and Alberto Toscano (London: Continuum, 2004), 226, 223. See also idem, "Meditation Fifteen: Hegel," in *Being and Event*.

77. Badiou, "The One and the Multiple," in *Being and Event*, 29.

78. Michel Foucault, *The Archaeology of Knowledge and the Discourse on Language*, trans. A. M. Sheridan Smith (New York: Pantheon, 1972), 235.

79. Ibid., 236.

80. Ibid., 236–37.

81. Ibid., 235.

82. Badiou, "Meditation Fifteen: Hegel," 163.

83. Ibid., 169.

84. Foucault, *Archaeology*, 236. Foucault exemplifies (a) the assimilation of Greek, Christian, and modern concepts of philosophy and reason that requires (b) the recent dawning of history, in announcing that, although "History" has existed "from the beginnings of the Ancient Greek civilization," a historicity that shatters Greco-Christian unity qua providence arrives only in the nineteenth century (*Order of Things*, 367).

85. Jacques Derrida, "Différence," in *Margins of Philosophy*, trans. Alan Bass (Chicago: University of Chicago Press, 1982). See Kulak, "Kierkegaard, Derrida, and the Context of Context(s)."

CHAPTER SIX

1. Immanuel Kant, "An Answer to the Question 'What Is Enlightenment?'," in *Kant: Political Writings*, trans. H. B. Nisbet (Cambridge: Cambridge University Press, 1970), 54.

2. See Anthony Pagden, *The Enlightenment and Why It Still Matters* (Oxford: Oxford University Press, 2013), and Alex Schulman, *The Secular Contract: The Politics of Enlightenment* (New York: Continuum, 2011).

3. For an account of this rationalism insofar as it culminates in Spinoza, see Carlos Fraenkel, *Philosophical Religions from Plato to Spinoza: Reason, Religion, and Autonomy* (Cambridge: Cambridge University Press, 2012).

4. Nietzsche, *Genealogy of Morals*, First Essay, §13.

5. In being distinguished from the logic of the one and the many, the principle of the all qua inclusion is in distinction from the all of a whole and its parts. For an illuminating treatment of this idea, see Slavoj Žižek, "Subtraction: Jewish and Christian," in *The Puppet and the Dwarf* (Cambridge, MA: MIT Press, 2003), 132–33.

6. Benedictus de Spinoza, *Political Treatise*, trans. Samuel Shirley (Indianapolis: Hackett, 2000), 39.

7. Jonathan I. Israel, *Radical Enlightenment: Philosophy and the Making of Modernity, 1650–1750* (New York: Oxford University Press, 2001), vi.

8. Ibid., 15.

9. Benedictus de Spinoza, *Theological-Political Treatise*, 2nd ed., trans. Samuel Shirley (Indianapolis: Hackett, 2001), 75–76.

10. Israel, *Radical Enlightenment*, vi.

11. Leo Strauss, "How to Study Spinoza's *Theologico-Political Treatise*," in *Persecution and the Art of Writing* (Chicago: University of Chicago Press, 1952), 184–90.

12. Steven B. Smith, *Spinoza, Liberalism, and the Question of Jewish Identity* (New Haven, CT: Yale University Press, 1997), 197, 200.

13. Israel, *Radical Enlightenment*, 230.

14. Louis Althusser, "The Only Materialist Tradition, Part I: Spinoza," in *The New Spinoza*. ed. Warren Montag and Ted Stolze (Minneapolis: University of Minnesota Press, 1977), 3–20; Alexandre Matheron, *Individu et communauté chez Spinoza* (Paris: Éditions de Minuit, 1969); Antonio Negri, *The Savage Anomaly*, ed. and trans. Michael Hardt (Minneapolis: University of Minnesota Press, 1991); Étienne Balibar, *Spinoza and Politics*, trans. Peter Snowdon (New York: Verso, 1998); Warren Montag, *Bodies, Masses, Power: Spinoza and His Contemporaries* (New York: Verso, 1999); and Hasana Sharp, *Spinoza and the Politics of Renaturalization* (Chicago: University of Chicago Press, 2011).

15. On Strauss and Smith, see Nancy Levene, "Ethics and Interpretation, or How to Study Spinoza's *Tractatus Theologico-Politicus* without Strauss," *Journal of Jewish Thought and Philosophy* 10 (2000): 57–110.

16. Negri, *Savage*, xix.

17. Sharp, *Spinoza and the Politics of Renaturalization*, 5.

18. Spinoza, *Ethics*, in *Collected Works*, part 2, proposition 13, 457. Hereafter references to the *Ethics* will be abbreviated as follows: pt. = part, prop. = proposition, ax. = axiom, cor. = corollary, def. = definition, def. aff. = definition of the affects, pref. = preface, schol. = scholium., and app. = appendix.

19. Balibar, *Spinoza and Politics*, 4.

20. Spinoza, *Ethics*, pt. 1, app., 441.

21. Margaret C. Jacob, *The Radical Enlightenment: Pantheists, Freemasons and Republicans* (London: Allen and Unwin, 1981), xiv.

22. The word materialist has a modern provenance, being first used in a 1668 dialogue by the Cambridge Platonist Henry More to refer to his character Hylobares as "a young, witty, and well-moralized *Materialist*" (Henry More, *Divine Dialogues Containing Disquisitions concerning the Attributes and Providence of God* (London, 1668), [xxviii]. Bishop George Berkeley used "materialism" in his *Three Dialogues between Hylas and Philonous* (London, 1713), the question being whether "materialism disposes men to believe the creation of things" (154), but the concept goes back at least as far as Epicurus, arguably the first materialist.

23. Spinoza, *Ethics*, pt. 3, pref., 491.

24. See Spinoza, *Ethics*, pt. 3, pref., 491–92.

25. Pierre Bayle, *Historical and Critical Dictionary*, trans. Richard H. Popkin (Indianapolis: Hackett, 1991), 296–97.

26. Ibid., 301.

27. Negri, *Savage*, xvii.

28. Spinoza, *Theological-Political Treatise*, 164.

29. Montag, *Bodies, Masses, Power*, xv.

30. Ibid., xvii.

31. Althusser, "Only Materialist Tradition, Part I: Spinoza," 12.

32. Montag, *Bodies, Masses, Power*, xiv.

33. Spinoza, *Political Treatise*, 42.

34. On pantheism and its mobility, see especially Jacob, *Radical Enlightenment*.

35. See Spinoza, *Theological-Political Treatise*, chaps. 19–20. For a critique of Spinoza the liberal, see Balibar, *Spinoza and Politics*, 27.

36. Montag, *Bodies, Masses, Power*, xxi. This reversal is also Sharp's. See Sharp, *Spinoza and the Politics of Renaturalization*, especially chap. 2. Both Montag and Sharp have in mind Spinoza's theory of mind and body as two dimensions of existence—"man consists of a Mind and a Body" (Spinoza, *Ethics*, pt. 2, prop. 13, cor., 457)—that are "one and the same thing, which is conceived now under the attribute of Thought, now under the attribute of Extension" (*Ethics*, pt. 3, prop. 2, schol., 494).

37. Images of Spinoza the contemplative tend to read him through the lens of Aristotle in conceiving of this virtue as the end of wisdom. See R. J. Delahunty, *Spinoza* (London: Routledge, 1985), 275. On the divergent aims of philosophy and politics with respect to the multitude and "the happy few," see Yirmiyahu Yovel, *Spinoza and Other Heretics: The Marrano of Reason* (Princeton, NJ: Princeton University Press, 1992), chap. 5.

38. Spinoza, *Ethics*, pt. 4, prop. 18, schol., 555.

39. Spinoza, *Ethics*, pt. 4, prop. 18, schol., 556.

40. Plato, *Republic*, bk. 6, 164.

41. Spinoza, *Ethics*, pt. 2, ax. 2, 448.

42. Descartes, *Meditations*, 20.

43. Compare the "Phaedo": "The lovers of learning know that when philosophy gets hold of their soul, it is imprisoned in and clinging to the body, and that it is forced to examine other things through it as through a cage and not by itself" (Plato, "Phaedo," 121) to Romans 8:6: "To set the mind on the flesh is death, but to set the mind on the Spirit is life and peace"; and to Romans 7:25: "So then, with my mind I am a slave to the law of God, but with my flesh I am a slave to the law of sin." Spinoza is consistent with Paul in insisting that the difference between what he calls "carnal man" and the man of reason (*Theological-Political Treatise*, 51) is a difference internal to desire ("the consciousness" of appetite), not between reason and the body (*Ethics*, pt. 3, def. aff. I, 531).

44. Spinoza, *Ethics*, pt. 4, pref., 543–46.

45. Karl Marx, "German Ideology," in *Marx-Engels Reader*, 155. Nietzsche, *Genealogy of Morals*, First Essay, §13.

46. Nietzsche, *Genealogy of Morals*, First Essay, §13.

47. See Spinoza, *Theological-Political Treatise*, chap. 16.

48. Spinoza, *Theological-Political Treatise*, chap. 16, 179. For a different view of fish and other nonhumans in Spinoza, see Sharp, *Spinoza and the Politics of Renaturalization*.

49. Spinoza, *Theological-Political Treatise*, chap. 16, 173.

50. Spinoza, *Ethics*, pt. 1, prop. 29, schol., 434.

51. Spinoza, *Ethics*, pt. 1, ax. 1, 410.

52. The concept of what is finite (*finitus*) is central in the *Ethics*. It first occurs in the second definition of part 1: "That thing is said to be finite in its own kind that can be limited by another of the same nature" (*Ethics*, pt. 1, def. 2, 408). When speaking about human power in concert with others, however, Spinoza uses *singularis*, singular, as in, "There is no singular thing in Nature that is more useful to man than a man who lives according to the guidance of reason" (*Ethics*, pt. 4, prop. 35, cor. 1, 563).

53. Spinoza, *Political Treatise*, 43.

54. Spinoza, *Ethics*, pt. 3, def. aff. I, 531.

55. Spinoza, *Political Treatise*, 101.

56. See Spinoza, *Theological-Political Treatise*, chaps. 16–17, especially 177–79, 185: "In a democratic state nobody transfers his natural right to another so completely that thereafter he is not to be consulted; he transfers it to the majority of the entire community of which he is a part. In this way all men remain equal, as they were before in a state of nature" (179).

57. Spinoza, *Political Treatise*, 40. In addition to the *Political Treatise*, Spinoza discusses the story of Adam and Eve in the *Theological-Political Treatise*, chap. 4, 53–54, 55–56, and the *Ethics*, pt. 4, prop. 68, schol., 584–85.

58. Spinoza, *Political Treatise*, 36.

59. Spinoza, *Theological-Political Treatise*, chap. 16, 181.

60. Spinoza, *Political Treatise*, 44.

61. Spinoza, *Theological-Political Treatise*, chap. 16, 175.

62. Spinoza, *Political Treatise*, introduction, 9.

63. See Nancy Levene, *Spinoza's Revelation: Religion, Democracy, and Reason* (Cambridge: Cambridge University Press, 2004); and idem, "Does Spinoza Think the Bible Is Sacred?" *Jewish Quarterly Review* 101, no. 4 (Fall 2011): 545–73.

64. Spinoza, *Theological-Political Treatise*, chap. 5, 64–65.

65. Ibid., chap. 4, 50.

66. Spinoza, *Ethics*, pt. 4, prop. 35, schol., 563.

67. See Levene, *Spinoza's Revelation*, chap. 4. On this issue I have learned from Étienne Balibar, "*Jus-Pactum-Lex*: On the Constitution of the Subject in the *Theological-Political Treatise*," in *The New Spinoza*, ed. Montag and Stolze, 171–205. For the alternative view that the modern compact is a purely secular one, see Schulman, *Secular Contract*.

68. Spinoza, *Theological-Political Treatise*, chap. 4, 50.

69. Ibid., chap. 16, 182 (pact with God) and 175 (pact between human beings).

70. Ibid., chap. 4, 49.

71. Ibid., chap. 4, 182.

72. Ibid., chap. 4, 55.

73. That human beings are "part of nature" is declaimed throughout Spinoza's three major works. In *Ethics*, see pt. 4, prop. 4.

74. Spinoza, *Theological-Political Treatise*, chap. 16, 174.

75. Spinoza, *Ethics*, pt. 4, prop. 68, 584: "If men were born free, they would form no concept of good and evil so long as they remained free."

76. Ibid., pt. 4, prop. 73, 587.

77. Ibid., pt. 3, def. 2, 493.

78. Spinoza, *Political Treatise*, 40.

79. Spinoza, *Ethics*, pt. 3, def. aff. II, 531.

80. Spinoza, *Political Treatise*, 40.

81. Ibid., 41.

82. On Spinoza and Hegel, see Hasana Sharp and Jason E. Smith, *Between Hegel and Spinoza: A Volume of Critical Essays* (New York: Bloomsbury, 2012).

83. Spinoza, *Ethics*, pt. 4, pref., 545–46.

84. Spinoza, *Political Treatise*, 36.

85. Spinoza, *Theological-Political Treatise*, chap. 4, 48–50.

86. Spinoza, *Ethics*, pt. 4, prop. 4, cor., 549.

87. Ibid., pt. 4, prop. 35, cor. 1 and 2, 563.

88. Ibid., pt. 4, pref., 545.

89. Plato, "Phaedo," 121. See Brayton Polka, *Between Philosophy and Religion: Spinoza, the Bible, and Modernity*, 2 vols. (Lanham, MD: Lexington Books, 2007), 2:185.

90. Spinoza, *Political Treatise*, 41.

91. Ibid., 62.

92. Montag, *Bodies, Masses Power*, xvii.

93. Spinoza, *Theological-Political Treatise*, chap. 19, 213.

94. Spinoza discusses the biblical prophets in chapters 1 and 2 of the *Theological-Political Treatise*, but they are subjects throughout the book.

95. Spinoza, *Theological-Political Treatise*, chap. 12, 147.

96. Kant, *Critique of Pure Reason*, 99.

97. Ibid.

98. One thinks of G. W. F. Hegel's *Phenomenology of Spirit*, trans. A. V. Miller (New York: Oxford University Press, 1977), and Karl Marx's *Capital: A Critique of Political Economy*, vol. 1, trans. Ben Fowkes (New York: Penguin Books, 1976).

99. Kant, *Critique of Pure Reason*, 114.

100. Ibid., 398.

101. Ibid., 140.

102. Ibid., 102.

103. Deut. 30:11–14.

104. Ex. 32:1.

105. Ex. 32:4.

106. Deut. 30:10.

107. Kant, *Critique of Pure Reason*, 110.

108. Kant, *Groundwork*, 53.

109. Ibid., 59–60.

110. Ibid., 55.

111. Ibid., 56.

112. Ibid.

113. Ibid., 59.

114. Kant, *Critique of Pure Reason*, 118.

115. Kant, *Groundwork*, 17.

116. Ibid.

117. Ibid., 16.

118. Compare with Plato's doctrine of recollection, according to which what is known is what has always been known, that is, never known insofar as we have a body. See Plato, "Phaedo," 110–15.

119. Kant, *Groundwork*, 56.

120. Ibid.

121. Ibid., 57.

122. The phrase is from Milton, *Paradise Lost*, bk. 2, line 916. The invocation is of hell, "this wilde Abyss, / The Womb of nature and perhaps her Grave," unless "the Almighty Maker them ordain / His dark materials to create more worlds." Writer Philip Pullman uses it to name his fantasy series on other worlds embedded in this one. For a recent take on multiplication of worlds, see Mary-Jane Rubenstein, *Worlds without End: The Many Lives of the Multiverse* (New York: Columbia University Press, 2015).

123. Kant, *Groundwork*, 57.

124. Ibid.

125. Ibid.

126. Ibid.

127. Ibid., 56.

128. Kant, *Critique of Pure Reason*, 385–86.

129. Immanuel Kant, *Religion within the Boundaries of Mere Reason*, trans. and ed. Allen Wood and George Di Giovanni (Cambridge: Cambridge University Press, 1998).

130. Kant, *Groundwork*, 59.

131. Stevens, "The Sail of Ulysses," in *Collected Poetry and Prose*, 464.

CHAPTER SEVEN

1. William Rasch, "Introduction: The Self-Positing Society," in Niklas Luhmann, *Theories of Distinction: Redescribing the Descriptions of Modernity*, trans. Joseph O'Neil et al. (Stanford, CA: Stanford University Press, 2002), 1–2.

2. Ibid., 1–3.

3. Ibid., 3.

4. Niklas Luhmann, "I See Something You Don't See," in *Theories of Distinction*, 192.

5. See Taylor, *Secular Age*. In resistance to the totality of these corrosions and in criticism of modernity qua secular reason as their signature, see also Milbank, *Theology and Social Theory*. Several recent books follow Taylor's and Milbank's drift in taking up the story of modernity with an emphasis on its medieval and early modern roots in such a way as to give the earlier period contextual, conceptual, and/or evaluative priority. See Brad Gregory, *The Unintended Reformation: How a Religious Revolution Secularized Society* (Cambridge, MA: Belknap Press of Harvard University Press, 2012); Thomas Pfau, *Minding the Modern:*

Human Agency, Intellectual Traditions, and Responsible Knowledge (Notre Dame, IN: University of Notre Dame Press, 2013); and Andrew Cole, *The Birth of Theory* (Chicago: University of Chicago Press, 2014).

6. Luhmann, "I See Something You Don't," 192.

7. Rasch, "Introduction," 6.

8. Spinoza, *Ethics*, 491.

9. The duck-rabbit illusion describes a figure that looks now like a duck and now like a rabbit, but not both at once. First noted by Joseph Jastrow in 1899, the optical trick is used by Wittgenstein in "Philosophy of Psychology: A Fragment" to explore the question of the world as it is and as how we take it, if that is indeed the correct question. See *Investigations*, 204.

10. This is a vast field. Six heavyweights are Hans Blumenberg, *The Legitimacy of the Modern Age*, trans. Robert M. Wallace (Cambridge, MA: MIT Press, 1983); Amos Funkenstein, *Theology and the Scientific Imagination from the Middle Ages to the Seventeenth Century* (Princeton, NJ: Princeton University Press, 1986); Marshall Berman, *All That Is Solid Melts into Air: The Experience of Modernity* (New York: Penguin Books, 1988); Stephen Toulmin, *Cosmopolis*; Pierre Manent, *An Intellectual History of Liberalism*, trans. Rebecca Balinski (Princeton, NJ: Princeton University Press, 1996); and Dror Wahrman, *The Making of the Modern Self: Identity and Culture in Eighteenth-Century England* (New Haven, CT: Yale University Press, 2004). On religion and modernity, see Louis Dupré, *Passage to Modernity: An Essay in the Hermeneutics of Nature and Culture* (New Haven, CT: Yale University Press, 1993); Gillespie, *Theological Origins of Modernity*; and Eric Nelson, *The Hebrew Republic: Jewish Sources and the Transformation of European Political Thought* (Cambridge, MA: Harvard University Press, 2010).

11. Dogmatic Constitution on Divine Revelation, *Dei Verbum* (1965), chap. 2, §8.

12. For an argument that "periodization must come undone" in the light of the politics of history, see Kathleen Davis, *Periodization and Sovereignty: How the Ideas of Feudalism and Secularism Govern the Politics of Time* (Philadelphia: University of Pennsylvania Press, 2008), 134.

13. Madeleine L'Engle, *A Wind in the Door* (New York: Crosswicks Ltd., 1973), 157–58.

14. Latour, *We Have Never Been Modern*.

15. This is how I understand criticisms of democracy in the work of thinkers such as Wendy Brown, Chantal Mouffe, David Harvey, Slavoj Žižek, and Alain Badiou.

16. These are transcriptions of courses listed on Sheehan's website at the University of California, Berkeley: http://history.berkeley.edu/people/jonathan-sheehan.

17. See Jonathan Sheehan and Dror Wahrman, *Invisible Hands: Self-Organization and the Eighteenth Century* (Chicago: University of Chicago Press, 2015).

18. I have written elsewhere on this "when," also in relation to Sheehan, among others. See Nancy Levene, "Commentaries on Our Age," a review of

Michael Warner, Jonathan VanAntwerpen, and Craig Calhoun, eds., *Varieties of Secularism in a Secular Age,* on "The Immanent Frame," http://blogs.ssrc.org /tif/2010/07/08/commentaries-on-our-age/.

19. Stevens, "The Poems of Our Climate," in *Collected Poetry and Prose,* 178–79, and idem, "Esthétique du Mal," 277.

20. Kant, "Conjectures on the Beginning of Human History," in *Kant: Political Writings,* 221. Friedrich Nietzsche, *The Gay Science,* trans. Walter Kaufmann (New York: Vintage Books, 1974), §34.

21. Homer, *The Iliad,* trans. Richmond Lattimore (Chicago: University of Chicago Press, 1951). See, for example, book 22, lines 105–10, 438; Plato, *Gorgias,* trans. Donald J. Zeyl (Indianapolis: Hackett, 1987), 50–61.

22. Nietzsche, *Gay Science,* §125.

CHAPTER EIGHT

1. Winnifred Sullivan, *The Impossibility of Religious Freedom* (Princeton, NJ: Princeton University Press, 2005), 3.

2. Ibid., 158–59.

3. For a variety of responses to this question, see the essays in *Politics of Religious Freedom,* ed. Winnifred Sullivan, Elizabeth Shakman Hurd, Saba Mahmood, and Peter G. Danchin (Chicago: University of Chicago Press, 2005). See also Matthew Scherer, *Beyond Church and State: Democracy, Secularism, and Conversion* (Cambridge: Cambridge University Press, 2013).

4. Sullivan, *Impossibility of Religious Freedom,* 147.

5. Michael Sandel, "Religious Liberty: Freedom of Choice or Freedom of Conscience," in *Secularism and Its Critics,* ed. Rajeev Bhargava (New Delhi: Oxford University Press, 1998), 93.

6. Sullivan, *Impossibility of Religious Freedom,* 154.

7. Ernst H. Kantorowicz, *The King's Two Bodies: A Study in Medieval Political Theology* (Princeton, NJ: Princeton University Press, 1957), 7. See also Eric Santner, *The Royal Remains: The People's Two Bodies and the Endgames of Sovereignty* (Chicago: University of Chicago Press, 2011).

8. For the view that the Radical Enlightenment made nature the operative issue, see Margaret C. Jacob, *The Radical Enlightenment: Pantheists, Freemasons and Republicans* (London: George Allen and Unwin, 1981).

9. On Protestantism as the prelude to a modernity of consumption, see Gregory, *Unintended Reformation.* See also William Arnal and Russell McCutcheon, "Contemporary Reinventions of Religion: Disney and the Academy," in *Sacred Is the Profane,* and Kathryn Lofton, *Oprah: The Gospel of an Icon* (Berkeley: University of California Press, 2011). On modernity and the unencumbered self, see Taylor, *A Secular Age.* On modernity in light of its scapegoats, see Gil Anidjar, *The Jew, the Arab: A History of the Enemy* (Stanford, CA: Stanford University Press, 2003), and idem, *Blood: A Critique of Christianity* (New York: Columbia University Press, 2014). Anidjar argues for a Christianity that is emblem of the primitive dualism (monism, contagion) I identify with the nonmodern, on the one hand, and with modernity insofar as it confuses its principle, on the

other. He therefore sees one dualism where I see two; that is, he sees none where I see one.

10. The reference is to the final lines of Milton's *Paradise Lost*, book 12, line 649.

11. For variations on this theme see Partha Chatterjee, *Empire and Nation: Selected Essays* (New York: Columbia University Press, 2010), especially "Our Modernity" (136–52); Ranajit Guha, *Dominance without Hegemony: History and Power in Colonial India* (Cambridge, MA: Harvard University Press, 1997); and Chakrabarty, *Provincializing Europe*.

12. See Kant, *Groundwork*, 35: "Here, then, we see philosophy put in fact in a precarious position, which is to be firm even though there is nothing in heaven or on earth from which it depends or on which it is based. Here philosophy is to manifest its purity as a sustainer of its own laws, not as herald of laws that an implanted sense or who knows what tutelary nature whispers to it."

13. Paul Bloom, "Is God an Accident?," *Atlantic*, December 2005. For a book-length study of the dualism at play in this article, see Bloom, *Descartes' Baby: How the Science of Child Development Explains What Makes Us Human* (New York: Basic Books, 2005).

14. Bloom, "Is God an Accident?," 1. (The page numbers refer to the printed online version of the article.)

15. Ibid., 2.

16. Ibid., 13.

17. Ibid., 1.

18. Ibid., 8.

19. Ibid., 10.

20. Ibid., 10–11.

21. Ibid., 17–18.

22. Ibid., 11.

23. Kant, *Groundwork*, 57.

24. See Paul Bloom, "Scientific Faith Is Different from Religious Faith," *Atlantic*, November 24, 2015.

25. Bloom, "Is God an Accident?," 15. See Stewart Guthrie, *Faces in the Clouds: A New Theory of Religion* (Oxford: Oxford University Press, 1995).

26. Bloom gives an account of nature's moral reasoning in *Just Babies*.

27. Durkheim, *Elementary Forms*, 156–57.

28. *Here's the Thing*: http://www.wnyc.org/shows/heresthething/; *This American Life*: http://www.thisamericanlife.org/.

29. Erich von Däniken, *Chariots of the Gods: Unsolved Mysteries of the Past*, trans. Michael Heron (New York: Berkley Books, 1999).

30. Billy Collins, "The Afterlife," in *Questions about Angels: Poems* (Pittsburgh: University of Pittsburgh Press, 1999).

31. Jonathan Boyarin and Daniel Boyarin, *Powers of Diaspora: Two Essays on the Relevance of Jewish Culture* (Minneapolis: University of Minnesota Press, 2002), 1.

32. Ibid., 1–2.

33. Ibid., 2.

34. Bloom, "Is God an Accident?," 1.

35. Karen Armstrong, *Fields of Blood: Religion and the History of Violence* (New York: Anchor Books, 2014), 393.

36. Ex. 12:14–20.

37. "And you shall guard [observe] the matzah" (*u shmartem et ha-matzot*) (Ex. 12:17). See http://www.chabad.org/holidays/passover/pesach_cdo/aid/1682 /jewish/The-Difference-between-Shmurah-Matzah-and-Regular-Matzah.htm.

38. Spinoza, *Theological-Political Treatise*, 213.

39. For a bracing take on this something else, see Christine Hayes, *What's Divine about Divine Law? Early Perspectives* (Princeton, NJ: Princeton University Press, 2015).

40. At the end of a Sabbath before the ordinary work week: *Barukh atah Adonai, Eloheinu, melekh ha'olam, hamav'dil bein kodesh l'chol.* At the end of a Sabbath before a festival . . . *bein kodesh l'kodesh.*

41. Slavoj Žižek makes this observation throughout his work. In the light of themes here, see "Subtraction Jewish and Christian," in *Puppet and the Dwarf*, 134–35.

42. See Judith Butler, *Parting Ways: Jewishness and the Critique of Zionism* (New York: Columbia University Press, 2012), especially the introduction, "Self-Departure, Exile, and the Critique of Zionism." For the distinctiveness of a Jewish contribution to philosophy, see Bruce Rosenstock, *Philosophy and the Jewish Question: Mendelssohn, Rosenzweig, and Beyond* (New York: Fordham University Press, 2010).

43. On the defense (and defensiveness) of modern Judaism in the light of Christian critiques of it, see Rose, *Judaism and Modernity.*

44. See Aamir Mufti's introduction to *Enlightenment in the Colony: The Jewish Question and the Crisis of Postcolonial Culture* (Princeton, NJ: Princeton University Press, 2007). See also Saba Mahmood, *Religious Difference in a Secular Age: A Minority Report* (Princeton, NJ: Princeton University Press, 2015).

Index